Sovereignty and Justice

Sovereignty and Justice: Balancing the Principle of Complementarity between International and Domestic War Crimes Tribunals

By

Mark S. Ellis

CAMBRIDGE SCHOLARS PUBLISHING

Sovereignty and Justice:
Balancing the Principle of Complementarity
between International and Domestic War Crimes Tribunals,
by Mark S. Ellis

This book first published 2014

Cambridge Scholars Publishing

12 Back Chapman Street, Newcastle upon Tyne, NE6 2XX, UK

British Library Cataloguing in Publication Data
A catalogue record for this book is available from the British Library

ISBN (10): 1-4438-5704-1, ISBN (13): 978-1-4438-5704-8

TABLE OF NATIONAL CASES

Norway

NCIS Norway v. Charles Bandora, (Case No. 11-050224ENE-OTIR/01)

Rwanda

Ituri District Military Prosecutor v. Kahwa Panga Mandro, (RMP No. 227/PEN/2006)

Israel

Attorney General of the Government of Israel v. Adolf Eichmann (Supreme Court (1962) 36 ILR 277)

United Kingdom

Al-Skeini and Others v. Secretary of State for Defence, [2007] UKHL 26

Brown and others v. Government of Rwanda and Secretary of State for the Home Department, [2009] EWCA 770

Re. Pinochet Ugarte [1998] All ER (D) 629; [1998] EWJ No. 2878

The Prosecutor v. Morris Kallon and Brima Bazzy Kamara, (Case No. SCSL-2004-15-AR72(E) and Case No. SCSL-2004-16-AR72(E))

The Prosecutor v. Joseph Kony, Vincent Otti, Okot Odhiambo, Dominic Ongwen, (Case No. ICC-02/04-01/05)
The Prosecutor v. Thomas Lubanga Dyilo, (Case No. ICC-01/04-01/06)
The Prosecutor v. Francis Kirimi Muthaura, Uhuru Muigai Kenyatta and Mohammed Hussein Ali, (Case No. ICC-01/09-02/11)
The Prosecutor v. William Samoei Ruto and Joshua Arap Sang, (Case No. ICC-01/09-01/11)

International Criminal Tribunal for the Former Yugoslavia (ICTY)
The Prosecutor v. Zejnil Delalić, Zdravko Mucić, Hazim Delic and Esad Landžo (*Čelebići* camp) (Case No. IT-96-21)
The Prosecutor v. Anto Furundzija, (Case No. IT-95-17/1)
The Prosecutor v. Enver Hadžihasanović and Amir Kubura, (Case No. IT-01-47)
The Prosecutor v. Ramush Haradinaj, Idriz Balaj and Lahi Brahimaj, (Case No. IT-04-84)
The Prosecutor v. Astrit Haraqija and Bajrush Morina, (Case No. IT-04-84-R77.4)
The Prosecutor v. Naser Oric (Case No. IT-03-68-AR73.2)
The Prosecutor v. Vojislav Šešelj, (Case No. IT-03-67)
The Prosecutor v. Duško Tadić, (Case No. IT-94-1)

International Criminal Tribunal for Rwanda (ICTR)
The Prosecutor v. Jean-Baptiste Gatete, (Case No. ICTR-2000-61-R11*bis*)
The Prosecutor v. Gaspard Kanyarukiga, (Case No. ICTR-2002-78-R11*bis*)
The Prosecutor v. Prosper Mugiraneza, (Case No. ICTR-99-50-AR73)
The Prosecutor v. Bernard Munyagishari, (Case No. ICTR-2005-89-R11*bis*)
The Prosecutor v. Yussuf Munyakazi, (Case No. ICTR-97-36-R11*bis*)
The Prosecutor v. Bernard Ntuyahaga, (Case No. ICTR-98-40-T)
The Prosecutor v. Jean-Bosco Uwinkindi, (Case No. ICTR-2001-75-I)

International Military Tribunal
France, United Kingdom, United States and USSR v. Hermann Goering et al. (1946) 22 IMT 203

Special Court for Sierra Leone (SCSL)
The Prosecutor v. Alex Tamba Brima, Ibrahim Bazzy Kamara and Santigie Borbor Kanu (AFRC case) (Case No. SCSL-2004-16)

Neumeister v. Austria, (Application No. 1936/63) Series A No. 8, 1 EHRR 191 (27 June 1968)
Scordino v. Italy (No. 1) (Application No. 36813/97) ECHR 2006-V (29 March 2006)

Human Rights Committee
Gonzalez del Rio v. Peru, Communication No. 263/1987
Karttunen v. Finland, Communication No. 387/1989
Rogerson v. Australia, Communication No. 802/1998, 2002
Rouse v. The Philippines, Communication No. 1089/2002

International Court of Justice (ICJ)
Legality of the Threat or Use of Nuclear Weapons, ICJ Reports (8 July 1996)
Monetary Gold Removed from Rome in 1943 (Italy v. France, United Kingdom of Great Britain and Northern Ireland and United States of America), ICJ Reports (15 June 1954)
Questions of Interpretation and Application of the 1971 Montreal Convention Arising from the Aerial Incident at Lockerbie (Libyan Arab Jamahiriya v. United Kingdom) ICJ Reports (1992)
Questions relating to the Obligation to Prosecute or Extradite (Belgium v. Senegal), ICJ Reports (2009)

International Criminal Court
The Prosecutor v. Abdallah Banda Abakaer Nourain and Saleh Mohammed Jerbo Jamus, (Case No. ICC-02/05-03/9)
The Prosecutor v. Omar Hassan Ahmad Al Bashir (Case No. ICC-02/05-01/09)
The Prosecutor v. Bahar Idriss Abu Garda, (Case No. ICC-02/05-02/09)
The Prosecutor v. Jean-Pierre Bemba Gombo, (Case No. ICC-01/05-01/08)
The Prosecutor v. Muammar Mohammed Abu Minyar Gaddafi, Saif Al-Islam Gaddafi and Abdullah Al-Senussi, (Case No. ICC-01/11-01/11)
The Prosecutor v. Saif Al-Islam Gaddafi and Abdullah Al-Senussi, (Case No. ICC-01/11-01/11)
The Prosecutor v. Laurent Gbagbo, (Case No. ICC-02/11-01/11)
The Prosecutor v. Ahmad Muhammad Harun and Ali Muhammad Al Abd-Al-Rahman, (Case No. ICC-02/05-01/07)
The Prosecutor v. Germain Katanga and Mathieu Ngudjolo Chui, (Case No. ICC-01/04-01/07)
The Prosecutor v. Uhuru Muigai Kenyatta (Case No. ICC-01/09-02/11)

TABLE OF INTERNATIONAL CASES

African Commission on Human and Peoples' Rights

Constitutional Rights Project v. Nigeria, Communication No. 60/91 (1995)

Extraordinary Chambers in the Courts of Cambodia (ECCC)

The Prosecutor v. Ieng Sary, (Case No. 002/19-09/2007)

European Court of Human Rights

Arap Yalgin and others v. Turkey, (Application No. 33370/96) ECHR (25 September 2001)

Bejer v. Poland, (Application No. 38328/974) ECHR (4 October 2001)

Bottazzi v. Italy, (Application No. 34884/97) ECHR 1999-V (28 July 1999)

Eckle v. Germany (Application No. 8130/78) Series A No. 51, 5 EHRR 1 (15 July 1982)

Dimitrov and Hamanov v. Bulgaria, (Application Nos 48059/06 and 2708/09) ECHR (10 May 2011)

Foucher v. France, (Application No. 22209/93) [1997] II ECHR

Fortunat v. Slovenia (Application No. 42977/04) ECHR 348 (18 April 2013)

Frydlender v. France (Application No. 30979/96) ECHR 2000-VII (27 June 2000)

Jorgic v. Germany, (Application No. 74613/01) 2007-IX ECHR 583, (12 July 2007)

Krasuski v. Poland, (Application No. 61444/00) ECHR 2005-V (14 June 2005),

Lobo Machado v. Portugal, (Application No. 15764/89) EHRR 1996-I (20 February 1996)

Kovačič v. Slovenia, (Application No. 24376/08) ECHR 355 (18 April 2013)

Messina v. Italy, (Application No. 13803/88) Series A257-H (26 February 1993)

Morel v. France, (Application No. 34130/96) ECHR 2000-VI (6 June 2000)

Chapter Six 238
International Financial and Professional Support for Domestic War Crimes Courts
Introduction
I. International Technical Assistance Office
A. Fair, Impartial and Effective Trials
B. Substantive Legal and Procedural Issues
C. Trial Observations
D. Judicial Nominations
E. Training
F. Gender Diversity
G. Victim and Witness Support
H. Post-Trial Sentencing
I. Judicial Selection
J. Defence Attorneys
K. Victim Compensation
L. Other Issues

Conclusion 286

Appendix 299

Index 319

Chapter Three 112
The Principle of Complementarity Under Article 17 of the Rome State and States' Ability to Prosecute
Introduction
I. Conflict
II. Weak Judicial System
III. No Implementing Legislation
IV. Fairness and Impartiality
A. Witnesses
B. Defence Rights

Chapter Four 152
The Principle of Complementarity and the Issue of Enforcement
Introduction
I. A Case History: the UNSC and the ASP on the arrest of Omar Al Bashir
II. *Ad hoc* Tribunals: the ICTY and ICTR
A. ICTY
B. ICTR
III. International Pressure

Chapter Five 177
Admissibility Challenges
Introduction
I. Timing of Admissibility Challenges
A. Uganda
II. Self-referral and Withdrawal
III. Non-State Parties: The Libya Situation
A. Saif Al-Islam Gaddafi
B. Abdullah Al-Senussi
IV. Sudan
V. Article 16
VI. Article 127, Withdraw
VII. Creating a Third Party to Determine a State's 'Unwillingness' and 'Inability' to Investigate

TABLE OF CONTENTS

Table of International Cases x

Table of National Cases xiv

Acknowledgements xv

Preface xvi

Introduction 1

Chapter One 12
The Principle of Complementarity: Its History and Function
Introduction
I. The International Law Commission and Post Development
II. How does Complementarity work in practice?
III. Complementarity and Universal Jurisdiction
IV. Complementarity and Admissibility Standards, Interest of Justice, Gravity
A. Interest of Justice
B. Gravity

Chapter Two 62
The Principle of Complementarity Under Article 17 of the Rome Statute and States' Willingness to Prosecute
Introduction
I. Understanding the Concepts of Unwillingness and Inability
II. Willingness to Prosecute
A. Shielding
B. Unjustified Delays
C. Impartiality
i. Judges

To Talbot 'Sandy' D'Alemberte, Justice Richard J. Goldstone, Monsignor William A. Kerr, and Justice Sandra Day O'Connor who have fought courageously for justice while others have retreated.

To the victims of atrocities whose voices are now silent but to whom we owe justice.

And to my son Andrew – may you grow to be firm in your convictions, to show empathy for those who suffer, and be filled with the grace of love and humility throughout your life.

ACKNOWLEDGMENTS

I want to express my deep appreciation to Rein Mullerson, Professor of International Law at King's College (now President of the Academy of Law at Tallinn University, Estonia), who acted as my dissertation supervisor during my PhD studies. His keen insight and guidance were invaluable. Similarly, Jane Henderson, Senior Lecturer in Law at King's College provided valuable judgement on early drafts, which clearly made the end product significantly better!

This book would not have seen the light of day had it not been for Stephen Dycus, internationally renowned Professor of law at Vermont Law School. During numerous summer fly-fishing trips to Colorado with George, Jim, Johnny, Wayne, LeRoy, and the Judge, he somehow had the time to focus on my career – rather than catch fish - and concluded that I should publish this work.

During the last year, I have been fortunate to work with some very bright students who conducted research for me and assisted me in drafting this publication. I want to thank Matthew Bogunovich, Phillippa White, Matt Sands, Alex Green, and particularly Gillian Quinn.

This book would not have been possible without the tremendous assistance of Mandy Lee, Helen Taylor and Kim Folliott. As my assistant, Mandy kept me on track and helped with endless logistical challenges. I simply could not have completed this book without her help. Helen and Kim bore the unenviable task of typing this manuscript through rewrites. Laurie Bromberg did her usual masterful job on editing this text. She is a saint. Steven Kay provided unsurpassed insight on the Kenya situation. Cathy Hagle ensured that I was upgraded on endless flights so I would have the time and comfort to write the manuscript. My brother Scott remained supportive. Homer Moyer and George Hagle encouraged me to press on when I was in doubt. Their friendship is a rare gift.

Finally, I want to thank the Carney family for their years of support and love. Even in tough times, they were always there for me. I am truly blessed.

PREFACE

Since Nuremberg, the world has turned to international criminal tribunals to address the most far-reaching crimes: genocide, crimes against humanity, and other war crimes. The *ad hoc* tribunals for the International Criminal Tribunal for the former Yugoslavia (ICTY) and the International Criminal Tribunal for Rwanda (ICTR) were created in 1993 and 1994, respectively. Other UN supported tribunals were created for Lebanon (the Special Tribunal for Lebanon – STL), Cambodia (the Extraordinary Chambers in the Courts of Cambodia – ECCC), East Timor (Ad-Hoc Court for East Timor) and Sierra Leone (Special Court for Sierra Leone). In 2002, the world community established the International Criminal Court (ICC), a permanent court to address these international crimes. However, eleven years after the creation of the ICC, the world is relying more and more on domestic war crimes courts to handle the investigation and prosecution of such cases. This trend toward domestic war crimes tribunals (e.g., Iraq, Croatia, Serbia, Kenya, Bangladesh) has arisen not despite the ICC but rather because of it.

The drafters of the ICC's founding document, the Rome Statute, foresaw what would become the main challenge to the ICC's legitimacy: that the Court would violate principles of national sovereignty and show disrespect for the legal traditions of a given state's domestic courts. To address this concern, the drafters of the Rome Statute added the principle of complementarity to the ICC's jurisdiction, in that the Court's jurisdiction merely complements the exercise of jurisdiction by the domestic courts of the Statute's member states. Specifically, the ICC will exercise jurisdiction over a given case only if it is at sufficient gravity and where the pertinent state is *unwilling* or *unable genuinely* to do so. Although the ICC may obtain jurisdiction through a UN Security Council referral, such a referral affects a non-State Party only in those circumstances where the state doesn't address the matter itself. For State Parties that have implemented the Rome Statute through domestic legislation, the ICC is honouring the authority of those states to conduct their own trials.

The purpose of this book is (a) to demonstrate the rise of this new trend toward domestic war crimes courts and (b) to elaborate on how the ICC can best implement the complementarity principle with domestic prosecutors. In analysing the current situation, and in making his case for the future direction of domestic courts, the author draws on his work with the ICTY, the ICC, the ECCC, the Iraqi War Crimes Tribunal, and his service as Legal Advisor to the OSCE for the creation of the Serbian War Crimes Court. This book asserts that the principle of complementarity is the key legal underpinning for domestic jurisdiction of international crimes. The principle is both dynamic and powerful. It provides the most effective framework that emphasises the cooperation between international and domestic accountability mechanisms.

However, the book shows how the goals of complementarity have not been fully achieved. In theory, the idea of domestic trials to prosecute individuals for committing gross violations of international criminal law is a laudable one. In practice, it is fraught with difficult challenges. If the principle of complementarity is to be applied, states must ensure that their own judicial systems and trials are consistent with international standards of independence and fairness. At a minimum, states will have to adhere to standards of due process found in international human rights instruments.

In addition, for complementarity to work, the ICC must be willing to actively support, embrace, and implement the principle. If the Court holds on too tightly to a self-aggrandising view of its role in promoting international justice, then it will lose all credibility in the eyes of nation states. Consequently, the international legal community will face the two most dramatic and contentious issues embodied in the principle of complementarity: (1) How exactly is a national judicial system deemed to have met or have failed to meet the international standards necessary to conduct credible and fair domestic war crimes cases? (2) Who should make this assessment and final determination – the ICC or the state? This book will answer both questions and set forth several innovative recommendations to strengthen and unify the principle of complementarity between the ICC and nation states.

Furthermore, the international community, in calling on states to address war crimes committed within their borders, must provide some of the financial, technical, and professional resources that many struggling states need in this endeavour. This should include the creation of an internationally maintained training centre, so that states can benefit from international assistance as they create domestic war crimes courts.

Finally, State Parties to the ICC face enormous political and culture-based opposition when establishing domestic war crimes courts. Consequently, the book explores how the international community can act sensitively to help states overcome these domestic challenges. The book sets forth several innovative recommendations to strengthen and unify the principle of complementarity between the ICC and nation states and presents a course of action that will make future domestic war crimes courts work more effectively.

INTRODUCTION

> *'[T]he most serious crimes of concern to the international community as a whole must not go unpunished and... their effective prosecution must be ensured by taking measures at the national level and by enhancing international cooperation'.*[1]

Since 1945 there have been 253 distinct armed conflicts in which an estimated minimum of 7.8 million people have lost their lives.[2] However, it is estimated that if victims of repressive authoritarian state regimes were included, the total may be as high as 101 million victims between 1946 and 2008;[3] this figure does did not include those who lost their lives as a *consequence* of armed conflict or state repression. Their inclusion would increase the total to 202 million victims for the same period.[4] Nor does this figure include those injured or displaced by armed conflict or state repression as such numbers are inestimable, although unquestionably extensive. Equally distressing is the fact that during this same period of time, only 823 persons had been indicted by international and regional courts for violations of international humanitarian law.[5]

The disparity between these numbers is staggering and has consistently confounded expectations. In 2012 alone, research suggests that at least 92,600 people were killed or injured as a direct result of armed conflict,

---

[1] *See* Rome Statute of the International Criminal Court, Rome, opened for signature 17 July 1988, 2187 UNTS 90 (entered into force 1 July 2002) UN Doc. A/CONF.183/9 (hereinafter, ICC Statute or Rome Statute), Preamble [emphasis added].

[2] This is a composite based on an assessment of a number of sources, analysis of which can be found in Appendix I.

[3] M. Cherif Bassiouni, 'Assessing Conflict Outcomes: Accountability and Impunity' in M. Cherif Bassiouni (ed.), *The Pursuit of International Criminal Justice: A World Study on Conflicts, Victimization, and Post-Conflict Justice*, 2 vols. (Oxford: Intersentia, 2010), vol. 1, p. 3.

[4] *Ibid.*

[5] *Ibid.*

and 6.5 million people were displaced.[6] Projected into the future, the need to focus on accountability and international justice becomes paramount. This solemn realisation undoubtedly reverberated with the international community. International justice took a leap forward on 1 July 2002 with the establishment of the International Criminal Court (ICC). Created as a permanent institution to prosecute individuals accused of the most egregious international crimes, namely genocide, war crimes, and crimes against humanity; this vanguard court is a remarkable development in international law.

To date, 122 countries have ratified the Rome Statute of the International Criminal Court (hereinafter ICC Statute or Rome Statute) and are bound, as States Parties, by its various mandates. The Court embodies a number of goals, including being '[m]indful that during this century millions of children, women and men have been victims of unimaginable atrocities that deeply shock the conscience of humanity, [and] [r]ecognizing that such grave crimes threaten the peace, security and well-being of the world'.[7]

One of the Court's laudable tenets is to provide uniformity in the exercise of jurisdiction over international crimes by domestic war crimes courts. It is reasonable and appropriate to debate the role of domestic courts in handling the most heinous of international crimes. Should gross violations of international criminal law only be tried through international courts or should domestic national courts also undertake this role? As I will address in this publication, any ambiguity over this debate is now resolved. Evidence showing that national accountability for international crimes has been lethargic and largely ignored is unequivocal.[8] However, this trend is being reversed. With the ongoing evolution of the ICC, indigenous national criminal jurisdictions are in the process of becoming the 'accountability centres' for international criminal trials.

There is one paramount reason for this growth of accountability and that is the ICC's reliance on the principle of *complementarity*. The

[6] Kate Halff, 'Persons displaced internally by conflict and violence in 2012', in Stuart Casey-Maslen (ed.), *The War Report 2012* (Oxford: Oxford University Press, 2013), p. 272.
[7] ICC Statute, Preamble.
[8] *See* Mark S. Ellis, 'Combating Impunity and Enforcing Accountability as a Way To Promote Peace and Stability – The Role of International War Crimes Tribunals' (2006) 2 *Journal of National Security Law and Policy*, 111, 112.

principle of complementarity is the single core attribute in support of the devolution of judicial authority, ensuring that domestic war crimes courts undertake the majority of war crimes trials. The ICC Statute's Preamble and Article 1 affirm the fundamental importance of this principle by establishing that the Court 'shall be complementary to national criminal jurisdictions'.[9] The principle places, within national courts, the primary authority to prosecute individuals who have committed gross violations of international criminal law. Again, the Statute's Preamble refers to 'the duty of every state to exercise its criminal jurisdiction over those responsible for international crimes'.[10] As Judge Fausto Pocar, former President of the International Criminal Tribunal for the former Yugoslavia (ICTY) (also former Chairman of the United Nations Human Rights Committee), stated: '[d]eveloping domestic capacity for the prosecution of international crimes and the application [by domestic judiciaries] of international law as clarified by international courts is... a primary objective to be achieved'.[11]

The principle of complementarity also addresses the presumed conflict between state sovereignty and the pursuit of supranational justice for the most pernicious international crimes; between a nation's right to control and enforce its own laws and the victims' right to objective justice. These considerations are not simply a matter of policy. Specific and succinct legal mechanisms have been built into the ICC Statute to uphold the principle of complementarity and give preference to the sovereignty of individual states. Thus, future systematic and widespread atrocities will likely be addressed by domestic courts, who will undertake a major role in fulfilling the universal duty for judicial accountability. Under the principle of complementarity, nation states possess the primary and preferred responsibility to suppress international crimes by bringing to account those who have perpetuated the crimes.

The first ICC Prosecutor, Luis Moreno-Ocampo, clearly addressed this issue when he stated: '[n]ational investigations and prosecutions, where they can properly be undertaken, will normally be the most effective and efficient means of bringing offenders to justice; states themselves will

---

[9] ICC Statute, Preamble and Article 1.

[10] *Ibid.*, Preamble.

[11] Judge Fausto Pocar, 'Dialogue with Member States on rule of law at the international level organised by the Rule of Law Unit: UN Approach to Transitional Justice', (2 December 2009), p. 2, available at www.unrol.org/files/TJ%20panel%20discssion%20-%20FP%20statement.pdf.

normally have the best access to evidence and witnesses'.[12] He went on to say that: '[i]n cases of concurrent jurisdiction between national systems and the ICC, the former have priority'.[13] The Prosecutor was making clear that his office would undertake investigations 'only where there is a clear case of failure to take national action' by a state.[14] It should come as no surprise that the majority of nation states' citizens also believe it is better to institute prosecutions in local courts than in international courts.[15]

Thus, the ICC *will not* undermine national sovereignty, nor interfere with judicial matters that naturally fall within the jurisdiction of states. The principle of complementarity will likely push states to retain control over investigating and prosecuting nationals charged with gross violations of international criminal law. Both States Parties and non-States Parties will stress the pre-eminence of domestic jurisdictions over international jurisdiction where they have the capacity to undertake domestic war crime trials. They certainly will argue that the primary responsibility for investigating and prosecuting international crimes should remain part of national sovereignty.

State sovereignty is a powerful, and at times tempestuous, concept in international law. States will be reluctant to admit to judicial inadequacies that would result in transferring a case to the ICC. Therefore, states will hold firm to retaining control over domestic prosecutions unless it is in the clear self-interest of the state to delegate these matters to the Court. This might happen if it is politically more appropriate to transfer a suspect to the ICC rather than undertake a domestic trial. For instance, transferring a former head of state to the Court could have a demulcent effect in a politically charged post-conflict environment. However, for most other situations, it is almost inconceivable that a state with a functioning legal system would not at least investigate alleged crimes. The risks are high if a state fails to maintain control over the proceedings; a state risks losing its jurisdictional control. Thus, States Parties will likely aggressively pursue

---

[12] ICC-Office of the Prosecutor (ICC-OTP), 'Paper on Some Policy Issues Before the Office of the Prosecutor' (September 2003), p. 2, available at www.icc-cpi.int/NR/rdonlyres/1FA7C4C6-DE5F-42B7-8B25-60AA962ED8B6/143594/030905_Policy_Paper.pdf.
[13] *Ibid.*, p. 4.
[14] *Ibid.*, p. 5.
[15] *See* a discussion on Serbia's views on the ICTY in Diane F. Orentlicher, *Shrinking the Space for Denial: The Impact on the ICTY in Serbia* (Open Society Justice Initiative, 2008).

domestic prosecutions of international crimes so as not to trigger ICC jurisdiction. The influence of the general principle of complementarity is creating a direct paradigm shift among States Parties who could find themselves under possible ICC investigation.

This trend is indisputable. Three examples of this phenomenon will be discussed in this publication: the Democratic Republic of Congo (DRC); Kenya; and most recently, Libya. When the first ICC Prosecutor announced he was opening an investigation into crimes committed in the countries, all three governments responded aggressively, asserting their desire to conduct the trials within their own domestic courts. The motivation was ostensibly geared at sidestepping ICC jurisdiction. The Kenyan Parliament passed a motion to withdraw from the ICC because of the Court's decision to indict individuals rather than allowing Kenya to try the individuals through a domestic war crimes court.[16] The motion also resolved to table a law that would repeal the International Crimes Act, a Kenyan Act that domesticated the Rome Statute.[17] Now that the motion has been passed, a bill to this effect is expected to be introduced soon.[18]

Before his capture and death, the new transitional government for Libya had made it clear that it wanted to try Muammar Gaddafi in Libya, despite the fact that the ICC had already indicted him on charges of crimes against humanity. Most recently, the Libyan government has declared that it would also try Gaddafi's son – Saif Al-Islam Gaddafi – and Abdullah Al-Senussi for war crimes. Reports state that Al-Senussi and Gaddafi have been charged with murder and other offences in relation to Libya's 2011 civil war, and that a trial date has been set.

For non-States Parties to the Rome Statute as well, the possibility of surrendering jurisdiction to the ICC through a UN Security Council

---

[16] *See* Parliament of Kenya, 'Kenya National Assembly Motions 2010', (22 December 2010), p. 40, available at http://www.parliament.go.ke/plone/archive/archive-10th-Parliament/motions/motion-tracker-2010/at_multi_download/item_files?name=Motion%20Tracker%202010%20as%20at%2022-12-10.pdf. The motion is not binding. *See also* 'Kenya MPs Vote to Withdraw from ICC', *BBC News*, (5 September 2013) available at http://www.bbc.co.uk/news/world-africa-23969316.

[17] Charles C. Jalloh, 'Kenya Should Reconsider Proposed Withdrawal from the ICC', *Jurist*, (13 September 2013), available at http://jurist.org/forum/2013/09/charles-jalloh-kenya-icc.php.

[18] *Ibid.*

referral is a powerful impetus for holding to account perpetrators of international crimes through domestic prosecutions. Non-States Parties cannot circumvent the possibility of ICC jurisdiction over domestic crimes by simply deciding *not* to sign and ratify the Rome Statute. In my opinion, the principle of complementarity actually applies to non-States Parties and States Parties alike. A state that fails to undertake genuine investigations and prosecutions of international crimes can still find itself within the ICC's reach via a UN Security Council referral. This is exactly what happened to Sudan when the government failed to end, and hold accountable those who committed, the atrocities in Darfur. The same occurred with Libya when the Security Council referred the humanitarian crisis in Libya to the ICC for investigation and prosecution.

Through the principle of complementarity, the ICC dramatically expands the role of national courts in trials involving international crimes. The reason is that the ICC has jurisdiction only if there is a breakdown in the national system of justice or if a States Party simply fails to prosecute. The ICC *must* defer its jurisdiction to national courts, except in situations where national jurisdictions have been 'genuinely unable' or 'unwilling' to investigate and/or prosecute the accused.[19] This is an irrevocable principle. Consequently, the ICC's impact on domestic law and national capacity building will be significant and far-reaching. Most dramatic will be the increase in the number of domestic war crimes courts, even in non-States Party jurisdictions. The international community is already witnessing this burgeoning trend.[20]

The decision by an increasing number of countries to conduct domestic war crimes trials provides significant insight into the pursuit of a domestic policy of accountability. However, the trend for states to retain control over prosecuting nationals charged with crimes that fall under the ICC Statute is not without legal constraints. In theory, establishing domestic trials to prosecute individuals for committing gross violations of international criminal law is a laudable aspiration. In practice, however, it is fraught with difficult challenges. If the principle of complementarity is to be applied, states must ensure that their own judicial systems, and subsequent trials, are consistent with international standards of independence

---

[19] ICC Statute, Article 17(1)(a).

[20] Including in the Democratic Republic of the Congo, Kenya, Mexico, Poland, Estonia, Latvia, Lithuania, Chile, Argentina, Senegal, Peru, Bolivia, Iraq, Bangladesh, Burundi, Ecuador, Guatemala, Uruguay, Liberia, Croatia, Serbia, Bosnia, Macedonia, Lebanon and Rwanda.

and fairness. At a minimum, states will have to adhere to standards of due process found in international human rights instruments.

The investigation and prosecution of war crimes has proven to be a highly complicated and difficult task. Although domestic war crimes courts can and do operate under special conditions, history shows that states can find it difficult to successfully bring war criminals to justice.[21] There remains doubt as to whether states can hold credible war crimes trials.[22] Nearly every national war crimes prosecution has been heavily criticised by human rights institutions for failing to remain independent from the political institutions.[23] Generally, these trials fail on several counts that are fundamental to a fair trial. Local investigations are often not feasible. The options for gathering evidence in post-conflict environments are limited. Sitting regimes are not always willing to cooperate, because there is simply a lack of political will to prosecute war crimes suspects. The investigations run the risk of being manipulated by the very people who should be held accountable, which is completely antithetical to the prosecution process. Moreover, governments may have an interest in providing biased information about members of their own party or members of the opposition. This can easily lead to an utter absence of transparency, resulting in 'sham trials'.

Courts will also confront the issue of security, particularly in post-conflict environments. For instance, in Iraq at least 210 lawyers and judges were killed between the fall of Saddam Hussein in 2003 and 2007.[24] A

---

[21] Eric Wiebelhaus-Brahm, 'Summary of Regional and Thematic Studies' in Bassiouni, *The Pursuit of International Criminal Justice,* vol. 1, pp. 114-118.

[22] *See* Dominic Raab, 'Evaluating the ICTY and its Completion Strategy: Efforts to Achieve Accountability for War Crimes and Their Tribunals', (2005) 3 *Journal of International Criminal Justice* 82, 93–94.

[23] Including the Humanitarian Law Center and the Belgrade Center for Human Rights. *See* John Ryan, 'Last Stop Belgrade', (2012) 13 *Law Dragon* 36, 50.

[24] *See* 'IRAQ: Justice delayed as lawyers live under threat', *IRIN News*, (30 April 2007) available at www.irinnews.org/Report.aspx?ReportId=71864. Since its publication, this figure has been quoted many times in the press, including in 2010: *see* 'Post-invasion Iraq – the facts', *New Internationalist*, (1 March 2010), p. 432 available at www.newint.org/features/2010/05/01/post-invasion-iraq-facts. Also in 2010, Amnesty International reported that 'a number of lawyers, judges and prosecutors have been murdered by armed groups' in Iraq, without offering a figure. *See* Amnesty International, *Iraq: Human rights Briefing,* (2010), p. 8, available at www.amnesty.org/en/library/asset/MDE14/004/2010/en/c2bb7123-1e17-4abf-8202-6f6f81448644/mde140042010en.pdf.

hostile security environment is also a clear threat to witnesses. Without a stable security environment, court proceedings will not be legitimate.

Yet, if structured properly, domestic war crimes courts can play an indisputable role in supporting post-conflict reconciliation. I realised the need for structural reform for domestic war crimes courts while acting as an expert for the Organisation for Security and Co-operation in Europe (OSCE) to Serbia in 2003. I was commissioned to conduct an assessment on whether Serbia was capable of conducting domestic war crimes trials. During the assessment mission, it was clear the Serbian judicial system had neither the knowledge nor expertise to undertake the enormous task of creating a domestic war crimes court. There was much to do, particularly in areas fundamental to ensuring a credible fair trial.

Two years later I encountered the same issues, complications, challenges, and questions while working with the newly created Iraqi War Crimes Court, created to bring to justice Saddam Hussein and his cohorts. Once again, this domestic court faced an intellectual 'black hole' on issues dealing with defence representation, judicial selection, witness protection, and the Court's perceived legitimacy.

This book asserts that the principle of complementarity is the key legal underpinning for domestic jurisdiction of international crimes. The principle is both dynamic and powerful. It provides the most effective framework that emphasises the cooperation between international and domestic accountability mechanisms. Complementarity aims to regulate, organise, and leverage the existing body of international criminal law, encouraging domestic courts to effectively make use of their own inherent jurisdiction over the most serious international crimes committed within their own territory.

However, complementarity only works under two conditions. First, national judicial systems must incorporate, embrace and enforce international judicial norms. The importance of stressing *international standards of justice* is paramount. This type of 'due process' approach reasons that a domestic system's disregard for international standards of fair trial amounts to being 'unwilling or unable' and renders a case admissible before the ICC.[25] Yet, many disagree with this approach,

---

[25] Dawn Yamane Hewett, 'Recent Developments: Sudan's Courts and Complementarity in the Face of Darfur', (2006) 31 *Yale Journal of International Law* 276, 277: 'a State may be considered 'unwilling' to prosecute, even if

including the ICC's Office of the Prosecutor (OTP), which argues that the Court is not a human rights monitoring body, and 'its role is not to ensure perfect procedures and compliance with all international standards [at the domestic level]'.[26] Others have expanded this assertion by arguing that it is not necessary for domestic courts to guarantee such fundamental principles as witness protection. They reason that since the ICC adheres to more stringent due process requirements than many domestic jurisdictions, there is a danger that the Court 'will become a tool for overly harsh assessments of the [judicial proceedings and non-judicial transitional justice mechanisms] in developing countries'.[27] These scholars reject the 'due process thesis', disavowing the role of the ICC as a human rights monitor.[28] Instead, a state is 'unwilling or unable' 'only if its legal proceedings are designed to make a defendant more difficult to convict'.[29] Thus, so long as domestic procedures are aimed at bringing to justice those

---

domestic trials are taking place... or if the proceedings failed to accord with international due process norms'. *See also* Mark S. Ellis, 'The International Criminal Court and its Implication for Domestic Law and National Capacity Building', (2002) 15 *Florida Journal of International Law*, 215.

[26] ICC-OTP, 'Informal Expert Paper: The Principle of Complementarity in Practice' (2003), p. 15, available at www.icc-cpi.int/iccdocs/doc/doc654724.pdf; *see also* International Center for Transitional Justice (ICTJ), *Uganda: Impact of the Rome Statute and the International Criminal Court* (May 2010), p. 4, available at http://ictj.org/sites/default/files/ICTJ-Uganda-Impact-ICC-2010-English.pdf.

[27] *See* William A. Schabas, *An Introduction to the International Criminal Court*, 2nd edn (Cambridge: Cambridge University Press, 2004), p. 86 (ICC may find truth commissions are unacceptable, even though productive); *see also* Kevin Jon Heller, 'The Shadow Side of Complementarity: The Effect of Article 17 of the Rome Statute on National Due Process' (2006) 17 *Criminal Law Forum*, 255, 256–257, ensuring due process in domestic proceedings, (higher ICC standards regarding defendants' match the International Covenant on Civil and Political Rights). However, if non-judicial process is genuine, the OTP is unlikely to investigate. *See also* Ellis, 'The International Criminal Court and its Implication for Domestic Law', 230.

[28] *See* Office of the Public Counsel for the Defence (OPCD) oral arguments in *The Prosecutor v. Saif Al-Islam Gaddafi and Abdullah Al-Senussi*, Doc. ICC-01/11-01/11-T-2-Red-ENG, 'Hearing Transcript', (9 October 2012), pp. 3-5. The Pre-Trial Chamber heard from Libya, the OTP, the OPCV, the OPCD, and Libya again. *See also* Heller, 'The Shadow Side of Complementarity'; Gregory S. McNeal, 'ICC Inability Determinations in Light of the Dujail Case', (2006) 39 *Case Western Reserve Journal of International Law*, 325.

[29] Heller, 'The Shadow Side of Complementarity', 257.

who have committed crimes, the ICC must allow the state to proceed 'no matter how unfair those proceedings may be'.[30]

It may be tantalising to accept these lesser standards because newly created domestic war crimes courts will most likely emerge in post-conflict environments where legal systems are weaker. However, creating a bifurcated system of measurable justice would be illogical and a mistake. It would exacerbate a perception that the principle of justice can somehow be split between a 'north-south' divide, allowing developing countries and post-conflict countries to meet a lesser standard of justice. Domestic war crimes courts should be foursquare in adhering to certain inviolable standards established and accepted by the international community as a whole.

Secondly, the ICC must be willing to actively support, embrace and implement the principle of complementarity. If the Court holds on too tightly to a self-aggrandising view of its role in promoting international justice, then it will lose all credibility with nation states. The Court's recent admissibility decisions over cases in Kenya and Libya are examples of this worrisome trend. The decisions have caused significant animosity towards the Court. For example, the African Union (AU) has claimed that the ICC process had degenerated into 'race hunting' and objected to the 'flawed' process where '99%' of those indicted by the ICC were African.[31]

The purpose of this book, therefore, is: (a) to demonstrate the rise of this new trend towards domestic prosecutions; and (b) to elaborate on how the ICC can best implement the complementarity principle domestic war crimes courts. Assessing these two issues will also bring to the forefront the two most dramatic and contentious issues embodied in the principle of complementarity. First, how exactly is a national judicial system deemed to have met or have failed to meet the international standards necessary to conduct credible and fair domestic war crimes cases? Secondly, who should make this assessment and final determination – the ICC or the state?

---

[30] *Ibid. But see* Ellis, 'The International Criminal Court and its Implication for Domestic Law', 226 (seemingly supporting ICC ensuring due process in domestic proceedings).

[31] 'African Union Accuses ICC of 'Hunting' Africans', *BBC News*, (27 May 2013), available at www.bbc.co.uk/news/world-africa-22681894.

The international community, in calling on states to address war crimes committed within their borders, must also provide some of the financial, technical and professional resources that many struggling states need in this endeavour. The assistance can be supplied through an internationally maintained training centre, so that states can benefit from international assistance, as they create domestic was crimes courts. This too will be covered in the upcoming chapters.

States Parties to the ICC also face enormous political and cultural-based opposition when establishing domestic war crimes courts. Consequently, this book explores how the international community can act sensitively to help states overcome these domestic challenges. The book sets forth several innovative recommendations to strengthen and unify the principle of complementarity between the ICC and nation states and presents a course of action that will make future domestic war crimes courts work more effectively.

CHAPTER ONE

THE PRINCIPLE OF COMPLEMENTARITY: ITS HISTORY AND FUNCTION

Introduction

The International Criminal Court (ICC), and its principle of *complementarity,* ensures primary jurisdiction and accountability at the state level. The ICC is a court of last resort. Its existence and codifying legislation are designed to support a cooperative process to end impunity for international crimes. This is the crucible for domestic war crimes courts and international law.

The Rome Statute, the textual source and enabling treaty of the ICC, does not offer a robust definition of the term 'complementarity'. Yet complementarity is clearly embodied in the Statute, and is of paramount importance if *nation states* (the Statute does not refer to regional courts) are to pursue justice against perpetrators of the most injurious international crimes.

The Preamble to the Rome Statute sets forth that:

> the most serious crimes of concern to the international community as a whole must not go unpunished and that their effective prosecution must be ensured by taking measures at the national level and by enhancing international cooperation.[1]

Article 1 of the Statute also states that the Court:

> shall have the power to exercise its jurisdiction over persons for the most serious crimes of international concern . . . and shall be *complementary* to national criminal jurisdiction', since it is 'the duty of every state to

---

[1] Rome Statute of the International Criminal Court, Rome, opened for signature 17 July 1988, 2187 UNTS 90 (entered into force 1 July 2002) UN Doc. A/CONF.183/9 (hereinafter, ICC Statute or Rome Statute), Preamble.

> exercise its criminal jurisdiction over those responsible for international crimes[2] [emphasis added].

The history of the principle of complementarity is often viewed within the early drafting stages of the Rome Statute as embodied in Draft Statute for an International Criminal Court with commentaries (1994).[3] However, the majority of commentators and academics have ignored a much earlier debate on the complementarity principle that emerged in 1943 during the creation and operation of the United Nations War Crimes Commission (UNWCC).[4] It was actually the UNWCC that laid the grounds for the current design and interpretation of the principle of complementarity.

The UNWCC was established on 20 October 1943 by seventeen Allied nations to work towards 'the detection, apprehension, trial and punishment of suspected war criminals' during World War II.[5] The United Nations War Crimes Commission was charged with investigating crimes. The investigating function of the UNWCC was envisaged in the Moscow Declaration of 1 November 1943.[6] However, since it had no machinery for

---

[2] ICC Statute, Article 1.

[3] 'Draft Statute for an International Criminal Court with Commentaries', (1994) 2 1 *Yearbook of the International Law Commission*, 26.

[4] The principle of complementarity and the UNWCC is also examined in a upcoming publication, by the author Dr. Mark S. Ellis, entitled 'Assessing the Impact of the United Nations War Crimes Commission on the Principle of Complementarity and Fair Trial Standards', which will be published in *Criminal Law Forum* later this year.

[5] The States Parties to the UNWCC included; Australia, Belgium, Canada (Canada was not represented on the Commission), China, Czechoslovakia, France, Greece, India, Luxembourg, the Netherlands, New Zealand, Norway, Poland, the United Kingdom, the United States, Yugoslavia and South Africa (South Africa took part in the creation of the UNWCC, but did not hold national trials and was not represented on the Commission); United Nations War Crimes Commission (UNWCC), 'Progress Report adopted by the Commission on 19th September 1944', Doc. C.48(1) (19 September 1944), p. 1. UNWCC Documents are available at http://www.legal-tools.org/en/go-to-database/ltfolder/0_28425/#results. Denmark later joined the UNWCC in July 1945; *See* Dan Plesch and Shanti Sattler, 'Changing the Paradigm of International Criminal Law: Considering the Work of the United Nations War Crimes Commission of 1943-1948' (2013) 15 2 *International Law Community Review*, 203.

[6] UNWCC, 'Annex V – Establishment of closer cooperation between the UNWCC and the National Offices', Doc. NOC.5 (2 June 1945), p. 1; 'Declaration of Four Nations on General Security' reprinted in 'Great Britain-Soviet Union-United States Tripartite Conference in Moscow' (1944) 38 1 (Supp.) *The American*

investigation, the UNWCC was responsible for simply investigating statements sent into it by the Allied governments to determine whether a further prima facie case of war crimes existed and then subsequently report back to the relevant governments. This was the primary function of the Commission from the onset.[7] The UNWCC was referred to as an 'arbitrator', an 'intermediary' and as an advisor – demonstrating that the 'root idea of self-help' is maintained by the United Nations and that the states have the pre-eminent right to punish their own nationals.[8]

The focus on complementarity was most prominent in the make-up of the National Offices for each Allied country of the UNWCC. Each Allied government[9] established a National Office for the purpose of preparing charges against alleged war criminals and 'transmitting them with the relevant information and material for the substantiation of the charges for examination by the Commission. These National Offices were to be in

---

Journal of International Law, pp. 3-8 (hereinafter Moscow Declaration). *See also* UNWCC, 'Declarations by United Nations Governments and Leaders on the Subject of War Crimes', Doc. C.29 (14 June 1944). Under the Moscow Declaration, 'those German officers and men and members of the Nazi party who have been responsible for or have taken a consenting part in the above atrocities, massacres and executions will be sent back to the countries in which their abominable deeds were done in order that they may be judged and punished according to the laws of these liberated countries and of free governments which will be erected therein'. Thus, those who committed crimes 'will know they will be brought back to the scene of their crimes and judged on the spot by the peoples whom they have outraged'.

[7] UNWCC, 'Progress Report', Doc. C.48(1), p. 1; UNWCC, 'Annex VI – Chairman's Introductory Speech', Doc. NOC.6 (31 May 1945), p. 5.

[8] UNWCC, 'Amendment of Paragraph 1 of Committee III's Draft Recommendation Regarding the SA, SS, and the Gestapo (Document C35)', Doc. C.35(1) (4 August 1944), p. 1; 'Each of the United Nations has the right, either on the basis of its present criminal law or on the basis of new legislation, to punish its own nationals who became members of the SA; SS; or Gestapo, irrespective of their rank as members and of the territories in which they served. Each of the United Nations has also the right to punish German or foreign members of the above-mentioned organisations who have committed crimes in their territories' [emphasis added]. The term 'United Nations' refers to the Allied nations following the adoption of the Declaration by United Nations (signed 1 January 1942).

[9] 'Each Allied Government' refers to each government that was party to the UNWCC; Australia, Belgium, China, Czechoslovakia, France, Greece, India, Luxembourg, Netherlands, New Zealand, Norway, Poland, South Africa, United Kingdom, United States and Yugoslavia.

close touch with the Commission'.[10] As succinctly stated by the Belgian representative on the Commission (Marcel de Baer), '[i]t cannot enough be stressed that if the National Offices wish to see a just punishment imposed upon these men they should investigate these cases themselves and bring charges against them'.[11] His remarks reflected the high level of responsibility that was afforded to the National Offices. Thus, it was the national courts that had 'primary jurisdiction' to try war criminals and that '[t]he majority of cases ought to be tried by national courts…'.[12]

> Consonant with the Moscow Declaration, 1st November, 1943, the principle is accepted by the United Nations War Crimes Commission that, with the exception of major war criminals, whose offences have no particular geographical localization, war criminals, upon apprehension, will be sent back to the countries in which their crimes were committed in order that they may be judged by the courts of such countries. **The mentioned countries thus have a paramount right to such criminals and their courts have primary jurisdiction**[13] [emphasis added].

The UNWCC recognised that the appropriate jurisdiction for the prosecution and trial of such crimes would ostensibly be the **national courts**.[14] With the exception of 'major' war criminals, the accused persons established on the War Crimes Commission's Lists '*should be handed over without delay to the country that has requested their surrender*',[15] and the Commission '*should take every step, within its jurisdiction, to ensure that the surrender is effectively carried out*'.[16] The very notion of the UNWCC system was rooted in the idea of self-help and 'that the [Allied countries] should each do its own work in bringing to justice those

[10] UNWCC, 'Progress Report', Doc. C.48(1), p. 1.

[11] UNWCC, 'Annex IV – Cooperation between National Offices and the War Crimes Commission', Doc. NOC.4, (2 June 1945), p. 2.

[12] UNWCC, 'Notes of Unofficial Preliminary Meeting of the United Nations Commission for the Investigation of War Crimes', (26 October 1943), p. 3, available at http://www.legal-tools.org/doc/ad8990/.

[13] UNWCC, 'Recommendation in favour of the establishment by Supreme Military Commanders of Mixed Tribunals for the Trial of War Criminals', Doc. C.52(1), (26 September 1944), p. 1.

[14] UNWCC, 'Draft Convention for the Establishment of a United Nations War Crimes Court', Doc. C.50(1), (30 September 1944), p. 1 [emphasis added].

[15] UNWCC, 'Annex IX – Statement presented to the Representatives and Reservations made at the last meeting of Conferences', Doc. NOC.10, (19 June 1945), p. 1 [emphasis added].

[16] UNWCC, 'Annex IX', Doc. NOC.10, p. 1 [emphasis added].

enemies who committed offences against their nationals'.[17] The Commission went even further and noted that the national courts should decide what laws and what procedure were applicable.[18]

The UNWCC can also be seen as a precursor to the current structural and statutory relationship between the ICC and States Parties. Although the national courts were afforded primary jurisdiction, the UNWCC called for close cooperation between the states and the Commission. For instance, the Commission stressed that major war criminals, as defined by the Moscow Declaration, should be tried at an international level. 'There was a class of persons who had directed criminal policies on the high level, or who could not be adequately punished by some national courts, and for them an inter-allied court was needed'.[19] On the subject of high-level perpetrators, the Commission reported that:

> [t]he judging of a certain, be it limited, number of the most prominent criminals, such as HITLER, HIMMLER, GOEBBELS, GOERING, MUSSOLINI, CIANO, etc., etc., could take place much better by an International Criminal Court than by any National Court of Law, however high its standing and however undoubted, its integrity might be. It can even be said that the trial of these individuals if it is to give general satisfaction, can and may only take place through the medium of an International Organ.[20]

Most important, and most relevant, to the current complementarity structure of the ICC is the fact that the UNWCC made certain that states that were *unable or unwilling* to try alleged war criminals would surrender the suspects in order for them to be tried by an international court:

> There was need of both courts, though not simultaneously. The cases so far could all be tried by national courts under the Moscow system; but there was a class of persons who had directed criminal policies on the high

[17] UNWCC, 'Annex VI – Chairman's Introductory Speech', Doc. NOC.6, (31 May 1945), p. 5.
[18] *Ibid.*
[19] UNWCC, 'Minutes of the Thirtieth Meeting', Doc. M.30, (5 September 1944), p. 2 [emphasis added].
[20] UNWCC, 'Report on the Constitution of and the Jurisdiction to be conferred on an International Criminal Court (submitted to the London Assembly by Dr JM de Moor)', Doc. SC II/3, (25 February 1944), p. 4.

level, *or who could not be adequately punished by some national courts*, and for them an inter-allied court was needed[21] [emphasis added].

Those individuals whom the governments are 'unable to punish (owing to the lack of national laws), or whom they do not wish to try in their own courts' would be able to transfer them to an international court'.[22]

Although not notable in the eyes of the public, the UNWCC actually contemplated the idea of establishing an international court to try war criminals.[23] These discussions followed an earlier debate in 1937 in the League of Nations, which focused on the creation of the *Convention for the Creation of an International Criminal Court*.[24] The idea of this Convention was raised by the French government in 1934, in a letter to the League of Nations. The Convention was attached to the *Convention for the Repression of Terrorism*.[25] Under the Convention, the court would be a permanent body that would deal with wilful acts against heads of states, destruction of public property of another state, terrorist activities and war crimes – when a state might 'prefer to surrender that person to an international court'.[26] The Convention aimed to address 'offences of an international character' and the offences listed in the *Convention for the*

---

[21] UNWCC, 'Minutes of the Thirtieth Meeting', p. 2.

[22] UNWCC, 'Minutes of the Thirty-first Meeting', Doc. M.31, (12 September 1944), p. 3 [emphasis added].

[23] One important issue that was raised was the fact that as the Allied courts were unable to try Germans who committed crimes in Germany, members of Commission argued that the creation of an inter-Allied court would offer a solution; '[t]he campaign of racial extermination of the Jews has special features which do not generally fall within the scope of the National Offices, as for instance the case of German Jews murdered in Germany'; UNWCC, 'Annex VI', Doc. NOC.6, p. 6.

[24] League of Nations, 'Convention for the Prevention and Punishment of Terrorism and the Convention for the Creation of an International Criminal Court (Geneva, 16 November 1937)' (1938) 19 *League of Nations Official Journal* 36; United Nations General Assembly (UNGA), 'Historical Survey of the Question of International Criminal Jurisdiction - Memorandum submitted by the Secretary-General', UN Doc. A/CN.4/7/Rev.1 (1949) 16-18; UNWCC (ed.), *History of the United Nations War Crimes Commission and the Development of Laws of War* (His Majesty's Stationary Office, 1948) (hereinafter *History of the UNWCC*), pp. 440-441.

[25] *Ibid.*

[26] UNWCC, *History of the UNWCC*, p. 440.

Repression of Terrorism. Although the Convention was adopted, it never entered into force.[27]

During the UNWCC discussions, the role of the national system was again examined. An initial draft convention (*Draft Convention for the Creation of an International Criminal Court*) was adopted by the London International Assembly in February 1944.[28] Article 3 of the *Draft Convention for the Creation of an International Criminal Court* stated that '[a]s a rule, no case shall be brought before the Court when a domestic Court of any one of the [Allied governments] has jurisdiction to try the accused and it is *in a position and willing to exercise such jurisdiction*' [emphasis added].[29] In April 1944, the American delegates drafted the *Draft Convention on the Trial and Punishment of War Criminals*[30], which took the London International Assembly's Draft Convention into account.[31] According to Mohamed M. El Zeidy, the *Draft Convention on the Trial and Punishment of War Criminals* 'retained the jurisdiction of national courts', and the court was designed to try cases 'where national courts lacked jurisdiction under international law or as a result of a gap in domestic legislation'.[32] As noted below, this draft served as the basis of future discussions on the creation of a war crimes court.[33]

The *Draft Convention on the Trial and Punishment of War Criminals* was redrafted following several recommendations.[34] The end result was the *Draft Convention for the Establishment of a United Nations War Crimes Court*,[35] which reflects the work of the UNWCC and shows,

---

[27] *Ibid.*, pp. 440-441.

[28] UNWCC, 'Draft Convention for the Creation of an International Criminal Court, submitted to the London International Assembly', Doc. II/2, (14 February 1944).

[29] *Ibid.*, Article 3.

[30] UNWCC, 'Draft Convention on the Trial and Punishment of War Criminals', Doc. II/11, (14 April 1944).

[31] El Zeidy notes that although the Draft Convention was 'inspired' by the League of Nations' Draft Convention (1937), there is no 'direct evidence to suggest that it was intended to base it on the 1937 League of Nations provision' relating to a complementarity mechanism. *See* Mohamed M. El Zeidy, *The Principle of Complementarity in International Criminal Law; Origin, Development and Practice* (Leiden: Martin Nijhoff Publishers, 2008) p. 72.

[32] *Ibid.*

[33] *Ibid.*, p. 71; UNWCC, *History of the UNWCC,* p. 443.

[34] UNWCC, 'Report on the Constitution', p. 4.

[35] UNWCC, 'Draft Convention', Doc. C.50(1); Original draft by Committee II of the UNWCC, 'Draft for the Establishment of a United Nations Joint Court', Doc.

unequivocally, that it played an antecedent role to the Rome Statute on the complementarity principle. The Preamble reflects this sentiment stating, in part, that:

> Recognizing that in general the appropriate tribunals for the trial and punishment of such crimes will be national courts of the United Nations, Mindful of the possibility that cases may occur in which such crimes cannot be conveniently or effectively punished by a national court, Have decided to set up an Inter-Allied Court before which the Governments of the United Nations may at their discretion bring to trial persons accused of an offence to which the Convention applies in preference to bringing them before a national court[36] [emphasis added].

Thus, from the earliest stage of the modern drafting process for the Rome Statute, the conveners, knowingly or unknowingly, followed the precedence of the UNWCC and decreed that the ICC should have jurisdiction over only the most 'serious crimes', emphasising national prosecutions.[37] As initially drafted, the Preamble of the Rome Statute, together with key commentary and articles, was unambiguous in stating that the Court would complement national criminal justice systems if and when a suspect had no prospect of being tried at the national level or a fair trial is not possible.[38]

C.50 (22 September 1944). *See* UNWCC, 'Explanatory Memorandum to Accompany the Draft Convention for the Establishment of a United Nations War Crimes Court', Doc. C.58, (6 October 1944).

[36] UNWCC, 'Draft Convention', C.50(1).

[37] UNGA, 'Report of the International Law Commission on the Work of its Forty-Sixth Session, Draft Statute for an International Criminal Court', UN Doc. A/49/355, (1 September 1994). Preamble: 'The States Parties to this Statute, Desiring to further international cooperation to enhance the effective prosecution and suppression of Draft Code of Crimes against the Peace and Security of Mankind crimes of international concern, and for that purpose to establish an international criminal court; Emphasizing that such a court is intended to exercise jurisdiction only over the most serious crimes of concern to the international community as a whole; Emphasizing further that such a court is intended to be complementary to national criminal justice systems in cases where such trial procedures may not be available or may be ineffective; Have agreed as follows…'.

[38] *See* 'Draft Statute for an International Criminal Court with Commentaries' for commentary to the Preamble; UNGA, 'Report of the International Law Commission on the Work of its Forty-Sixth Session (1994)' UN Doc. A/CN.4/464/Add.1, (22 February 1995), para. 7: 'Above all, it was emphasized that the Draft Statute must provide further assurances that the proposed Court would be complementary to national courts and that the new system would not undermine existing law enforcement efforts'.

During the drafting process, Britain advocated for an 'exceptional and restrictive role for the ICC',[39] whereby it would only prosecute if a state acted in 'bad faith or there were unconscionable delay in the investigation, prosecution or request for extradition'.[40] Germany and Slovenia proposed an additional restriction, giving the ICC jurisdiction only when a state failed in its duty to prosecute.[41] Both restrictions ultimately made their way into the final draft of the Rome Statute, establishing the Court's mandate as one of reinforcing the independence and effectiveness of *national courts*. The final version actually drew upon an earlier International Law Commission (ILC) draft, which had been careful to give primacy to national courts and extended ICC jurisdiction only in specific, limited circumstances.[42] The draft became the cornerstone for the construction of the notion of complementarity.[43] The ILC's replacement, the Preparatory Committee (PrepCom) reaffirmed this approach.[44] However, it is important to stress that the complementarity principle was not a certainty during these initial negotiations, even with the rich history of the UNWCC.

I. The International Law Commission and Post Development

In 1950, the International Law Commission asked its Special Rapporteur Ricardo J. Alfaro to consider the issue of state sovereignty in relation to an international court. Alfaro assumed that an international court would require states to surrender their own nationals to an external

---

[39] Christopher Keith Hall, 'The First Two Sessions of the UN Preparatory Committee on the Establishment of the International Criminal Court', (1997) 91 1 *American Journal of International Law*, 177, 181.

[40] *Ibid.*

[41] *Ibid.* These states argued that the ICC should be able to decide whether to exercise jurisdiction when a state's proceedings were not impartial or independent or when prosecution was not diligent.

[42] The United Nations International Law Commission (ILC) had placed the principle of complementarity in the preamble of its draft statute; UNGA, 'Report of the International Law Commission', Preamble.

[43] Mohamed M. El Zeidy, 'The Principle of Complementarity; A New Machinery to Implement International Criminal Law', (2001-2002) 23 *Michigan Journal of International Law*, 869, 892.

[44] *Ibid.*, citing *Report of the Preparatory Committee on the Establishment of an International Criminal Court,* Official Records of the General Assembly, Fifty-first Session, Supplement No. 22, Vol. I, UN Doc. A/51/22[Vol.I] (1996), para. 154.

jurisdiction, but recognised that this would be seen to challenge state sovereignty.[45] However, he believed that the 'principle of absolute sovereignty is incompatible with the present organisation of the world'.[46] The very existence of the United Nations demonstrated that states were willing to delegate elements of sovereignty to an international body. As argued by Alfaro, states were now part of an interdependent community in which the rights of everyone are limited by the rights of others. He went as far as to state that '[t]he sovereignty of the State is subordinated to the supremacy of international law'.[47] Not surprisingly, Alfaro's view was not universally accepted. Many members of the Commission argued that nations would refuse to relinquish their territorial jurisdiction or submit to the compulsory jurisdiction of an international court.[48] Years later, this same debate would engulf the Rome Conference. Alfaro's proposition would not hold. State Parties to the Rome Statute would ensure that the new international criminal court would not trump the jurisdiction of national courts unnecessarily.

Arguing for the primacy of domestic prosecutions, Australia proffered that national courts should take precedence if they were 'able and willing' to deal with the alleged criminal conduct.[49] Likewise, Kazakhstan argued that it wanted 'to maintain and consolidate its sovereignty' when addressing jurisdictional claims.[50] China went so far as to declare that complementarity was 'the most important guiding principle of the Statute'.[51]

Not every representative in Rome agreed. One of the most outspoken opponents was Judge Gabrielle Kirk McDonald, the representative from the International Criminal Tribunal for the former Yugoslavia (ICTY). She

---

[45] 'Report on the Question of International Criminal Jurisdiction by Ricardo J. Alfaro, Special Rapporteur', UN Doc. A/CN.4/15 and Corr.1, (3 March 1950), at 129.
[46] *Ibid.*
[47] *Ibid.*
[48] 'Report of the International Law Commission on its Second Session, 5 June to 29 July 1950', UN Doc. A/CN.4/34, (July 1950), at 137.
[49] United Nations Diplomatic Conference of Plenipotentiaries on the Establishment of an International Criminal Court, 'Summary Record of the 2nd Plenary Meeting', UN Doc. A/CONF.183/SR.2, (20 November 1998), para. 9.
[50] United Nations Diplomatic Conference of Plenipotentiaries on the Establishment of an International Criminal Court, 'Summary Record of the 3rd Plenary Meeting', UN Doc. A/CONF.183/SR.3, (20 November 1998), para. 1.
[51] *Ibid.*, para. 37.

argued strenuously that the 'unequivocal obligation [of states] to comply with orders, not just requests, by the International Criminal Court was essential [as was] the Prosecutor and defence counsel be[ing] able to conduct interviews and on-site investigations on the territories of states without any unwarranted interference by a national authority'.[52] The ICTY, through Judge Kirk McDonald, also criticised the draft Statute for its attempts to advance community interests by consensus rather than advance the hard principle of justice. This was seen by the ICTY as a flawed approach to ensuring accountability.[53] The adoption of the complementarity principle would, in its eyes, permanently abnegate the 'primary' jurisdiction principle that was at the heart of the ICTY and International Criminal Tribunal for Rwanda (ICTR).[54]

In the end, however, the state delegates prevailed. Whereas the original Preamble stated: '*Emphasizing further* that such a court *is intended to be* complementary to national criminal justice systems', the final draft was changed to read 'that such a court *shall be* complementary'[55] [emphasis added].

Thus, following explicit challenges and debates during the drafting process, the complementarity framework developed into a procedural and substantive safeguard against the possibility that a supranational institution might curtail the sovereign rights of nations. Today, the principle ensures that judgements by a domestic court are not replaced by the judgements of

---

[52] *Ibid.*, para. 107.

[53] *Ad hoc* Committee on the Establishment of an International Criminal Court, 'Comments Received Pursuant to Paragraph 4 of General Assembly Resolution 49/53 on the Establishment of An International Criminal Court', delivered to the General Assembly, UN Doc. A/AC.244/1, (20 March 1995), para. 8, p. 27.

[54] For example, the ICTY has primacy over the national courts and does not need to concern itself with any state claims of sovereignty. This means that at any stage of proceedings, the ICTY can request the national courts to defer a case to the ICTY. The ICTY is not, therefore, designed to be complementary to the national courts and it does not require consent of the states involved in order for it to hear a case. *See* Article 9(2) Statute of the International Tribunal for the Prosecution of Persons Responsible for Serious Violations of International Humanitarian Law Committed in the Territory of the former Yugoslavia since 1991, UN Doc. S/RES/827(1993) (hereinafter ICTY Statute).

[55] United Nations Diplomatic Conference of Plenipotentiaries on the Establishment of an International Criminal Court, 'Official Records', UN Doc. A/CONF.183/13 (Vol. III) 13; *see* China concerns in *Ad hoc* Committee, 'Comments Received', UN Doc. A/AC.244/1, pp. 8-12.

an international court. Complementarity has been affirmed by the international legal community as the best form of jurisdiction for an international institution.[56] It places international courts, like the ICC, in a 'complementary' role to national courts and does not circumvent the intrinsic responsibility of states to prosecute international crimes.[57] The principle is designed to keep the focus on *domestic courts* while the ICC remains a secondary institution, empowered to act if and when domestic institutions are unable to fulfil their obligation to prosecute.

The balance between international and domestic jurisdiction is also maintained by the fact that the ICC, both structurally and conceptually, is not designed to handle mass volumes of cases. The type of criminal acts that can be handled by the Court, as well as its position as a court of last resort, guarantees that only a small number of cases will move before the ICC for investigation. Considering that the Court has completed only **two** cases in ten years, this may be an understatement. The ICC will not adjudicate **all** cases involving international crimes, but rather states will be encouraged, by the mere presence of the ICC, to prosecute these crimes through their own domestic courts.

In part, there is a preference for national prosecutions because domestic war crimes courts enjoy several benefits that international courts do not. For example, domestic adjudication can be more efficient when conducting trials. Domestic courts tend to have better access to evidence and witnesses, both of which are generally found within the territory of a state where the perpetrator resides or where of the crime took place.[58] In addition to advantages of access and ability to preserve evidence, domestic courts often enjoy a sense of legitimacy among local populations that international courts do not.[59] Citizens understand their own legal system.

---

[56] Mark S. Ellis, 'International Justice and the Rule of Law: Strengthening the ICC through Domestic Prosecutions', (2009) 1 *Hague Journal on the Rule of Law*, 79, 81.
[57] *Ibid.*
[58] Robert Cryer, Håkan Friman, Darryl Robinson and Elizabeth Wilmhurst, *An Introduction to International Criminal Law and Procedure*, 2nd edn (Cambridge: Cambridge University Press, 2007). *See also* Neil J. Kritz, 'Coming to Terms with Atrocities: A Review of Accountability Mechanisms for Mass Violations of Human Rights', (1996) 59 *Law and Contemporary Problems* 127, 133 (noting that 'domestic courts can be more sensitive to the nuances of local culture').
[59] Steven R. Ratner and Jason S. Abrams, *Accountability for Human Rights Atrocities in International Law: Beyond the Nuremberg Legacy*, 2nd edn (Oxford: Oxford University Press, 2001).

They have lived with the nuances of their own judiciary. They know the judges, prosecutors and lawyers and they can more easily follow the court proceedings in the local setting and in their own language. Moreover, 'the effectiveness and local impact' of reconciliatory mechanisms is 'undoubtedly enhanced by… physical presence in the territory'.[60] Supranational enforcement mechanisms also risk being seen as 'an instrument of hegemony for powerful states'.[61]

A recent review of Serbia's domestic war crimes court by John Ryan provides one of the more authoritative assessments of this phenomenon. Ryan argues that, in public opinion polls, Serbs viewed their domestic war crimes court as more 'legitimate' than the ICTY.[62] A court run by Serbs, prosecuting crimes committed in Serbian territory was viewed as an exercise of sovereignty and, thus, more 'legitimate'. It follows that a domestic judicial process stands a greater chance of being viewed as a genuine attempt to bring perpetrators to justice rather than being a politically motivated action or example of 'victor's justice'.[63] These advantages, including procedures and personnel familiar to a domestic population, are critical to establishing universality of norms of accountability.

However, for domestic prosecutions to work, pursuant to the principle of complementarity, they must reflect international norms of justice. Despite the theoretical logic of complementarity, there remain serious concerns as to how the principle will be applied in post-conflict environments.[64] The fact is that domestic actors can thwart the course of justice, jeopardizing both the legitimacy and the universality of international norms.[65] Again, Serbian compliance was seen as largely disingenuous and having more to do with the desire for membership in the

---

[60] William W. Burke-White, 'A Community of Courts: Toward a System of International Criminal Law Enforcement', (2002) 24 *Michigan Journal of International Law* 1, 88 citing Kritz, 'Coming to Terms with Atrocities', 131.
[61] *Ibid.*, 88.
[62] John Ryan, 'Last Stop Belgrade', (2012) 13 *Law Dragon* 36, 50.
[63] *Ibid.*
[64] *See* Open Society Foundations, *Putting Complementarity into Practice: Domestic Justice for International Crimes in Democratic Republic of Congo, Uganda, and Kenya*, (New York: Open Society Foundations, 2011), p. 5.
[65] Jelena Subotic, *Hijacked Justice: Dealing with the Past in the Balkans*, (New York and London: Cornell University Press, 2009), p. 6.

European Union than a sincere desire to punish offenders.[66] It was only later, following a change in political leadership and pressure from the international community that Serbia began to show a willingness to bring perpetrators to justice.[67]

The challenge for the international community is to preserve the balance between state and international authority while strengthening the ability of domestic war crimes courts to prosecute gross violations of international law according to a set of universally accepted, binding legal mechanisms. While the Rome Statute elaborates a useful framework, the path to achieving this goal may be circuitous and painful. The current 'battle' between Libya and the ICC regarding who should prosecute Saif Al-Islam Gaddafi is a case in point.

As will be discussed throughout this book, valid questions remain regarding whether the Rome Statute is sufficiently clear and robust for complementarity to be successfully implemented. This goes to the heart of validating the presumption that domestic war crimes courts will ostensibly be responsible for justice over serious international crimes. To that end, this book provides a retrospective on how the ICC has applied complementarity provisions in current situations and how this affects the functioning and efficacy of domestic war crimes courts. Ultimately, whether the ICC or a domestic court prosecutes a case will depend largely on how the ICC and nation state interpret their respective powers under the concept of complementarity.

II. How does Complementarity Work in Practice?

The principle of complementarity attempts to balance the integrity of domestic adjudications of international crimes on the one hand, and authorising a supranational court, on the other, to exercise power when domestic legal systems are ineffective. Rather than overwhelming domestic jurisdictions, complementarity is best viewed as restricting trials at the international level.

---

[66] *Ibid.*, referred to by Ryan, *Last Stop Belgrade*, 51.

[67] Mark S. Ellis, 'Coming to Terms with its Past - Serbia's New Court for the Prosecution of War Crimes', (2004) 22 *Berkeley Journal of International Law*, 165, 168-169.

The Rome Statute creates a complex set of jurisdictional guidelines that limit ICC authority and defer to the good faith investigative efforts and prosecutorial discretion of domestic courts. Thus, absent a referral of a situation by the UN Security Council to the ICC, complementarity ensures that the ICC can gain jurisdiction over a situation **only** when a state fails the 'admissibility test' by, for example, being *unwilling or genuinely unable* to carry out an investigation or prosecution of an accused individual.[68] Under the concept of complementarity, the ICC cannot hear a case when a state has made a decision to act. If the case is genuinely being investigated by a state with jurisdiction, the ICC simply cannot intervene. The ICC has jurisdiction only if there is a breakdown in the national system of justice or a state is reticent to act. The Court will not interfere with judicial matters that naturally fall within the jurisdiction of states and are equally handled through principles of due process. In this way, the ICC is prevented from exercising jurisdiction without the consent of a nation state. Only where prosecutions are unattainable within the domestic legal system will the principle of complementarity provide a forum to ensure that serious international crimes do not go unpunished.

For domestic war crimes courts created in countries that are States Parties to the ICC, authority and jurisdiction are linked to the Rome Statute. It is a fundamental premise of treaty law that states are bound to a treaty only in so far as they voluntarily relinquish part of their sovereign rights by signing and implementing the treaty within their own domestic laws.[69]

Under the Rome Statute, States Parties have agreed to transfer their sovereign right to investigate and adjudicate vertically to the ICC should they not adequately pursue the case themselves. The only two exceptions to this deferral principle are (1) when the UN Security Council refers a situation (including in the jurisdiction of a non-State Party) to the Court (which the Council can do so long as the situation is a 'threat to peace and security' pursuant to Chapter VII of the UN Charter), and (2) when the

---

[68] *See* ICC Statute, Article 17(1)(a).

[69] This principle can be found in the Vienna Convention on the Law of Treaties, which itself codifies customary law. Under Article 11, the consent of a State to be bound may be given by signature, exchange of instruments constituting a treaty, ratification, acceptance, approval or accession, or by any other means if they have been agreed upon. Vienna Convention on the Law of Treaties, (1979) 1155 UNTS 331.

Court exercises jurisdiction in cases where only one party has consented to the Court's jurisdiction.

The effect of this last exception is controversial. To preserve state sovereignty and support the role of domestic war crimes courts, the principle of complementarity places specific restraints on the ICC's exercise of power over non-States Parties. Article 12 of the Rome Statute clearly sets out preconditions for the exercise of the Court's jurisdiction.[70] However, Article 12 still permits the Court to investigate crimes where only **one** party has specifically requested the Court to take jurisdiction.

Some states view the Article 12 clause on jurisdiction as a violation of the aforementioned principle that international treaties may not impose obligations on non-States Parties without their consent.[71] Article 34 of the Vienna Convention on the Law of Treaties states: '[a] treaty does not create either obligations or rights for a third State without its consent'. The question is how can a third state be bound by the Statute if it has not specifically consented by a method permitted under Article 11 of the Convention?

Additionally, by permitting an international court to try such cases, the Rome Statute seems to be in breach of the *Monetary Gold*[72] principle. The

---

[70] ICC Statute, Article 12 reads:
1. A State which becomes a Party to this Statute thereby accepts the jurisdiction of the Court with respect to the crimes referred to in article 5.
2. In the case of article 13, paragraph (a) [cases referred to the Prosecutor by a State Party] or (c) [*proprio motu* investigations initiated by the Prosecutor], the Court may exercise its jurisdiction if one or more of the following States are Parties to this Statute or have accepted the jurisdiction of the Court in accordance with paragraph 3:
(a) The State on the territory of which the conduct in question occurred or, if the crime was committed on board a vessel or aircraft, the State of registration of that vessel or aircraft;
(b) The State of which the person accused of the crime is a national.
3. If the acceptance of a State which is not a Party to this Statute is required under paragraph 2, that State may, by declaration lodged with the Registrar, accept the exercise of jurisdiction by the Court with respect to the crime in question.

[71] Dapo Akande, 'The Jurisdiction of the International Criminal Court over Nationals of Non- Parties: Legal Basis and Limits', (2003) 1 *Journal of International Criminal Justice* 618, 620.

[72] *Monetary Gold Removed from Rome in 1943 (Italy v. France, United Kingdom of Great Britain and Northern Ireland and United States of America),* Judgment,

principle would suggest that an international court cannot exercise jurisdiction where the rights or responsibilities of a non-consenting third party are the subject of the dispute.[73] The International Court of Justice (ICJ) in the *Monetary Gold* case reasoned that exercising jurisdiction over a third state party without its consent would 'run counter to a well-established principle of international law embodied in the Court's Statute'.[74] It is logical to argue that the ICJ was implying that this principle is applicable to all courts that apply international law. In fact, the International Law Commission (ILC) has reasoned that the principle is generally applicable to international courts including the ICJ and the ICC.[75]

The United States had been one of the main proponents of this principle, arguing that territorial jurisdiction cannot be delegated to an international court.[76]

Again, looking back at the early stages of the draft Statute, the issue of imposing obligations on third parties was hotly debated during the Rome Conference. The view that the consent of either the territorial state where the crime was committed or the state of the accused (the latter having to be a States Party) was the only valid '*jurisdictional nexus*' had wide support

---

ICJ Reports (15 June 1954), pp. 31-32. The International Court of Justice heard a question concerning which country owns gold taken from Albania by Nazi Germany. The Court was called on to decide which country should receive the gold: Italy or the United Kingdom. To decide this question, though, it first had to decide whether Albania, a third party, had committed any international wrong against Italy, and was, therefore, obligated to pay Italy compensation. Considering that Albania had not consented to adjudication, yet her legal interests would form the very subject matter of the decision, the Court found it could not adjudicate any aspect of the case.

[73] Akande, 'The Jurisdiction of the International Criminal Court', 621.

[74] *Case of the Monetary Gold Removed from Rome in 1943*, pp. 31-32.

[75] Dapo Akande, *Prosecuting Aggression: The Consent Problem and the Role of the Security Council*, (Oxford Institute for Ethics, Law and Armed Conflict: Working Paper, 2010) p. 19, available at http://www.elac.ox.ac.uk/downloads/dapo%20akande%20working%20paper%20may%202010.pdf.

[76] David Scheffer, 'International Criminal Court: The Challenge of Jurisdiction, address at the Annual Meeting of the American Society of International Law' (26 March 1999), repeated in: Michael P. Scharf, 'The ICC's Jurisdiction over the Nationals of Non-Party States: A Critique of the US Position', (2001) 64 *Law and Contemporary Problems*, 67, 69.

during the Rome Conference.[77] However, states, as sovereign entities, have primacy over their own territories; this includes prosecuting any crimes that occur within it, even if caused by a non-national.[78] Moreover, there is no prohibition in international law against a state transferring a case over which it has jurisdiction to an international court. This is the territorial principle of jurisdiction found in international law.[79]

Philippe Kirsch, the Chairman of the Rome Diplomatic Conference, argued that the ICC Statute does no more than render people subject to the criminal laws of other states when in their territories, including any laws arising from treaty obligations.[80] Just as a domestic court does not require consent of the foreign national's state to try him for a crime committed on its soil, so too in the Rome Statute is the requirement of consent selective not cumulative.[81]

Dapo Akande in his article '*The Jurisdiction of the International Criminal Court over Nationals of Non- Parties: Legal Basis and Limits*' suggests that the Statute does not impose any obligations on, nor create any duties for, non-States Parties. Rather, that it is merely their political interests, which are affected.[82] Likewise, Michael Scharf, a former attorney for UN Affairs, submits that while treaty obligations could affect the sovereign interests of states, they are not legally binding, and thus are beyond the remit of Article 34 of the Vienna Convention of the Law of

---

[77] Mr Choi Tae-Hyun (Republic of Korea), the United Kingdom and France are just a few examples of States in support of this proposition, *see* United Nations Diplomatic Conference of Plenipotentiaries on the Establishment of an International Criminal Court, 'Summary Record of the 7th Meeting', UN Doc. A/CONF.183/C.1/SR.7, (25 January 1999), para. 53. A relatively lone opposition voice was Iran's who espoused the 'fundamental importance' of state consent, *see* United Nations Diplomatic Conference of Plenipotentiaries on the Establishment of an International Criminal Court, 'Summary Record of the 8th Meeting', UN Doc. A/CONF.183/C.1/SR.8, (25 January 1999), para. 69.

[78] Stéphane Bourgon, 'Jurisdiction *Ratione Loci*' in A. Cassese, P. Gaeta, J. Jones (eds.) *The Rome Statute of the International Criminal Court: A Commentary*, 2 vols. (Oxford: Oxford University Press, 2002), vol. 1, p. 562.

[79] *Ibid.*

[80] Philippe Kirsch, 'The Rome Conference on the International Criminal Court: A Comment', *ASIL Newsletter* (November/December 1998), 1.

[81] 'Summary Record of the 7th Meeting', UN Doc. A/CONF.183/C.1/SR.7, para. 53.

[82] Akande, 'The Jurisdiction of the International Criminal Court', 620.

Treaties.[83] Non-States Parties are under no obligation to cooperate with the Court.[84] Supporters of this position would point to Article 12(3), which specifically allows for *ad hoc* compliance by non-states, as evidence that the Statute is not designed to bind third party states.[85]

Dapo Akande circumvents the *Monetary Gold* doctrine by stating that the ICC does not *explicitly* determine state responsibility.[86] Instead while state responsibility might 'flow' from the fact that an official of the state has committed an international crime, the focus is on the personal responsibility of individuals.[87] Scharf claims that 'the one who owes the obligation [to the international community] is the individual not the state'.[88] Placing the individual at the heart of the criminal process arises from the desire to hold people responsible for their actions, rather than allowing them to hide behind the 'state'. After all, *'[c]rimes against international law are committed by men, not by abstract entities…'*.[89]

Despite this argument, it remains difficult to separate the individual from the state. For *states* that have not endorsed the ICC and yet find themselves under its jurisdiction, Article 12 remains understandably controversial.

We see a prime example of this in the 2008 conflict between Georgia and Russia, when Georgia invaded the Russian-backed unrecognised entity of South Ossetia.[90] There were various reports of war crimes committed by both sides, including rape, unlawful killing and the use of

[83] Scharf, 'The ICC's Jurisdiction over the Nationals of Non-Party States', 98.
[84] 'Summary Record of the 7th Meeting', UN Doc. A/CONF.183/C.1/SR.7, para. 51; France supported this, *see* 'Summary Record of the 8th Meeting', UN Doc. A/CONF.183/C.1/SR.8, para. 48.
[85] Gennday M. Danilenko, 'ICC Statute and Third States', in Cassese, Gaeta, Jones (eds.) *The Rome Statute of the International Criminal Court: A Commentary*, vol. 2, pp. 1889-1890.
[86] Akande, 'The Jurisdiction of the International Criminal Court', 634-635.
[87] *Ibid*, 636.
[88] Scharf, 'The ICC's Jurisdiction over the Nationals of Non-Party States', 74.
[89] *France et al. v. Goering et al.*, 22 IMT 411, 466 [emphasis added].
[90] The armed conflict between the three regions stems from long simmering tensions between the right of South Ossetia to self-determination versus the territorial integrity of Georgia. While South Ossetia was a part of Georgia, both before the latter's consumption into the USSR and again once the USSR had been dismantled, South Ossetia has claimed independence.

cluster bombs by Russian and Georgian military.[91] Although Russia is not a signatory to the Rome Statute, the ICC could exercise jurisdiction because Georgia is a State Party to the Rome Statute,[92] and the alleged crimes were committed on the territory of **that** state. It is legally irrelevant that the alleged crimes were committed by citizens of a non-State Party (i.e. Russia) as this situation is clearly anticipated by the language of Article 12, which specifically permits the Court to exercise jurisdiction if 'one or more' of the states is a party to the Rome Statute.[93] The Court can exercise jurisdiction over a national of a non-State Party if the crime was committed on the territory of a State Party.

As stated earlier, the ability of the Court to obtain jurisdiction over a non-State Party is based on the theory of territorial criminal jurisdiction.[94] However, the Court would still need to determine that South Ossetia is either Georgian or an independent state that could secure ICC jurisdiction. Such a designation clearly is not self-evident and would be subject to dispute. Whether based on *declarative* or *constitutive* theories of state recognition, it is unlikely that South Ossetia would be considered a state under international law.[95] Apart from Russia, South Ossetia has been

---

[91] The fighting in August 2008 killed hundreds of soldiers and civilians and displaced an estimated 160,000 people from their homes. For further detail *see* Amnesty International, *Civilians in the Line of Fire: The Georgia-Russia Conflict*, (London: Amnesty International Publications, 2008).

[92] Article 13(a) of the ICC Statute states: '[t]he Court may exercise its jurisdiction with respect to a crime…if: (a) A situation in which one or more of such crimes appears to have been committed is referred to the Prosecutor by a State Party..'.

[93] Article 12(2)(a) of the ICC Statute states: '[t]he Court may exercise its jurisdiction if one or more of the following states are Parties to this Statute . . .(a) The state on the territory of which the conduct in question occurred . . . .'.

[94] *See* M. Cherif Bassiouni, *The Legislative History of the International Criminal Court: Introduction, Analysis and Integrated Text*, 3 vols. (Transnational Publishers, 2005).

[95] An EU report concluded that there was no prima facie case for statehood. Firstly, including the fact that 'no state had recognised it before the outbreak of the war' and most importantly, South Ossetia itself had not unambiguously and consistently claimed to be a state and acted as such. While some residents claimed to be a sovereign nation they have conversely sought unification with Russia and North Ossetia. As such, the existence of a stable group with a common nationality is doubtful. Additionally, South Ossetia does not have a sufficiently independent government, either 'inwardly', in respect to the people who live there, nor 'outwardly' in regards its relationship with other states. Finally, following the constitutive theory, there is almost no international recognition of South Ossetia as a state. Russia is one of two countries who has declared its recognition of the State

recognised by only five UN member states: Tuvalu, Vanuatu (which only recognised Abkhazia), Nauru, Venezuela and Nicaragua.[96]

From the perspective of international law, South Ossetia and Abkhazia are part of Georgia's sovereign territory; the ICC thus has jurisdiction over crimes committed in this disputed region.

However, even if the legal argument over jurisdiction over non-States Parties to the Rome Statute is reconciled, there remains the practical hurdle of investigating crimes committed by a national of a non-State Party. Despite the language of Article 12, a non-State Party such as Russia owes **no** duty to cooperate with the Court. Without Russia's cooperation, the ICC Prosecutor is forced to rely on other states and entities to collect evidence and pursue an investigation.

As can be seen in the Ossetia-Abkhazia case, assignment of jurisdiction can pose significant challenges to the Court. The OTP's Preliminary Examination into the Georgia-Russia conflict began in August 2008. Six and a half years later, the Preliminary Examination is still ongoing. The latest information released by the ICC is contained in its 'Report on Preliminary Examination Activities 2012', published in November of that year.[97] On its website, the ICC publishes a list of preliminary examinations

---

of South Ossetia and has been widely criticised by the EU and NATO for doing so. *See* Independent International Fact-Finding Mission on the Conflict in Georgia, *Report*, 3 vols. (2009) vol. 2, p. 129, available at http://www.ceiig.ch/.

[96] On Vanuatu's recognition of Abkhazia *see* D. Flitton, 'Australia lashes Russia over aid', *The Age*, (17 October 2011), available at www.theage.com.au/national/australia-lashes-russia-over-aid-20111016-1lrjv.html; B. Abbott, 'Transparency calls for naming of Vanuatu diplomats 'on commission'', *Radio Australia*, (10 January 2012), available at www.radioaustralia.net.au/international/radio/onairhighlights/transparency-calls-for-naming-of-vanuatu-diplomats-on-commission. On Nauruan and Latin American recognition of Abkhazia *see* 'Pacific island recognises Georgian rebel region', *Reuters*, (15 December 2009) available at http://in.mobile.reuters.com/article/idINIndia-44730620091215?irpc=932.

[97] ICC-OTP, 'Report on Preliminary Examination Activities 2012' (November 2012), paras 120-140, pp. 29-32, available at http://www.icc-cpi.int/NR /rdonlyres/C433C462-7C4E-4358-8A72-8D99FD00E8CD/285209/OTP2012 ReportonPreliminaryExaminations22Nov2012.pdf.

leading to a court decision; there is still no mention of the case of Russia-Georgia.[98]

Both Russia and Georgia are conducting their own national investigations. Russia states that its investigation is active, but has been held up by a lack of cooperation from Georgia and the fact that key Georgian officials have been given immunity.[99] Georgia cites a lack of access to the crime scenes and a lack of cooperation from South Ossetian and Russian authorities.[100] The ICC is waiting on results from these investigations before it makes its own decision regarding admissibility.

The situation in Sudan, which was referred to the ICC by the UN Security Council in 2005, is the same.[101] Because Sudan is not party to the Rome Statute and does not consider itself obliged to cooperate, the parties have been unable to effectively investigate or access witnesses in Darfur.

Recently, defence counsel in the *The Prosecutor v. Abdallah Banda Abakaer Nourain and Saleh Mohammed Jerbo Jamus* case filed a request to temporarily stay the proceedings, arguing that circumstances made a fair trial impossible.[102] The defence cited, *inter alia*, lack of cooperation from Sudan, and the inability of the OTP to investigate and/or disclose potentially exculpatory evidence and witness testimony. Given this infringement on the rights of the accused to disclosure, to enter witness testimony on their own behalf and to present other evidence, the defence argued there could be no fair trial.[103] The Court had to decide whether a fair trial was possible if the parties are unable, due to a lack of state cooperation, to carry out on-site investigations and contact potential witnesses according to the principle of equality of arms.

---

[98] ICC-OTP, 'Communications, Referrals and Preliminary Examinations', (2014) available at http://www.icc-cpi.int/en_menus/icc/structure%20of%20the%20court /office%20of%20the%20prosecutor/comm%20and%20ref/Pages/communications %20and%20referrals.aspx.

[99] ICC-OTP, 'Report on Preliminary Examination Activities 2012', para. 133, p. 31.

[100] *Ibid.*, para. 136, pp. 31-32.

[101] *The Prosecutor v. Abdallah Banda Abakaer Nourain and Saleh Mohammed Jerbo Jamus*, Doc. ICC-02/05-03/09-274, 'Defence Request for Temporary Stay of Proceedings', (6 January 2012), paras 4–15.

[102] *Ibid.,* para. 47.

[103] *Ibid.,* para. 1.

In a letter in support of the defence application, Justice Richard J. Goldstone[104] stated that: 'to conduct trial proceedings in circumstances where the defence is denied this investigative opportunity – through no fault of its own – is, in my view, a breach of an accused's right to such an extent as to render a fair trial not possible'.[105]

The fact is that the ICC cannot expect non-States Parties to provide an accurate, unbiased assessment of events. Non-government organisations (NGOs) and court monitoring groups following the ICC have expressed concern over this predicament; in the Russian/Georgian conflict there is doubt that either national investigation is a genuine effort.[106] The OTP, in its most recent (2012) Report, concludes:

> The Office is seeking clarification as to whether the respective national investigations have halted; whether any additional information remains to be provided to the Office; and whether the lack of cooperation identified as an obstacle both by the Russian and Georgian authorities may be overcome through enhanced mutual legal assistance between the two States.[107]

It is conceivable that the Preliminary Examination stage over non-States Parties could go on for years. According to the ICC '[t]here are no timelines provided in the Statute for a decision'.[108] Moreover, the OTP 'aims' (i.e., but is not necessarily obliged) 'to issue regular reports on its activities' and to 'provide reasoned responses for its decisions to either proceed or not proceed with investigations'.[109]

---

[104] Justice Goldstone was a Justice of the Constitutional Court of South Africa (Retired), former Chief Prosecutor of the ICTY and ICTR, and Honorary President of the International Bar Association's Human Rights Institute.

[105] *The Prosecutor v. Abdallah Banda Abakaer Nourain and Saleh Mohammed Jerbo Jamus*, Doc. ICC-02/05-03/09-274-AnxO, 'Annexure O', (6 January 2012), p. 3.

[106] ICC-OTP, 'Report on Preliminary Examination Activities 2012', para. 139, p. 32.

[107] *Ibid.*, para. 140.

[108] ICC-OTP, 'Policy Paper on Preliminary Examinations', (November 2013), para. 14, available at http://www.icc-cpi.int:80/en_menus/icc/press%20and%20media/press%20releases/Documents/OTP%20Preliminary%20Examinations/OTP%20-%20Policy%20Paper%20Preliminary%20Examinations%20%202013.pdf.

[109] *Ibid.*, para. 15.

As problematic as territorial jurisdiction can be, as seen in the Russia-Georgia case, the notion of *universal jurisdiction* is even more controversial.

III. Complementarity and Universal Jurisdiction

The principle of complementarity represents a distinct departure from past international criminal courts.[110] ICC jurisdiction does not – and never was intended to – rise to the level of *full* universal jurisdiction. As noted, the ICC operates with an express presumption in favour of national jurisdiction. However, it would be inaccurate to state that there is not an *element* of universal jurisdiction within the Rome Statute.

In fact, the Rome Statute incorporates a theory of *universal international jurisdiction* that permits the Court, in limited circumstances, to apply international laws that are universal and without geographical restrictions.[111] Some States Parties have already recognised this reality:

> For some Governments, the legitimacy of universal jurisdiction...was borne out by the measures deployed at the domestic level to ratify and implement the Rome Statute, including steps taken to establish universal respect of clearly defined crimes of international concern and providing the means of enforcement allowing the national courts to exercise jurisdiction over such crimes.[112]

As stated earlier, even in the case of non-States Parties, the ICC can feasibly assume primary jurisdiction when the UN Security Council refers a case under Chapter VII of the UN Charter and the Prosecutor decides to act.[113] In other words, by virtue of a referral from the Security Council, a non-State Party loses its presumptive sovereignty.

---

[110] For an excellent overall discussion, *see* Philippe Sands, 'After Pinochet: The Role of National Courts', in Philippe Sands (ed.), *From Nuremberg to The Hague: The Future of International Criminal Justice*, (Cambridge: Cambridge University Press, 2003), pp. 68-108.

[111] *See* Leila N. Sadat and S. Richard Carden, 'The New International Court: An Uneasy Revolution', (2000) 88 *The Georgetown Law Journal*, 381, 407.

[112] UN Secretary-General, 'The Scope and Application of the Principle of Universal Jurisdiction', UN Doc. A/65/181, para. 24.

[113] *See* ICC Statute, Article 13(b) reads 'a situation in which one or more of such crimes appears to have been committed is referred to the Prosecutor by the Security Council acting under Chapter VII of the Charter of the United Nations'.

Of course, a Security Council referral must be based on a substantial threat to international peace and security, and it is likely that any state targeted for a referral is already hostile to the ICC. The landmark decision to issue an arrest warrant for Sudanese President Omar Hassan Ahmad Al Bashir is a case in point. When the Darfur situation was referred, Sudan protested vehemently. Although it is not a State Party to the ICC, Sudan is a UN member state and is thereby legally obliged to cooperate with the ICC.[114]

Nonetheless, because complementarity is based on limited jurisdictional authority, the ICC does not impose coercive primary jurisdiction upon states, even a non-State Party that is referred to by the Security Council to the Court. Thus, the Court still must assess the case situation through the lens of the complimentary principle and permit the referred state to show that is it willing and able to prosecute.

Complementarity currently incorporates the most effective elements of primary and universal jurisdiction. It does so within a framework that emphasizes the cooperation of states and domestic war crime courts in adhering to international criminal law. Complementarity aims to regulate, organise and leverage the existing body of international criminal law, inducing domestic courts to effectively make use of their own inherent jurisdiction over core international crimes committed within their territory or by their nationals.[115] It bolsters the idea that domestic prosecution is the first line of defence in countering impunity.[116] The desired result, as stated earlier, is that domestic courts will adjudicate the vast majority of international war crimes prosecutions. Complementarity gives domestic war crimes courts the 'first bite of the apple'. In essence, the ICC is a fallback institution for the remainder of cases but only after a determination has been made regarding the sufficiency domestic prosecution.

---

[114] Article 25 of the UN Charter states that 'the members of the UN agree to accept and carry out the decisions of the Security Council in accordance with the present Charter', Charter of the United Nations, (24 October 1945) 1 UNTS XVI (hereinafter UN Charter).

[115] *See* William W. Burke-White, 'Proactive Complementarity: The International Criminal Court and National Courts in the Rome System of Justice', (2008) 49 *Harvard International Law Journal* 53; El Zeidy, 'The Principle of Complementarity: A New Machinery To Implement International Criminal Law', 869-975.

[116] Jann K. Kleffner, *Complementarity in the Rome Statute and National Criminal Jurisdiction*, (Oxford: Oxford University Press, 2008), p. 96.

Complementarity provides a legal structure that is predictable and rational for states. By allowing a central authority to ensure accountability for the most egregious atrocities, yet tempering that authority through the principle of complementarity, international law is strengthened.

International law is further reinforced when states adopt domestic legislation to mirror the *ratione materiae* of the Rome Statute, particularly regarding points of criminalisation and enforcement as listed in the Statute. The principle of complementarity also encourages states to bolster their own domestic judicial processes. The interest of the international community is served when national legal systems adhere to and enforce international standards within their own jurisdiction. By encouraging domestic adjudication of international crimes, the principle of complementarity actually achieves greater domestic stability within the context of international criminal law. The Rome Statute specifically requires States Parties to 'ensure that there are procedures available under their national law for all of the forms of cooperation'.[117]

IV. Complementarity and Admissibility Standards, Interest of Justice, Gravity

The complementarity principle is merely a part of the more expansive admissibility requirements followed by the ICC. Together, these requirements effectively give domestic war crimes courts primary jurisdiction. The concept of admissibility operates as a limitation on jurisdiction: the challenging party acknowledges that the Court has jurisdiction over the alleged events, but asserts that the Court is precluded from exercising its jurisdiction under one of the avenues of inadmissibility.[118] These admissibility requirements preserve and enhance the principle of complementarity in favour of domestic prosecutions.

It is important to emphasise that an 'admissibility test' is part of the Court review process that arises from an investigation. While this focuses in part on whether the state is willing and able to undertake prosecution, the admissibility test also refers to the *gravity* and *interest of justice* threshold that all ICC cases must meet. This part of the test is shouldered

---

[117] *See* ICC Statute, Article 88.

[118] Megan A. Fairlie, 'Establishing Admissibility at the International Criminal Court: Does the Buck Stop with the Prosecutor, Full Stop?' (2005) 39 *The International Lawyer,* 817, 837-838.

by the Prosecutor when deciding whether to institute an investigation. In my opinion, this part of the admissibility test is crucial in supporting the primacy of national prosecutions over ICC prosecutions. It allows states to undertake prosecution of 'lesser' international crimes and prosecutions that might be of particular interest to a state.

The Prosecutor undertakes a *preliminary* examination of a situation to determine whether to proceed with a *proprio motu* investigation. In doing so, the Prosecutor assesses the seriousness and relevance of the information received. For this purpose, the Prosecutor is vested with the authority to seek information from any source that he or she feels is relevant in determining if an investigation is warranted. Thus, the Prosecutor can 'seek additional information from States, organs of the United Nations, intergovernmental or non-governmental organisations, or other reliable sources that he or she deems appropriate, and may receive written or oral testimony at the seat of the Court'.[119] The Prosecutor will likely conduct an exhaustive review of open source information including reports from international and domestic human rights groups. This occurred in the *Gaddafi* case where the Prosecutor, and ultimately the Court, relied heavily on formal third party submissions (e.g., Human Rights Watch reports).[120]

An investigation may also begin at the behest of others. In Nigeria, for example, a non-governmental organisation urged the Prosecutor to investigate *proprio motu* allegations that more than 300 people were killed during violence between Muslims and Christians in January 2010.[121] Another example is when the OTP was petitioned in more than 240 communications to investigate war crimes committed in the Iraqi conflict.[122] In December 2013, representatives of the previous Egyptian

[119] ICC Statute, Article 15(2). The same provision is repeated in Rule 104 of the ICC Rules of Procedure and Evidence as a remedy to the lack of coordination between Article 15(2) and Article 53(1) of the ICC Statute. ICC, 'Rules of Procedures and Evidence', Doc. ICC-ASP/1/3 (Part.II-A) (hereinafter 'ICC Rules of Procedure and Evidence').

[120] *The Prosecutor v. Said Al-Islam Gaddafi and Abdullah Al-Senussi*, Doc. ICC-01/11-01/11-344-Red, 'Decision on the admissibility of the case against Saif Al-Islam Gaddafi', (31 May 2013), paras 177-181.

[121] *See* Steve Dotterer, 'Nigeria rights group urges ICC to investigate Jos violence', *Jurist*, (2 February 2010), available at http://jurist.law.pitt.edu/paperchase/2010/02/nigeria-rights-group-urges-icc-to.php.

[122] *See* Response of Luis Moreno-Ocampo, Chief Prosecutor of the International Criminal Court, Regarding Iraq (9 February 2006), p. 1, available at

government, headed by the Muslim Brotherhood, filed a petition with the Court to open an investigation into crimes committed during the country's civil strife following the military's removal of President Morsi in July 2013. Documents submitted to the Court allege the killing of hundreds of protesters, consistent with crimes against humanity.[123] Egypt is not a party to the Rome Statute, so it can only come within ICC jurisdiction pursuant to either UNSC referral, which is unlikely, or by an Article 12(3) declaration accepting the Court's jurisdiction. However, with the current governmental crisis in Egypt, the ICC has stated that it has no jurisdiction to investigate without Egyptian authorities' consent.[124]

The purpose of a preliminary examination is to determine whether or not to open a full investigation in accordance with statutory requirements; this does not need prior Court authorisation.[125] The method for the preliminary examination is outlined in Article 15(2) of the Rome Statute. Currently, the Prosecutor has announced ten preliminary investigations.[126]

---

http://www.iccnow.org/documents/OTP_letter_to_senders_re_Iraq_9_February_2006.pdf.

[123] 'Egypt's ousted cabinet seeks ICC arbitration', *Al Jazeera* (7 January 2014) available at www.aljazeera.com/news/middleeast/2014/01/egypt-ousted-cabinet-seeks-icc-arbitration-201416194523921578.html.

[124] Amer Sultan, 'No jurisdiction to investigate crimes in Egypt: *ICC' Ahram Online* (17 January 2014) available at http://english.ahram.org.eg/NewsContent/1/64/91808/Egypt/Politics-/No-jurisdiction-to-investigate-crimes-in-Egypt-ICC.aspx.

[125] According to the ICC-OTP, a preliminary examination can be distinguished from a formal investigation. The former is a phrase where the OTP assesses whether crimes falling under the ICC jurisdiction may have been, or are possibly being, committed in a given situation; whether genuine investigations and prosecutions are carried out by the competent authorities in relation to these crimes; and whether the possible opening of an investigation by the Prosecutor would not go against the *interests of justice*. During this phase, the Office evaluates all information on alleged crimes from multiple sources, including information from individuals and groups also known as 'communications' and submissions from parties concerned. The triggering of a preliminary examination does not imply that an investigation will eventually be opened. *See* ICC-OTP, 'Report on Preliminary Examination Activities 2013', (November 2013), available at http://www.icc-cpi.int/en_menus/icc/press%20and%20media/press%20releases/Documents/OTP%20Preliminary%20Examinations/OTP%20-%20Report%20%20Preliminary%20Examination%20Activities%202013.PDF.

[126] Afghanistan, Colombia, Comoros, Federal Republic of Nigeria, Georgia, Guinea, Honduras, Côte d'Ivoire, Central African Republic, and Republic of Korea. ICC-OTP, 'Preliminary Investigations' (2014) available at http://www.icc-

For example, in April 2010, the Prosecutor issued a statement that he was considering opening an investigation into alleged crimes against humanity perpetrated in Côte d'Ivoire. Two months later the Prosecutor submitted a request to the Court to begin an investigation into the country's political conflict, and has since visited to collect information about alleged crimes. At the time, Côte d'Ivoire was not a party to the Rome Statute, but nonetheless affirmed the Court's jurisdiction.[127] In March 2013, Côte

---

cpi.int/en_menus/icc/structure%20of%20the%20court/office%20of%20the%20prosecutor/comm%20and%20ref/Pages/communications%20and%20referrals.aspx. The latest preliminary investigation is against North Korea. The former ICC Chief Prosecutor Luis Moreno-Ocampo announced a preliminary investigation to evaluate if two incidents allegedly committed by North Korea on the territory of the Republic of Korea constitute war crimes under ICC jurisdiction. These are: 'a) the shelling of Yeonpyeong Island on the 23 November 2010 which resulted in the killing of South Korean marines and civilians and the injury of many others; and b) the sinking of a South Korean warship, the Cheonan, hit by a torpedo allegedly fired from a North Korean submarine on 26 March 2010, which resulted in the death of 46 persons'. *See* ICC-OTP, 'ICC Prosecutor: Alleged War Crimes in the Territory of the Republic of Korea under Preliminary Examination', (6 December 2010), p. 1, available at http://www.icc-cpi.int/NR/rdonlyres/40BB19F9-3193-4A76-9E70-EB8BE39363B3/282744/KoreaEng1.pdf. The investigation was launched after the Office of the Prosecutor received communications regarding the potential war crimes, but it was not requested by South Korea. *See also* 'International court could launch N. Korea war crimes case', *AFP News* (6 December 2010), available at http://www.google.com/hostednews/afp/article/ALeqM5j9fY9fDcOPs6yg-X10qDVNa0xY6g?docId=CNG.e3bf3baa7c2b266ab97088b6237362e9.3b1. Recently, the Commission of Inquiry on Human Rights in the Democratic People's Republic of North Korea published its findings, concluding that crimes against humanity are widespread in North Korea. *See* UNGA, 'Situation of human rights in the Democratic People's Republic of North Korea', UN Doc. A/HRC/RES/22/13 (9 April 2013); UNGA, 'Report of the Commission of Inquiry on Human Rights in the Democratic People's Republic of Korea', UN Doc. A/HRC/25/63 (17 February 2014).

[127] The Côte d'Ivoire is not a party to the Rome Statute of the International Criminal Court, having signed but not ratified the treaty, but President Laurent Gbagbo formally accepted the jurisdiction of the Court pursuant to Article 12(3) of the ICC Statute. *See* 'Déclaration de reconnaissance de la Compétence de la Cour Pénale Internationale', (April 2003), available at http://www.icc-cpi.int/NR/rdonlyres/CBE1F16B-5712-4452-87E7-4FDDE5DD70D9/279779/ICDE.pdf. *See also* 'Confirmation de la Déclaration de reconnaissance', (14 December 2010), available at http://www.icc-cpi.int/NR/rdonlyres/498E8FEB-7A72-4005-A209-C14BA374804F/0/ReconCPI.pdf.

d'Ivoire became a Party to the Rome Statute.[128] Its cooperation with the Court soon followed. In March 2014, the country transferred Charles Blé Goudé to the ICC.[129] The Court issued an arrest warrant for Blé Goudé in December 2011 for alleged crimes against humanity committed during the post-election violence in Côte d'Ivoire between December 2010 and April 2011.[130]

In February 2014, the Prosecutor, Mrs Fatou Bensouda, announced that her office will open a preliminary investigation into the current situation in the Central African Republic (CAR).[131]

Recently, the ICC released its Report on Preliminary Examination Atrocities in Afghanistan.[132] This report exemplifies the extensive nature of these types of investigations. It reported that over 14,300 civilians had been killed in Afghanistan between January 2007 and June 2013. It further found that both anti-government and government armed forces had been recruiting children in attacks, especially to carry out suicide attacks.[133] The report stated that 'war crimes and crimes against humanity were and continue to be committed in Afghanistan'.[134] However, one of the major deficiencies in these preliminary investigations is the length of the investigations themselves. The inquiry has gone on for six years, longer than any other publicly pending ICC inquiry in such an early phase of examination.[135]

---

[128] ICC, 'ICC Welcomes Côte d'Ivoire as a New State Party', Doc. ICC-CPI-20130319-PR884, (19 March 2013).

[129] 'Ivory Coast suspect Ble Goude in ICC custody' *Al Jazeera*, (22 March 2014) available at http://www.aljazeera.com/news/africa/2014/03/ivory-coast-suspect-ble-goude-icc-custody-201432213515 2889545.html.

[130] *See The Prosecutor v. Charles Blé Goudé*, Doc. ICC-02/11-02/11-1, 'Warrant of Arrest for Charles Blé Goudé', (30 September 2013).

[131] ICC, 'Statement of the Prosecutor of the International Criminal Court Fatou Bensouda, on opening a new Preliminary Examination in Central African Republic', (7 February 2014), available at http://www.icc-cpi.int/en_menus/icc/press%20and%20media/press%20releases/Pages/otp-statement-07-02-2014.aspx.

[132] ICC-OTP, 'Report on Preliminary Examination Activities 2013', paras 19-56.

[133] *Ibid.*, para. 34.

[134] *Ibid.*, para. 18.

[135] Human Rights Watch, *Afghanistan: ICC Prosecutor Finds Grave Crimes*, (1 December 2013), available at http://www.hrw.org/news/2013/12/01/afghanistan-icc-prosecutor-finds-grave-crimes.

The extent of powers afforded to the Prosecutor under Article 15(2) to conduct the preliminary investigation is subject to the parameters of Article 53(1) of the Statute. As such, the Prosecutor is entitled to collect information and receive testimony until she is satisfied that: (1) there is a reasonable basis to believe that a crime exists and that the Court would have jurisdiction over the crime;[136] (2) the case meets the admissibility requirements of Article 17;[137] and (3) the crime is of sufficient gravity to justify further action by the Court.[138]

Determining whether the Court has jurisdiction over the alleged crimes requires an assessment of whether the Court has jurisdiction over the state itself. The complexity of this assessment arises particularly when a non-State Party seeks jurisdiction of the ICC through Article 12(3) of the Rome Statute. Article 12(3) reads:

> If the acceptance of a State, which is not a Party to this Statute, is required under paragraph 2, that State may, by declaration lodged with the Registrar, accept the exercise of jurisdiction by the Court with respect to the crime in question.

To date, there have been two declarations made by non-States Parties pursuant to Article 12(3). Both situations have resulted in important, and insightful, decisions by the Prosecutor. The first declaration was made by Côte d'Ivoire in 2003 'accepting the jurisdiction of the Court for the purpose of identifying, investigating and trying the perpetrators and accomplices of acts committed on Ivorian territory since events of 19 September 2002'.[139]

What makes this case interesting is the fact that Côte d'Ivoire ratified the Rome Statute in 2013. This led the defence to challenge the authority of the Court by arguing that the Court lacked jurisdiction over crimes committed after 2003 since the Article 12(3) declaration was limited to past, not future crimes. However, the Pre-Trial Chamber dismissed the defence's assertion, finding that the Ivorian 2003 Declaration submitted to the ICC pursuant to Article 12(3) relates to the overall 'situation' in the

---

[136] ICC Statute, Article 53(1)(a).
[137] *Ibid.*, Article 53(1)(b).
[138] *Ibid.*, Article 53(1)(c).
[139] 'Déclaration de reconnaissance de la Compétence de la Cour Pénale Internationale'.

country and does not limit the temporal scope of the acceptance of jurisdiction.[140] The decision was upheld by the Appeals Court.[141]

The potential consequence of the decision has yet to be seen. However, it is possible that future non-States Parties may be reluctant to seek jurisdiction of the ICC through an Article 12(3) declaration because they lose the flexibility to frame the Court's jurisdiction around a particular jurisdictional time frame. As Mohamed M. El Zeidy has argued, Article 12(3) was designed to give 'states that are not parties to the Statute, but that have a nexus to the crimes committed (as either the territorial state or the perpetrator's state of nationality), the opportunity to accept the Court's jurisdiction on an *ad hoc* basis and without putting the states under pressure to accede to the Statute itself'.[142] However, the Côte d'Ivoire decision indicates a possible shift where the non-State Party making a declaration under Article 12(3) is doing so for an indeterminate period of time. Does this mean that the state is de facto, if not de jure, a State Party because it has no control over stipulating the period of jurisdiction to be investigated by the Court?[143]

There seems to be merit in the prospect of this outcome when viewed within the context of the Rules of Procedure and Evidence Rule 44(2), which states:

> when a State lodges (…) a declaration with the Registrar pursuant to Article 12, paragraph 3, (…) the Registrar shall inform the State concerned that the declaration under Article 12, paragraph 3, has as a consequence

[140] *The Prosecutor v. Laurent Gbagbo*, Doc. ICC-02/11-01/11-212, 'Decision on the Corrigendum of the challenge to the jurisdiction of the International Criminal Court on the basis of articles 12(3), 19(2), 21(3), 55 and 59 of the Rome Statute filed by the Defence for President Gbagbo (ICC-02/11-01/11-129)', (15 August 2012), para. 61.

[141] *The Prosecutor v. Laurent Gbagbo*, Doc. ICC-02/11-01/11-321, 'Judgement on the appeal of Mr Laurent Koudou Gbagbo against the decision of the Pre-Trial Chamber I on jurisdiction and stay of proceedings', (12 December 2012), para. 106.

[142] Carsten Stahn, Mohamed M. El Zeidy, and Héctor Olásolo, 'The International Criminal Court's *Ad hoc* Jurisdiction Revisited', (2005) 99 *American Journal of International Law,* 421, 422.

[143] This question is more difficult in the Côte d'Ivoire case because the 2003 Declaration stated that it is to have effect for an indeterminate (*pour une durée indéterminé*) period. *See* 'Déclaration de reconnaissance de la Compétence de la Cour Pénale Internationale'.

> the acceptance of jurisdiction with respect to the crimes referred to in Article 5 of relevance to the situation and the provisions of Part 9, and any rules thereunder concerning States Parties, shall apply.[144]

In the same vein, the Pre-Trial Chamber recalled in its decision in *Gbagbo*[145] that 'Rule 44 of the Rules was adopted in order to ensure that states that chose to stay out of the treaty could not use the Court 'opportunistically'', and that he Court could not be used as a political tool allowing a state to accept the jurisdiction of the Court selectively 'in respect of certain crimes or certain parties to a conflict'.[146]

Thus, scholars who have argued that Article 12(3) gives non-States Parties the discretion to make a declaration only when in their favour[147] are clearly mistaken. I would argue that a country that is not party to the Rome Statute has the same obligation to cooperate with the Court under Article 12(3) as a State that signed and ratified the Rome Statute.

The second declaration was made by the Minister of Justice of the Government of Palestine in January 2009, recognising the jurisdiction of the Court with respect to acts committed on the territory of Palestine since 1 July 2002.[148] The Prosecutor announced that he would 'carefully examine all relevant issues including [the scope of the Court's] jurisdiction'.[149] More than 260 individuals and organisations made similar demands for the ICC to launch an investigation into alleged war crimes committed by Israeli troops during that conflict. However, the decision by

---

[144] ICC Rules of Procedure and Evidence, Rule 44(2).

[145] *The Prosecutor v. Laurent Gbagbo*, Doc. ICC-02/11-01/11-212, 'Decision on the Corrigendum of the challenge to the jurisdiction of the International Criminal Court on the basis of articles 12(3), 19(2), 21(3), 55 and 59 of the Rome Statute filed by the Defence for President Gbagbo (ICC-02/11-01/11-129)', (15 August 2012).

[146] *Ibid.*, para. 56.

[147] James Chan, 'Judicial Oversight over Article 12(3) of the ICC Statute', *FICHL Policy Brief Series*, No. 11, 2013, p. 1, (Torkel Opsahl Academic Epublisher, 2013).

[148] *See* 'Declaration recognizing the Jurisdiction of the International Criminal Court', (21 January 2009) available at
http://www.icc-cpi.int/NR/rdonlyres/74EEE201-0FED-4481-95D4-C8071087102C/279777/20090122PalestinianDeclaration2.pdf.

[149] ICC-OTP, 'The Office of the Prosecutor, Visit of the Minister of Justice of the Palestinian National Authority, Mr. Ali Khashan, to the ICC' (22 January 2009), available at http://www.icc-cpi.int/NR/rdonlyres/4CC08515-D0BA-454D-A594-446F30289EF2/280869/PNAMFA130209.pdf.

the OTP to institute a preliminary investigation was legally vague. Most unsettling was the fact that it raised unrealistic expectations that the ICC had jurisdiction to investigate alleged crimes committed in Gaza. It did not. Immediately after the announcement by the Prosecutor, I wrote an article setting out why the ICC did not have jurisdiction.[150]

As mentioned earlier, the Rome Statute is unequivocal regarding the Court's jurisdiction to investigate breaches of international criminal law. Unless the UN Security Council refers a situation to the Court, which will never happen in the Gaza situation because of the veto power held by the United States, the Court has jurisdiction only over a state that is a Party to the Rome Statute. Thus, the alleged crimes must have occurred on the territory of a State Party, or by a person who is a national of that state.

Israel fell outside the Court's jurisdiction because it has not ratified the Rome Statute. More problematic was the status of the West Bank and Gaza.[151] In its request for an investigation, the Palestinian National Authority relied on Article 12(3) of the Statute. However, there were two interpretive problems with this in relation to Gaza. The first was the political and legal uncertainty of suggesting that the Fatah faction of the Palestinian National Authority, which controlled the West Bank, could speak for the interest of the Hamas-controlled Gaza strip. The second problem, and by far the most perplexing, was whether Palestine could be recognised as a state within the meaning of the Rome Statute.

The key word in Article 12(3) is *state*. Only a state may accept, by declaration, the Court's jurisdiction. The Palestinian territories certainly did not constitute a state under international law at the time of the Article 12(3) referral. Moreover, the 1998 Rome diplomatic conference, which

---

[150] Mark Ellis, 'The ICC and the Gaza Conflict', *EQ: Equality of Arms Review*, Issue 3, (International Bar Association, July 2009), pp. 1, 3 and 4.

[151] The International Court of Justice approached the issue in a 2004 Advisory Opinion, but refrained from making any comment on the legal status of the Occupied Palestinian Territories. *Legal Consequences of the Construction of a Wall in the Occupied Palestinian Territory*, Advisory Opinion, ICJ Reports (9 July 2004) 136, paras 89-101. As noted by Brubacher, 'the fact that [even] the Security Council ha[s] not made a similarly emphatic political determination on the Israeli-Palestinian conflict makes the ICC more sensitive to the potential political effects of its decisions'. *See* Matthew R. Brubacher, 'Prosecutorial discretion within the International Criminal Court', (2004) 2 *Journal of International Criminal Justice* 71, 83.

established the ICC, invited only UN member states to participate as signatories to the Statute. Palestine was given observer status; it was not designated a potential signatory.

For the OTP to have considered jurisdiction over the Gaza conflict, it would have had to invalidate the legal status of the territories and effectively recognise the Palestinian state. There was no legal basis for such a decision. The only possibility was for Palestine to obtain UN Security Council recognition.

After a lengthy three year period, the Prosecutor finally announced his decision. It reflected my position in 2009. In summary, the Prosecutor determined that Palestine could not be considered a state under international law and as an observer to the United Nations, it would be beyond the scope of the ICC to afford state status to Palestine.[152]

In reaching this conclusion, the OTP ruled that it was for the UN Secretary General to determine the scope of the term 'state' in accordance with Article 12. In addition, the OTP noted that it would be for the UN or the Assembly of States Parties (ASP) to determine whether Palestine qualified as a state for the purposes of acceding to the Rome Statute under Article 12(1).

However, in its 2012 finding, the OTP also concluded that, 'should the competent organs of the UN (or the Assembly of States Parties to the Rome Statute) resolve the legal issues underlying the applicability of Article 12(3) to the Palestinian Declaration, the situation could change'.[153] On 29 November 2012, the UN General Assembly, by 138 votes to 9, with 41 states abstaining, decided 'to accord to Palestine non-member observer State status in the United Nations'.[154] It remains to be determined if the General Assembly's promotion of Palestine to a 'non-member observer state' is sufficient to enable Palestine to either join the ICC as a full party or re-file an Article 12(3) *ad hoc* declaration. In order to provide for the ICC's *ad hoc* jurisdiction under Article 12(3), Palestine would have to

---

[152] ICC-OTP, 'Situation in Palestine', (3 April 2012), available at http://www.icc-cpi.int/NR/rdonlyres/C6162BBF-FEB9-4FAF-AFA9-836106D2694A/284387/SituationinPalestine030412ENG.pdf

[153] Andreas Zimmermann, 'Palestine and the International Criminal Court *Quo Vadis*?' (2013) 11, *Journal of International Criminal Justice*, 303, 305.

[154] UNGA, 'Status of Palestine in the United Nations', (4 December 2012) UN Doc. A/RES/67/19, p. 3.

either submit a new declaration or, reconfirm the 2009 Declaration. However, the recognition of statehood remains a complex and, at times, confusing area of international law. A decision by the ICC on this issue would be equally complicated.

For instance, while the UN resolution seems to recognise the 'State of Palestine' on the basis of the pre-1967 borders (including the West-Bank and Gaza)[155], a number of analysts have pointed out that the territory of Palestine, and thus the scope of the ICC's territorial jurisdiction, is not clearly defined.[156]

Furthermore, since the Oslo Accords gave Israel exclusive criminal jurisdiction over all Israelis both in the Palestinian-controlled and Israeli-controlled areas of the West Bank, it could be argued that it would be problematic for Palestine to confer its jurisdiction over the West Bank to the ICC since it does not possess it.[157]

The Gaza situation highlights the potential problem when a Prosecutor proceeds with a preliminary inquiry prior to a *proprio motu* investigation. It shows how important it is for the ICC to have 'a check' on the Prosecutor's discretion. Without the eventual required review by the Pre-Trial Chamber, the principle of complementarity could easily be weakened. The Rome Statute was deliberately crafted to give the Court specific and limited jurisdiction. If the Court were to expand its jurisdictional boundaries unilaterally, it would be seen as political and reckless, and would have grave implications for the principle of complementarity and international law. The Gaza situation also plays into the hands of those countries that question the non-political nature of the Court.

Opponents of the Court in the United States used the Prosecutor's decision to review the Gaza conflict as a strong justification for why the US should not ratify the Rome Statute. An influential US foundation has concluded that the Court's

---

[155] Zimmermann, 'Palestine and the International Criminal Court *Quo Vadis*?', 308.

[156] *See* Maryne Rondot, 'The ICC and the Israel-Palestine conflict: Current Developments, Implications and Future Scenarios', (7 August 2013), available at http://www.amicc.org/docs/the_icc_and_the_israel-palestine_conflict.pdf.

[157] *Ibid.*, p. 15.

> broad autonomy and jurisdiction invite politically motivated indictments .... Efforts to use the Court apply pressure to inherently political issues and supersede the foreign policy prerogatives of sovereign nations [such as the Prosecutor's decision to consider Israel's actions in Gaza] undermine the Court's credibility . . . .[158]

As mentioned earlier, the Court is again facing another potential political firestorm as the result of the ousted Egyptian Muslim Brotherhood government and Freedom and Justice Party filing a complaint to the ICC in regards to alleged abuses committed by military authorities.[159] Although Egypt signed the Rome Statute in December 2000, it did not ratify it, rendering the Court's jurisdiction ineffective. However, the two parties issued a declaration pursuant to Article 12(3) of the Rome Statute accepting *ad hoc* jurisdiction of the Court in respect to alleged crimes against humanity committed since the 3 July 2013 coup. The parties claim that the Muslim Brotherhood remains the legitimate government.

At some point, the OTP will have to make a decision as to whether to open an investigation into the Egyptian case. This will clearly implicate the OTP in questions of democratic legitimacy, which it is not in a position to answer.

These types of political interventions into the Court's potential jurisdiction are actually very common. The Office of the Prosecutor has received 597 communications between 1 November 2012 and 31 October 2013 dealing with requests for investigations. The OTP noted that 503 of these communications 'were outside the Court's jurisdiction'; 41 were linked to a situation that was already under Court analysis; 21 communications required 'further analysis' and 32 were linked to a current Court prosecution or investigation.[160]

---

[158] Brett D. Schaefer and Steven Groves, 'The US Should Not Join the International Criminal Court', p. 20, (*Heritage Foundation*, 17 August 2009), available at http://s3.amazonaws.com/thf_media/2009/pdf/bg2307es.pdf.

[159] Paul Waldie, 'Egypt's Muslim Brotherhood appeals to world criminal court', *The Globe and Mail*, 06.01.2014, available at http://www.theglobeandmail.com/news/world/lawyers-file-claim-in-icc-against-egypts-military-backed-regime/article16204039/.

[160] *See* ICC-OTP, 'Report on Preliminary Examination Activities 2013', (November 2013), available at http://www.icc-cpi.int/en_menus/icc/press%20and%20media/press%20releases/Documents/OTP%20Preliminary%20Examinations/OTP%20-%20Report%20%20Preliminary%20Examination%20Activities%202013.PDF.

A. Interest of Justice

In deciding on the contentious issue of admissibility, the Prosecutor must give consideration to the interest of justice. Thus, just as the Prosecutor must take into account the gravity of the crimes when deciding to pursue an investigation, she must also take into account the '*interests of justice*', and decide whether 'there are nonetheless substantial reasons to believe that an investigation would not serve' such an interest [emphasis added].[161] *Interests of justice* is not defined in the Statute. In fact, in 2007 the OTP issued a policy paper in which it expounded on its own interpretation of the meaning of 'interests of justice'. At the outset the OTP recognised that as a mere policy document, it remains subject to subsequent authoritative interpretations of law from the Court itself.[162]

The OTP acknowledges that the Rome Statute gives neither definition nor 'clear guidance' on 'the interests of justice', and Article 53(1)(c) 'represents one of the most complex aspects of the Treaty'.[163] The Court thus far has given the concept very little attention.

There has yet to be a case in which the Prosecutor has determined that 'the interests of justice' **not** to investigate outweighs the gravity of a crime and the victims' interests. Consequently, the Court has so far been able to offer little by way of interpretation of the phrase 'interests of justice'. In fact, when the Court did review the procedural aspects of Article 53(1)(c), it seemed to suggest that there would always be a presumption in favour of prosecution. The Prosecutor should only embrace the *interests of justice* principle in exceptional circumstances and 'as a course of last resort'.[164] There should be a presumption in favour of investigation or prosecution where the criteria in Articles 53(1)(a) and (b) are met.

In March 2010, Pre-Trial Chamber II considered the 'interests of justice' provision when ruling on the Prosecutor's request, by his own motion, for its authorisation to investigate the post-election events in Kenya in 2007. In a majority decision upholding his request, the Court concluded that the provision imposes **no positive** requirement for the

---

[161] ICC Statute, Article 53(1)(c).
[162] ICC-OTP, 'Policy Paper on the Interests of Justice', (September 2007), p. 2, available at http://www.icc-cpi.int/NR/rdonlyres/772C95C9-F54D-4321-BF09-73422BB23528/143640/ICCOTPInterestsOfJustice.pdf.
[163] *Ibid.*
[164] *Ibid.*, p. 9.

Prosecutor 'to establish that an investigation is actually in the interests of justice', and therefore 'the Prosecutor does not have to present reasons or supporting material in this respect'.[165] The Court stated that:

> It is only when the Prosecutor decides that an investigation would **not** be in the interests of justice that he or she is under the obligation to notify the Chamber of the reasons for such a decision, thereby triggering the review power of the Chamber[166] [emphasis added].

The Prosecutor later adhered to this line of reasoning when deciding to institute proceedings in the Libyan situation. Prior to the formal opening of an ICC investigation into the situation in Libya, the Prosecutor evaluated the available information and held that the statutory criteria for opening an investigation had been met.[167] As part of this evaluation, the OTP found no evidence that there was any genuine national investigation or prosecution of the alleged perpetrators and consequently found that the cases 'clearly appeared to meet the threshold of gravity required'; and that there was 'no substantial reasons to believe that [an ICC] investigation would not serve the interests of justice'.[168]

However, there are still circumstances in which the Prosecutor might decide not to investigate or prosecute based on the interests of justice. It is conceivable that the Prosecutor could consider other 'relevant factors', for instance the circumstances of the defendant (who might be terminally ill, for instance, or 'subject of abuse amounting to serious human rights violations') or issues relating to 'peace and security'.[169] This could include: the availability of other suitable justice mechanisms, which would

---

[165] *Situation in the Republic of Kenya*, Doc. ICC-01/09-19, 'Decision Pursuant to Article 15 of the Rome Statute on the Authorization of an Investigation into the Situation in the Republic of Kenya', (31 March 2010), para. 63.
[166] *Ibid.*
[167] Luis Moreno-Ocampo, Prosecutor of the International Criminal Court, 'Statement of the Prosecutor on the opening of the investigation into the situation in Libya', (3 March 2011), available at http://www.icc-cpi.int/NR/rdonlyres/EA019818-B8C1-44C8-8C7B-4398F33FF029/283045/StatementLibya_03032011.pdf.
[168] ICC-OTP, 'Report on Preliminary Examination Activities', (13 December 2011), para. 118, available at http://www.icc-cpi.int/NR/rdonlyres/63682F4E-49C8-445D-8C13-F310A4F3AEC2/284116/OTPReportonPreliminaryExaminations13December2011.pdf.
[169] ICC-OTP, 'Policy Paper on the Interests of Justice', pp. 7-8.

address the impunity gap (such as truth seeking, reparations, and traditional justice mechanisms).[170]

The latter – other transitional justice mechanisms – will likely become a major issue for the Court. The establishment of truth commissions is one of the more common forms of extra-judicial proceedings that will undoubtedly be a focus for states in the future. Given that they are restorative rather than retributive, truth commissions tend to be created as an *alternative* to prosecutions. They could easily be seen as being incompatible with the ICC's duty to prosecute and, more cynically, as a mechanism to avoid justice.[171]

If a state uses alternative accountability mechanisms, such as a truth commission, to deal with low-level perpetrators, it is likely that the Court will accept it. As mentioned earlier, the Court is not focused on low-level perpetrators. Yet, how should the Court respond if the jurisdictional scope of a truth commission was broadened to include leaders and organisers of genocide? An unwillingness to prosecute persons most responsible for an egregious crime under international law would violate the complementarity principle. In such a case, it would be in the interests of justice for the Court to assume jurisdiction.

There is also the contentious issue of judgements rendered through indigenous methods of accountability. The most prominent example of such a 'traditional accountability method' is the *Gacaca* courts established in Rwanda after the 1994 genocide.[172] The Rwandan government believed

---

[170] *Ibid.*

[171] Mark S. Ellis, 'The International Criminal Court and its Implication for Domestic Law and National Capacity Building', (2002) 15 *Florida Journal of International Law*, 215, 229.

[172] In the aftermath of the 1994 genocide in Rwanda, the new Rwandan Patriotic Front (RPF) government faced the daunting task of pursuing justice for the deaths of between 800,000 and 1,000,000 Rwandans. Reports vary on the number of perpetrators, for example some Rwandan officials claim that as many as three million perpetrators participated in the massacre. *See* Scott Straus, 'How Many Perpetrators were there in the Rwandan Genocide? An Estimate', (2004) 6 *Journal of Genocide Research*, 85 (citing Philip Gourevitch, *We Wish to Inform You that Tomorrow We Will Be Killed with Our Families: Stories from Rwanda*, (New York: Farrar Straus and Giroux, 1998), p. 244). *See also* M. Mamdani, *When Victims Become Killers: Colonialism, Nativism, and the Genocide in Rwanda*, (Princeton: Princeton University Press, 2001), p. 7; C. Scherrer, *Genocide and Crisis in Central Africa: Conflict Roots, Mass Violence, and Regional War*

that the *Gacaca* courts would engage the majority of Rwandan citizens 'in the process of accounting for a genocide that involved mass societal participation'.[173]

In 2001, the Rwandan government adopted a law creating a new system of *gacaca* courts designed to prosecute crimes of genocide and crimes against humanity committed between 1 October 1990 and 31 December 1994.[174] The law was amended to fully establish the organisation, competence, and functions of the *Gacaca* courts.[175] This involved the

---

(Westport: Praeger Publishers, 2002); J. Waller, *Becoming Evil: How Ordinary People Commit Genocide and Mass Killing* (Oxford: Oxford University Press, 2002); *see also* Jeevan Vasagar, 'Grassroots Justice', *The Guardian*, (17 March 2005), available at http://www.guardian.co.uk/world/2005/mar/17/worlddispatch.rwanda (noting that the latest official reports concluded that at least 761,000 perpetrators participated in the genocide).

173 Traditionally, *Gacaca* courts have been used as a dispute resolution mechanism in Rwanda with a focus on providing reconciliation within a given community. As such, their primary purpose is to mediate between the disputing parties. Any sentences imposed were of a compensatory nature, rather than punitive, and could not be imposed without prior acceptance of the sentence by both parties. *See* Amnesty International, *Gacaca: A Question of Justice* (December 2002), pp. 125–126 available at http://www.amnesty.org/en/library/asset/AFR47/007/2002/en/b65d04e4-d769-11dd-b024-21932cd2170d/afr470072002en.pdf. Customarily, *Gacaca* shunned the use of law within this reconciliation process and relied instead on societal and tribal norms to dictate the appropriate redress for the dispute. Voluntary participation by members of the community was crucial to the traditional *gacaca* method of dispute resolution, as were the premises of collective responsibility and the higher value of the best interests of the community as a whole, rather than individual interests. *See also* Maya Goldstein-Bolocan, 'Rwandan Gacaca: an Experiment in Transitional Justice' (2004) 2 *Journal of Dispute Resolution*, 355; Maya Sosnov, 'The Adjudication of Genocide: Gacaca and the Road to Reconciliation in Rwanda' (2008) 36 *Denver Journal of International Law and Policy* 125, 145.

174 'Organic Law No. 40/2000 of 26/01/2001 Setting Up 'Gacaca Jurisdictions' and Organising Prosecutions for Offences Constituting the Crime of Genocide or Crimes Against Humanity Between October 1, 1990 and December 31, 1994' (26 January 2001). *See also* Jacques Fierens, 'Gacaca Courts: Between Fantasy and Reality', (2005) 3 *Journal of International Criminal Justice* 896, 901.

175 Organic Law No. 33/2001 of 22/06/2001; Organic Law No 16/2004 of 19/06/2004; Organic Law No. 13/2008 of 19/05/2008.

election of approximately 260,000 judges across 751 jurisdictions.[176] Rwanda thus transformed its traditional method of dispute resolution into a quasi-judicial forum for prosecuting those accused of committing egregious crimes, creating what some have called the 'most ambitious transitional justice measure ever attempted'.[177]

However, the more complex challenge with any alternative method of accountability is to ensure that it does not abnegate the responsibility to carry out an independent and impartial process, as outlined in Article 17(c) of the Rome Statute. As discussed earlier, the Court must still undertake an admissibility test to determine whether the requirements of Article 17 are met. The *Gacaca* system demonstrates how difficult it is to meet those requirements. The *Gacaca* court system contains limited assurances of fair trial standards and due process for suspects.[178]

One major criticism of the system is the absence of trained legal professionals to advise the accused during proceedings.[179] The independence

---

[176] Yves Beigbeder, *Judging Criminal Leaders: The Slow Erosion of Impunity,* (The Hague/London/New York: Martinus Nijhoff Publishers, 2002); Erin Daly, 'Between Punitive and Reconstructive Justice: the Gacaca Courts in Rwanda', (2002) 34 *New York University Journal of International Law and Policy*, 355, 372; Jeremy Sarkin, 'The Tension Between Justice and Reconciliation in Rwanda: Politics, Human Rights, Due Process and the Role of the Gacaca Courts in Dealing with Genocide', (2001) 45 *Journal of African Law*, 143; Sosnov, 'The Adjudication of Genocide', 135; Amnesty International, *Gacaca*; 'Rwanda: Gacaca genocide trials to begin in May 2002', *IRIN News*, (12 December 2001), available at http://www.irinnews.org/Report.aspx?ReportId=29083. *See also* Chiseche Mibenge, 'Enforcing International Humanitarian Law at the National Level: the Gacaca Jurisdictions of Rwanda', *TMC Asser Institute*, available at http://www.asser.nl/default.aspx?site_id=9&level1=13337&level2=13363.

[177] Lars Waldorf, 'Transitional Justice and DDR: The Case of Rwanda' (International Center for Transitional Justice: June 2009), p. 3, available at http://ictj.org/sites/default/files/ICTJ-DDR-Rwanda-ResearchBrief-2009-English_0.pdf. *See also* Straus, 'How Many Perpetrators'; Mamdani, *When Victims Become Killers*; Scherrer, *Genocide and Crisis*; Waller, *Becoming Evil*; Vasagar, 'Grassroots Justice'.

[178] Amnesty International, *Gacaca*, pp. 30-40; *see also* 'Rusizi: District Plagued by Corruption of Gacaca Judges', *Hirondelle News Agency*, (6 October 2008), available at http://www.hirondellenews.com/content/view/11515/309/.

[179] Human Rights Watch, *Justice Compromised: The Legacy of Rwanda's Community-Based Gacaca Courts*, (31 May 2011), p. 1, available at http://www.hrw.org/node/99177/section/1 (citing remarks of President Paul Kagame at the International Peace Institute, New York, September 21, 2009).

and impartiality of the judges has also been criticised. Moreover, *Gacaca* judges are not trained lawyers, but rather 'persons of integrity' from the community.[180] In the early stages of the legal process, *Gacaca* judges in Rwanda received only six days of training, no compensation for their work, and no resources to fulfil their duties.[181] Allegations of corruption on the bench also plagued the *Gacaca* proceedings.[182]

Despite recognition by some governments that *Gacaca* courts 'are tribunals to which the international human rights instruments . . . apply',[183] the numerous weaknesses found in the Rwandan courts would provide the ICC, if it had jurisdiction, grounds to initiate an investigation under the interest of the justice concept. This would be the case even if the alternative dispute mechanism were seen as a viable way to find a peaceful resolution to an existing conflict. So as to avoid the charge of ignoring an investigation for political reasons, the OTP has stated that 'there is a difference between the concepts of the interests of justice and the interests of peace and that the latter falls within the mandate of institutions other than the Office of the Prosecutor'.[184] Simply stated, politics is a pestilence that the Court wants to avoid.

Finally, there is an issue of whether the Prosecutor can reconsider her decision not to pursue an investigation. Although Article 53 relates to the initiation of an investigation, Section 4 of this Article reads, in part: '[t]he Prosecutor may, *at any time*, reconsider a decision *whether* to initiate an *investigation or prosecution* based on new facts or information' [emphasis added].[185] This procedure seems to give the Prosecutor discretion to resurrect an investigation that she previously had declined or to suspend an

---

[180] Organic Law No. 13/2008 of 19/05/2008, Article 3. *See also* Human Rights Watch, *Justice Compromised*, pp. 65-66.

[181] Donald L. Hafner and Elizabeth B. L. King, 'Beyond Traditional Notions of Transitional Justice: How Trials, Truth Commissions, and other Tools for Accountability Can and Should Work Together', (2007) 30 *Boston College International and Comparative Law Review*, 91, 107.

[182] Amnesty International, *Gacaca*, p. 16; *see also* 'Rusizi: District Plagued by Corruption of Gacaca Judges', *Hirondelle News Agency*.

[183] Republic of Rwanda, *Reply to Amnesty International's Report: Rwanda: The Troubled Course of Justice* (2000) (obtained from Sosnov, 'The Adjudication of Genocide', 132).

[184] ICC-OTP, 'Paper on Some Policy Issues', p. 1.

[185] ICC Statute, Article 53(4).

investigation or prosecution in favour of national prosecution.[186] The latter part of this discretionary power is the most relevant and interesting. It suggests the possibility of 'transferring' an existing investigation back to a state, based on complementarity. Therefore, in the *interests of justice* or due to new information, the Prosecutor can reconsider whether an *ongoing* investigation or prosecution is still admissible. Senior ICC staff appear to give the Section 4 provision a narrow meaning, suggesting that 'an investigation can't be suspended unless there is reason to believe that it would not be in the interests of justice'.[187] Such a decision would of course be subject to approval by the Pre-Trial Chamber.[188] The only real hurdle to this interpretation is that the phrase 'in the interests of justice', as indicated earlier, lacks definition in the Rome Statute. Consequently, a decision to suspend could be seen as politically motivated and that ultimately undermines an investigation or prosecution.[189]

B. Gravity

Like the *interests of justice* concept, the concept of *gravity* is also poorly defined in the Rome Statute and the ICC's Rules of Procedure and Evidence. However, those crimes that fall within the Court's jurisdiction—genocide, crimes against humanity, war crimes—would act as the basis for determining gravity. Pursuant to Article 53, the Prosecutor must distinguish between 'major' and 'minor' war criminals, or in some way grade the heinousness of an offence.[190] She must also take into account the number of victims. It is likely that a crime with few victims

---

[186] Morten Bergsmo and Pieter Kruger, 'Article 53: Initiation of an Investigation', in Otto Triffterer (ed.), *Commentary on the Rome Statute of the International Criminal Court: Observers' Notes, Article by Article,* 2nd edn (München: CH Beck, Hart and Nomos, 2008), p. 1076.

[187] Josefine Volqvartz, 'ICC under fire over Uganda Probe', *CCN World*, (23 February 2005), available at http://edition.cnn.com/2005/WORLD/africa/02/23/uganda.volqvartz/index.html.

[188] ICC Statute, Article 53(1)(c) reads in part: '[i]n deciding whether to initiate an investigation, the Prosecutor shall consider whether: . . . Taking into account the gravity of the crime and the interests of victims, there are nonetheless substantial reasons to believe that an investigation would not serve the interests of justice. If the Prosecutor determines that there is no reasonable basis to proceed and his or her determination is based solely on subparagraph (c) above, he or she shall inform the Pre-Trial Chamber [of the decision and the reasons for the conclusion as articulated in Article 53(2)(c)]'.

[189] ICC-OTP, 'Policy Paper on the Interests of Justice', p. 2.

[190] *See* Sadat and Carden, 'The New International Court', 419.

would not meet the gravity criteria and jurisdiction would remain with the state. Because of the gravity requirement, the threshold for admissibility to the ICC is high. This is an important element of the Rome Statute that supports national prosecutions and the complementarity principle.

In *The Prosecutor v. Thomas Lubanga Dyilo*, the Trial Chamber established that the gravity threshold must be met upon *initiation* of an investigation and again once a case *arises from* the investigation of a situation.[191] For a determination of gravity, the Court ruled that conduct must amount to a systematic or large-scale pattern of incidents; isolated instances of criminal activity are not sufficient.[192] It is interesting to note that this is the same jurisdictional language that is used to characterise the systematic nature of crimes against humanity.

Perhaps recognising the lack of clarity in defining the term gravity the Court also tried to establish another tantalising way to evaluate the term: 'due consideration' must be given to the 'social alarm such conduct might have caused in the international community' when assessing the gravity of a crime.[193] The major drawback, however, is that the Court did not elaborate on what is meant by 'social alarm'. Thus, the Court introduced a new term to its jurisprudence without offering guidance as to its meaning. Academics weighed in, suggesting that social alarm means 'the extent of global concern over a particular type of crime because that crime affronts widely shared, fundamental values, whether or not it causes many deaths'.[194] Thus, social alarm could be seen as the *global* concern around a crime, rather than the impact of a crime on the community or nation where it occurred.[195] Examples of these types of crimes could include attacks on UN peacekeepers and torture.[196]

---

[191] *The Prosecutor v. Thomas Lubanga Dyilo*, Doc. ICC-01-04-01/06-8-US-Corr, 'Decision concerning Pre-Trial Chamber I's Decision of 10 February 2006 and the Incorporation of Documents into the Record of the Case against Mr Thomas Lubanga Dyilo', (24 February 2006), para. 41.

[192] *Ibid.*, para. 46.

[193] *Ibid.*

[194] Mark Osiel, 'How Should the ICC Office of the Prosecutor Choose its Cases? The Multiple Meanings of Situational Gravity', *The Hague Justice Portal*, (5 March 2009), p. 2, available at http://www.haguejusticeportal.net/Docs/Commentaries%20PDF/Osiel_ICC_EN.pdf.

[195] Susana SáCouto and Katherine Cleary, 'The Gravity Threshold of the International Criminal Court', (2007) 23 *American University International Law Review*, 807, 812.

[196] Osiel, 'How Should the ICC Office of the Prosecutor Choose its Cases?', p. 2.

The Court added further confusion to terminology used in assessing gravity by implying that social alarm is specifically attributed 'to the international community by the extent of the practice of enlisting and conscripting into armed groups and using to participate actively in hostilities children under the age of fifteen'.[197] By fusing the phrases 'social alarm' and 'international community', the Court presumably believes that the relevant crime affronts global norms and should be assessed in the context of the Article 17(1)(d) gravity threshold.

Yet interestingly, the Court did not stop with the assessment of global norms. It went further. The Court required that a suspect be among the 'most senior leaders' for the crimes.[198] To initiate a case, the Court stipulated that the Prosecutor must consider the *position* of the person, the extent to which the person contributed, either through acts or omissions, to the systematic or large-scale crimes committed by the state entity, the organisation or armed group to which he or she belonged, and the contribution of the given state entity, organisation or armed group to the overall commission of the crimes.[199] The Court explained these requirements by stating:

> [t]he Chamber considers that the application of these three elements results from the fact that those persons who, in addition to being at the top of the State entities, organisations or armed groups allegedly responsible for the systematic or large-scale commission of crimes... play a major role by acts or omissions in the commission of such crimes are the ones who can most effectively prevent or stop the commission of those crimes.[200]

However, the Appeals Chamber dismantled the lower court's decision. It dismissed the Chamber's ruling because its test 'blur[red] the distinction between the jurisdictional requirements for war crimes and crimes against humanity that were adopted when defining the crimes that fall within the jurisdiction of the Court'.[201] The Appeals Chamber further noted that the test contradicted the Rome Statute drafters' intent and would incorrectly

[197] *The Prosecutor v. Thomas Lubanga Dyilo*, 'Decision concerning Pre-Trial Chamber I's Decision', para. 66.
[198] *Ibid.*
[199] *Ibid.*, paras 41-63.
[200] *Ibid.*, para. 53.
[201] *Situation in the Democratic Republic of the Congo*, Doc. ICC-01/04-169, 'Judgment on the Prosecutor's Appeal Against the Decision of Pre-Trial Chamber I Entitled 'Decision on the Prosecutor's Application for Warrants of Arrest, Article 58'', (13 July 2006), para. 70.

limit the Court's jurisdiction over war crimes.[202] The Appeals Chamber also completely rejected the 'social alarm' requirement. It did so for primarily one reason - the term is not mentioned anywhere in the Rome Statute. Thus, the resulting subjective assessment made by the Trial Chamber was without merit and should play no role in determining the admissibility of a case pursuant to Article 17 (1)(d) of the Statute.[203]

Most importantly, the Appeals Chamber rejected the rather sophomoric notion set forth by the Trial Chamber that there should be some test to determine the 'most responsible' parties. The Appeals Chamber argued that the Court must be free to prosecute **all** levels of offenders in order to prevent categorical impunity for low-ranking offenders and creative crime commissions designed to preclude the Court's jurisdiction.[204] This seems like sound logic considering that the Rome Statute makes no mention of prosecuting those *most responsible* for committing a crime.[205] However, the Court to date has focused on perpetrators deemed to have been in a 'command' position; it has shown no interest in pursuing rank-and-file offenders. Thus, despite sound legal reasoning, the Appeals Chamber ruling conflicts with the reality of the Court's jurisprudence. Unfortunately, the Appeals Chamber did not outline an alternative test for 'sufficient gravity'.

The confusion over the definition of 'gravity' gained further traction in the case of *Jean-Pierre Bemba Gombo* of the Central African Republic where Mr Gombo challenged the charges against him, arguing that 'co-perpetration' did not meet the requirement of gravity.[206] The Appeals Chamber side-stepped the issue of defining 'sufficient gravity', and in its decision responded to the defence challenge with only one paragraph. It stated that the Pre-Trial Chamber was obliged only to determine whether there is sufficient evidence to 'establish substantial grounds to believe that the person committed crimes charged'.[207] Since the Pre-Trial Chamber had already decided that the case fell within ICC jurisdiction and was admissible, it implicitly found that it met the gravity threshold. In essence,

---

[202] *Ibid.*, para. 71.
[203] *Ibid.*, para. 72.
[204] *Ibid.*, paras 73-79.
[205] *Ibid.*, para. 79.
[206] *The Prosecutor v. Jean-Pierre Bemba Gombo*, Doc. ICC-01/05-01/08-704-Red3-tENG, 'Application Challenging the Admissibility of the Case pursuant to Articles 17 and 19(2)(a) of the Rome Statute', (25 February 2010), paras 132-149.
[207] ICC Statute, Article 61(7).

the Court found that 'sufficient gravity' was inherent in the confirmation.[208] Importantly, the Court's rationale completely ignores the requirement to determine gravity as a condition to, rather than inherent in, the finding of admissibility.

The gravity threshold issue came up again when Pre-Trial Chamber I in the Sudan situation issued a 'Decision on the Confirmation of Charges' in the case of *Bahar Idriss Abu Garda*.[209] Unlike the *Gombo* case, the Pre-Trial Chamber in the *Abu Garda* case noted that simply because the accused was charged with the most serious crimes, the case did not automatically meet the gravity threshold. The Court held that not only quantitative but also qualitative factors must be taken into account.[210] According to the Court, Rule 145(1)(c) of the Rules of Procedure and Evidence could serve as a 'guideline'.[211] Relevant factors for a qualitative approach would be 'the extent of the damage caused, in particular the harm caused to the victims and their families, the nature of the unlawful behaviour and the means employed to execute the crime; the degree of participation of the convicted person; the degree of intent; the circumstances of manner, time and location'.[212] Thus, in the eyes of the Court, these factors are extremely relevant to determining 'gravity' under Article 17(1)(d) of the Statute.

More recently, Mr Mohammed Hussein Ali brought a new challenge before the Court, asserting that his case is inadmissible because the

---

[208] *The Prosecutor v. Jean-Pierre Bemba Gombo*, Doc. ICC-01/05-01/08-802, 'Decision on the Admissibility and Abuse of Process Challenges', (24 June 2010), para. 249.

[209] *The Prosecutor v. Bahar Idriss Abu Garda,* Doc. ICC-02/05-02/09-243-Red, 'Decision on the Confirmation of Charges' (8 February 2010), paras 30-34.

[210] *Ibid*., para. 31.

[211] Rule 145(1)(c) of ICC Rules of Procedure and Evidence reads: '[i]n addition to the factors mentioned in article 78, paragraph 1, give consideration, *inter alia*, to the extent of the damage caused to the victims and their families; the nature of the unlawful behaviour and the means employed to execute the crime; the degree of participation of the convicted person; the degree of intent; the circumstances of manner, time and location; and the age, education, social and economic condition of the convicted person'.

[212] *The Prosecutor v. Abu Garda*, Doc. ICC-02/05-02/09-243-Red, 'Decision on the Confirmation of Charges', para. 32.

Prosecution failed to demonstrate 'sufficient gravity'[213] under the Pre-Trial Chamber's *Lubanga* test.[214] Mr Ali used the *Lubanga* test because the Court had yet to endorse any other clear test.[215] Thus, the defence argued that the conduct in question was not systematic or large scale and that Mr Ali was not one of the most senior leaders in this case[216] and that the Prosecution provided no support that Ali was one of the parties most responsible for the conduct in this case.[217]

The Court correctly rejected Ali's argument, finding that the alleged crimes met the gravity threshold as outlined in Article 17(1)(d).[218] This was an easy decision considering that Mr Ali relied on a test declared flawed by the Appeals Chamber in the *Lubanga* case.[219] Instead, the Court in the *Ali* case looked at factors such as the 'scale, nature, and manner of commission of the alleged crimes, their impact on victims, and the existence of any aggravating circumstances' to determine if the crimes met the gravity threshold.[220] Because the crimes in the current situation were committed in two locations over many days, that there were numerous deaths, and that the manner of the commission of the crimes was

---

[213] *The Prosecutor v. Francis Kirimi Muthaura, Uhuru Muigai Kenyatta and Mohammed Hussein Ali,* Doc. ICC-01/09-02/11-356, 'Prosecution's Response to the Defence Challenges to Jurisdiction', (14 October 2011), para. 50.

[214] *The Prosecutor v. Francis Kirimi Muthaura, Uhuru Muigai Kenyatta and Mohammed Hussein Ali*, Doc. ICC-01/09-02/11-338, 'Defence Challenge to Jurisdiction, Admissibility and Prosecution's Failure to Meet the Requirements of Article 54', (19 September 2011), para. 60.

[215] *Ibid.*

[216] *See Situation in the Republic of Kenya*, Doc. ICC-01/09-02/11-257-AnxA, 'Documents Containing the Charges', (19 August 2011), paras 20-21. 'Alleging that Kenyatta and Muthaura facilitated a series of pre-election meetings with Mungiki leaders and senior PNU government officials, politicians, and businessmen, for the purpose of obtaining their support in retaliatory attacks against perceived ODM supporters in the Rift Valley) never possessed the ability to control Kenyan government policies'. *See The Prosecutor v. Muthaura Francis Kirimi Muthaura, Uhuru Muigai Kenyatta and Mohammed Hussein Ali*, Doc. ICC-01/09-02/11-338, 'Defence Challenge to Jurisdiction', p. 23.

[217] *Ibid.*, para. 67.

[218] *The Prosecutor v. Francis Kirimi Muthaura, Uhuru Muigai Kenyatta and Mohammed Hussein Ali*, Doc. ICC-01/09-02/11-382-Red, 'Decision on the Confirmation of Charges Pursuant to Article 61(7)(a) and (b) of the Rome Statute', (23 January 2012), para. 50.

[219] *Ibid.*, para. 44.

[220] *Ibid.*, para. 50.

particularly brutal, the Court found the crimes did in fact meet the gravity threshold of Article 17(1)(d).[221]

Once it is decided that the case can move forward, having found that the case is of sufficient gravity and would serve the interest of justice, the Court then assesses the complementarity principle under a second test. This test, as discussed in Chapters 2 and 3, is emerging as the most challenging and most controversial element in the Rome Statute.

[221] *Ibid.*

CHAPTER TWO

THE PRINCIPLE OF COMPLEMENTARITY UNDER ARTICLE 17 OF THE ROME STATUTE AND STATES' WILLINGNESS TO PROSECUTE

Introduction

It is useful to view the ICC's 'admissibility test' as constituting two parts. We have discussed the *gravity* and *interests of justice* part of the test. The second part goes to the very core of the complementarity principle. It goes to the very core of complementarity because the Court must determine whether a fair and judicious trial is most likely to be conducted in a national, or international setting. This requires an assessment on a state's *willingness* and *ability* to undertake a trial based on international standards. This second part of the test also has two subcomponents, the first of which is straightforward. The Court needs to determine whether there exists an ongoing investigation or prosecution at the domestic level.[1]

A case is inadmissible to the ICC if it is being *adjudicated* or *investigated* by a state that has jurisdiction or the accused has already been tried or punished domestically for the same offence.[2] This last point is the *double jeopardy*, or *ne bis in idem*, principle. It is important to note that under a *ne bis in idem* challenge, a state can postpone the surrender of an

---

[1] Rome Statute of the International Criminal Court, Rome, opened for signature 17 July 1988, 2187 UNTS 90 (entered into force 1 July 2002) UN Doc. A/CONF.183/9 (hereinafter, ICC Statute or Rome Statute), Article 17(1)(a).

[2] The key is the underlying facts of the crime rather than the legal terminology. Thus, a domestic court could try the suspect for mass murder, even though the ICC might try him for crimes against humanity.

individual to the ICC but must still carry out the ICC's arrest warrant until the court's decision on admissibility is finalised.[3]

The Court has not spent considerable time on this component of the test. However, in the *Lubanga* case, the Pre-Trial Chamber ruled that state inaction or delay may prevent the case from being declared inadmissible under Article 17 of the Statute.[4] Indeed, the Court stated that a 'case would be admissible only if those States with jurisdiction over it have remained ***inactive*** in relation to that case ***or*** are unwilling or unable within the meaning of Article 17(1)(a) to (c), 2 and 3 of the Statute'[5] [emphasis added]. I think the Trial-Chamber was absolutely correct in its reasoning. The same reasoning has been repeated and accepted by the Pre-Trial Chamber in the *Gaddafi* case.[6] However, not everyone has agreed with the Court's assessments.

Surprisingly, some international experts[7] have accused the Court of unwarranted judicial activism, reasoning that the Court *created* 'inactivity' as a third 'unwritten' element of admissibility.[8] One pre-eminent expert states that the Article 17 complementarity test has only two 'well-known' requirements: that a state must be *unwilling* or *unable genuinely* to

---

[3] *See* Robert Cryer, Håkan Friman, Darryl Robinson and Elizabeth Wilmhurst, *An Introduction to International Criminal Law and Procedure*, 2nd edn (Cambridge: Cambridge University Press, 2007) p. 519; ICC Statute, Articles 18(2) and 89(2).
[4] *The Prosecutor v. Thomas Lubanga Dyilo*, Doc. ICC-01/04-01/06-8-US-Corr, 'Decision Concerning Pre-Trial Chamber I's Decision of 10 February 2006 and the Incorporation of Documents into the Record of the Case against Mr Thomas Lubanga Dyilo' ('Annex I - Decision on the Prosecutor's Application for a Warrant of Arrest, Article 58, (10 February 2006)'), (24 February 2006), paras 30-40.
[5] *Ibid.*, para. 30.
[6] *The Prosecutor v. Saif Al-Islam Gaddafi and Abdullah Al-Senussi*, Doc. ICC-01/11-01/11-344-Red, 'Decision on the admissibility of the case against Saif-Al-Islam Gaddafi', (31 May 2013), paras 199-218.
[7] *See* Mahnoush Arsanjani and W. Michael Reisman, 'The Law-in-Action of the International Criminal Court' (2005) 99, *American Journal of International Law*, 385 as *quoted* in Darryl Robinson, 'The Inaction Controversy – Neglected Words and New Opportunities' in Carsten Stahn and Mohamed M. El Zeidy (eds.) *The International Criminal Court and Complementarity From Theory to Practice*, 2 vols. (Cambridge: Cambridge University Press, 2011) vol. 1, pp. 478-483.
[8] William A. Schabas, 'The Rise and Fall of Complementarity' in Stahn and El Zeidy, *The International Criminal Court and Complementarity*, vol. 1, p. 159.

undertake proceedings in order for the case to be admissible before the Court.[9]

However, the allegation of political activism is a bit harsh. Arguably, the Pre-Trial Chamber in the *Lubanga* case, and now in the *Gaddafi* case, was not creating a third avenue to render a case admissible, but instead the Court was applying Article 17 of the Rome Statute – which frames the requisite factors of admissibility in the negative – by listing requirements to render a case *in*admissible.

The same position was upheld three years later (2009) in the *Katanga* case.[10] The Appeals Chamber in *Katanga* laid out a two-step analysis and specified that an assessment of inability or unwillingness only follows a determination that the state is conducting or has conducted an investigation.

> To do otherwise would be to put the cart before the horse. It follows that in case of inaction, the question of unwillingness or inability does not arise; inaction on the part of a State having jurisdiction (that is, the fact that a State is not investigating or prosecuting, or has not done so) renders a case admissible before the Court, subject to article 17 (1) (d) of the Statute.[11]

The following year, the Appeals Chamber in *Bemba* echoed this reasoning and affirmed that the state must have completed an investigation or be actively investigating, before the Court can determine 'the issues of inability and unwillingness' pursuant to Article 17.[12] Other Court decisions have also supported this position.[13]

---

[9] William A. Schabas, 'Prosecutorial Discretion v. Judicial Activism at the International Criminal Court' (2008) 6 *Journal of International Criminal Justice*, 731, 757.

[10] *The Prosecutor v. Germain Katanga and Mathieu Ngudjolo Chui*, Doc. ICC-01/04-01/07-1497, 'Judgment on the Appeal of Mr Germain Katanga against the Oral Decision of Trial Chamber II of 12 June 2009 on the Admissibility of the Case', (25 September 2009), para. 78.

[11] *Ibid.*

[12] *The Prosecutor v. Jean-Pierre Bemba Gombo*, Doc. ICC-01/05-01/08-962, 'Judgment on the appeal of Mr Jean-Pierre Bemba Gombo against the decision of Trial Chamber III of 24 June 2010 entitled 'Decision on the Admissibility and Abuse of Process Challenges'', (19 October 2010), paras 107-109.

[13] Other cases also state that inactivity is a ground for admissibility *The Prosecutor v. Thomas Lubanga Dyilo*, Doc. ICC-01-04-01/06-8-US-Corr, 'Decision concerning Pre-Trial Chamber I's Decision of 10 February 2006 and the Incorporation of Documents into the Record of the Case against Mr Thomas Lubanga Dyilo', (24 February 2006), para. 29; *The Prosecutor v. Ahmad*

As Darryl Robinson, one of the Statute drafters notes, 'the real mystery is why this proposition is controversial'.[14] The only way the counter analysis makes sense is to ignore the majority of the text. Robinson highlights the 'fifty-five words' of Article 17 which make clear that it is only when proceedings are commencing, or have done, that issues of unwillingness and inability can be considered.[15] These words include the first fifteen words of Article 17(1)(a), namely that '[t]he case is being investigated or prosecuted by a State which has jurisdiction over it....'.[16] Subsection 17(1)(b) also only applies when '[t]he case has been investigated by a State..' and 17(1)(c) when '[t]he person concerned has already been tried for [the same] conduct...'.[17]

It seems clear, particularly after the decision in the *Gaddafi* case, that there exists a subcomponent in the complementarity test that focuses solely on the active or inactive status of a state's investigation or prosecution of a case.[18]

A case at the domestic level must also include charges against the *same individuals* and for the *same conduct* as identified by the ICC.[19] 'Same conduct' has been interpreted as needing to be 'substantially the same

---

Muhammad Harun and Ali Muhammad Al Abd-Al-Rahman, Doc. ICC-02/05-01/07-1, 'Decision on the Prosecution Application under Art 58(7) of the Statute', (27 April 2007), paras 19-25; *The Prosecutor v. Omar Hassan Ahmad Al Bashir*, Doc. ICC-02/05-01/09-3, 'Decision on the Prosecution's Application for a Warrant of Arrest against Omar Hassan Ahmad Al Bashir', (4 March 2009), paras 48-49; and implicitly, *The Prosecutor v. Jean-Pierre Bemba Gombo*, Doc. ICC-01/05-01/08-14-tENG 'Decision on the Prosecution's Application for a Warrant of Arrest against Jean-Pierre Bemba Gombo', (10 June 2008) and *Situation in Uganda*, Doc. ICC-02/04-01/05-53, 'Warrant of Arrest for Joseph Kony Issued on 8 July 2005 as Amended on 27 September 2005', (27 September 2005); which were helpfully listed by Robinson, 'The Inaction Controversy – Neglected Words and New Opportunities', p. 461.

[14] Robinson, 'The Inaction Controversy – Neglected Words and New Opportunities', p. 460.

[15] *Ibid.*, pp. 463-464.

[16] ICC Statute, Article 17(a).

[17] *Ibid.*, Articles 17(1)(b) and 17(1)(c).

[18] *The Prosecutor v. Said Al-Islam Gaddafi and Abdullah Al-Senussi*, Doc. ICC-01/11-01/11-344-Red, 'Decision on the admissibility of the case against Saif Al-Islam Gaddafi', (31 May 2013), paras 53-55.

[19] ICC Statute, Article 17(1)(a). *See also The Prosecutor v. Thomas Lubanga Dyilo*, Doc. ICC-01/04-01/06-8-US-Corr, 'Decision Concerning Pre-Trial Chamber I's Decision', para. 37.

conduct'[20] in both the domestic and international cases. The Kenyan situation is a good example of this issue. In December 2010, the Prosecutor requested summonses for six high-ranking Kenyan officials most responsible for the post-election violence.[21] They became known as the 'Ocampo Six'. The six men were tried in two separate cases. The first involved three who were members of the government, at the time that the confirmation of charges were released,[22] and the second included three who were leaders of the opposition.[23]

The Kenyan government appealed the ICC's admissibility decision and requested the transfer of both cases to the Kenyan courts.[24] The government argued that under Article 19(2)(b) of the Rome Statute, it had the ability and willingness to investigate and prosecute those responsible for the atrocities committed during the country's post-election violence, and to do so consistent with international standards of fair trials.[25] The

---

[20] *The Prosecutor v. Said Al-Islam Gaddafi and Abdullah Al-Senussi*, Doc. ICC-01/11-01/11-344-Red, 'Decision on the admissibility of the case against Saif Al-Islam Gaddafi', (31 May 2013), para. 76, *citing The Prosecutor v. Francis Kirimi Muthaura, Uhuru Muigai Kenyatta and Mohammed Hussein Ali*, Doc. ICC-01/09-02/11-274, 'Judgment on the Appeal of the Republic of Kenya against the decision of Pre-Trial Chamber II of 30 May 2011 entitled 'Decision on the Application by the Government of Kenya Challenging the Admissibility of the Case Pursuant to Article 19(2)(b) of the Statute'', (30 August 2011) (hereinafter 'Kenya Admissibility Decision'), para. 39.

[21] *See* ICC-OTP, 'Kenya's Post Election Violence: ICC Prosecutor Presents Cases Against Six Individuals for Crimes Against Humanity', Doc. ICC-OTP-20101215-PR615, (15 December 2010). In December 2010, the six included William Samoei Ruto (former minister of Higher Education, Science and Technology); Henry Kiprono Kosgey (member of the Kenyan Parliament); Joshua Arap Sang (Head of Operations); Francis Kirimi Muthaura (Head of Public Service and Secretary to the Cabinet); Uhuru Muigai Kenyatta (Deputy Prime Minister) and Mohamed Hussein Ali (Chief Executive of Postal Corporation of Kenya). See *The Prosecutor v. Francis Kirimi Muthaura, Uhuru Muigai Kenyatta and Mohammed Hussein Ali*, Doc. ICC-01/09-02/11-382-Red, 'Decision on the Confirmation of Charges Pursuant to Article 67(1)(a) and (b) of the Rome Statute' (20 January 2012).

[22] Uhuru Muigai Kenyatta, Francis Kirimi Muthaura and Mohamed Hussein Ali.

[23] William Samoei Ruto, Henry Kiprono Kosgey and Joshua Arap Sang.

[24] *Situation in the Republic of Kenya*, Doc. ICC-01/09-01/11-19, 'Application on Behalf of the Government of the Republic of Kenya Pursuant to Article 19 of the ICC Statute', (31 March 2011).

[25] *Ibid.*, paras 1, 2 and 30. *See also The Prosecutor v. Francis Kirimi Muthaura, Uhuru Muigai Kenyatta and Mohammed Hussein Ali*, Doc. ICC-01/09-02/11-67, 'Filing of Annexes of Matrials to the Application of the Government of Kenya

Kenyan government stressed that the Pre-Trial Chamber had wrongly interpreted the requirements under Article 17(1)(a) of the Statute which provides that 'the Court shall determine that a case is inadmissible where the case is being investigated [...] by a state which has jurisdiction over it'.[26]

Kenyan Cabinet Minister Mutula Kilonzo stated: '[w]e can say that Kenyan judges meet the best international standards...Why on earth should a Kenyan go to The Hague?'[27] His remarks are backed up by international observers who report that 'Kenya has strong capacity in many parts of its justice sector' and 'all agreed that there are no insurmountable technical challenges to the conduct of credible investigations, prosecutions and trials for international crimes in Kenya'.[28] Kenya argues that it has made steps towards a more effective judicial system – including the appointment of a new chief justice, the establishment of a Supreme Court, and a new process for vetting its judges.[29] However, the Court can counter these arguments with reports (including one by the International Bar Association (IBA)) that suggest Kenya's legal system is paralyzed by corruption, judicial interference and a complete absence of public confidence in the judicial system, and does not function effectively enough to undertake domestic war crimes trials.[30]

Pursuant to Article 19 of the Rome Statute' (21 April 2011); *The Prosecutor v. Francis Kirimi Muthaura, Uhuru Muigai Kenyatta and Mohammed Hussein Ali*, Doc. ICC-01/09-02/11-67-Anx3, 'Annex 3', (21 April 2011). The Kenyan government argued that these filings provided evidence that the cases before the ICC were being investigated in Kenya.

[26] *Ibid.*, paras 26-28; ICC Statute, Article 17(1)(a).

[27] 'Kenyans Question ICC Authority', (2010) 18 *Human Rights Brief*, p. 49 available at http://www.wcl.american.edu/hrbrief/18/181.pdf.

[28] Open Society Foundations, *Putting Complementarity into Practice: Domestic Justice for International Crimes in Democratic Republic of Congo, Uganda, and Kenya*, (New York: Open Society Foundations, 2011), pp. 84, 86.

[29] W. Davidson, 'African Union Summit Backs Return of Kenyan ICC Cases', *Bloomberg*, (27 May 2013), available at http://www.bloomberg.com/news/2013-05-27/african-leaders-set-to-back-return-of-kenyan-icc-cases.html.

[30] *See* International Bar Association Human Rights Institute (IBAHRI) and International Legal Assistance Consortium (ILAC), *Restoring Integrity: An Assessment of the Needs of the Justice System in the Republic of Kenya*, (February 2010), p. 54, available at
http://www.ibanet.org/Article/Detail.aspx?ArticleUid=EB1896B1-3494-4E9D-BF39-A49072685F06.

Even Kenya's own legal profession has questioned whether Kenya's judiciary is capable of undertaking such complex cases.[31]

In its decision, the Appeals Chamber seemed to be impervious to Kenya's effusive statements about its own legal system. Instead, the Chamber focused on a more nuanced position, ruling that the case is inadmissible only 'if the suspects are being investigated in Kenya for substantially the same conduct'.[32] The Chamber held that the words '*being investigated*' mean taking steps to ascertain whether the suspects are responsible for the conduct, such as interviewing witnesses and suspects, analysing forensic information, and collecting documentary evidence.[33] The Chamber was unconvinced that investigations against the six suspects were actually taking place. The Appeals Chamber made clear that it was not sufficient for the state to merely be prepared to take such steps, or to be investigating other suspects.[34] The Appeals Chamber upheld the Pre-Trial decision on admissibility of the case.

I. Understanding the Concepts of Unwillingness and Inability

As noted earlier, the complementarity principle gives nation states and their domestic courts complete authority to bring perpetrators of international crimes to justice. However, the Court is obliged to determine the capacity of domestic courts to carry out this duty. This is another succinct and decisive component of the admissibility test. This step considers whether a state is unwilling or unable genuinely to carry out the investigation or prosecution.[35] The assessment is made separately for

---

[31] 'Uhuru Kenyatta and William Ruto named in Kenya TJRC report', *BBC News*, (22 May 2013) available at www.bbc.co.uk/news/world-africa-22622408. *See also* Truth, Justice and Reconciliation Commission of Kenya (TJRC), 'Report of the Truth, Justice and Reconciliation Commission of Kenya', 6 vols, (Kenya: Truth, Justice and Reconciliation Commission, 2013).

[32] *The Prosecutor v. Francis Kirimi Muthaura, Uhuru Muigai Kenyatta and Mohammed Hussein Ali*, Doc. ICC-01/09-02/11-274, 'Kenya Admissibility Decision', para. 40.

[33] *Ibid.*, para. 1.

[34] *Ibid.*, para. 40.

[35] *The Prosecutor v. Said Al-Islam Gaddafi and Abdullah Al-Senussi*, Doc. ICC-01/11-01/11-344-Red, 'Decision on the admissibility of the case against Saif Al-Islam Gaddafi', (31 May 2013), para. 58, *citing The Prosecutor v. Germain Katanga and Mathieu Ngudjolo Chui*, Doc. ICC-01/04-01/07-1497, 'Judgment on

'unwillingness' and 'unable' (i.e., inability). Thus, if the Pre-Trial Chamber determines that a state is genuinely unable to carry out an investigation or prosecution (to be discussed in Chapter 3), it does not need to address the state's 'unwillingness' to do so.[36] The reverse is also true.

The factors enumerated for determining if a state is *unwilling* to prosecute include whether the judicial proceedings are undertaken for the purpose of protecting an individual from criminal responsibility; whether there is an unjustified delay in the proceedings; or whether the proceedings are being conducted without respect to independence or impartiality.[37]

How is a judicial system deemed unable or unwilling to undertake a successful trial? How will these decisions be rendered in a consistent and objective manner? The standards for admissibility determinations are an obvious weakness in the Rome Statute. The concepts *unable* and *unwilling* are not clearly defined and certainly not objective. Most recently, the admissibility hearings for Libya again illustrate the ongoing confusion for both the Court and states regarding implementation of the complementarity principle.

In its argument for ICC jurisdiction over Saif Al-Islam Gaddafi, the Office of Public Counsel for the Defence (OPCD) focused on Gaddafi's custody. To date, he has been held in Libya by a faction of the Zintan militia forces hostile to the Libyan government.[38] This has had clear negative repercussions in terms of Gaddafi's access to domestic legal representation and the government's ability to try him domestically. The OPCD argued that the militia showed 'a clear unwillingness' to transfer Gaddafi to the National Transitional Council (NTC) in Tripoli.[39] However,

---

the Appeal of Mr Germain Katanga against the Oral Decision of Trial Chamber II', paras 1 and 75-79.

[36] *The Prosecutor v. Said Al-Islam Gaddafi and Abdullah Al-Senussi*, Doc. ICC-01/11-01/11-344-Red, 'Decision on the admissibility of the case against Saif Al-Islam Gaddafi', (31 May 2013), para. 138.

[37] ICC Statute, Article 17.

[38] Kevin Jon Heller, 'Libya Admits (Again) It Should Lose Its Admissibility Challenge', *Opinio Juris*, (4 March 2013), available at http://opiniojuris.org/2013/03/04/libya-again-admits-it-should-lose-its-admissibility-challenge/.

[39] *The Prosecutor v. Saif Al-Islam Gaddafi and Abdullah Al-Senussi*, Doc. ICC-01/11-01/11-190-Corr-Red, 'Public Redacted Version of the Corrigendum to the 'Defence Response to the Application on behalf of the Government of Libya

this argument conflated the Zintan militia forces and the government to suggest a violation of Article 17(2)(c) of the Statute. In my opinion, the OPCD's argument was misplaced. You cannot impugn the government's willingness to prosecute based on the acts of a militia group that has no alliance with that government. The OTP, on the other hand, argued that the Libyan government was '**unable** to move the case forward'[40] so long as this situation persists. It correctly and expressly mentioned Article 17(3), arguing that the *inability* of the State to obtain custody of defendants would constitute grounds for declaring the case admissible.

Still more perplexing are the contradictory positions taken by the OTP and the OPCD. For example, the OPCD has argued that Libya is *unwilling* to prosecute Gaddafi. However, the Libyan government has found support on this very issue from the OTP, which expressed the view that Libya has taken 'concrete' investigative steps and that there is 'no evidence' to suggest that it is 'not genuine in its investigation and prosecution of Saif Al-Islam'.[41] The Prosecutor's main concern has been with Libya's *ability* to prosecute.

The subjective nature of the admissibility review is reinforced by the fact that Article 17(1)(a) of the Rome Statute adds the word 'genuinely' after the word 'unable'. By connoting an act in good faith, this gives the Court some leeway in interpretation.[42] However, subjectivity cannot be haphazard. Consistency is crucial to the Court's legitimacy, especially

---

pursuant to Article 19 of the ICC Statute'', (31 July 2012), para. 360 (hereinafter 'Corrigendum to the 'Defence Response to the Application on behalf of the Government of Libya'').

[40] *The Prosecutor v. Saif Al-Islam Gaddafi and Abdullah Al-Senussi*, Doc. ICC-01/11-01/11-167-Red, 'Prosecution Response to Application on behalf of the Government of Libya pursuant to Article 19 of the ICC Statute', (5 June 2012), para. 8 [emphasis added].

[41] *Ibid.*, para. 46.

[42] For a discussion on the drafting history of the ICC Statute, *see* Mohamed M. El Zeidy, *The Principle of Complementarity in International Criminal Law; Origin, Development and Practice* (Leiden: Martin Nijhoff Publishers, 2008) pp. 129-130; Mohamed M. El Zeidy, 'The Principle of Complementarity; A New Machinery to Implement International Criminal Law', (2001-2002) 23 *Michigan Journal of International Law*, 869, 899-900; William A. Schabas, *An Introduction to the International Criminal Court*, 2nd edn (Cambridge: Cambridge University Press, 2004), p. 86. *See also* Vienna Convention on the Law of Treaties, (1979) 1155 UNTS 331. (Treaties must be interpreted using the ordinary usage of terms and their context, in consideration of the treaty's goals).

considering charges of Western bias and serious tensions with the African Union.[43] Indeed, as critics have said, 'the Court cannot apply one standard to Kenya and another to Libya'.[44] Surprisingly, the Court has indicated a willingness to uphold such inconsistency by suggesting that a country's ability to carry out proceedings should be 'assessed in the context of the relevant national system and procedures'.[45] This strikes me as a dangerous precedent. It creates a stunning degree of subjectivity in the assessment process.

The subjective nature of Article 17(1)(a) is tempered by some basic parameters set forth in the Rome Statute. First, a decision regarding admissibility is informed by the findings of several parties at different stages of the investigative process. The Prosecutor has the first opportunity to judge whether a domestic prosecution is genuine or not. In addition, the Prosecutor will determine whether there is a reasonable basis to believe that a crime within the Court's jurisdiction has been, or is being, committed (as discussed earlier).[46] And of course, the Prosecutor has to decide whether to initiate an investigation *proprio motu* (of his own independent initiative) for crimes falling within the jurisdiction of the Court.[47]

Kenya was the first situation before the ICC where the Prosecutor used his *proprio motu* power to initiate formal investigations after obtaining authorisation from the Pre-Trial Chamber. This was a milestone in the Court's development. Before the Prosecutor can proceed with an investigation, he **must** obtain authorisation from the Pre-Trial Chamber.

---

[43] *See* 'Is Africa on trial?', *BBC News*, (27 March 2012), available at http://www.bbc.co.uk/news/world-africa-17513065. The African Union is considering pulling out of the ICC, in favour of establishing a court with parallel jurisdiction.

[44] *The Prosecutor v. Saif Al-Islam Gaddafi and Abdullah Al-Senussi*, Doc. ICC-01/11-01/11-T-3-Red-ENG, 'Hearing Transcript', (10 October 2012) (hereinafter '10 October Transcript'), at 7:11.

[45] *The Prosecutor v. Said Al-Islam Gaddafi and Abdullah Al-Senussi*, Doc. ICC-01/11-01/11-344-Red, 'Decision on the admissibility of the case against Saif Al-Islam Gaddafi', (31 May 2013), para. 200.

[46] ICC Statute, Article 53(1)(a).

[47] *Ibid.*, Article 15(2) reads: '[t]he Prosecutor shall analyse the seriousness of the information received. For this purpose he or she may seek additional information from States, organs of the United Nations, intergovernmental or non-governmental organisations, or other reliable sources that he or she deems appropriate, and may receive written or oral testimony at the seat of the Court'.

And to do so, he must prove that there is a reasonable basis to believe that a crime exists and that the Court would have jurisdiction over the crime.[48] The burden is on the Prosecutor to convince the Chamber that 'there is a reasonable basis to proceed with an investigation' after presenting an application for authorisation along with any supporting material. Limiting the power of the Prosecutor in this regard is a legal mechanism that regulates Court decisions to pursue cases that would otherwise be under the jurisdiction of states and reduces the risk of politically motivated investigations.

However, by permitting the Prosecutor to initiate investigations *proprio motu*, states are less likely to allow the most serious crimes to go unpunished. So long as the Court considers first the possibility of a state-based prosecution, the legal mechanism permitting the Prosecutor to initiate a case does not undermine the concept of complementarity. In fact, it might help the state to focus on post-conflict reconstruction rather than a complicated domestic war crimes trial. Leaving this responsibility to the ICC could best serve the interests of justice, particularly if a trial is directed at a high-profile political leader. This was precisely the situation in Kenya that led the government initially to cooperate with the ICC.

Again, the Prosecutor serves as an intermediary between the ICC and states wishing to investigate and prosecute crimes that might also fall under the jurisdiction of the ICC. The Prosecutor must notify all interested states at the time an investigation is to commence.[49] Article 18 of the Rome Statute relates to the **commencement of an investigation**, initiated where the Prosecutor has a reasonable basis to believe a crime has been

[48] Once the Prosecutor concludes that there is a 'reasonable basis to proceed with an investigation' and submits a request for the Pre-Trial Chamber (PTC) to authorize an investigation, a majority of the judges in the PTC must agree on the ruling. This is thus a situation where '[t]he functions of the Pre-Trial Chamber shall be carried out . . . by three judges of the Pre-Trial Division' rather than by 'a single judge of that division' (*Ibid.* Article 39(2)(b)(iii)). Upon examination of the request and supporting material, if the PTC agrees that there is a 'reasonable basis to proceed with an investigation and that the case appears to fall within the jurisdiction of the Court, it shall authorize the commencement of the investigation, without prejudice to subsequent determinations by the Court with regard to the jurisdiction and admissibility of a case' (*Ibid.*, Article 15(4)).

[49] *Ibid.*, Article 18(1).

committed.[50] Article 18, therefore, applies in the preliminary stages of an investigation.

The notification requirement extends not only to States Parties but to '*those states . . . [which] would normally exercise jurisdiction over the crimes concerned*' [emphasis added].[51] This language suggests that all states that have a direct link to the crime or the accused will be placed on notice. This requirement provides a legal mechanism that mandates notice of a potential investigation by the ICC so as to allow an interested state to exercise jurisdiction by invoking the principle of complementarity.

It is interesting to note that, although the Prosecutor must notify the states concerned, she may limit the information provided (such as the suspects' identity) when such disclosure could disadvantage the investigation. As any investigation is likely to concern those in government and military roles, there may be various reasons for withholding information at this stage. Furthermore, Rule 52 of the Rules of Procedure and Evidence does not require the Prosecutor to disclose the details of his investigation; it only requires that 'notification shall contain information about the acts that may constitute crimes referred to in Article 5, relevant for the purposes of Article 18, Paragraph 2'.[52]

Upon notification of an investigation, a state has one month to request a deferral. If the state notifies the ICC of its own investigation (Article 17(1)), the ICC is divested of jurisdiction and the domestic investigation is automatically given primacy unless the Prosecutor submits an application to the Pre-Trial Chamber. The language of Article 18 is unequivocal: '[t]he Prosecutor *shall* defer to the state's investigation of those persons unless the Pre-Trial Chamber, on the application of the Prosecution, decides to authorise the investigation' [emphasis added].[53] The decision to defer to the state is reviewed after six months or whenever there has been a

---

[50] John T. Holmes, 'Complementarity: National Courts *versus* the ICC' in A. Cassese, P. Gaeta, J. Jones (eds.) *The Rome Statute of the International Criminal Court: A Commentary*, 2 vols. (Oxford: Oxford University Press, 2002), vol. 1, p. 681.

[51] ICC Statute, Article 18(1). The Prosecutor would do so through the Jurisdiction, Complementarity and Cooperation Division (JCCD).

[52] ICC, 'Rules of Procedures and Evidence', Doc. ICC-ASP/1/3 (Part.II-A) (hereinafter 'ICC Rules of Procedure and Evidence'), Rule 52(1).

[53] ICC Statute, Article 18(2).

'significant change of circumstances based on the State's unwillingness or inability to genuinely carry out the investigation'.[54]

Even if the Prosecutor decides to pursue the investigation with the Pre-Trial Chamber's authorisation, the state in question can still provide the Court with information to support its own claim to jurisdiction over the investigation.[55] Such information will likely reinforce the state's argument that it is willing and able to try the suspect.

In essence, there exist statutory mechanisms that limit the actions of the Prosecutor in the interest of preserving the primacy of domestic war crimes courts. A series of independent assessments combine to determine admissibility, with the Court as final arbiter.[56] Determinations thus rest with the Prosecutor, the Pre-Trial Chamber, the Trial Chamber, and the Appeals Chamber. Each applies the admissibility test criteria, depending on when the question of admissibility arises.[57]

II. Willingness to Prosecute

Before assessing the statutory requirements concerning a state's willingness to prosecute, it is useful to look at willingness in terms of a state's political will to prosecute. The importance of *political will* in bringing individuals to justice cannot be underestimated.

Lack of *political will* to try persons accused of international crimes is nothing new. Since 1945, there have been 253 distinct armed conflicts in which an estimated minimum 7.8 million people have been lost their lives[58], twice the number of victims in World War I and II combined.[59] Yet to date, only 823 persons have been indicted by international or regional

---

[54] *Ibid.*, Article 18(3).
[55] ICC Rules of Procedure and Evidence, Rules 52(2), 53, 55 and 56(2).
[56] Jann K. Kleffner, *Complementarity in the Rome Statute and National Criminal Jurisdiction*, (Oxford: Oxford University Press, 2008), p. 102, *citing* Holmes, 'Complementarity: National Courts Versus the ICC', p. 672.
[57] *Ibid.*, pp. 102, 163-235.
[58] This is a composite based on an assessment of a number of sources, analysis of which can be found in Appendix I.
[59] Christopher Mullins, 'Conflict Victimization and Post-Conflict Justice 1945-2008' in M. Cherif Bassiouni (ed.), *The Pursuit of International Criminal Justice: A World Study on Conflicts, Victimization, and Post-Conflict Justice*, 2 vols. (Oxford: Intersentia, 2010), vol. 1, p. 67.

courts.[60] The fact is that prosecution of international crimes has been an 'historical anomaly'.[61] Whether acting out of political expediency or deliberately undermining the rule of law, states have too often let international crimes go unpunished. More problematic is the difficulty in bringing to justice senior military and political commanders accused of crimes. One US Ambassador, speaking of war crimes committed in Sri Lanka, stated:

> There are no examples we know of a regime undertaking wholesale investigations of its troops or senior officials for war crimes while that regime or government remains in power.[62]

In times of conflict, decision-makers may also be so desperate to achievc peace and stability in the short-run that they broker deals with the very leaders who committed atrocities. For instance, Bosco Ntaganda has been wanted by the ICC since 2006 for war crimes committed in Ituri.[63] In 2009, the DRC government was seen to openly negotiate with Ntaganda.

The same thing happened in former Yugoslavia when the international community sat at the bargaining table with Slobodan Milošević rather than insist that he be apprehended and tried for war crimes. It is often argued that such a non-punitive process with perpetrators of atrocities is a necessary concession to bring an end to violence. Afghanistan is another example. In March 2010, the Afghan government enacted a law providing blanket pardon for all war crimes and human rights violations that occurred before December 2001.[64] Unfortunately, war criminals do not disappear; they re-emerge to commit new atrocities. We saw this in former Yugoslavia and are beginning to see it again in Afghanistan.

---

[60] *Ibid.*

[61] *See* Jonathan I. Charney, 'International Criminal Law and the Role of Domestic Courts', (2001) 95 *American Journal of International Law*, 120.

[62] Confidential message by US Ambassador to Colombia, Patricia Butenis, reported in 'An Era of Sri Lanka's President: From Mullivaikal to Oxford Union—Groundviews', *Tamil News Network*, (24 December 2010), available at http://www.tamilnewsnetwork.com/2010/12/24/an-era-of-sri-lankas-president-from-mullivaikal-to-oxford-union-groundviews/.

[63] Bosco Ntaganda's warrant for arrest was unsealed on 28 April 2008. *See The Prosecutor v. Bosco Ntaganda*, Doc. ICC-01/04-02/06-2, 'Warrant of Arrest' (22 August 2006).

[64] *See* 'Afghanistan Says It Enacted Law to Pardon War Crimes', *Reuters*, (16 March 2010), available at www.nytimes.com/2010/03/17/world/asia/17kabul.html.

Nearly twenty years after the 1994 Rwandan genocide, there remain nine ICTR indictees who are still fugitives.[65] The UN Security Council has called on all member states to assist in bringing them to justice.[66] Recently, the President of the ICC urged the international community to increase its efforts to bring perpetrators of international crimes to justice. He stated:

> Make no mistake—the ICC faces threats today as real as ever before. There are those who seek to undermine the international justice movement, who politicise its action, who question its value, and who purport to speak for the victims it serves. There are those who refuse to cooperate, leaving more than ten ICC suspects still at large.[67]

Recently, I visited Burma where I met with Nobel Peace Prize winner and opposition political leader Aung San Suu Kyi. I discussed with her the issue of accountability for past crimes committed in the country. Her response was both revealing and surprising. Presently, she said, there is simply not sufficient political will in the country to support an accountability mechanism. Even more disturbing is that Aung San Suu Kyi herself expressed no appetite for advocating for such a policy. She was clearly more interested in looking to the future and not dealing with the past. However, as we have seen time and time again, ignoring past crimes is short-sided; they come back to haunt society.

Where political leaders fail to demonstrate support for war crimes trials, domestic or international, radical elements can also easily derail a fragile peace.[68] This could certainly occur in Burma. In preventing the resumption of conflict, it is thus vital to find the political will to uphold accountability over impunity.

---

[65] *See* United Nations Mechanism for International Criminal Tribunals, 'Searching for Fugitives', (2014) available at http://unmict.org/searching-for-fugitives.html.

[66] UN Security Council, UN Doc. S/RES/2080 (2012), (12 December 2012); *See* Dan Taglioli, 'UN extends terms of Rwanda criminal tribunal justices', *Jurist*, (13 December 2012) available at http://jurist.org/paperchase/2012/12/un-extends-terms-of-rwanda-criminal-tribunal-justices.php.

[67] ICC, 'Statement from the President: International Criminal Justice Day', (16 July 2013), available at http://www.icc-cpi.int/en_menus/icc/press%20and%20media/press%20releases/Pages/statement-16-07-2013.aspx.

[68] 'Politicians Stymie Belgrade War Crimes Trials', *Institute for War and Peace Reporting*, (15 February 2010), available at http://iwpr.net/report-news/politicians-stymie-belgrade-war-crimes-trials.

Under Article 17(2), unwillingness can be established if 'the proceedings' were for the purpose of shielding the person concerned;[69] or there is an unjustified delay 'in the proceedings'[70] or 'proceedings' have not been conducted 'independently or impartially'.[71]

As noted earlier, the term 'unwilling' is not clearly defined in the Rome Statute. As described by Mohamed M. El Zeidy, the issue was unsettled during the drafting process, with the Court ultimately being given significant leeway in 'deciding on states' unwillingness'.[72] At minimum, the term would require a state to act in 'good faith' to prosecute.[73] The Statute includes general parameters to assist the Court in deciding if a state is unwilling to conduct investigations.

Article 17(2) of the Statute provides that:

> In order to determine unwillingness in a particular case, the Court shall consider, having regard to the principles of due process recognized by international law, whether *one or more* of the following exist, as applicable: [emphasis added]
>
> (a) The proceedings were or are being undertaken or the national decision was made for the purpose of shielding the person concerned from criminal responsibility for crimes within the jurisdiction of the Court . . . ;
>
> (b) There has been an unjustified delay in the proceedings, which in the circumstances is inconsistent with an intent to bring the person concerned to justice;
>
> (c) The proceedings were not or are not being conducted independently or impartially, and they were or are being conducted in a manner which, in the circumstances, is inconsistent with an intent to bring the person concerned to justice.[74]

While these represent separate and distinct criteria, the Court to date has tended to consider them together. This is not surprising since all three scenarios can be seen as attempts by a state to avoid bringing a person to justice. Furthermore, a review of all three is more effective because not

---

69 ICC Statute, Article 17(2)(a).

70 *Ibid.*, Article 17(2)(b).

71 *Ibid.*, Article 17(2)(c).

72 El Zeidy, *The Principle of Complementarity in International Criminal Law*, p. 163.

73 *Ibid.*, p. 165.

74 ICC Statute, Article 17(2).

every situation will be easy to prove.[75] However, the 'one or more' wording in the Statute conveys a clear intention that only one of these situations is sufficient to demonstrate 'unwillingness'. Consequently, for the purpose of better understanding the three principles each will be assessed independently.

A. Shielding

The first test under Article 17(2)(a) concerns whether the domestic proceedings are simply *shielding* the accused from prosecution. This particular test grew from the situation in the former Yugoslavia where a competent judiciary was 'politically unwilling to prosecute'.[76] Required here is an assessment of the nature of the state's action, with a keen focus on the facts of each case. Is the state acting with specific intent to undermine an individual's public persona, or taking the necessary action to investigate or prosecute?

It is important to note that when a state assumes jurisdiction of a case, it is incumbent upon the domestic war crimes court to proceed with a legitimate effort to bring perpetrators to justice. The principle of complementarity would **not** allow a state to obtain control over a case and then refuse to investigate, or to conduct an investigation without intent to bring the case to trial. However, deference to domestic courts also requires the ICC to recognise the fact-finding and investigative outcomes conducted by states, assuming they were not undertaken to circumvent prosecutions. The ICC must accept not only the substantive legal rules of the domestic jurisdiction but also the procedures to implement those rules.[77]

---

[75] El Zeidy, *The Principle of Complementarity in International Criminal Law*, p. 181.

[76] *See* Claire Brighton, 'Avoiding Unwillingness: Addressing the Political Pitfalls Inherent in the Complementarity Regime of the International Criminal Court', (2012) 12 *International Criminal Law Review*, 629, 640.

[77] Britain provides a recent example of how the deferral mechanism works under the principle of complementarity. The situation involved the conduct of British soldiers in Iraq, who were accused of having unlawfully killed and tortured Iraqi civilians during British occupation. The case was brought to the attention of the ICC. However, Britain readily assumed jurisdiction over the matter and proceeded with a domestic investigation and prosecution of the soldiers. The ICC Prosecutor did not request authorisation to conduct a subsequent investigation, finding the British adjudication sufficient to meet ICC standards under the principle of

A good example of shielding occurred in the Democratic Republic of the Congo (DRC). The District Military Court had sentenced Yves Panga Mandro Kahwa to 20 years' imprisonment for crimes against humanity.[78] The Court of Appeals reversed the District Court and acquitted Kahwa on the grounds that the offences were covered by the Law on Amnesty as acts of war and political offences.[79] In essence, the Court relied on an amnesty

---

complementarity. *See* Response of Luis Moreno-Ocampo, Chief Prosecutor of the International Criminal Court, Regarding Iraq (9 February 2006), p. 1, available at http://www.iccnow.org/documents/OTP_letter_to_senders_re_Iraq_9_February_2006.pdf. The Prosecutor did not proceed to the issue of adequacy of national proceedings as, under Article 53(1)(a), he was not satisfied that the gravity requirement had been met. He said: '[i]n light of the conclusion reached on gravity, it was unnecessary to reach a conclusion on complementarity' (*Ibid.*, p. 9). A communication by the American Non-Governmental Organizations Coalition for the International Criminal Court (AMICC) draws the same conclusion. *See* AMICC, 'Communications to the ICC Regarding the Situation in Iraq', (28 July 2009), available at
http://www.amicc.org/docs/Iraq.pdf. *See also Al-Skeini and Others v. Secretary of State for Defence*, [2007] UKHL 26.

[78] Trial, 'Yves Mandro Kahwa Panga', (2014) available at http://www.trial-ch.org/en/resources/trial-watch/trial-watch/profiles/profile/576/action/show/controller/Profile/tab/legal-procedure.html. Military Garrison Court of Ituri at Bunia, Yves Mandro Kahwa Panga is a former member of the Union of Congolese Patriots (UPC) of Thomas Lubanga, and in 2003 founded the Party for Unity and Safeguarding of the Integrity of Congo (PUSIC). PUSIC was a militia group identified with the Hema ethnicity and was one of the controlling groups in the northeast zones, including Ituri, which were involved in local conflicts. Despite measures to end violence, and the signing of an agreement in 2002 ending the civil war in most parts of the country, Ituri remained volatile due to continued militia activity of groups, including PUSIC. During an ethnic conflict from January 2002 to March 2003 between the Hema and another ethnic group, PUSIC allegedly attacked villages, under the command of Kahwa Panga, resulting in about 500 civilian deaths and the destruction of 24 villages. Between 15-16 October 2002, under the command of Kahwa, PUSIC was alleged to have attacked the Zumbe, a remote village in Ituri. Mines were planted, killing several civilians ('including the then-Mayor of the Djugu Township and relatives of the 13 persons who were joined in the proceedings as *parties civiles*'); 573 homes were destroyed and a health centre, three schools and churches were burned along with other severe property damage (Trial, 'Yves Mandro Kahwa Panga', (2013) available at http://www.trial-ch.org/en/ressources/trial-watch/trial-watch/profils/profile/576/action/show/controller/Profile.html; *see also Ituri District Military Prosecutor v. Kahwa Panga Mandro*, RMP No. 227/PEN/2006).

[79] *Ibid.*

law to acquit the defendant of massacres against the civilian population. This is shielding.

Kenya is another example where the ICC intervened because Kenyan authorities appeared to be shielding perpetrators. During the 2007 general election, targeted ethnic violence resulted in more than 1,200 people being killed, 3,600 people injured and between 350,000 to 650,000 people displaced from their homes.[80] The violence was widespread, organised and sustained. The international community called for an immediate investigation by the ICC into alleged crimes against humanity.[81]

Soon after, the OTP made it known that it had an interest in ensuring that the perpetrators were brought to justice. The OTP left no doubt that it had jurisdiction over the situation in Kenya, since Kenya is a State Party to the Rome Statute.[82] However, the OTP also made clear that 'the primary responsibility for investigating and prosecuting these crimes' is with Kenya.[83]

---

[80] ICC, 'Press Conference by the Prosecutor of the International Criminal Court, Luis Moreno-Ocampo', (26 November 2009), available at http://www.icc-cpi.int/NR/rdonlyres/AC13413D-D097-4527-B0AE-60CF6DBB1B68/281313 /LMOINTROstatement26112009_2_2.pdf. *See* Commission of Inquiry into the Post Election Violence (CIPEV), 'Final Report', (16 October 2008), available at http://reliefweb.int/sites/reliefweb.int/files/resources/15A00F569813F4D54925760 7001F459D-Full_Report.pdf. The CIPEV was established in May 2007 and is also known as the 'Waki' Commission, after the chairman, Justice Philip Waki. *See also* Kenyan National Commission on Human Rights, 'On the Brink of the Precipice: A Human Rights Account of Kenya's Post-2007 Election Violence', (August 2008) available at http://kenyastockholm.files.wordpress.com/2008/08/pev-report-as-adopted-by-the-commission-for-release-on-7-august-20081.pdf; J. Wingard, 'Kenyans Wait for Justice in Election Violence Trial', *Deutsche Welle*, (26 October 2012), available at http://www.dw.de/kenyans-wait-for-justice-in-election-violence-trial/a-1633 6263; Human Rights Watch, 'Kenya: ICC Judges OK Election Violence Trials', (23 January 2012), available at http://www.hrw.org/news/2012/01/23/kenya-icc-judges-ok-election-violence-trials.

[81] Including this author, *see* Mark S. Ellis, 'Atrocities in Kenya Must Not Go Unpunished', *The Times* (6 February 2008).

[82] ICC-OTP, 'OTP Statement in Relation to Events in Kenya', (5 February 2008) available at http://www.icc-cpi.int/NR/rdonlyres/1BB89202-16AE-4D95-ABBB-4597C416045D/0/ICCOTPST20080205ENG.pdf.

[83] ICC, 'ICC Prosecutor receives materials on post-election violence in Kenya', Doc. ICC-OTP-20090716-PR438, (16 July 2009).

The Kenyan government could not escape the Court's mandate and decided to counterbalance potential ICC jurisdiction by creating the Commission of Inquiry on Post-Election Violence ('the Waki Commission'), which subsequently recommended the establishment of a Truth, Justice and Reconciliation Commission (TJRC) and the creation of a Special Tribunal for Kenya.[84]

The Waki Commission concluded that politicians on all sides had organised and funded attacks on supporters of their opponents. The Kenyan government initially agreed to keep the ICC Prosecutor updated on the status of investigations and prosecutions and to provide any information requested by the ICC to perform its own preliminary examinations.[85]

Most important, the Kenyan government agreed to refer jurisdiction to the ICC if the Kenyan Parliament did not agree on a judicial mechanism to deal with the crimes.[86] This promise became the tipping point in the strained relationship between the Court and Kenya.

In the end, the constitutional amendment needed to establish a Special Tribunal, as recommended by the Waki Commission, failed to gain consensus in Parliament. This meant that the Kenyan government missed the agreed upon deadline, September 2009, for initiating prosecutions.

The government then focused on establishing the TJRC and relying on ordinary criminal courts to undertake prosecutions. This, however, was a vexing issue for the Court. Would an extra-judicial process constitute a violation of Article 17(2)(a) by 'shielding' the person from criminal responsibility? The principal concern here is how the admissibility rules of Article 17 of the Rome Statute relate to the 'judgments' of alternative

---

[84] CIPEV, 'Final Report', pp. 22, 472-475.
[85] ICC, 'Agreed Minutes of the Meeting Between Prosecutor Moreno-Ocampo and the Delegation of the Kenyan Government', (3 July 2009), available at http://www.icc-cpi.int/NR/rdonlyres/AA9AC1FD-112F-4582-84D8-AA6C58445D98/280560/20090703AgreedMinutesofMeetingProsecutorKenyanDele.pdf. Subsequently, the Kenyan attorney general delivered a report and six boxes of documents and supporting materials compiled by the Commission to the ICC Prosecutor. This coincided with the decision by UN Secretary-General Kofi Annan to deliver the names of those believed responsible for the post-election violence to the ICC Prosecutor.
[86] ICC, 'ICC Prosecutor receives materials on post-election violence in Kenya'.

methods of accountability.[87] The TJRC's mandate was to create an historical record of the crimes committed since Kenya's independence in 1963, but with a specific focus on the violence following the 2007 election. However, the TJRC quickly struggled against a serious credibility gap and was not seen as an appropriate alternative to domestic war crimes proceedings by the Court.[88] Recently though, the TJRC issued a report that found the two highest level government officials 'plan[ned] incitement and financ[ed] violence during the 2007/2008 post-election violence'.[89] However, in spite of its terms of reference, the Commission's report has made no recommendation about action against the two.[90]

In the end, despite overwhelming evidence of war crimes committed during the country's election violence, no 'concrete actions' were taken by Kenyan authorities to bring those responsible to justice.[91] Kenyan authorities were 'remarkably consistent in evading their legal obligations to undertake credible criminal investigations'.[92] Their actions are characteristic of a pervasive political unwillingness to cooperate.

With the failure to create a domestic Tribunal and the rejection of TJRC, the ICC Prosecutor stood firm in insisting that he had a right to initiate a *proprio motu* investigation if Kenya failed to undertake prosecutions. The Prosecutor argued that there were no active or pending proceedings against 'those bearing the greatest responsibility for the crimes…'.[93] The Pre-Trial Chamber agreed, and confirmed the Court's jurisdiction based on 'a lack of national proceedings in the Republic of Kenya or in any third state with respect to the main elements which may

---

[87] Benjamin Perrin, 'Making Sense of Complementarity: The Relationship between the International Criminal Court and National Jurisdictions', (2006) 18 *Sri Lanka Journal of International Law*, 301, 309.
[88] *See* ICTJ, 'New Calls for resignation of TJRC Chair', (24 February 2010) available at http://www.ictj.org/en/news/press/release/3477.html.
[89] TJRC, 'Report of the Truth, Justice and Reconciliation Commission of Kenya', vol. 4, pp. 172-173.
[90] *Ibid.*
[91] Human Rights Watch, 'World Report 2012: Kenya', (January 2012) available at http://www.hrw.org/world-report-2012/world-report-2012-kenya.
[92] 'ICC's Kenya decision is no cause for celebration', *Al Jazeera*, (31 January 2012), available at http://www.aljazeera.com/indepth/opinion/2012/01/2012128125931617297.html.
[93] *Situation in the Republic of Kenya*, Doc. ICC-01/09-19, 'Decision Pursuant to Article 15 of the Rome Statute on the Authorization of an Investigation into the Situation in the Republic of Kenya', (31 March 2010), para. 183.

shape the Court's potential case(s)'.[94] Although not articulated in this way, the Prosecutor was arguing that Kenya was *shielding* those responsible for atrocities.

Consequently, in 2009, the Prosecutor requested authority from the PTC to conduct investigations into the Kenya situation. In 2010, the PTC gave the Prosecutor authority to investigate crimes that might have occurred in Kenya between 1 June 2005 (the date Kenya accepted ICC jurisdiction) and 26 November 2009.[95]

Although not under the ICC's jurisdiction, Sri Lanka offers another example of a state purposely shielding perpetrators following the twenty-five-year civil war between the government and the Liberation Tigers of Tamil Eelam. I concluded for UK *Channel 4 News* in London that there was prima facie evidence that the Sri Lankan government was complicit in war crimes and possible crimes against humanity during Sri Lanka's civil war.[96] Despite calls by UN Secretary-General Ban Ki-Moon and the Council of the European Union for a 'proper investigation'[97], the Sri Lankan government ignored these requests.[98] Instead, the government created an internal Commission to investigate abuses.[99] International

---

[94] *Ibid.*, para. 184.

[95] *Ibid.*, para. 207.

[96] This assessment was made for UK *Channel 4 News* and was based on my viewings of videos showing graphic footage of atrocities being committed against individuals by what purports to be military personnel. *See* 'Sri Lanka 'war crimes' video: who are these men?', *Channel 4 News*, (2 December 2010), available at http://www.channel4.com/news/sri-lanka-war-crimes-video-who-are-these-men.

[97] United Nations, 'Secretary-General's press encounter following the Security Council's informal interactive discussion on Sri Lanka', (5 June 2009), available at http://www.un.org/sg/offthecuff/?nid=1296; Council of the European Union, 'Council Conclusions on Sri Lanka', (18 May 2009), available at http://www.consilium.europa.eu/uedocs/cms_data/docs/pressdata/en/gena/107873.pdf.

[98] 'Sri Lanka says UN panel 'will not be allowed' to enter', *BBC News*, (24 June 2010) available at http://www.bbc.co.uk/news/10405996. *See also* Press Release of the Presidential Secretariat of Sri Lanka, 'Government opposes UN Panel', (23 June 2010) available at http://www.priu.gov.lk/news_update/Current_Affairs/ca201006/20100623govt_opposes_un_panel.htm.

[99] The Sri Lankan Lessons Learnt and Reconciliation Commission (LLRC) was created in May 2010, with the ostensible purpose of investigating violations of human rights and the laws of war by government forces and the Liberation Tigers

organisations immediately questioned the efficacy of the Commission, noting its failure to satisfy certain criteria generally used to assess the value of such commissions.[100] The criteria included independence, impartiality and competence of commission members, a mandate broad enough to allow for full investigations of allegations, and adequate protection of witnesses.[101]

In March 2010, Secretary-General Ban Ki-moon stated his intention to set up a UN panel to investigate the allegations of human rights abuses in Sri Lanka, but Sri Lanka's President Mahinda Rajapaksa rejected it as 'totally uncalled for and unwarranted'.[102] The United Nations Special Rapporteur on Extra-judicial Executions, Philip Alston, was among the first to dismiss the Commission as ineffective without a mandate to investigate war crimes or breaches of human rights law.[103] Sri Lanka has since refused to allow the UN to conduct its own war crimes probe, ordering that any investigation be managed in cooperation with the

---

of Tamil Eelam during Sri Lanka's civil war. For more information *see* the website of Lessons Learnt Reconciliation Commission available at http://www.llrc.lk/index.php. The LLRC was established following international calls for an investigation into the alleged violations, but was soon criticised by civil society as inadequate. Some international groups have stated that the LLRC was only established to prevent United Nations intervention, and have cited concerns about the LLRC's adequacy on grounds of impartiality, procedure, and a limited mandate. *See* e.g. Human Rights Watch, 'Sri Lanka: Report Fails to Advance Accountability' (16 December 2011) available at http://www.hrw.org/news/2011/12/16/sri-lanka-report-fails-advance-accountability.

[100] Human Rights Watch, 'Letter to Secretary Clinton on the Sri Lanka's Lessons Learnt and Reconciliation Commission (LLRC)' (27 May 2010) available at http://www.hrw.org/en/news/2010/05/27/letter-secretary-clinton-sri-lankas-lessons-learnt-and-reconciliation-commission-llr.

[101] US Mission to the UN, 'Statement by US Ambassador Susan E. Rice on Sri Lanka's Announcement of a Commission on Lessons Learned and Reconciliation', (10 May 2010), available at http://usun.state.gov/briefing/statements/2010/141657.htm.

[102] Ministry of Defence and Urban Development Sri Lanka, 'Special Panel on Sri Lanka uncalled for and unwarranted – President to Ban Ki-moon', (6 March 2010), available at http://www.defence.lk/new.asp?fname=20100306_05.

[103] 'Sri Lanka's Commission convenes as US calls for independent investigations', *TamilNet*, (11 August 2010), available at http://www.tamilnet.com/art.html?catid=13&artid=32384.

Commission.[104] In 2013, the UN Human Rights Council issued a resolution requiring the Sri Lankan government to report back by March 2014 on alleged violations of international law during the civil war.[105] To date, the Government has brushed aside the request. Most recently, the Public Interest Advocacy Centre's (PIAC's) International Crimes Evidence Project (ICEP) released a report in February 2014 alleging the commission of war crimes and crimes against humanity during the end of the Sri Lankan civil war. The report concludes that there are reasonable grounds to conclude that members of the Sri Lankan Security Forces (SFs) and Liberation Tigers of Tamil Eelam (LTTE) committed violations of international law amounting to war crimes and crimes against humanity.[106]

Similarly, in February 2014 Navanethem Pillay, UN High Commissioner for Human Rights (OHCHR), issued a report on advice and technical assistance for the Government of Sri Lanka on promoting reconciliation and accountability in Sri Lanka.[107] The final report concluded that the steps taken by Sri Lanka towards recovery had not satisfied the requirements for an independent and credible investigation into allegations of serious human rights violations.[108] Pillay's report expressed the damning conclusion that the lack of progress could not be attributed to lack of time or capacity but was instead indicative of lack of political will, and again called for an independent and credible international investigation into alleged violations of international human rights and humanitarian law. Both reports will undoubtedly be ignored by the Sri

---

[104] 'Sri Lanka says UN panel cannot conduct own war crimes probe', *Reuters*, (30 December 2010), available at http://www.reuters.com/article/idUSTRE6BT13B20101230.

[105] *See* UNGA, 'Report of the Office of the United Nations High Commissioner for Human Rights on advice and technical assistance for the Government of Sri Lanka on promoting reconciliation and accountability in Sri Lanka', UN Doc. A/HRC/22/38, (11 February 2013).

[106] *See* Public Interest Advocacy Centre (PIAC) and International Crimes Evidence Project (ICEP), 'Island of impunity? Investigation into international crimes in the final stages of the Sri Lankan civil war', (February 2014), para. 1.6, available at http://www.piac.asn.au/sites/default/files/publications/extras/island_of_impunity.pdf. A recent report suggests that near Mullaitivu, there were over 40,000 people killed, many civilians, as people were trying to flee from government forces. *See The Economist*, (8 March 2014), at 53.

[107] *See* UNGA, 'Promoting reconciliation and accountability in Sri Lanka', UN Doc. A/HRC/25/23, (24 February 2014).

[108] *Ibid*., para. 65.

Lankan government.[109] In March 2014, the UN Human Rights Council voted to launch an investigation into alleged human rights violations committed during the Sri Lankan civil war.[110]

The Sri Lankan government has stated that only Sri Lankan courts will be permitted to investigate the crimes.[111] It argues that the country has a 'robustly independent judiciary' that is capable of undertaking domestic investigations.[112] Acting External Affairs Minister D.E.W. Gunasekera made it very clear: it would 'not under any circumstances, allow any others to impose on us their advice or solution'.[113] Any outside help to investigate violations of international humanitarian law would be resisted.[114] A government-sponsored protest opposing the resolution drew thousands of people.[115]

---

[109] *Ibid.*, paras 72, 74.

[110] Ann Schober, 'UN rights body votes to investigate Sri Lanka war crimes' *Jurist* (28 March 2014) available at http://jurist.org/paperchase/2014/03/un-rights-body-votes-to-investigate-sri-lanka-war-crimes.php.

[111] International Institute for Strategic Studies (IISS), 'Winning counter-insurgency campaigns: Q&A', (31 May 2009), (Response from Rohitha Bogollagama, Minister of Foreign Affairs, Sri Lanka) available at http://www.iiss.org/conferences/the-shangri-la-dialogue/shangri-la-dialogue-2009/plenary-session-speeches-2009/fifth-plenary-session/qa/; *see also* 'Sri Lanka refuses external probes into alleged human rights violations', *Jurist*, (31 May 2009), available at http://jurist.org/paperchase/2009/05/sri-lanka-refuses-external-probes-into.php.

[112] Ministry of Defence and Urban Development Sri Lanka, 'Government strongly opposes the appointment of the Sri Lanka – Panel of experts by the UNSG', (23 June 2010), available at http://www.defence.lk/new.asp?fname=20100623_08; *See also* 'Sri Lanka pro-government protesters demand end to UN Panel', *Jurist*, (6 July 2010), available at http://www.jurist.org/paperchase/2010/07/sri-lanka-pro-government-protesters-demand-end-to-un-panel.php.

[113] 'After Geneva, government must evolve clear-cut policy', *The Sunday Times* (Sri Lanka), (25 March 2012), available at http://sundaytimes.lk/120325/Columns/political.html.

[114] 'Sri Lanka rejects UN war resolution', *Al Jazeera*, (24 March 2012), available at http://www.aljazeera.com/news/asia/2012/03/201232323325912421.html.

[115] *See* Jamie Davis, 'Thousands in Sri Lanka protest proposed UN war crimes resolution', *Jurist*, (27 February 2012) available at http://www.jurist.org/paperchase/2012/02/thousands-in-sri-lanka-protest-proposed-un-war-crimes-resolution.php.

Though various foreign-based Tamil groups have submitted detailed reports to the ICC urging action,[116] there has been no detailed response from the OTP, except to remind parties that the Office does not have jurisdiction in Sri Lanka without a referral by the UN Security Council.[117] Not surprisingly, there has been little indication that the Security Council would refer these crimes to the ICC.[118]

The former Yugoslavia offers one of the most revealing and disturbing examples of a country that created an entire state structure for the purpose of shielding those responsible for atrocities to be brought to justice.

In 2003, I conducted a study for the Organisation for Security and Co-operation in Europe (OSCE) regarding Serbia's intent to bring war criminals to justice. I reported that 'the most serious deterrent to undertaking domestic war crimes trials [in Serbia] was the lack of *political* will', and that '[i]ndividuals in Serbia do not see any reason why local citizens accused of war crimes should be held accountable because, in the eyes of many individuals, these citizens remain heroes'.[119] For example, seventy-eight percent of Serbs would *not* have given up Ratko Mladić had they known where he was hiding.[120] After the war, the Serbian government supported a climate of impunity.[121] Political obstructionism was pervasive.

---

[116] 'Denmark Tamils take legal step to file war-crimes charges', *TamilNet*, (30 October 2010), available at http://www.tamilnet.com/art.html?catid=13&artid=32911.

[117] ICC-OTP, 'Clarification regarding the situation in Sri Lanka', Doc. ICC-OTP-20100607-PR541, (7 June 2010).

[118] The International Crisis Group has written that as the government maintains the support of China and Russia, securing such a referral will be very difficult. *See* International Crisis Group, 'War Crimes in Sri Lanka', (17 May 2010), Asia Report No. 191, p 34, available at http://www.crisisgroup.org/~/media/Files/asia/south-asia/sri-lanka/191%20War%20Crimes%20in%20Sri%20Lanka.ashx.

[119] Mark S. Ellis, 'Coming to Terms with its Past - Serbia's New Court for the Prosecution of War Crimes', (2004) 22 *Berkeley Journal of International Law*, 165, 168 [emphasis added].

[120] Human Rights Watch, 'ICTY: Q&A on the Case against Ratko Mladic', (31 May 2011), available at http://www.hrw.org/news/2011/05/31/icty-qa-case-against-ratko-mladic.

[121] I also argued that the Serbian judiciary lacked the capacity to conduct fair trials, and I stated that one of OSCE's main priorities should be to assist Serbia, through capacity-building programmes, to conduct domestic war crimes trials (*see* Ellis, 'Coming to Terms with its Past', 168).

For more than a decade, the Serbian government maintained a 'non-cooperation' policy with the ICTY, adopting a 'Milošević-era, nationalist mind set', and refusing even to acknowledge Serbia's role in atrocities.[122]

Justice Richard J. Goldstone, the ICTY's first Prosecutor, stated:

> The leaders of Serbia rejected the legality of and justification for the ICTY. They regarded it as representing an act of discrimination against their people.[123]

Professor Diane Orentlicher, an international law expert, also noted that the ICTY had little direct impact on the development of a war crimes court in Serbia. It was the eventual change in government that caused Serbia to institute the necessary legal reforms to develop the War Crimes Chamber in Serbia.[124] However, even with the creation of the War Crimes Chamber in July 2003, the early failure of Serbian politicians to back war crimes prosecutions severely hampered the work of the new court, and attacks from powerful nationalist politicians opposed to war crimes prosecutions weakened the resolve and effectiveness of the Court, the Office of the War Crimes Prosecutor, and the special war crimes investigation unit of the police.[125] The climate of impunity was evident within the Ministry of Interior, which oversaw the actual investigations.[126] Police, under the authority of the ministry, were not willing to cooperate with the Prosecutor because most of the war crimes perpetrators were police officers.[127] For example, the Serbian government refused to investigate, or even acknowledge, the cremations, by Serbian police and security forces, of the more than 710 bodies found in a mass grave at a police training facility near Belgrade.[128] The government's support of

---

[122] *See* International Crisis Group, 'Update Briefing: Serbia: Spinning its Wheels', Europe Briefing No. 39, (23 May 2005), p. 3, available at http://www.crisisgroup.org/~/media/Files/europe/b039_serbia___spinning_its_wheels.pdf.

[123] Richard J. Goldstone, 'South-East Asia and International Criminal Law', Occasional Paper Series No. 2 (2010), (Torkel Opsahl Academic EPublisher, 2011), p. 7.

[124] *See* Raab, 'Evaluating the ICTY', 94; Ellis, 'The Legacy of the ICTY', p. 143.

[125] *Ibid.*

[126] *Ibid.*

[127] *Ibid.*

[128] *Ibid.*

domestic war crimes trials was sporadic, at best. There were only a handful of low-level convictions.[129]

It is interesting to note that Article 17 of the Rome Statute does not address state issued amnesties. I would argue that legislation supporting outright amnesties for international crimes reflects an unambiguous decision by a state not to cooperate with the Court. Indeed, such amnesties or impunities are antithetical to achieving accountability for grave international crimes. Immunities, at least functional immunities, have already been ruled as inconsistent with customary international law. The Special Court for Sierra Leone articulated this principle clearly: 'there is a crystallising international norm that a government cannot grant amnesty for serious violations of crimes under international law…'.[130] Thus, government officials are not protected if charged with international crimes, whether in international or domestic courts.[131]

Pardons are also not addressed in the Rome Statute, yet are relevant to newly created domestic war crimes courts. It would be inconsistent with the meaning of the Statute if a state were permitted to use pardons as a way to circumvent justice. Penalties must be appropriate to the crime. However, it is possible that over a period of time, a government may decide to pardon an individual for reasons other than 'shielding'. For instance, a case may have involved a miscarriage of justice or disproportionate sentence. Such a scenario is more likely, however, given a significant time lapse between sentencing and pardon.

In my opinion, a state offer of outright amnesty or pardon to perpetrators of international crimes constitutes an act of 'shielding' under Article 17(2)(c)(a) of the Statute, and would be *per se* illegal. However,

---

[129] *Ibid.*

[130] *See The Prosecutor v. Morris Kallon and Brima Bazzy Kamara,* Case Nos SCSL-2004-15-AR72(E) and SCSL-2004-16-AR72(E), 'Decision on Challenge to Jurisdiction: Lomé Accord Amnesty', (13 March 2004) para. 82. *See also* 'Report of the Secretary-General on the Establishment of a Special Court for Sierra Leone', UN Doc. S/2009/915, (4 October 2000), para. 24.

[131] *See Attorney General of the Government of Israel v. Adolf Eichmann*, 'Appeal Judgement', (Supreme Court of Israel (1962) 36 ILR 277) when the Court ruled that 'only in one eventuality has a fugitive offender a right of immunity;' where the State requesting extradition tries the offender for a different offence than the one he was extradited for. The Court noted that the right of asylum and immunity belong to the country of asylum, and not to the offender as an individual. *See* also *Re. Pinochet Ugarte* [1998] All ER (D) 629; [1998] EWJ No. 2878.

when I interviewed the newly appointed Chief Prosecutor, Fatou Bensouda, she indicated that amnesties and other impunity mechanisms could be permissible under certain circumstances.[132] She focused on the timing of the ICC indictment. Once an indictment is issued, it becomes a 'red line' that cannot be crossed; a state cannot offer any form of amnesty or immunity and it must cooperate with the Court. However, prior to indictment, the Prosecutor stated that she would have no problem if the person under investigation obtained an 'immunity or amnesty deal'.[133] Moreover, the Prosecutor stated that an individual not under investigation by the Court would be 'encouraged to enter into negotiations with the relevant state', and that could include an offer of amnesty.[134]

I understand the practicality of this approach. Individuals not under ICC investigation are simply not the Court's concern. Similarly, a person under investigation is not the same as an indicted suspect. However, this approach seems to minimise and undermine the more general principle of accountability that is the foundation of both international justice and the ICC.

The Preamble of the Rome Statute affirms the duty of the Court 'to put an end to impunity for the perpetrators of these crimes and thus to contribute to the prevention of such crimes'.[135] Set in this framework, the Court serves a purpose larger than simply prosecuting the small number of perpetrators who find themselves within the Court's jurisdiction. I would argue that the new ICC Prosecutor is actually advocating 'shielding' for any suspect not of direct concern to the Court. This position seems deficient in both principle and effect.

B. Unjustified Delays

The second measure the ICC will consider when determining a state's 'unwillingness' to prosecute is whether there have been *unjustified delays* in the domestic proceedings (Article 17(2)(b)). Here again, the Rome Statute does not specify what constitutes 'unjustified' delays. However, it would surely cover both substantive and procedural due process aimed at bringing the accused to Court. A reasonable time might be that set forth by international standards and bodies. However, interpretation of 'unjustified

[132] Interview with Fatou Bensouda, ICC Chief Prosecutor, (Paris, 20 March 2013).
[133] *Ibid.*
[134] *Ibid.*
[135] ICC Statute, Preamble.

delay' gives states considerable latitude in determining exactly when to initiate legal proceedings. European jurisprudence has been particularly robust in setting forth acceptable causes for delay. The jurisprudence of the European Court of Human Rights (ECtHR) assesses 'reasonable' length of proceedings in light of the 'circumstances of the case and the criteria laid down in the Court's case-law, in particular the complexity of the case, the applicant's conduct and that of the competent authorities, and the importance of what was at stake for the applicant in the dispute'.[136]

The ICTR has also provided some insight into how to determine if there has been an unjustified delay. The Court set out several factors, including: 1) 'The length of the delay; 2) The complexity of the proceedings, such as the number of charges, the number of accused, the number of witnesses, the volume of evidence, the complexity of facts and law; 3) The conduct of the parties; 4) The conduct of the relevant authorities; 5) The prejudice to the accused if any'.[137]

The International Court of Justice also weighed in on the issue of unjustified delay in the case of *Belgium v. Senegal.*[138] Belgium filed a claim against Senegal claiming that Senegal failed in its obligation, under the Convention against Torture and customary international law, to prosecute Hissène Habré or extradite him to Belgium for the purpose of standing trial. As of 2014, Senegal had neither extradited nor tried Habré. The Court ruled that the Convention against Torture gives no indication of the timeframe for performance of the obligation to try or extradite, but it is

---

[136] *See*, among many other authorities, *Scordino v. Italy* (No. 1) (Application No. 36813/97) ECHR 2006-V (29 March 2006), para. 177; *Kovačič v. Slovenia*, (Application No. 24376/08) ECHR 355 (18 April 2013), para. 36; *Fortunat v. Slovenia* (Application No. 42977/04) ECHR 348 (18 April 2013), para. 43; *Dimitrov and Hamanov v. Bulgaria*, (Application Nos 48059/06 and 2708/09) ECHR (10 May 2011), para. 71; *Frydlender v. France* (Application No. 30979/96) ECHR 2000-VII (27 June 2000), para. 43; *Eckle v. Germany* (Application No. 8130/78) Series A No. 51, 5 EHRR 1 (15 July 1982), para. 80.

[137] *The Prosecutor v. Prosper Mugiraneza*, Case No. ICTR-99-50-AR73, 'Decision on Prosper Mugiraneza's Interlocutory Appeal from Trial Chamber II Decision of 2 October 2003 Denying the Motion to Dismiss the Indictment, Deman Speedy Trial and for Appropriate Relief', (27 February 2004), pp. 2-3.

[138] *Questions relating to the Obligation to Prosecute or Extradite (Belgium v. Senegal)*, Provisional Measures, Order of 28 May 2009, ICJ Reports 2009, p. 139; *Questions relating to the Obligation to Prosecute or Extradite (Belgium v. Senegal*), 'Judgment', ICJ Reports 2012, p. 422 (hereinafter *Belgium* v. *Senegal*, 'Judgment').

implicit in the text that it is to be 'implemented in a reasonable time in a manner compatible with the object and purpose of the Convention'.[139] The Court stated:

> The object and purpose of the Convention is 'to make more effective the struggle against torture'. It is for this reason that proceedings should be taken without delay, which Senegal has failed to do until now and must remedy that.[140]

The Court found that Senegal was obliged to take all measures necessary to try or extradite Habré, as soon as possible, once the first complaint was filed against him in 2000. Having failed to do so, Senegal was in breach of its obligation under the Convention.[141]

In assessing unjustified delay, the clock 'begins to run as soon as a person is 'charged''.[142] While the standard normally applied is the ECtHR 'specific case' approach, there are two exceptions. First, if 'the case has occurred in a context of repeated breaches of the reasonable-time requirement by the defendant state, reflecting organisational failure of its judicial system',[143] a more summary standard is applied. In this context, the ECtHR is exempted from assessing in greater detail 'the circumstances of the case'.[144]

The 'complexity of the case' represents a unique factor that may influence the ICC's complementarity assessment. If procedural complexity stems from 'organisational complexity of national procedure' the respondent state could be held responsible, as it is under ECtHR jurisprudence.[145] However, there are criteria that could support a *justified* delay. Relevant issues taken into account by the Court could include, *inter alia*, a 'large

---

[139] *Belgium* v. *Senegal*, 'Judgment', para. 11.
[140] *Ibid.*, para. 68.
[141] *Ibid.*, para. 463.
[142] *Eckle v. Germany*, para. 73.
[143] Frédéric Edel, *The length of civil and criminal proceedings in the case-law of the European Court of Human Rights*, 2nd edn, Human Rights Files No. 16, (Strasbourg: Council of Europe Publishing 2007), pp. 34 and 36-39.
[144] *Bottazzi v. Italy*, (Application No. 34884/97) ECHR 1999-V (28 July 1999), paras 22 and 23.
[145] Edel, *The length of civil and criminal proceedings in the case-law of the European Court of Human Rights*, p. 42.

number of defendants',[146] 'the seriousness of the charges',[147] 'the number of witnesses,[148] the ability to interact with the witnesses,[149] the need to secure expert witnesses,[150] and, more generally, all matters related to the '*administration des preuves*'.[151]

Intent is a crucial element of Article 17(2)(b). The Court must assess the state's *intent* to bring a person to justice. If a delay in proceedings is based on the state's reticence to bring the person concerned to trial, then, regardless of the reasons, it should be condemned as *unjustified*. In essence, ill intent by the state negates the possibility of legitimate delay.

The complexity of determining 'unjustified delay' is on full display in the *Gaddafi* admissibility proceedings before the ICC. In its submission to the Court, the OPCD (the Office of the Defence for the ICC) highlighted 'significant delays' in Libya's investigation which are 'inconsistent with a genuine intent' to bring Gaddafi to justice.[152] Necessary investigative steps include notifying Gaddafi of the charges against him, bringing him before a judge, and facilitating his domestic legal representation.[153] But what yardstick should be used to determine an 'unjustified delay'? As discussed earlier in relationship to ECtHR rulings, Libya is on solid ground with respect to the current delays. The government has, I believe, rightfully argued that 'the timeframe for the prosecution of Mr Gaddafi is justifiable and intended to achieve justice'.[154] Libya does not have authority over the

[146] *Arap Yalgin and others v. Turkey*, (Application No. 33370/96) ECHR (25 September 2001), para. 27.
[147] *Ibid.*
[148] *Bejer v. Poland*, (Application No. 38328/974) ECHR (4 October 2001), para. 49.
[149] *Neumeister v. Austria*, (Application No. 1936/63) Series A No. 8, 1 EHRR 191 (27 June 1968), para. 20.
[150] *Krasuski v. Poland*, (Application No. 61444/00) ECHR 2005-V (14 June 2005), para. 56.
[151] *Bejer v. Poland,* para. 49. *See also*, among other authorities, *Messina v. Italy*, (Application No. 13803/88) Series A257-H (26 February 1993), para. 28.
[152] *The Prosecutor v. Saif Al-Islam Gaddafi and Abdullah Al-Senussi*, Doc. ICC-01/11-01/11-190-Corr-Red, 'Corrigendum to the 'Defence Response to the Application on behalf of the Government of Libya'', para. 160.
[153] *Ibid.*, para. 161.
[154] *The Prosecutor v. Saif Al-Islam Gaddafi and Abdullah Al-Senussi*, Doc. ICC-01/11-01/11-293-Red, 'Libyan Government's consolidated reply to the responses of the Prosecution, OPCD, and OPCV to its further submissions on issues related

tribal forces holding Gaddafi. Furthermore, the Libyan government claims to have 'taken all necessary steps to stay the hand of vengeance in favour of a fair trial, and was genuinely committed to justice', as demonstrated by the judicial action taken to date.[155]

C. Impartiality

A third measure, elaborated in Article 17(2)(c), is whether domestic proceedings are being conducted *independently* and *impartially*, consistent with intent to uphold justice. Here again the state's *intent* to conduct proceedings *fairly* is crucial. Interestingly, this provision was originally meant to be part of Article 17(3) dealing with a state's **inability** to undertake prosecutions.[156] This makes sense because a state's failure to conduct independent judicial proceedings would clearly suggest an overall inability to prosecute. However, the drafters of the Rome Statute retained this provision under the rubric of 'unwillingness'.

As will be discussed, the minimum standard for judicial independence is an impartial judicial system in which court decisions are respected and enforced, free from government interference.[157] These standards would **also** apply in determining whether a state is *genuinely unable* to prosecute.

i. Judges

Judges must be independent and, equally important, must be viewed as independent. The selection of judges, in fact, is one of the most important factors in ensuring a fair trial. If judicial selection does not adequately demonstrate that the bench is independent, the trial will not be perceived as fair, and the legitimacy of all of the judge's decisions will be undermined.

---

to the admissibility of the case against Saif Al-Islam Gaddafi', (4 March 2013), para. 77.

[155] *The Prosecutor v. Saif Al-Islam Gaddafi and Abdullah Al-Senussi*, Doc. ICC-01/11-01/11-130-Red, 'Application on behalf of the Government of Libya pursuant to Article 19 of the ICC Statute', (1 May 2012), para. 95.

[156] El Zeidy, *The Principle of Complementarity in International Criminal Law*, p. 195.

[157] Matthew Stephenson, *Judicial Independence: What is it, How can it be Measured, Why it Occurs,* (2001), available at http://siteresources.worldbank.org/INTLAWJUSTINST/Resources/JudicialIndependence.pdf.

In post-conflict states, it is likely that government figures will have played some role, whether active or passive, in the conflict. Questions of impartiality, therefore, are critical when national courts take on international criminal prosecutions. Without unequivocal judicial independence,[158] judgements may be seen as 'victor's justice', leaving both the bench and the legal process tainted.

Additionally, prolonged conflict invariably causes large numbers of educated legal professionals to flee, leaving a shortage of qualified judges to undertake domestic war crimes trials. We know that countries such as Uganda, Kenya, the DRC, and Iraq have all struggled to identify well-trained judges experienced in international criminal law. Such fragile judicial sectors leave observers, victims and suspects doubting the fairness of proceedings and verdicts.[159] National war crimes courts will require practical guidelines for the selection of qualified, independent judges as well as procedures to ensure that these judges, once selected, maintain their independence.

Standards for judicial independence and impartiality are codified in a number of international instruments and court decisions. The ICTY spent considerable time reviewing ECtHR decisions and adopted similar principles regarding judicial impartiality.[160] In the future, the ICC will undoubtedly refer to these guidelines as well. However, it is interesting to note, that after careful review of the ICC's decisions, the Court has, to date, made no explicit mention of any ECtHR standards of **judicial independence** in its decisions. The Court has only referred generally to judiciary independence when assessing a courts degree of impartiality. But this will likely change, with the Court making reference to ECtHR standards of judicial independence and fair trial rights more broadly

---

[158] Independence can be defined as the ability of a judge to decide matters without interference from the executive, legislature, the parties involved, or any other person or entity with an interest in the process or outcome of the case. Impartiality focuses on the judge's ability to remain open-minded and unprejudiced in deciding matters involved in the dispute. *See* Suzannah Linton, 'Safeguarding the Independence and Impartiality of the Cambodian Extraordinary Chambers', (2006) 4 *Journal of International Criminal Justice*, 327.

[159] Patricia M. Wald, 'Reflections on Judging: At Home and Abroad', (2005) 7 *University of Pennsylvania Journal of Constitutional Law*, 219, 222.

[160] *See The Prosecutor v. Anto Furundzija*, Case No. IT-95-17/1-A, 'Judgement', (21 July 2000).

because there have been various submissions **to** the Court along these same lines.

For example, as discussed earlier, in the case of the *The Prosecutor v. Saif Al-Islam Gaddafi and Abdullah Al-Senussi*, both the Libyan government and the defence have made reference to standards of judicial independence set out in European Convention on Human Rights (ECHR) legislation and ECtHR judgments.[161] The Libyan government argued that there is a requirement to adhere 'to the principles of due process recognised by international law' in determining the unwillingness of a State to genuinely prosecute under Article 17 of the Rome Statute.[162] This would include 'relevant provisions of international instruments defining human rights and humanitarian standards' including 'regional conventions such as ECHR, Article 6'.[163] In contrast, the defence for Mr Gaddafi, in its submissions to the Court concerning the failure of the Libyan government to evidence that it is investigating the case, also relied on ECtHR decisions to support its position.[164]

In the 'Decision on the Admissibility of the Case Against Al-Senussi'[165] the defence tried to argue that the same judges hearing the *Al-Senussi* case also took part in the 'special courts' of the Gaddafi era and, thus, lacked independence. However, the Court still ruled that Libya's judicial system was independent and impartial. The Court spent considerable time identifying elements showing Libya's reliance on an

[161] *See The Prosecutor v. Saif Al-Islam Gaddafi and Abdullah Al-Senussi*, Doc. ICC-01/11-01/11-190-Corr-Red, 'Corrigendum to the 'Defence Response to the Application on behalf of the Government of Libya''; *The Prosecutor v. Saif Al-Islam Gaddafi and Abdullah Al-Senussi,* Doc. ICC-01/11-01/11-307-Red2, 'Application on behalf of the Government of Libya in the case of Abdullah Al-Senussi pursuant to Article 19 of the ICC Statute', (2 April 2013).
[162] *The Prosecutor v. Saif Al-Islam Gaddafi and Abdullah Al-Senussi,* Doc. ICC-01/11-01/11-307-Red2, 'Application on behalf of the Government of Libya in the case of Abdullah Al-Senussi pursuant to Article 19 of the ICC Statute', (2 April 2013), para. 111.
[163] *Ibid.*
[164] *The Prosecutor v. Saif Al-Islam Gaddafi and Abdullah Al-Senussi*, Doc. ICC-01/11-01/11-190-Corr-Red, 'Corrigendum to the 'Defence Response to the Application on behalf of the Government of Libya'', para. 76.
[165] *The Prosecutor v. Saif Al-Islam Gadaffi and Abdullah Al-Senussi*, Doc. ICC-01/11-01/11-466-Red, 'Decision on the Admissibility of the Case Against Abdullah Al-Senussi', (11 October 2013), para. 246.

independent judiciary.[166] Although the Court's finding of judicial independence is suspect, its decision sheds light on the importance of considering the independence of the judiciary when considering Article 17 of the Rome Statute.

Furthermore, in the case of *Lubanga*, the Defence made reference to 'the principle of adversarial justice' and cited the ECtHR decisions of *Lobo Machado v. Portugal* and *Morel v. France* as a legal basis for this principle.[167] Similarly, the Defence in *Chui* relied on the ECtHR case of

---

[166] *Ibid.*, for example, para 248: '[t]he Chamber observes that the independence and impartiality of the judiciary is recognised in articles 32 and 33 of Libya's Constitutional Declaration of 3 August 2011'. *See also* paras 249-50:

> '249. Further, as submitted by Libya, the National Transitional Council (NTC) 'issued Law 3 of 2011 adjusting law 6 of 2006 on the judiciary, with the aim of insulating the judiciary from the executive', and, by NTC Resolution no. 17 of 2 April 2011, the Internal Security Agency and the State Security Court were abolished and numerous political prisoners were released.
>
> 250. The Chamber also notes that the Supreme Judicial Council is now composed only of members of the judiciary and is chaired by the President of the Supreme Court instead of the Minister of Justice'.

The Chamber also took note of a decision of the Libyan Supreme Court, which unanimously determined that People's Court procedures could not be applied to criminal cases. *See* para. 251:

> 'Considering that the intervention of the Supreme Court took place upon motion of the lawyer of Abu Zaid Omar Dorda (Muammar Gaddafi's former prime minister and head of the External Security Agency at the time of the 2011 revolution), in whose case the Prosecutor-General had sought to apply the People's Court procedure, the Chamber finds significant the following statement made in the decision of 23 December 2012: 'there is no room for pleading that crimes viewed by the People's Court had special gravity and political considerations, since the type of crime and degree of gravity do not justify the laws' violation of the constitutional rules which are superior to them'.

See also para. 256:

> 'The Chamber also considers relevant that the hearing before the Accusation Chamber held on 19 September 2013 in the case against Mr Al-Senussi and another 37 officials of the former Gaddafi regime has been adjourned to 3 October 2013, upon request of some defence teams, in order to allow them to view the accusation file'.

[167] *The Prosecutor v. Thomas Lubanga Dyilo*, Doc. ICC01/04-01/06-1464-tENG, 'Defence response to the 'Prosecution's application to lift the stay of proceedings' dated 11 July 2008', (1 September 2008), para. 29, *citing Lobo Machado v. Portugal*, (Application No. 15764/89) EHRR 1996-I (20 February 1996), para. 31;

Foucher v. France in support of its submissions relating to the right to adequate time and facilities for preparation of the defence, further to the Article 6 of the ECHR relating to the right to a fair trial.[168]

These examples demonstrate that **parties** before the ICC do rely on ECtHR jurisprudence relating to fair trial rights and judicial independence – both specific provisions and broad principles. Most importantly, because the ECHR and the jurisprudence of the ECtHR are both reliable and representative of international standards, the ICC is bound to include them as instructive for its own determination of a country's ability to undertake fair proceedings under an Article 19 admissibility assessment.

In 1985, the *United Nations Basic Principles on the Independence of the Judiciary* (Basic Principles) was established to ensure the right to a fair hearing before a competent, independent, and impartial judiciary and provides practical guidelines to that effect.[169] The Basic Principles even characterise an independent and impartial court as a human right, enshrined in the Universal Declaration of Human Rights.[170]

The Principles recognise the unique role played by judges, who are charged with making 'the ultimate decision over life, freedoms, rights, duties and property of citizens'.[171] The Principles were agreed upon as a set of general guidelines, two key principles of which are set out in the first two paragraphs:

> Principle 1: Independence of the Judiciary shall be guaranteed;
> Principle 2: The Judiciary shall decide matters impartially...without any restriction, improper influence, inducements, pressures, threats or interferences...[172]

Morel v. France, (Application No. 34130/96) ECHR 2000-VI (6 June 2000), para. 27.

168 *The Prosecutor v. Mathieu Ngudjolo Chui*, Doc. ICC-01/04-02/12-40-tENG, 'Urgent application by Mathieu Ngudjolo's Defence seeking the Appeals Chamber's instructions on the modalities of preparation for the appeals procedure in view of Mathieu Ngudjolo's current situation (Article 67 of the Rome Statute)', (20 March 2013) para. 21, *citing Foucher v. France*, (Application No. 22209/93), ECHR 1997-II, para. 36.

169 United Nations Basic Principles on the Independence of the Judiciary, UN Doc. A/CONF.121/22/Rev.1, p. 59 (1985), Preamble.

170 *Ibid.*

171 *Ibid.*

172 *Ibid.*, Principles 1 and 2.

The *Basic Principles* also require that the judiciary decide matters impartially based on facts and according to law - without any restrictions, improper pressure or interference.[173] This provision is one of the most important to maintaining the integrity of a court. Identical guarantees are made in the ECHR,[174] the American Convention on Human Rights,[175] and the African Charter on Human and Peoples' Rights.[176] Indeed, the UN Human Rights Committee has stated that the guarantee of impartiality 'is an *absolute right that may suffer no exceptions*' [emphasis added].[177] The International Covenant on Civil and Political Rights (ICCPR) further underscores the notion that a fair hearing requires an impartial judge where all people are equal before the court.[178]

---

[173] *Ibid.*, Principle 2.

[174] European Convention for the Protection of Human Rights and Fundamental Freedoms, 4 November 1950, in force 3 September 1953, ETS 5; 213 UNTS 221. Article 6(1) reads 'everyone is entitled to a fair and public hearing within a reasonable time by an independent and impartial tribunal established by law'.

[175] American Convention on Human Rights, 22 November 1969, in force 18 July 1978, OAS Treaty Series No. 36; 1144 UNTS 123; 9 ILM 99 (1969). Article 8(1) reads '[e]very person has the right to a hearing, with due guarantees and within a reasonable time, by a competent, independent and impartial tribunal'.

[176] African Charter on Human and Peoples' Rights, 27 June 1981, in force 21 October 1986, OAU Doc. CAB/LEG/67/3 rev. 5; 1520 UNTS 217; 21 ILM 58 (1982). Article 7(1) reads '[e]very individual shall have the right to have his cause heard. This comprises: [...] (d) the right to be tried within a reasonable time by an impartial court or tribunal'. *See* e.g., *Constitutional Rights Project v. Nigeria*, African Commission on Human and Peoples' Rights, Communication No. 60/91 (1995), para. 14 ('Regardless of the character of the individual members of the of such tribunals, its composition alone creates the appearance, of not actual lack, of impartiality. It thus violates Article 7.1(d)').

[177] *Gonzalez del Rio v. Peru,* Communication No. 263/1987, UN Doc. CCPR/C/46/D/263/1987 (28 October 1992), para. 5.1.

[178] International Covenant on Civil and Political Rights, 16 December 1966, in force 23 March 1976, GA Res. 2200A (XXI), 21 UN GAOR Supp. (No. 16) at 52, UN Doc. A/6316 (1966); 999 UNTS 171; 6 ILM 368 (1967), (hereinafter ICCPR), Article 14(1). The notion of 'impartiality' in Article 14(1) 'implies that judges must not harbour preconceptions about the matter put before them, and that they must not act in ways that promote the interests of one of the parties', *Karttunen v. Finland*, Communication No. 387/1989, UN Doc. CCPR/C/46/D/387/1989, (5 November 1992), para. 7.2; *see also* supporting comments in *Rogerson v. Australia*, Communication No. 802/1998, UN Doc. CCPR/C/74/D/802/1998, (3 April 2002), para. 7.4. On the consideration of judicial competence, *see Rouse v. The Philippines*, Communication No. 1089/2002, UN Doc. CCPR/C/84/D/1089/2002, (5 August 2005), para. 7.2.

I would argue that, as part of an Article 17(2)(c) assessment, the ICC should look for clearly written statutes and rules governing judicial independence in state courts. The ICC must be assured that domestic courts are free of government pressure and can focus on the trial process without being distracted by vague or conflicting legislative provisions. Failure in this regard would severely hinder national prosecutions.

The Iraqi Court, which I assessed daily as legal commentator for *CNN International*, illustrates what happens when statutory guarantees of independence fail. One of many problems that hampered the Iraqi War Crimes Court was the inconsistency of language between the Court's statute and its rules. Iraq's Constitution guaranteed independence of the judiciary.[179] The Court's Rules of Procedure and Evidence stated that:

> Each Judge shall act independently and shall not be submitted to or response (sic) to the instructions or the directions issued by the Presidency of the Republic or the cabinet or from any other governmental department, or from any other source in its judicial functions.[180]

Moreover, while the Rules required evidence to support a party's request for disqualification of a judge, the Court's Statute allowed the executive to transfer a judge *for any reason*.[181] The Statute prohibited former members of the Ba'ath Party (the Political Party of Saddam Hussein) from holding any position on the Court.[182] Even those 'suspected' of being Ba'athists were prohibited from being appointed to the Court, and there was no investigative process to prove party membership.[183] What resulted was a highly subjective purging process.

---

[179] Doustour Joumhouriat al-Iraq (The Constitution of the Republic of Iraq), (15 October 2005). Under Article 87, the judiciary is independent and will be represented by courts of different kinds and levels, and they will issue their rulings according to law. Under Article 88, judges are independent, with no authority over them in their rulings except the law. No authority can interfere in the judiciary or in the affairs of justice.

[180] Rules of Procedure and Evidence of the Iraqi Special Tribunal, *Al-Waqa'I Al-Iraqiya* (The Official Gazette of Iraq), (18 October 2005), (hereinafter Iraq Rules of Procedure and Evidence), Rule 7.

[181] *Ibid.*, Rule 8.

[182] Law of the Iraqi Higher Criminal Court, *Al-Waqa'I Al-Iraqiya* (The Official Gazette of Iraq), (18 October 2005), (hereinafter Iraq Statute), Article 33.

[183] Sonya Sceats, *The Trial of Saddam Hussein*, Chatham House Briefing Paper No. 05/02 (2005), p. 5, available at http://www.chathamhouse.org/sites/default/files/public/Research/International%20 Law/bptrialhussein.pdf.

Strong statutory guarantees help ensure that national judges are free from undue pressure from the executive and the legislature, both of which may have an interest in the outcome of the proceedings.[184] It is important not only to have a clear, precisely written statute, but also to ensure that it works *with*, and not against, the court's rules. These guarantees are important because political interference in judicial processes is all too common.[185]

The procedure for selecting judges for the Iraqi War Crimes Court was contained in the Iraqi High Criminal Court Law, which states that 'Judges [...] shall be of high moral character, integrity and uprightness. They shall possess experience in criminal law and shall fulfil the appointment requirements stipulated in the Judicial Organisation Law No. 160 of 1979'.[186]

Judges for the Court were nominated by the Iraqi Supreme Judicial Council and chosen by a governing Council. However, the Council of Ministers had to approve the nominations and render a decision on their appointment by the Presidency Council.[187] This opened the door to government interference, ultimately weakening the independence and integrity of the Court. As reported by Human Rights Watch at the time:

> Since the formation of the Interim Governing Council, control over the [Court] has been the subject of political disputation and interference by Iraqi Political factions. Interference has taken the form of attempts by Iraqi political leaders to dismiss or appoint [Court] officials and judges thought to be loyal to one faction or another. The [Court's] first administrative director, Salem Chalabi, was dismissed in September 2004, and there were reportedly attempts to have 'Chalabi loyalists' removed from the [Court] and replaced by personnel selected by officials in the government headed by interim Prime Minister Ayad Allawi. Subsequently, under the government of Prime Minister Ibrahim Ja'fari, further attempts were made to effect widespread dismissals within the personnel of the [Court] through the 'de-Ba'athification' process, which was led by Deputy Prime Minister,

---

[184] *Gonzalez del Rio v. Peru*, para. 5.1.
[185] Nisha Valabhji, 'Political Interference and Judicial Misconduct Impede Justice in Cambodia', *Jurist*, (6 December 2011), available at http://jurist.org/hotline/2011/12/nisha-valabhji-cambodian-interference.php.
[186] Iraq Statute, Article 4(1). It is unusual for a civil law state to recruit judges from the pool of lawyers and prosecutors. Recruitment of judges is typically done through competitive exams and merit. The recruitment of experienced lawyers for judicial posts is a method of selection routinely used in common law jurisdictions.
[187] Iraq Statute, Article 4(3).

> Ahmad Chalabi. This process resulted in the dismissal of nine administrative staff, including the then Administrative Director 'Ammar al-Bakri' (an Allawi appointee), but stopped short of dismissal of judicial personnel after intervention by both President Talabani and Prime Minister Ja'fari.[188]

For instance, the government explicitly influenced the selection and dismissal of several judges. Rizgar Amin, a Kurd, was selected as the first presiding judge over the Saddam Hussein trial. However, he resigned five days into the trial after the government accused him of being too lenient. His replacement, Sayeed Hamashi, was also removed because the government accused him of having been a member of the Ba'ath Party. He was replaced by Judge Ra'uf Rasheed Abdul-Rahman, a man tried and convicted *in absentia* under Saddam Hussein for having been a member of the Kurdish party and opposing the regime. Rule 11(4) of the Court's Rules of Procedure and Evidence requires that 'a judge must withdraw from any case in which his impartiality or independence might reasonably be doubted'.[189] Yet, Judge Abdul-Rahman was permitted to serve on the Saddam trial and the following trials.[190] In future assessments, the ICC should question the impartiality of a national war crimes court that tolerates or is complicit in the government's attempt to control the selection process.

It should be stressed that the degree of political interference in the Iraq War Crimes Court was pervasive. During the *Dujail* trial, for instance, the government pressured the presiding judge to resign because he was seen to be too accommodating to the defendant, Saddam Hussein. Another judge was removed during deliberations because he reportedly opposed the death penalty.[191] Also, throughout the trial, government leaders made disparaging remarks about the trial process. Former Interim President, Iyad Allawi, and other prominent officials issued frequent press releases claiming that trials must commence immediately. Many commentators, including Salem Chalabi, former Chief Administrator of the Court,

---

[188] Human Rights Watch, *The Former Iraqi Government on Trial: A Human Rights Watch Briefing Paper,* (16 October 2005), p. 17.

[189] Iraq Rules of Procedure and Evidence, Rule 11(4).

[190] Mark S. Ellis, 'Can Saddam's Trial be Salvaged?', *International Herald Tribune*, (10 February 2006).

[191] *See* Chatham House, 'Discussion Group Summary of The Iraqi Tribunal: The Post-Saddam Cases', p. 5, (4 December 2008) available at https://www.chathamhouse.org/sites/default/files/public/Research/International%20Law/il041208.pdf.

correctly accused Mr Allawi of manipulating the Court by calling for hasty pre-election trials in an effort to boost his popularity and hold on to power.

Mr Allawi also tried to influence the Court by dismissing senior Court officials and appointing political loyalists in their place. Again, Salem Chalabi accused the interim government of 'attempting to politicize the Tribunal to such a large extent that…the policies of a fair, independent judicial process, inherent in the Statute of the Iraqi Special Tribunal' will be disregarded.[192] He added that '[s]how trials followed by speedy executions may help the interim government politically in the short term but will be counterproductive for the development of democracy and the rule of law in Iraq in the long-term'.[193]

In 2006, the Iraqi Prime Minister unilaterally removed the presiding Court judge, citing an inferred bias behind his statement that Saddam Hussein 'was not a dictator'.[194] The UN Special Rapporteur on the Independence of Judges and Lawyers considered that the hostile dynamics between the Court and the Executive, and the dismissal of judges during this trial process, undermined the legitimacy and credibility of the judgment handed down in the *Dujail* trial.[195]

---

[192] Rajiv Chandrasekaran, 'Hussein's Trial Not Likely to Begin this Year, US Official Says', (25 September 2004), *Washington Post*, available at http://www.washingtonpost.com/wp-dyn/articles/A48640-2004Sep24.html.

[193] *Ibid.* The Interim Iraqi Justice Minister Malik Dohan al-Hassan, was also reported to have expressed concern that Iraqi government was rushing too quickly to bring to trial senior officials of the Saddam Hussein regime. Moreover, a member of the team of Americans advising the Tribunal criticised attempts by the Interim Iraqi Government to speed up the process. He observed that 'these are very difficult trials. These are command-responsibility cases… You have to follow the chain of command up. It takes time and it takes effort, and it's not self-evident, and there's no way around it. These cases proceed at their own pace' (*Ibid.*). This sentiment was echoed in the Iraqi Special Tribunal, Press Release (6 June 2005), available (in Arabic) at http://web.archive.org/web/20051202123153/http://www.iraq-ist.org/ar/press/releases/0016a.htm.

[194] Chatham House, 'Discussion Group Summary of The Iraqi Tribunal', p. 4. *See also* Mark S. Ellis, 'From the Saddam Trial, Vital Lessons', *International Herald Tribune* (4 August 2006); Ellis, 'Can Saddam's Trial be Salvaged?'

[195] UN Press Release, 'Expert on Judiciary Expresses Concern about Saddam Hussein Trial and Verdict and Calls for International Tribunal', (6 November 2006), available at http://www.ohchr.org/EN/NewsEvents/Pages/DisplayNews.aspx?NewsID=590&LangID=E.

Even with international assistance, national judicial proceedings can fail an Article 17(2)(c) assessment. At the Extraordinary Chambers in the Courts of Cambodia (ECCC), mixed panels of Cambodian and international judges sit in both the Trial and Appeals Chambers. There are additionally two Co-Investigating Judges, one of whom is an international appointment. In total, seven judges sit on the Appeals bench, five of whom are Cambodian. Five judges also sit in the Trial Chamber, three of whom are Cambodian. Though the majority in each chamber is Cambodian, the Agreement between the United Nations and the Royal Government of Cambodia (hereafter 'the Agreement')[196] requires a supermajority for all decisions, so that assent of at least one international judge is needed.

In negotiations preceding the establishment of the ECCC, it was agreed that the selection of Cambodian judges would be placed fully under national government control. The Cambodian judges on the ECCC were appointed directly by the Supreme Council of the Magistracy - without any international input.

The UN Secretary-General nominated twelve judges to serve on the ECCC.[197] The Cambodian Supreme Council of the Magistracy then selected the five international judges from this list.[198] The Supreme Council is comprised of nine members: the King of Cambodia, the Minister of Justice, the Head of the Supreme Court, the Prosecutor of the Supreme Court, the Head of Appeals Court, the Prosecutor of the Appeals Court, and three judges (elected by peers).[199]

On its face, the Supreme Council appeared to be representative, including both judicial expertise and executive oversight. Unfortunately, it remained deeply politicised, and the Cambodian government exploited its power to ensure that appointees to the ECCC were loyal to the Prime

---

[196] United Nations, 'Agreement Between the United Nations and the Royal Government of Cambodia Concerning the Prosecution Under Cambodian Law of Crimes Committed During the Period of Democratic Kampuchea', (6 June 2003) (hereinafter UN-Cambodia Agreement).

[197] *Ibid.*, Article 3(2) and 3(5).

[198] *Ibid.*, Article 3 (5).

[199] Khmer Institute of Democracy, 'Fair Trial Principles', (16 June 2006), p. 10, available at http://www.khmerrough.com/pdf/FairTrialPrinciples160606.pdf.

Minister.[200] The complete absence of transparency added to the secrecy of the nomination process and ultimately hid inescapable executive interference.

The UN Special Rapporteur on the Situation of Human Rights in Cambodia, Surya Subedi, strongly criticised government interference in the Cambodian judiciary, stating that 'both financial and political interference in the judiciary was undermining the faith that Cambodians had in their judicial institutions', and specified that such external interference could be 'political or interference by people in powerful positions within the society'.[201]

The Cambodian experience also illustrates the importance of judicial qualifications in Article 17(2)(c) assessments. Judges sitting in the ECCC were supposed to '[b]e persons of high moral character, impartiality and integrity who possess the qualifications required in their respective countries for appointment to judicial offices. They 'shall be independent in the performance of their functions and shall not accept or seek instructions from any government or any other source'.[202] Yet, the Cambodian government blatantly ignored these requirements.

Despite calls from a number of non-governmental organisations to establish clear criteria for selecting qualified judges,[203] the government of

---

[200] Human Rights Watch, *Cambodia: Government Interferes in Khmer Rouge Tribunal Donors Should Recognize How Government Tactics Threaten Entire Process,* (6 December 2006), available at http://www.hrw.org/en/news/2006/12/04/cambodia-government-interferes-khmer-rouge-tribunal.

[201] Mark Worley and Neou Vannarin, 'UN Envoy Says Judiciary 'Compromised'', *The Cambodia Daily*, (18 June 2010), pp. 1–2.

[202] UN-Cambodia Agreement, Article 3(3).

[203] For instance, the Cambodian Human Rights Action Committee (CHRAC) argued:

> 'The successful conduct of the ECCC will depend heavily on the quality of the judges and prosecutors appointed. CHRAC respectfully recommends that the Supreme Council of the Magistracy use the following criteria when they decide who to appoint. The appointees should: 1) Have completed their legal training and hold a university degree in law or an equivalent; 2) Have experience in significant criminal cases and have worked in criminal or international criminal courts as judge or prosecutor for at least three years; 3) Include all suitably qualified and skilled women judges and prosecutors to achieve gender balance; 4) Be persons of high moral

Cambodia did not choose candidates based on professional credentials alone.[204] It has been widely reported by international observers that some of the Cambodian judges on the ECCC have only the equivalent of a high school certificate.[205] In addition, very soon after the ECCC began operations, allegations of corruption began to surface. This led Human Rights Watch to argue that '[t]he Cambodian judges [...] receive their order directly or indirectly from Hun Sen [the Cambodian President]. They cannot act independently for fear of being removed or worse'.[206] The failure to deal with these allegations led critics to conclude that the Court was indeed corrupt and inherently biased. The Cambodian proceedings were reduced to a charade.

> character, impartiality and integrity; 5) Be capable of and aware of the need to act independently of the Government and any other person or organization; 6) Be unlikely to be repeatedly disqualified from cases because they have a personal interest in or personal association with any party in any case'.

CHRAC also recommended that to facilitate communication the Cambodian candidates be able to speak either French or English to a high standard. *See* Cambodian Human Rights Action Committee (CHRAC), 'Media Statement: Selection of Judges and Prosecutors for the Extraordinary Chambers in the Court of Cambodia', (2 May 2006), p. 1, available at http://www.licadho-cambodia.org/press/files/112PRCHRACJudgesKR06.pdf.

[204] *See* Open Society Justice Initiative, 'Progress and Challenges at the Extraordinary Chambers in the Courts of Cambodia', (June 2007), p. 8, available at http://www.soros.org/initiatives/justice/focus/international_justice/articles_publications/publications/cambodia_20070627/cambodia_20070627.pdf; 'UN Urges Cambodia's Judicial Reform', *Global Policy Forum*, (19 May 2006), available at http://www.globalpolicy.org/component/content/article/163/28908.html.

[205] *See* World Bank, 'Cambodia at the Crossroads', Report No. 30636-KH, (15 November 2004), para. 15. (According to the World Bank, only one in six of Cambodia's 117 judges and one in nine of the Supreme Court Judges had law degrees in 2004).

[206] As reported in Susan Postlewaite, 'Khmer Rouge Trial Threatened', *Asia Sentinel,* (24 April 2009), available at http://www.asiasentinel.com/society/khmer-rouge-trial-threatened/. *See also* Human Rights Watch, 'Cambodia: Political Pressure Undermining Tribunal', (22 July 2009), available at http://www.hrw.org/en/news/2009/07/22/cambodia-political-pressure-undermining-tribunal; Abigail Salisbury, 'Rights Group Urges Cambodia Tribunal to End Perception of Government Interference', *Jurist*, (23 July 2009), available at http://jurist.law.pitt.edu/paperchase/2009/07/rights-group-urges-cambodia-tribunal-to.php.

I wrote two damning reports about the lack of independence of the ECCC, stating that:

> Given that the first ECCC trial was seen as a compelling and rewarding event for many Cambodians, it may be tempting to set a presumption in favour of making the compromises necessary to simply establish a court, even a flawed court. Some could argue that even where the ECCC fails to meet international standards, it far exceeds the norm in Cambodia. However, more is at stake than increasing the legitimacy of a single trial. While scholars may debate the degree to which the ECCC is a success or failure, *there is no doubt that the UN has given its hallmark to a court whose independence fails to meet international standards of due process.* In resting the legitimacy of the ECCC on that of the Cambodian Judiciary, the ECCC has weakened the UN brand in the realm of international accountability.[207]

Such criticisms are bolstered by recent events[208] which indicate that heavy-handed government interference with the judicial independence of the ECCC is not an isolated incident, but symptomatic of a wider issue. Cambodia has previously come under international scrutiny for targeted criminal prosecutions of government critics, including stripping members of the political opposition of Parliamentary immunity for criminal

---

[207] Mark S. Ellis, *Safeguarding Judicial Independence in Mixed Tribunals: Lessons from the ECCC and Best Practices for the Future*, (London: International Bar Association, 2011), p. 46. *See also* Mark S. Ellis, *The ECCC – A Failure of Credibility,* (London: International Bar Association, 2012).

[208] *See* e.g. LICADHO – Cambodian League for the Promotion and Defense of Human Rights (hereinafter LICADHO), 'Press Release: Military special command unit deployed to crackdown on striking workers', (2 January 2014), available at http://www.licadho-cambodia.org/pressrelease.php?perm=333; LICADHO, 'Joint Media Statement: Civilians killed and injured by security forces amid civil unrest in Phnom Penh', (3 January 2014), available at http://www.licadho-cambodia.org/pressrelease.php?perm=334; LICADHO, 'Joint Media Statement: Civilians killed and injured by security forces amid civil unrest in Phnom Penh', (3 January 2014), available at http://www.licadho-cambodia.org/pressrelease .php?perm=334; 'Cambodia calls for calm as protests banned after deadly clash', *Xinhua*, (4 January 2013), available at http://news.xinhuanet.com/english/world/2014-01/04/c_133018723.htm; 'Cambodia opposition leaders summoned to court', *Al Jazeera*, (5 January 2014), available at http://www.aljazeera.com/news/asia-pacific/2014/01/cambodia-opposition-leaders-summoned-court-20141581039781458.html; LICADHO, 'Media Statement: Authorities must reveal whereabouts of detainees immediately', (6 January 2014), available at http://www.licadho-cambodia.org/pressrelease.php?perm=336.

prosecution,[209] trials and sentencing *in absentia*,[210] and convictions without sufficient evidence.[211] The Cambodian judiciary has been described as 'politically-controlled'[212] with Hun Sen 'exercis[ing] an iron grip over the courts'.[213] The Cambodian Center for Human Rights advocated for judicial reform with specific commitment to judicial independence, stating that:

> The judiciary is under the influence of outside sources in numerous ways. Judges and prosecutors are currently appointed by the Ministry of Justice, political influence pervades the courts, and corruption is endemic. Government influence on the courts can be seen in the number of politically-motivated cases seen in recent years ...[214]

The Cambodian Human Rights Action Committee (CCHR) concluded that '[t]he judiciary and the [Royal Government of Cambodia] (RGC)

---

[209] Office of the High Commissioner for Human Rights (OHCHR), 'The Special Representative expresses deep concern over the defamation verdicts against opposition leader Sam Rainsy', (27 December 2005), available at http://www.ohchr.org/EN/NewsEvents/Pages/DisplayNews.aspx?NewsID=4824&LangID=E; 'Sam Rainsy appeal on Cambodia', *BBC News*, (4 February 2005), available at http://news.bbc.co.uk/1/hi/world/asia-pacific/4235951.stm; 'US Condemns Detention of Cambodian Human Rights Activists', *IIP Digital*, (6 January 2006), available at http://iipdigital.usembassy.gov/st/english/article/2006/01/20060105141020tjkcollub0.7272455.html#axzz2piuYSjfU; LICADHO, 'Another Blow to Cambodia's Faltering Democracy: Lifting of SRP President Parliamentary Immunity', (16 November 2009), available at http://www.licadho-cambodia.org/pressrelease.php?perm=215.

[210] Human Rights Watch, 'Cambodia: Opposition Leader Sam Rainsy's Trial a Farce', (29 January 2010), available at http://www.hrw.org/news/2010/01/28/cambodia-opposition-leader-sam-rainsy-s-trial-farce.

[211] Human Rights Watch, 'Cambodia: Supreme Court keeps activist jailed', (29 March 2013), available at http://www.hrw.org/news/2013/03/29/cambodia-supreme-court-keeps-activist-jailed (*see* comment on Phnom Penh Municipal Court trial).

[212] *Ibid.*

[213] Human Rights Watch, 'Cambodia: Opposition Leader Sam Rainsy's Trial a Farce'.

[214] Cambodia Center for Human Rights (CCHR), 'CCHR Briefing Note – February 2013: Judicial Reform', (18 February 2013), p. 4, available at http://www.cchrcambodia.org/admin/media/analysis/analysis/english/2013-02-18-CCHR%20Briefing%20Note%20-%20Judicial%20Reform_en.pdf.

must make an immediate commitment to cease the judicial harassment of human rights defenders and activists'.[215]

Kenya is another case in which the desire to conduct domestic war crimes trials is undermined by the judicial selection process, which is 'neither transparent nor accountable'.[216] The International Bar Association, which I direct, conducted an assessment of the country's existing legal framework, focusing on the judiciary and its ability to support domestic war crimes prosecutions. The results were not encouraging. Under current arrangements, the Constitution fails to entrench judicial power exclusively in the judiciary or unambiguously guarantee its independence. The judiciary lacks any sense of financial autonomy, and effective court administration is undermined by the centralisation of power within the office of the Chief Justice. The IBA report concluded that: 'the absence of any open, competitive and merit-based process for the appointment of members of the judiciary of Kenya not only denies many interested and qualified lawyers the opportunity to serve in the judiciary, but also serves to undermine public confidence in the quality of those named to judicial office'.[217] As a result, there is an overwhelming 'lack of public confidence in the judicial system'.[218]

Also in Libya, judicial independence is a key element in the admissibility battle regarding jurisdiction over Saif Al-Islam Gaddafi. The OPCD attacked the laws promulgated by the interim National Transitional Council (NTC) as 'deliberately targeted at persons associated with the former Gaddafi regime', claiming they would 'completely deprive the defendant of the right to impartial and independent proceedings'.[219] It argued that NTC Law 26, by excluding from the bench anyone who lauded the former regime or stood against the February 2011 revolution, creates a

---

[215] *Ibid.*, p. 7.

[216] International Bar Association Human Rights Institute (IBAHRI) and International Legal Assistance Consortium (ILAC), *Restoring Integrity: An Assessment of the Needs of the Justice System in the Republic of Kenya*, (February 2010), p. 45, available at http://www.ibanet.org/Article/Detail.aspx?ArticleUid=EB1896B1-3494-4E9D-BF39-A49072685F06.

[217] *Ibid.*

[218] *Ibid.*, p. 54.

[219] *The Prosecutor v. Saif Al-Islam Gaddafi and Abdullah Al-Senussi*, Doc. ICC-01/11-01/11-190-Corr-Red, 'Corrigendum to the 'Defence Response to the Application on behalf of the Government of Libya'', para. 315.

'strong disincentive' for any judge to find in favour of Mr Gaddafi.[220] The OPCD also challenged the extra-legal nature of several official statements, notably the two million dollar 'dead or alive' bounty placed on Muammar Gaddafi's head by the NTC chairperson, despite the existence of an ICC indictment.[221]

However, in the battle for legal jurisdiction, the Libyan government has strenuously argued that the independence and impartiality of its judiciary is enshrined in Article 32 of the 2011 Libyan Constitutional Declaration, which ensures that 'the Judiciary Authority shall be independent'; courts 'shall issue their judgments in accordance with the law'; 'judges shall be independent, subject to no other authority but the law and conscience'; and that 'establishing Exceptional Courts shall be prohibited'.[222] In addition, the government has noted that judicial independence is codified in Article 52 of the country's Judicial System Law and Article 31 of the Freedoms Act.[223]

Gaddafi's OPCD-appointed defence attorney, Melinda Taylor, stated that any trial in Libya would not be 'motivated by a desire for justice' but rather by 'a desire for revenge', and that the Libyan court would be 'organised to convict rather than to achieve justice'; she concluded that 'it is abundantly clear that proceedings against Mr Gaddafi lack both independence and impartiality'.[224] Taylor supported her argument by highlighting a new law passed by the NTC stating that 'no child of Gaddafi will ever benefit from leniency'.[225] Additional evidence from international human rights organisations has suggested there is 'rampant torture of inmates in makeshift prisons operated by militias accused of seeking to exact revenge against the slain leader's former supporters... Various former rebel groups are holding as many as 8,000 prisoners in

---

[220] *Ibid.,* para. 324.
[221] *Ibid.,* para. 338.
[222] *The Prosecutor v. Saif Al-Islam Gaddafi and Abdullah Al-Senussi*, Doc. ICC-01/11-01/11-130-Red, 'Application on behalf of the Government of Libya pursuant to Article 19 of the ICC Statute', (1 May 2012), para. 53; National Transitional Council, *Constitutional Declaration of 2011*, (3 August 2011), Article 32.
[223] *Ibid.*, para. 55.
[224] 'Gaddafi's son facing gallows in Libya: lawyer', *ABC News*, (11 October 2012), available at http://www.abc.net.au/news/2012-10-10/gaddafis-son-will-be-hanged-lawyer/4306462.
[225] 'Libya crisis: ICC considers Gaddafi hearing venue', *BBC News*, (9 October 2012), available at http://www.bbc.co.uk/news/world-africa-19881863.

[sixty] detention centres around the country'.[226] In discussions with the Ministry of Justice during a trip to Libya in 2013, I was able to confirm this allegation. Amnesty International reached the same conclusion, noting that 'what we witness in Libya is revenge and not justice'.[227]

Under the admissibility test that the Court must follow, if it decides that the state is *willing* to undertake an investigation and prosecution, it must still assess the state's *ability* to do the same. This part of the admissibility equation is covered in the next chapter.

---

[226] *See* Rami Al-Shaheibi, 'Libya to Niger: Al-Saadi Gaddafi Must Be Handed Over', *The World Post*, (11 February 2012), available at http://www.huffingtonpost.com/2012/02/11/libya-niger-al-saadi-gaddafi_n_1270293.html. *See also* Human Rights Watch, 'Libya: New Government Should End Illegal Detention', (16 November 2012), available at http://www.hrw.org/news/2012/11/16/libya-new-government-should-end-illegal-detention.

[227] Amnesty International, 'Libya Must Seek Justice Not Revenge in Case of Former Al-Gaddafi Intelligence Chief', (18 October 2012), available at http://www.amnesty.org/en/news/libya-must-seek-justice-not-revenge-case-former-al-gaddafi-intelligence-chief-2012-10-18.

CHAPTER THREE

THE PRINCIPLE OF COMPLEMENTARITY UNDER ARTICLE 17 OF THE ROME STATE AND STATES' ABILITY TO PROSECUTE

Introduction

The other critical ground on which the ICC can counter a state's right to prosecute under the principle of complementarity is determining that a state is *unable* to conduct proceedings. Article 17(3) states:

> In order to determine inability in a particular case, the Court shall consider whether, due to a total or substantial collapse or unavailability of its national judicial system, the State is unable to obtain the accused or the necessary evidence and testimony or otherwise unable to carry out its proceedings.

In my opinion, this component is the most difficult aspect of the entire admissibility test. It also raises the most challenging questions for the ICC.

As we will see, the process for determining 'inability' is decidedly more objective than determining 'unwillingness', but no more undemanding.[1] Furthermore, it is important to keep in mind that a state's inability to prosecute assumes that the case is being considered for national prosecution. As stated earlier, if a state simply failed or refused to initiate proceedings, Article 17 regarding state *inaction* would apply.

In assessing and ultimately determining a state's inability to prosecute, the ICC would consider factors that might indicate a substantial degree of

---

[1] Mohamed M. El Zeidy, *The Principle of Complementarity in International Criminal Law; Origin, Development and Practice* (Leiden: Martin Nijhoff Publishers, 2008) p. 222.

collapse in a state's overall legal system.[2] The Rome Statute suggests a two-part test whereby any situation that renders a state incapable of gaining custody over the accused or obtaining the necessary evidence and testimony, or that renders the state otherwise unable to carry out the proceedings, would fall within the ICC's remit.[3] The phrase - '[o]therwise unable to carry out proceedings' - is clearly a catch-all clause for those unforeseen circumstances that would prevent a state from undertaking prosecutions.[4]

A review of the Preparatory Committee's debates on Article 17(3) confirms that these determinations are hardly straightforward. Despite what might seem to be a brief and clear articulation of what inability means as set forth in Article 17(3), further elaboration is needed. I would argue that states struggling with the ability to prosecute will likely be states that have experienced the following situations:

1. engaged in conflict, either domestic or international, that involves political unrest or economic crisis, or in a post-conflict transition, or
2. lack the type of judicial system that is required under the international standards of legal fairness, or
3. have failed to incorporate implementing legislation necessary to cooperate with the Court, or
4. have failed to ensure fair trial proceedings.

In each of these scenarios, where crimes falling under the Rome Statute have been committed, the ICC would likely be able to claim jurisdiction.

---

[2] *See* Rome Statute of the International Criminal Court, Rome, opened for signature 17 July 1988, 2187 UNTS 90 (entered into force 1 July 2002) UN Doc. A/CONF.183/9 (hereinafter, ICC Statute or Rome Statute), Article 17(3).

[3] *See* Jann K. Kleffner, *Complementarity in the Rome Statute and National Criminal Jurisdiction*, (Oxford: Oxford University Press, 2008), p. 153; *see also* Benjamin Perrin, 'Making Sense of Complementarity: The Relationship between the International Criminal Court and National Jurisdictions', (2006) 18 *Sri Lanka Journal of International Law*, 301, 303.

[4] El Zeidy, *The Principle of Complementarity in International Criminal Law*, p. 224.

I. Conflict

As to the first category, according to the Center for Defense Information, there currently are forty-two significant conflicts in the world.[5] The Failed States Index of 2012 lists a number of states plagued by disintegration, destruction, lawlessness, and chaos.[6] The methodology incorporates twelve key political, social, and economic indicators (split into sub-indicators) that are used to score 178 countries.[7] The indicators are Demographic Pressures, Refugees and IDPs, Group Grievance, Human Flight and Brain Drain, Uneven Economic Development, Poverty and Economic Decline, State Legitimacy, Public Services, Human Rights and Rule of Law, Security Apparatus, Factionalized Elites and External Intervention.[8] A state that has experienced or is embroiled in an armed conflict will likely score poorly in many, if not all, of these indicators. Consequently, the state would be severely limited in its ability to investigate, arrest, and try war crimes suspects. This deficit was certainly the catalyst for establishing the ICTR in Rwanda, where widespread violence in 2004 led to the total collapse of the country's domestic justice system.[9]

Equally important is the fact that political unrest in the form of military coups, rigged elections, or popular upheaval will undermine a state's adherence to the rule of law. In such situations the standards of judicial independence are also often ignored.[10]

---

[5] *See* Global Security, *Military: World at War*, (2014), available at http://www.globalsecurity.org/military/world/war/index.html.

[6] Fund for Peace, 'The Failed State Index 2012', (2012), available at http://ffp.statesindex.org/rankings-2012-sortable.

[7] *Ibid.*

[8] Fund for Peace, 'The Indicators', (2014), available at http://ffp.statesindex.org/indicators.

[9] *See* REDRESS, 'Reparation for Torture: A Survey of Law and Practice in 30 Selected Countries (Rwanda Country Report)', (May 2003), p. 6, available at http://www.redress.org/downloads/country-reports/Rwanda.pdf. During this time, many members of the judiciary fled the country, were killed, or were later charged with participating in the genocide and imprisoned. The judicial staff left in the country, including judges, prosecutors and investigators, decreased so dramatically that it was impossible for the courts to function. In addition, courts and other judicial infrastructure were either severely damaged or looted.

[10] In Argentina, political instability resulted in severe rights violations that amounted to crimes against humanity. Under Argentina's military junta (1976-1983) thousands of people were arrested and then disappeared. Most were left-

Post-conflict states are likely to be without a functioning judicial system for a significant amount of time and, therefore, unable to carry out proceedings as required by the Rome Statute. Transitioning from a failed legal system to a legitimate one is an arduous and difficult process that requires adjustment in all facets of government. New codes and legislation must be adopted and significant energy must be directed at training new judges and others involved in the judicial process. During this turbulent interim period, a state is unlikely to be able to handle proceedings at the national level.

There is also ample evidence to suggest that security concerns in post-conflict environments can compromise a state's ability to effectively adjudicate. This was the case in both Iraq and Libya. In Libya, credible reports have cited concerns about 'the overall lack of security in cities and around the courts as a hindrance to the reestablishment of the judiciary'.[11]

II. Weak Judicial System

The second category includes those states that simply ignore the fundamental principles of the rule of law. I would argue that this includes states that fail to uphold customary international law and human rights protection. To be effective, newly created domestic war crimes courts must draw from the experiences of existing international and mixed courts, and also adopt guidelines that integrate international norms of judicial independence and impartiality.

---

wing dissidents and innocent civilians unconnected with terrorism or any other crime. Yet Argentina is only one example. Similar atrocities took place in other parts of the world and throughout South America during this period. *See generally* Derechos, 'Argentina', (2014), available at
http://www.derechos.org/nizkor/arg/eng.html.

[11] *The Prosecutor v. Saif Al-Islam Gaddafi and Abdullah Al-Senussi*, Doc. ICC-01/11-01/11-190-Corr-Red, 'Public Redacted Version of the Corrigendum to the 'Defence Response to the Application on behalf of the Government of Libya pursuant to Article 19 of the ICC Statute'', (31 July 2012), (hereinafter 'Corrigendum to the 'Defence Response to the Application on behalf of the Government of Libya'') para. 384, *citing* United States Bureau of Democracy, Human Rights and Labour, 'Country Report on Human Rights Practices for 2011: Libya', (2012), p. 9, available at
http://www.state.gov/j/drl/rls/hrrpt/humanrightsreport/index.htm?dlid=186437.

This issue has taken centre stage at the admissibility hearings between Libya and the ICC. Despite credible allegations of torture and mistreatment in obtaining evidence, Libya has argued that the ICC, when conducting a complementarity enquiry, is required neither to 'scrutinise the proceedings from the exacting perspective of human rights court' nor 'to ensure and enforce compliance by the domestic court' with due process rights.[12] The Court's enquiry, Libya argues, should exclusively consider whether or not domestic proceedings are carried out genuinely.[13] This argument is baseless. International law does not permit a state to ignore a basic, inviolable prohibition (i.e., against torture) regardless of the state's good faith efforts to carry out domestic prosecutions.

Kenya and Syria also fall into this category. As discussed earlier, the 2007 general elections in Kenya led to the rape, torture, killing or enforced disappearance of thousands of people.[14] Despite these human rights violations, Kenyan courts have only handed down 'a handful of convictions for serious crimes' committed during the post-election violence.[15] In Syria, as civil war continues to rage, alternative 'courts' have been created in rebel-controlled areas, but these fall far short of the standards required by international law.[16]

---

[12] *The Prosecutor v. Saif Al-Islam Gaddafi and Abdullah Al-Senussi*, Doc. ICC-01/11-01/11-293-Red, 'Libyan Government's consolidated reply to the responses of the Prosecution, OPCD, and OPCV to its further submissions on issues related to the admissibility of the case against Saif Al-Islam Gaddafi', (4 March 2013), para. 84.

[13] *Ibid.*

[14] *See* Human Rights Watch, 'Kenya Country Summary', (January 2012), available at http://www.hrw.org/sites/default/files/related_material/kenya_2012.pdf.

[15] In a 2012 report, Human Rights Watch reported that although there were thousands of cases pending before Kenya's Directorate of Public Prosecutions, there were serious difficulties obtaining evidence. There was also impunity for police officials who were implicated in the crimes and the government did not show a 'serious commitment to ensuring fair, transparent and effective investigations of those who organised and financed the violence'. *See* Human Rights Watch, 'Perceptions and Realities: Kenya and the International Criminal Court', (14 November 2013) available at http://www.hrw.org/news/2013/11/14/perceptions-and-realities-kenya-and-international-criminal-court. *See also* Human Rights Watch, 'Turning Pebbles: Evading Accountabilty for Post-Election Violence in Kenya', (2011), p. 9, available at http://www.hrw.org/sites/default/files/reports/kenya1211webwcover_0.pdf.

[16] Ivan Watson and Raja Razek, 'Rebel court fills void amid Syrian civil war', *CNN*, (26 January 2013), available at

Rwanda is another example of a post-conflict state in transition. Crimes committed during the Rwandan genocide fell under the jurisdiction of the international *ad hoc* tribunal for Rwanda – the ICTR. Rwanda had requested that the ICTR transfer Yussuf Munyakazi to the Rwandan court system. The ICTR followed an assessment remarkably similar to the ICC's complementarity principle. Pursuant to Rule 11*bis*(A), the Court may agree to a referral to a state with jurisdiction (i.e., Rwanda) only if that state is 'willing and adequately prepared' to accept the case.[17] In fact, this same language is found in the ICTY Rules covering war crimes in the former Yugoslavia.[18] In addition, Rule 11*bis*(C) of the ICTR Rules requires the Court, prior to referral, to be satisfied that the accused will receive a fair trial in the state concerned.[19]

However, the ICTR denied the request for transfer because of concerns that the Rwandan judiciary was not fully independent and immune from outside pressure.[20] The Court made a similar determination when it denied the transfer of genocide suspect Jean-Baptiste Gatete to Rwanda's national courts. The ICTR commended Rwanda for taking steps to improve its judicial and penal systems but said it still had reservations about transferring cases to the country's courts:

> The Chamber concludes that the Republic of Rwanda has made notable progress in improving its judicial system. Its legal framework contains satisfactory provisions concerning jurisdiction and criminalizes Jean-Baptiste Gatete's alleged conduct. The death penalty has been abolished. However, the Chamber is not satisfied that Gatete will receive a fair trial if transferred to Rwanda. First, it is concerned that he will not be able to call witnesses residing outside Rwanda to the extent and in a manner which will ensure a fair trial. Second, it accepts that the Defence will face

http://edition.cnn.com/2013/01/25/world/meast/syria-rebel-court.

[17] Rules of Procedure and Evidence of the International Criminal Tribunal for Rwanda, Revision 19, (10 April 2013), UN Doc. ITR/3/Rev. 19 (2013), (hereinafter ICTR Rules of Procedure and Evidence), Rule 11*bis*(A)(iii).

[18] Rules of Procedure and Evidence of the International Criminal Tribunal for the former Yugoslavia, Revision 49, (22 May 2013), UN Doc. IT/32/Rev. 49 (2013), (hereinafter ICTY Rules of Procedure and Evidence), Rule 11*bis*(A)(iii).

[19] ICTR Rules of Procedure and Evidence, Rule 11*bis*(C).

[20] *The Prosecutor v. Yussuf Munyakazi,* Case No. ICTR-97-36-R11*bis*, 'Decision on the Prosecutor's request for the referral of the case to the Republic of Rwanda' (28 May 2008), para. 48. *See also* UN Security Council, 'Speakers in Security Council call for rapid completion of cases before tribunals, while stressing need for mechanisms to tackle residual tasks', (4 June 2009), 6134th Meeting, available at http://www.un.org/News/Press/docs/2009/sc9670.doc.htm.

problems in obtaining witnesses residing outside Rwanda because they will be afraid to testify. Third, there is a risk that Gatete, if convicted to life imprisonment there, may risk solitary confinement due to unclear legal provisions in Rwanda.[21]

As one would expect, the Rwandan government reacted vehemently against the ICTR decision, arguing that it undermined the country's judicial reforms and hindered national reconciliation. The government blamed 'erroneous, factually incorrect assessments' and occasional 'deliberate misrepresentations' of the country's human rights situation by advocacy groups for fuelling the negative impression of Rwanda's judiciary.[22]

I serve on the Board of Directors of an advocacy group that criticised Rwanda's judiciary.[23] The response from Rwanda's government was equally critical of our assessment.

Rwanda's weak judicial system was made apparent by the fact that third party states refused extradition requests. The Finnish government refused to extradite a suspect (Francois Bazaramba) accused of war crimes. The government argued that it was following the ICTR's finding that defendants would not receive a fair trial in Rwanda.[24] It is interesting to note that the Finnish government did not undertake a separate assessment of Rwanda's judiciary; it simply relied on the ICTR assessment:

---

[21] *The Prosecutor v. Jean-Baptiste Gatete*, Case No. ICTR-2000-61-R11*bis*, 'Decision on Prosecutor's Request for Referral to The Republic of Rwanda', (17 November 2008), para. 95.

[22] UN Security Council, 'Speakers in Security Council call for rapid completion of cases'. *See also* Andrew Morgan, 'Rwanda prosecutor criticizes ICTR refusal to transfer jurisdiction', *Jurist*, (5 June 2009), available at http://jurist.org/paperchase/2009/06/rwanda-prosecutor-criticizes-ictr.php.

[23] The International Legal Assistance Consortium (ILAC). The ILAC is a non-profit consortium established in the late 1990s to enable expert representatives of the international community to make assessments of post-conflict justice systems and to make recommendations as to judicial rehabilitation during post-conflict periods. The ILAC's stated mission is to rebuild justice systems, based on the rule of law and protection of human rights. It comprises fifty member organisations, representing more than three million judges, lawyers and academics worldwide. *See generally* http://www.ilac.se/.

[24] Finnish Ministry of Justice, 'Press Release: Genocide Suspect not to be released to Rwanda', (20 February 2009), available at http://www.government.fi/ajankohtaista/tiedotteet/tiedote/en.jsp?oid=254185.

> The Ministry of Justice states in its decision that it has neither any reason to question the conclusions of the ICTR nor any grounds to assess the prevailing circumstances in Rwanda any differently than the ICTR.[25]

Reference was also made to Finland's responsibility under the European Convention on the Protection of Human Rights and Fundamental Freedoms[26] to ensure that the right to a fair trial is protected for persons within its jurisdiction.[27]

The United Kingdom faced the same problem. Four Rwandans accused of genocide in Rwanda during the 1994 conflict appealed the lower court's ruling that the suspects be extradited back to Rwanda for trial. Appealing to the UK High Court, the four suspects argued that because of political interference and intimidation of witnesses, trials in Rwanda would not be impartial and independent and thus violated the European Convention on Human Rights. The UK High Court focused on whether a 'real risk of a flagrant denial of justice' would be suffered by the suspects should they be returned to Rwanda for trial. After consideration, the Court was satisfied that the four men 'would suffer a real risk of a flagrant denial of justice by reason of a likely inability to adduce the evidence of supporting witnesses;'[28] the High Court was also persuaded by evidence of political interference in Rwandan courts. Consequently, the High Court allowed the appeal and ordered the men released.

Sweden confronted a similar request. The Rwandan government requested extradition of Sylvere Ahorugeze, a man suspected of being a former chief of the Hutu Interahamwe militia, on charges of genocide and crimes against humanity allegedly committed during the 1994 genocide. Ahorugeze had argued that Swedish extradition law, and the European Convention for the Protection of Human Rights and Fundamental Freedoms, prevented his extradition, basing his argument in part on the shortcomings of Rwanda's judicial system.[29] Yet, in a move that was

---

[25] *Ibid.*

[26] Opened for signature 4 November 1950, entered into force 3 September 1953, ETS 5; 213 UNTS 221.

[27] Finnish Ministry of Justice, 'Press Release: Genocide Suspect not to be released to Rwanda'.

[28] *Brown and others v. Government of Rwanda and another* [2009] All ER (D) 98 (Apr), para. 139.

[29] Christian Ehret, 'Sweden High Court rules government may extradite Rwandan Hutu', *Jurist*, (29 May 2009), available at http://jurist.org/paperchase/2009/05/sweden-high-court-rules-that-government.php.

exactly the opposite of the decisions of Finland and the United Kingdom, Sweden's Supreme Court ruled that Rwanda's extradition request was allowed under both domestic and international law and that 'Rwanda's justice system, while flawed, has been continuously improving in recent years'.[30] The contradiction between this decision and that of both the United Kingdom and Finland on the same legal issue (i.e., Rwanda's ability to undertake prosecutions) is illustrative of the challenges that the ICC will face in implementing Article 17(3). It also points to the need for a more objective assessment of a country's domestic judicial system under the principle of complementarity.

In 2010, France was also consistently ruling against extradition to Rwanda. The courts declined to extradite Dr Eugene Rwamucyo, accused of genocide, and also Callixte Mbarushimana, the alleged leader of the Democratic Forces for the Liberation of Rwanda.[31] The French courts ruled that these individuals would not receive a fair trial in Rwanda.[32] However, by mid-2012, at least one French court was willing to extradite French-Rwandan citizens, Claude Muhayimana and Innocent Musabyimana, to Rwanda on charges of crimes against humanity, and was not concerned about fair trial issues.[33] An Appeals Court approved the extradition.[34] Claude and Innocent are two Rwandans wanted by Rwanda for their alleged role in the 1994 Rwandan genocide.[35] This was the first ruling where France has approved the extradition of genocide suspects to Rwanda itself.[36]

---

[30] *Ibid.*

[31] Ashley Hileman, 'France court orders Rwanda rebel leader to face ICC trial', *Jurist*, (3 November 2010), available at http://jurist.org/paperchase/2010/11/france-court-orders-rwanda-rebel-leader-to-face-icc-trial.php.

[32] Daniel Makosky, 'France court rejects Rwanda extradition request for war crimes suspect', *Jurist*, (15 September 2010) available at http://jurist.org/paperchase/2010/09/france-court-rejects-rwanda-extradition-request-for-war-crimes-suspect.php.

[33] *See* Jamie Davis, 'France approves first extradition to Rwanda', *Jurist*, (31 March 2012), available at http://jurist.org/paperchase/2012/03/france-approves-first-extradition-to-rwanda.php.

[34] 'French Court Backs Extradition of Rwanda Genocide Suspects', *Expatica*, (13 November 2013), available at http://www.expatica.com/fr/news/french-news/french-court-backs-extradition-of-rwanda-genocide-suspects_278365.html.

[35] *Ibid.*

[36] Samuel Franklin, 'France Appeals Court Approves Extradition of Rwandan Genocide Suspects', *Jurist* (13 November 2013), available at

However, on 26 February 2014, France's Court of Cassation issued a ruling blocking the extradition of the individuals.[37] The Court rejected the extradition of the suspects on the basis that the Rwandan Law, making genocide a punishable crime, only came into force in 1996: the men were charged with crimes committed in 1994. Thus, the Court ruled that there was no legal basis for extradition.[38]

The decision by the Court was, in my opinion, incorrect. The crime of genocide is embodied in the Convention on the Prevention and Punishment of the Crime of Genocide adopted by the UN General Assembly on 9 December 1948. I have written extensively on this issue and have argued that there now exists a considerable body of state practice, *opinio juris*, and international and domestic court decisions to support the position that the crime of genocide is subject to universal jurisdiction under customary international law.[39] Thus, there should have been no concern by the French Court about the retroactivity of the crime of genocide in Rwanda.

The failure to articulate clearly why a country is unable to undertake domestic prosecutions will inevitably lead to conflicts between international courts (including the ICC) and domestic courts. In the ICTR-Rwanda clash, the UN Security Council went so far as to express its 'disappointment' in the ICTR's failure to transfer some of the genocide cases to Rwanda as requested by the government. Expressing the importance of domestic prosecutions and its frustration with the ICTR, a UNSC spokesperson stated:

> [W]e do think that there is chance for more cases to be transferred to Rwanda to be tried locally because this makes the whole process faster and

---

http://jurist.org/paperchase/2013/11/france-appeals-court-approves-extradition-of-rwanda-genocide-suspects.php.

[37] 'Rwanda genocide: France blocks extraditions', *BBC News*, (26 February 2014) available at http://www.bbc.co.uk/news/world-africa-26356286.

[38] Decision No. 810 of 26 February 2014 (13-87888), Cour de Cassation, CR00810 (France) (26 February 2014) available at http://www.courdecassation.fr/jurisprudence_2/chambre_criminelle_578/810_26_28535.html.

[39] *See* Mark Ellis, 'Defining, Suppressing and Trying Genocide', in Willem J.M. van Genugten, Michael P. Scharf and Sasha E Radin (eds.), *Criminal Jurisdiction 100 Years After the 1907 Hague Peace Conference*, (The Hague: T.M.C. Asser Press, 2009), p. 53.

> less expensive. We are disappointed that this has not taken place so far, and it is having an impact on other cases.[40]

It was not until 2011, in the case of *Jean-Bosco Uwinkindi*, that the ICTR reversed its long-standing position and finally determined that Rwanda was capable of accepting and prosecuting an ICTR case.[41] However, it is interesting to note that the Court's decision seemed to suggest some lingering apprehension about Rwanda's legal system. In the last paragraph of its decision, the Court expressed marked uncertainty:

> Before parting with this decision, the Chamber expresses its solemn hope that the Republic of Rwanda, in accepting its first referral from this Tribunal, will actualise in practice the commitment it has made in its filings about its good faith, capacity and willingness to enforce the highest standards of international justice in the referred cases.[42]

A month later, a Norwegian court followed the ICTR's reasoning. In July 2011, the Oslo District Court ruled on Rwanda's request for the extradition of Charles Bandora, accused of participating in Rwanda's genocide.[43] The Court did not conduct its own on-ground assessment, but looked at the recent *Uwinkindi* case and ruled that the ICTR decision 'must be given great weight'.[44] Not surprisingly, the Court ruled in favour of the extradition request.

---

[40] Ambassador John Sawers, Head of Delegation of the visiting UN Security Council *quoted* in Edmund Kagire, 'UNSC Disappointed with ICTR's Failure to Transfer Genocide Cases', *The New Times*, (18 May 2009), available at http://www.newtimes.co.rw/news/index.php?i=13899&a=15785.

[41] The Court ruled that: 'Rwanda had made material changes in its laws and had indicated its capacity and willingness to prosecute cases referred by the ICTR adhering to internationally recognised fair trials standards enshrined in the ICTR Statute and other human rights instruments. In particular, the Chamber found that the issues which concerned previous Referral Chambers, namely the availability of witnesses and their protection, had been addressed to some degree in the intervening period', *The Prosecutor v. Jean-Bosco Uwinkindi*, Case No. ICTR-2001-75-R11*bis*, 'Decision on Prosecutor's Request for Referral to the Republic of Rwanda: Rule 11*bis* of the Rules of Procedure and Evidence', (28 June 2011), para. 222; ICTR, 'Press Release: Case of Jean Uwinkindi Referred for Trial to the Republic of Rwanda', Doc. ICTR/INFO-9-2-681.EN, (28 June 2011).

[42] *The Prosecutor v. Jean-Bosco Uwinkindi*, Case No. ICTR-2001-75-R11*bis*, 'Decision on Prosecutor's Request for Referral to the Republic of Rwanda: Rule 11*bis* of the Rules of Procedure and Evidence', (28 June 2011), para. 225.

[43] *NCIS Norway v. Charles Bandora*, Oslo District Court, Case No. 11-050224ENE-OTIR/01, (22 November 2011) [on file with author].

[44] *Ibid.*, para. 14.

By 2012, the ICTR had clearly established a new precedent in supporting the transfer of cases to Rwanda's own judiciary. In the case of Fulgence Kayishema, the Court again ruled that Rwanda was capable of accepting and prosecuting ICTR transfer cases. The Court also transferred the cases of Charles Sikubwabo and Ladislas Ntaganzwa to Rwanda.[45]

III. No Implementing Legislation

A third category of the 'inability test' arises where a state has failed to effectively incorporate the Rome Statute into its domestic body of criminal and procedural law. National proceedings are likely to be compromised where a state is neither able to exercise its complementary (national) jurisdiction, nor cooperate with the Court in the exercise of its jurisdiction, because it lacks supporting legislation. This can occur when a state: has simply failed to implement the Rome Statute; has implemented only one of two types of legislation (i.e., 'complementarity' or 'cooperation'); has implemented incomplete or defective legislation (e.g., omitting certain Rome Statute offences); or maintains other legislation inconsistent with the Statute (e.g., upholding immunity for heads of State).

Implementation of the Rome Statute is not a mere aspiration. In signing and ratifying the Statute, States Parties have accepted formal, express obligations to cooperate with the Court.[46] Article 88 of the Statute says that 'States Parties shall ensure that there are procedures available under their national law for all of the forms of cooperation which are specified under this Part'.[47] Similarly, Article 86 requires States Parties to 'cooperate fully with the Court in its investigation and prosecution of crimes within the jurisdiction of the Court'.[48]

In addition, there is a firm expectation in customary international law that states must honour treaty obligations of their own free will (*pacta sunt*

[45] *See* Sung Un Kim, 'ICTR transfers case of former mayor to Rwanda court', *Jurist*, (27 March 2012), available at http://jurist.org/paperchase/2012/03/ictr-transfers-case-of-former-mayor-to-rwanda-court.php; Rebecca DiLeonardo, 'Rwanda genocide tribunal transfers case to national court', *Jurist*, (25 June 2012), available at http://jurist.org/paperchase/2012/06/rwanda-genocide-tribunal-transfers-case-to-national-court.php.

[46] ICC Statute, Part 9.

[47] *Ibid.*, Article 88.

[48] *Ibid.*, Article 86.

servanda – meaning 'agreements must be kept'). This principle is echoed and given further force by Article 26 of the Vienna Convention.[49]

However, the extent of non-implementation among States Parties is surprisingly high. While state support for the ICC is an historical success in international law, actual implementation of the Rome Statute is poor. The Coalition for the International Criminal Court (CICC) is the authoritative body on this subject. According to its figures, the number of *signatory* states to the Rome Statute is 139, and the number of state *ratifications* is 122.[50] However, **only** 65 of these 122 States Parties have enacted complementarity or cooperation provisions; the number of states that have enacted both categories of legislation is obviously lower. A further group of approximately thirty-five states '[has] *some* form of advanced draft implementing legislation'[51] [emphasis added]. This means that of 122 total States Parties, the legislative progress of the remaining group of (roughly) twenty-two is either non-existent or falls short of the 'advanced drafting' stage; overall, some fifty-seven States Parties lack implementing legislation of any form.

The obligations contained in the Rome Statute require States Parties to adopt implementing legislation upon signing the Statute. Complete and effective implementation of the Rome Statute at the domestic level entails the enactment of *cooperation* and *complementarity* legislation.

Cooperation provisions support the ICC's ability to exercise its jurisdiction and function effectively as an international court. Domestic legislation must allow for the following: permit the ICC to sit in the State Party's territory;[52] extend immunity to senior ICC officials engaged in investigations;[53] assist the Court in identifying and locating suspects and interested persons;[54] ensure that the Court is able to seize and examine

---

[49] Vienna Convention on the Law of Treaties, (1979) 1155 UNTS 331. Article 26 reads '[e]very treaty in force is binding upon the parties to it and must be performed by them in good faith'.

[50] Coalition for the International Criminal Court (CICC), 'Home page', (2014), available at
http://www.iccnow.org/index.php?mod=home.

[51] CICC, 'Implementation of the Rome Statute', (2014), available at www.iccnow.org/index.php?mod=romeimplementation.

[52] ICC Statute, Articles 3(3) and 4(2).

[53] *Ibid.*, Article 48.

[54] *Ibid.*, Article 93(1)(a).

evidence;[55] provide witness protection;[56] and execute Court requests to arrest and surrender suspects found on the state's territory.[57]

The broader obligation to provide '[a]ny other type of assistance' necessary for the Court to investigate or prosecute jurisdictional crimes[58] may require additional legislative diligence by a State Party. This is especially true when there is reason to clarify the form of cooperation under domestic law.

In addition to the cooperation test, a State Party must incorporate the Rome Statute's substantive criminal law provisions into its domestic body of law. This is the *complementarity* part of the test. It requires States Parties to take steps such as criminalising all offences contained in the Statute, ensuring that the principle of command responsibility is incorporated into domestic legislation,[59] removing any statute of limitations for Rome Statute offences,[60] and, perhaps most importantly, denying immunity to heads of state.[61]

Where a Party's non-cooperation prevents the Court from exercising its powers, the Statute provides that 'the Court may make a finding to that effect and refer the matter to the Assembly of States Parties or, where the Security Council referred the matter to the Court, to the Security Council'.[62] The Court, in fact, acted on this provision in 2011. Pre-Trial Chamber I referred Malawi[63] and Chad[64] to the Security Council for

---

55 *Ibid.*, Article 93(1)(b) and (g).
56 *Ibid.*, Article 93(1)(e).
57 *Ibid.*, Article 59 and Part 9.
58 *Ibid.*, Article 93(1)(l).
59 *Ibid.*, Article 28.
60 *Ibid.*, Article 29.
61 *Ibid.*, Article 27.
62 *Ibid.*, Article 87(7).
63 *The Prosecutor v. Omar Hassan Ahmad Al Bashir*, Doc. ICC-02/05-01/09-139, 'Decision Pursuant to Article 87(7) of the Rome Statute on the Failure by the Republic of Malawi to Comply with the Cooperation Requests Issued by the Court with Respect to the Arrest and Surrender of Omar Hassan Ahmad Al Bashir', (12 December 2011), p. 21.
64 *The Prosecutor v. Omar Hassan Ahmad Al Bashir*, Doc. ICC-02/05-01/09-140-tENG, 'Decision Pursuant to Article 87(7) of the Rome Statute on the Failure by the Republic of Chad to Comply with the Cooperation Requests Issued by the Court with Respect to the Arrest and Surrender of Omar Hassan Ahmad Al Bashir' (13 December 2011), para. 14.

failure to detain Omar Al Bashir (President of Sudan) on his visits to both countries, contrary to standing and repeated ICC requests to States Parties to arrest and surrender him to the Court. Much to the world's consternation, the Security Council has eschewed any responsibility and has taken no action against Al Bashir; he remains at liberty. This objectionable UN policy will be discussed in Chapter 4.

Despite legal treaty obligations, there is a high rate of non-implementation among States Parties. To correct this, the Assembly of States Parties (ASP) has identified 'full implementation' of the Rome Statute as a key goal. As part of its 'Plan of Action', it has renewed its call to States Parties to report on technical and financial constraints that hamper implementation, constitutional obstacles to full implementation, and national and regional strategies to promote implementation.[65] Further, a broad range of international NGOs advise States Parties on political and technical dimensions of implementing legislation.[66] These issues will be further discussed in Chapter 6.

IV. Fairness and Impartiality

The final category regarding the assessment of a state's inability to prosecute includes states that fall short of ensuring that their national judicial systems meet international standards of fairness and impartiality. This category overlaps with the third and fourth categories discussed earlier, but focus less on 'states in transition' and more on the specific lack of fair trial guarantees. This category is also similar to the 'impartiality' assessment recognised under Article 17(2)(c). However, I would argue that the difference here is that a state's willingness to undertake investigations and trials may not be matched by its ability to ensure effective proceedings. If the judicial system is not sufficiently able to try international crimes, the state would fail to meet the requirements of complementarity.

---

[65] *See* ICC Assembly of States Parties (ICC-ASP), 'Plan of Action of the Assembly of States Parties for achieving universality and full implementation of the Rome Statute of the International Criminal Court', Doc. ICC-ASP/12/S/008, (13 February 2013).

[66] *See* ICC-ASP, 'Complementarity – Completed Projects', (2014), available at www.icc-cpi.int/en_menus/asp/complementarity/CompletedProjects/Pages/defaulf.aspx.

For instance, in the Libyan admissibility case before the ICC, the OPCD argued that the alleged repeated violations of Gaddafi's rights demonstrated an institutional lack of understanding of 'basic human rights or the role of the Defence'.[67] The UN International Commission of Inquiry in Libya echoed this point, reporting that few officials have demonstrated 'a real understanding of basic legal and human rights standards'.[68] The OPCD also pointed to admissions by government officials that 'Libyan authorities do not yet have the ability to properly gather evidence or present a case',[69] and the Defence noted that prosecuting authorities 'do not appear to have the capacity to verify or assess the credibility of witnesses'.[70] The OPCD identified the fundamental issue of the Libyan judiciary as lacking a secure method of implementing orders and decisions,[71] constituting a clear challenge to Libya's ability to initiate domestic trials.

This raises a challenging question for the ICC. Should the Court concede that states in post-conflict environments cannot be held to the same fair trial scrutiny as states in stable environments? In its admissibility challenge to the ICC, Libya argued this very point. In its submission to the Court, the Libyan government acknowledged that the transitional atmosphere will present difficulties because '[s]tates emerging from mass-

---

[67] *The Prosecutor v. Saif Al-Islam Gaddafi and Abdullah Al-Senussi*, Doc. ICC-01/11-01/11-190-Corr-Red, 'Corrigendum to the 'Defence Response to the Application on behalf of the Government of Libya'', para. 369.

[68] United Nations Human Rights Council (UNHRC), 'Report of the International Commission of Inquiry on Libya', UN Doc. A/HRC/19/68, (8 March 2012), para. 12.

[69] *The Prosecutor v. Saif Al-Islam Gaddafi and Abdullah Al-Senussi*, Doc. ICC-01/11-01/11-190-Corr-Red, 'Corrigendum to the 'Defence Response to the Application on behalf of the Government of Libya'', para. 373, *quoting* NTC official Fathi Baji interviewed in D. Kirkpatrick and M. Simons, 'Libya Resists International Court's Claim on War Crimes Case', *New York Times*, (21 March 2012), available at http://www.nytimes.com/2012/03/22/world/africa/libya-resists-the-hague-in-war-crimes-case.html?_r=0.

[70] *The Prosecutor v. Saif Al-Islam Gaddafi and Abdullah Al-Senussi*, Doc. ICC-01/11-01/11-190-Corr-Red, 'Corrigendum to the 'Defence Response to the Application on behalf of the Government of Libya'', para. 369.

[71] *Ibid.*, para. 406, *quoting The Prosecutor v. Saif Al-Islam Gaddafi and Abdullah Al-Senussi*, Doc. ICC-01/11-01/11-190-Anx12B, 'Interview Translation', Annex 12B, (24 July 2012).

atrocities will not possess a sophisticated or functional judicial system'.[72] Libya argued that, in the midst of transition, legal systems need not meet the highest standards of law to fairly try a case, and it would be contrary to the principle of complementarity and the role of the ICC 'to hold Libya's national legal system against an exacting and elaborate standard beyond that basically required for a fair trial'.[73] Libya's counsel, Philippe Sands, emphasized that the ICC should not function as a human rights court but is 'called only to determine whether there are genuine national proceedings or not'.[74]

Interestingly, Professor William Schabas expressed a similar view regarding the 'danger that the provisions of Article 17 will become a tool for overly harsh assessments of the judicial machinery in developing countries'.[75] Indeed, Libya referred to this argument in its submission. It is a widely held concern that complementarity might operate at the expense of poor, under-developed countries. As the Libyan government argued, complementarity affords transitional justice systems 'an opportunity for post-conflict judicial capacity-building in the broader context of national reconciliation and democratization'.[76]

It may be tantalising to accept these lesser standards in the interest of democratic change. However, creating a bifurcated system of justice would be illogical and a mistake. It would exacerbate the 'north-south' divide, allowing a different measure of justice for developing and post-conflict countries. Domestic war crimes courts should be four-square in

---

[72] *The Prosecutor v. Saif Al-Islam Gaddafi and Abdullah Al-Senussi*, Doc. ICC-01/11-01/11-130-Red, 'Application on behalf of the Government of Libya pursuant to Article 19 of the ICC Statute', (1 May 2012), para. 98.
[73] *Ibid.*, para. 99.
[74] *The Prosecutor v. Saif Al-Islam Gaddafi and Abdullah Al-Senussi*, Doc. ICC-01/11-01/11-T-2-Red-ENG, 'Hearing Transcript', (9 October 2012), at 43:17-18. The Pre-Trial Chamber heard from Libya, the OTP, the OPCV, the OPCD, and Libya again. The Chamber instructed the parties to address 'the status of domestic proceedings in Libya, the subject matter of the domestic investigation in Libya, issues of national law in Libya, and the authorities currently holding Saif Al-Islam Gaddafi in custody (*Ibid.*, at 6: 8-11).
[75] William A. Schabas, *An Introduction to the International Criminal Court*, 2nd edn (Cambridge: Cambridge University Press, 2004), p. 196.
[76] *The Prosecutor v. Saif Al-Islam Gaddafi and Abdullah Al-Senussi*, Doc. ICC-01/11-01/11-130-Red, 'Application on behalf of the Government of Libya pursuant to Article 19 of the ICC Statute', (1 May 2012), para. 98.

adhering to standards established and accepted by the international community.

The cost of a lesser standard of justice is high. States too often pursue accountability without due care for fair trial standards, leaving suspects languishing in detention while investigations proceed at a painfully slow pace, or failing to adequately consider the plight of victims, who typically are left without retributive or restorative justice. There is a risk that the cure may be worse than the disease. In these bathetic circumstances, states and the international community need to carefully balance the desire for accountability against the requirements to undertake trials pursuant to international standards. If international standards cannot be satisfied, then trials should not be conducted at the national level.

The Rome Statute actually anticipates the need for states to adhere to human rights standards under the complementarity principle. Article 21(3) of the Rome Statute provides that '[t]he application and interpretation of law pursuant to this article must be consistent with internationally recognized human rights'.[77] In the *Lubanga* case, the Appeals Chamber confirmed that Article 21(3) 'requires the exercise of the jurisdiction of the Court in accordance with internationally recognized human rights norms'.[78] The Court stated that:

> [h]uman rights underpin the Statute; every aspect of it, including the exercise of the jurisdiction of the Court. Its provisions must be interpreted and more importantly applied in accordance with internationally recognized human rights; first and foremost, in the context of the Statute, the right to a fair trial, a concept broadly perceived and applied, embracing the judicial process in its entirety.... Where a fair trial becomes impossible because of breaches of the fundamental rights of the suspect or the accused by his/her accusers, it would be a contradiction in terms to put the person on trial. Justice could not be done. A fair trial is the only means to do justice. If no fair trial can be held, the object of the judicial process is frustrated and the process must be stopped.[79]

[77] ICC Statute, Article 21(3).
[78] *The Prosecutor v. Thomas Lubanga Dyilo*, Doc. ICC-01/04-01/06-772, 'Judgment on the Appeal of Mr Thomas Lubanga Dyilo against the Decision on the Defence Challenge to the Jurisdiction of the Court pursuant to article 19(2)(a) of the Statute of 3 October 2006', (14 December 2006), para. 36.
[79] *Ibid.*, para. 37.

Moreover, Article 21(3) requires that the Statute be applied and interpreted consistently with internationally recognised human rights; so the Court in fact has no discretion to ignore human rights principles. The language of this particular article further weakens the position of any state that contends that Article 17(1) must be read *only* on its face, effectively in isolation, and not interpreted and applied in light of human rights principles.

Within Article 17(3), read with Article 21(3) of the Rome Statute, I believe there are two sub-categories that are fundamental to the requirement that trial proceedings are fair and impartial. These categories are 1) witness protection and 2) defence rights. Both of these categories project clear and incontrovertible measurements on whether a state is able to conduct fair and impartial proceedings consistent with the principle of complementarity. These two categories have been central to the success or failure of both international and national prosecutions since the creation of the ICTY and ICTR. Both categories will continue to be central to any state that desires to adhere to the complementarity principle.

A. Witnesses

In many ways witness protection overlaps with the security concerns discussed above regarding post-conflict environments. Lack of security can be a clear threat to witnesses. In Libya, for example, threats against Gaddafi regime supporters would inevitably affect the availability of defence witnesses during any trial held in Libya,[80] not to mention the safety of those that might decide to testify. Indeed, in its decision rejecting Libya's admissibility challenge, the Pre-Trial Chamber found that Libya lacked the capacity to obtain testimony due to the authorities' inability to adequately protect witnesses.[81]

However, witness protection in general is so crucial to a fair trial that it warrants particular attention. Courts cannot deliver justice to the victims

[80] *The Prosecutor v. Saif Al-Islam Gaddafi and Abdullah Al-Senussi*, Doc. ICC-01/11-01/11-190-Corr-Red, 'Corrigendum to the 'Defence Response to the Application on behalf of the Government of Libya'', para. 394.

[81] *The Prosecutor v. Said Al-Islam Gaddafi and Abdullah Al-Senussi*, Doc. ICC-01/11-01/11-344-Red, 'Decision on the admissibility of the case against Saif Al-Islam Gaddafi', (31 May 2013), para. 209.

unless all witnesses are protected.[82] Certainly domestic courts will not pass the 'complementarity test' without a witness protection programme that meets international standards. Such a programme must incorporate measures to protect witnesses prior to, during, and after trials.

These protective measures are found in international treaties and covenants, including the Universal Declaration of Human Rights,[83] the International Covenant on Civil and Political Rights,[84] and the International Covenant on Economic, Social and Cultural Rights.[85] Under these agreements, states must uphold witness rights to physical and mental integrity.

An effective witness protection programme not only increases the likelihood that justice will be served but is crucial to ensuring confidence in the judicial process. As David Tolbert, former Deputy Prosecutor of the International Criminal Tribunal for the former Yugoslavia (ICTY) stated:

> If witnesses are not protected in an appropriate fashion and either are intimidated or suffer harm as a result of providing evidence, etc., public confidence in the judicial system will suffer...[86]

---

[82] *See* e.g., Alex C. Lakatos, 'Evaluating the Rules of Procedure and Evidence for the International Criminal Tribunal for the former Yugoslavia: Balancing Witnesses' Needs Against Defendants Rights' (1995) 46 *Hastings Law Journal*, 909.

[83] Universal Declaration of Human Rights, 10 December 1948, UN Doc. A/RES/217(III), Article 3, ('Everyone has the right to life, liberty and security of person').

[84] International Covenant on Civil and Political Rights, 16 December 1966, in force 23 March 1976, GA Res. 2200A (XXI), 21 UN GAOR Supp. (No. 16) at 52, UN Doc. A/6316 (1966); 999 UNTS 171; 6 ILM 368 (1967), (ICCPR). Article 2(3)(a), ('Each party to state the present undertakes: [t]o ensure that any person whose rights or freedoms as herein recognized are violated shall have an effective remedy, notwithstanding that the violation has been committed by persons acting in an official capacity . . . .').

[85] International Covenant on Economic, Social and Cultural Rights, 10 December 1966, in force 3 January 1976, UN Doc. A/6316 (1966); 993 UNTS 3; 6 ILM 368 (1967), Article 9 ('The States Parties to the present Covenant recognize the right of everyone to social security, including social insurance').

[86] David Tolbert and Aleksandar Kontić, *Final Report of the International Criminal Law Services Experts on the Sustainable Transition of the Registry and International Donor Support to the Court of Bosnia and Herzegovina and the*

There have been many instances in which witnesses critical to a case have refused to testify because of the lack of protection.[87] In both Bosnia and Serbia, there was a failure to adequately protect witnesses; many continue to fear for their safety even today.[88] When drafting the law to create Serbia's domestic war crimes court, the Serbian government gave no priority to witness protection. The government viewed a Victims and Witnesses Unit as 'too complex, expensive, time consuming' to incorporate into the draft law.[89] The Serbian government naively believed that creating such a unit would delay the new Court. More generally, there were no witness protection measures outlined in the new law. This was a major weakness of the Serbian War Crimes Court, where it was absolutely critical that Bosnian and Croatian victims be encouraged to testify. The complete lack of trust in Serbian institutions also meant that prosecutors were unable to secure victims' participation in the trials.[90]

I recall visiting the Court in Belgrade and listening to the judge read out each witness's home address before examining him or her.[91] Only after strong pressure from international experts, including myself, did the Serbian government agree to create a department focused exclusively on

Prosecutor's Office of Bosnia and Herzegovina in 2009, (The Hague: International Criminal Law Services Foundation, 15 December 2008), para. 48.

[87] *See* e.g., Human Rights Watch, *Justice at Risk: War Crimes Trials in Croatia, Bosnia and Herzegovina, and Serbia and Montenegro*, (14 October 2004), available at http://www.unhcr.org/refworld/docid/42c3bcf70.html (discussing how lack of protection has deterred individuals from coming forward as witnesses in the war crimes courts of Croatia, Bosnia and Herzegovina, and Serbia and Montenegro).

[88] *See* Amnesty International, *Burying the Past: 10 Years of Impunity for Enforced Disappearances and Abductions in Kosovo* (2009), available at http://www.amnesty.org/en/library/asset/EUR70/007/2009/en/ccf25c64-d299-46ee-83d4-a8835f8bf970/eur700072009eng.pdf.

[89] Mark S. Ellis, 'Coming to Terms with its Past - Serbia's New Court for the Prosecution of War Crimes', (2004) 22 *Berkeley Journal of International Law*, 165, 183.

[90] *See* Humanitarian Law Center, 'Victim/Witness Counselling and Legal Representation: A Model of Support – Project Implementation Report', (22 February 2007), available http://www.hlc-rdc.org/?p=13582&lang=de.

[91] *See* Human Rights Watch, 'Unfinished Business – Serbia's War Crimes Chamber', (June 2007), p. 9, available at http://www.hrw.org/legacy/backgrounder/eca/serbia0607/serbia0607web.pdf.

witness and victim protection.[92] Unfortunately, its commitment to this endeavour was weak.

The President of the Court, Siniša Vazić did, however, create a victims and witness unit. It initially consisted of 'two nice ladies' who helped the witnesses, and did so effectively.[93] The Unit was not given a budget; the United States provided limited funding ($17,000) to assist witnesses with travel. The Unit did not have resources to provide other support, even during investigations.[94] It was not until 2006, when Serbia enacted the Law on the Protection of the Participants in Criminal Proceedings that witness protection was enhanced to provide protection before, during and after trials.[95] However, the Witness Protection Unit is still short-staffed and under-budgeted.[96] Witnesses remain reluctant to testify for fear of retaliation when they return home. They are also fearful of the Unit and the involvement of Serbian police. Consequently, a local NGO created a Witness/Victim Protection Team to escort the victims to and from the Court.[97] The Court continues to be pressed by NGOs to provide physical security and twenty-four-hour protection for the most vulnerable witnesses.[98]

Bosnia also faced challenges when it created its War Crimes Chamber of the State Court of Bosnia and Herzegovina. Although it has done a better job of protecting witnesses than other mixed courts, the Court still has a number of problems.[99] Witness intimidation is common; witnesses

---

[92] Ellis, 'Coming to Terms with its Past', 184. I pushed heavily for this change while advising the OSCE on the creation of Serbia's domestic war crimes court in 2002.

[93] Human Rights Watch, 'Unfinished Business – Serbia's War Crimes Chamber', p. 7.

[94] *Ibid.*, pp. 7-8.

[95] Law on the Protection Programme for Participants in Criminal Proceedings, *Official Gazette of the Republic of Serbia*, No. 85/05 (2005).

[96] Amnesty International, *Burying the Past*, pp. 13 and 25.

[97] *See* Humanitarian Law Center, 'Victim/Witness Counselling and Legal Representation'.

[98] Telephone Interview with Nataša Kandić, Executive Director the Humanitarian Law Center (20 April 2007).

[99] David Tolbert and Aleksandar Kontić, 'The International Tribunal for the former Yugoslavia ('ICTY') and the Transfer of Cases and Materials to National Judicial Authorities: Lessons in Complementarity' in Carsten Stahn and Mohamed M. El Zeidy (eds.) *The International Criminal Court and Complementarity From Theory to Practice*, 2 vols. (Cambridge: Cambridge University Press, 2011) vol. 2, p. 896.

fear for their safety and often change their statements between the initial investigation and their appearance in court.[100] As in Serbia, there were problems during the trial stage when witnesses' names and other identifying information were made public.[101]

The Court created a stand-alone Witness Protection Programme housed in a domestic agency—the Bosnian State Investigation and Protection Agency (SIPA). This was a positive development. The Witness Protection Department assesses each witness and then tailors an individual protection scheme. The Director of SIPA supervises enforcement of the Witness Protection Law as well as 'the promotion of cooperation and exchange of information with authorities of foreign States and international organisations responsible for the protection of witnesses'.[102]

It should be stressed that witness protection is extremely difficult under the best of circumstances; for a domestic court in a transitional or post-conflict environment it can seem impossible. In the newest ICC investigation in Kenya, allegations surfaced that several witnesses had been bribed to provide false evidence against government officials.[103] The witnesses signed affidavits stating that they received 'upkeep money', rent allowances, and the promise of relocation outside of Kenya.[104] Though Kenya enacted a Witness Protection Act in 2006,[105] it wasn't enough to counter the systematic criminality that existed after the 2007 election, or to

---

[100] *See* Human Rights Watch, 'Bosnia and Herzegovina: A Chance for Justice? War Crime Prosecutions in Bosnia's Serb Republic', (March 2006), pp. 33-35, available at http://www.hrw.org/reports/2006/bosnia0306/bosnia0306webwcover.pdf.

[101] Tolbert and Kontić, *Final Report of the International Criminal Law Services*, para. 50.

[102] 'Witness Protection Program Law', *Official Gazette of Bosnia and Herzegovina*, No. 29/04, Article 14.

[103] Sarah Miley, 'ICC Prosecutor Says Court Will Not Use Testimony of Allegedly Bribed Kenya Witnesses', *Jurist*, (17 November 2010), available at http://jurist.org/paperchase/2010/11/icc-prosecutor-says-court-will-not-use-testimony-of-allegedly-bribed-kenya-witnesses.php.

[104] Benjamin Muindi, 'We Were Induced to Implicate Ruto, Two Claim', *All Africa*, (11 November 2010), available at http://allafrica.com/stories/201011120111.html.

[105] 'The Witness Protection Act, 2006', No. 16/2006 (Kenya), available at http://www.kenyalaw.org/Downloads/Acts/The_Witness_Protection_Act_2006.pdf.

allay witnesses' fear of reprisals.[106] The ICC Prosecutor urged Kenya's government to take genuine steps to protect witnesses.[107] As a result, the parliament passed a bill in April 2010 amending the 2006 Witness Protection Act and establishing an independent Witness Protection Unit.[108] The new legislation was expected to include security and justice sector reform.[109]

However, charges against two of the original six accused in the Kenyan case - Henry Kiprono Kosgey and Mohammed Hussein Ali - were rejected by the ICC Pre-Trial Chamber II on 23 January 2012. The Chamber found that the Prosecutor's evidence failed to satisfy the requisite 'evidentiary threshold' in both cases and questioned in particular the decision to rely on an '*anonymous and insufficiently corroborated witness*' [emphasis added].[110]

---

[106] The ICTJ has already reported that a number of witnesses have been harassed and at least two killed since the ICC initiated an investigation. *See* ICTJ, *Kenya: Impact of the Rome Statute and the International Criminal Court*, (June 2010), para. 19, available at http://ictj.org/sites/default/files/ICTJ-Kenya-ICC-Impact-2010-English.pdf.

[107] ICC-OTP, 'OTP Press Conference on Kenya, Prosecutor Moreno-Ocampo's Statement', (1 April 2010), available at http://www.icc-cpi.int/en_menus /icc/structure%20of%20the%20court/office%20of%20the%20prosecutor/reports% 20and%20statements/statement/Pages/20100401.aspx.

[108] ICTJ, *Kenya: Impact of the Rome Statute and the International Criminal Court*, p. 6. The Attorney General reported to the Review Conference of the Rome Statute of the ICC that the President had assented to the Act, completing the legislative process. *See* 'Statement by Hon. S. Amos Wako, Attorney General of the Republic of Kenya, to the Review Conference of the Rome Statute of the International Criminal Court', (31 May 2010), available at http://www.icc-cpi.int/iccdocs /asp_docs/RC2010/Statements/ICC-RC-gendeba-Kenya-ENG.pdf. *See* 'The Witness Protection (Amendment) Act, 2010', No. 2/2010, (Kenya), available at http://kenyalaw.org/kl/index.php?id=513.

[109] Such reforms are crucial in circumstances where actors of the state are implicated in the violence. For instance, it was reported that the National Commission on Human Rights recorded the confessions of police officer, Bernard Kirinya, who said he had witnessed extra-judicial killings committed by the Police in 2008. Kirinya was subsequently shot dead, before he could testify. *See* Mary Kiio, 'New Bill to Improve State Witness Protection, If Passed', *Inter Press Service*, (10 March 2010), available at http://ipsnews.net/news.asp?idnews=50624.

[110] ICC, 'Summary of decision in two Kenya cases (Presentation for 23 January 2012 in Case 1 and 2)', (23 January 2013), available at http://www.icc-cpi.int/fr_menus/icc/press%20

The new ICC Prosecutor, Mrs Fatou Bensouda, submitted a notice to withdraw the charges against another suspect - Francis Muthaura, former Kenyan diplomat and civil service chief on 11 March 2013[111] (See Chapter 2). A pre-trial review of the available evidence led to the Prosecutor to conclude that the requisite level of proof could not be satisfied; namely that the accused's guilt must be established 'beyond all reasonable doubt', as set out in Article 66(3) of the ICC Statute.[112] Informing this decision, she emphasised, was the 'limited pool of potential witnesses, several of whom have been killed or died since the 2007-2008 post-election violence', which had created investigative issues.[113] She also criticised the Kenyan government for failing to fully cooperate in uncovering useful evidence. Finally, she stressed that 'a critical witness' against Mr Muthaura – 'Witness 4', whose testimony she had decided to drop a month beforehand - had recanted his testimony.[114] This protected witness allegedly lied in a number of statements, however this allegation has not been proven.[115]

In a statement released shortly after the decision was made, Mrs Bensouda explained that it was her 'responsibility as a Prosecutor' to withdraw the charges, under exceptional circumstances, if there was not a 'reasonable prospect of conviction'.[116] Indeed, this decision marks the first time charges were withdrawn against an ICC defendant set for trial. In view of the fact that three of the original six Kenyan officials charged have now been terminated on evidential grounds, commentators have criticised the ICC's dependency on witnesses as a form of evidence and contend that this is rooted in a problem with the selection of the cases that are being

---

and%20media/press%20releases/news%20and%20highlights/Pages/summary%20of%20decision%20in%20the%20two%20kenya%20cases.aspx.

[111] *The Prosecutor v. Francis Muthaura and Uhuru Muigai Kenyatta*, Doc. ICC-01/09-02/11-687, 'Prosecution notification of withdrawal of the charges against Francis Kirimi Muthaura', (11 March 2013).

[112] *Ibid.*, para. 10.

[113] *Ibid.*, para. 11.

[114] *Ibid.*

[115] Discussion with Steven Kay QC, Defence Attorney for Uhuru Kenyatta (27 March 2014).

[116] ICC, 'Statement of ICC Prosecutor on the Notice to withdraw charges against Mr Muthaura', (11 March 2013), available at http://www.icc-cpi.int/en_menus/icc/press%20and%20media/press%20releases/Pages/OTP-statement-11-03-2013.aspx.

prosecuted; and that the OTP should more carefully consider the likelihood of securing convictions before pursuing individuals.[117]

One week after the notice of withdrawal was issued by the Prosecutor, Trial Chamber V formally terminated the proceedings. In a partial dissenting opinion, Judge Eboe-Osuji described the reasons for the withdrawal as 'very troubling' and expressed the view that where there is 'credible evidence' connecting a defendant to conduct akin to witness bribery, withdrawal of charges is not the appropriate course of action, since this risks creating 'passports to impunity' for the other defendants.[118] Nevertheless, it was agreed that withdrawal was appropriate given the evidential and witness circumstances.

In light of these evidential issues that are clearly plaguing the OTP in the Kenyan cases (Judge Eboe-Osuji observed that 'the Prosecution had clearly indicated that their case against Mr Muthaura was not strong to begin with'[119]), criticism of the Prosecutor's basic approach to the cases she decides to prosecute appears to be warranted. The Prosecutor's decision has arguably served to highlight concerns about the very function of the ICC. The consequences of her decision were significant. One of the key Kenya defendants, President Uhuru Kenyatta, has filed a motion asking for a permanent stay of the ICC proceedings claiming that a fair trial is not possible because of the Prosecution's corrupt witnesses.[120] His argument won the day.

---

[117] Simon Jennings, 'ICC Under Fire Over Investigations', *Institute for War and Peace Reporting*, ARC Issue 343, (22 March 2013), available at http://iwpr.net/report-news/icc-under-fire-over-investigations.

[118] *The Prosecutor v. Francis Kirimi Muthaura and Uhuru Muigai Kenyatta*, Doc. ICC-01/09-02/11-698, 'Partial Dissenting Opinion of Judge Ozaki and Concurring Separate Opinion of Judge Eboe-Osuji to the Decision on the withdrawal of charges against Muthaura', (19 March 2013), para. 4, p. 9.

[119] *Ibid.*, para. 4, p. 7.

[120] *The Prosecutor v. Uhuru Muigai Kenyatta*, Doc. ICC-01/09-2/11-822-Red, 'Defence Application for a Permanent Stay of Proceedings due to Abuse of Process', (10 October 2013), para. 24. *See also The Prosecutor v. Uhuru Muigai Kenyatta*, Doc. ICC-01/09-2/11-903, 'Defence Response to the 'Prosecution submissions on the *ne bis in idem* principles' (ICC-01/09-02/1-899)' (17 February 2014), paras 6, 11, 36. Defence counsel for Kenyatta also argued that the OTP's 'disproportionate post-confirmation investigations and disclosure regime' led to repeated delays in the trial. In light of the above, the defence called for the termination of the proceedings and for 'the entry of a not guilty verdict in

The Prosecutor informed the Court that it no longer has sufficient evidence to proceed with the trial of President Kenyatta as scheduled. In 2014, the Prosecution requested an indefinite adjournment of the case pending a decision on an application of non-compliance against Kenya.[121] However, on 31 March 2014, the Court ordered that the trial should be adjourned until 7 October 2014 and deferred any determination of non-compliance.[122]

The Prosecution had removed a key trial witness from its list, and faced the likely withdrawal of a second witness. The result was that there was no longer sufficient evidence to proceed to trial. According to the Prosecution, the first witness 'recently admitted that he provided false evidence at the heart of the Prosecution's case'.[123] The second witness indicated that he was no longer willing to testify.[124] The Prosecution acknowledged that even if the witness agreed to testify, the evidence was insufficient.[125] He was a member of the Mungiki (variously described as a gang or sect) allegedly employed to commit much of the post-election violence.[126]

---

circumstances where the Prosecution's case has failed and there is insufficient evidence to proceed with trial' (para. 36).

[121] *See The Prosecutor v. Uhuru Muigai Kenyatta*, Doc. ICC-01/09-02/11-892, 'Prosecution opposition to the Defence request for the termination of the Kenyatta case', (31 January 2014), para. 29. *See also The Prosecutor v. Uhuru Muigai Kenyatta*, Doc. ICC-01/09-02/11-875, 'Notification of the removal of a witness from the Prosecution's witness list and application for an adjournment of the provisional trial date', (19 December 2013).

[122] *See The Prosecutor v. Uhuru Muigai Kenyatta*, Doc. ICC-01/09-02/11-908, 'Decision on Prosecution's applications for a finding of non-compliance pursuant to Article 87(7) and for the adjournment of the provisional trial date' (31 March 2014).

[123] *Ibid.*, para. 2.

[124] *Ibid.*

[125] *See The Prosecutor v. Uhuru Muigai Kenyatta*, ICC-01/09-02/11-892, 'Prosecution opposition to the Defence request for the termination of the Kenyatta case', (31 January 2014), para. 11.

[126] *The Prosecutor v. Uhuru Muigai Kenyatta*, Doc. ICC-01/09-2/11-839, 'Prosecution's amended order of witnesses following the Chamber's decision of 23 October 2013', (28 October 2013), para. 5; Kamore Maina, 'Mungiki witness reveals why he quit Uhuru case', *The Star*, (23 December 2013), available at http://www.the-star.co.ke/news/article-148281/mungiki-witness-reveals-why-he-quit-uhuru-case.

Earlier, in the same (*Kenyatta*) trial, the Prosecution announced the withdrawal of another witness to the Pre-Trial Chamber. The Prosecutor had expressed 'strong concerns for her personal safety and that of her family' if her identity were to become known.[127]

Although allegations of witness interference have been reported in a number of ICC cases[128] the OTP says that the situation in Kenya is unprecedented[129] and probably the most extreme case for these activities.[130] That seems to be a material understatement. The apparent lack of effective protection has led to fears for the safety of witnesses being questioned during the prosecution's investigation.[131] The Prosecution has alleged that '[m]any potential witnesses expressed a fear of being harmed or even killed if they cooperate with the prosecution, and

---

[127] *The Prosecutor v. Uhuru Muigai Kenyatta*, Doc. ICC-01/09/02/11-874, 'Prosecution communication of withdrawal of Witness 66', (16 December 2013), para. 1.

[128] For instance, in the *Bemba* trial, several cases of threats and witness intimidation have been reported since July 2011. These threats were allegedly made 'against prosecution witnesses and their families in connection with their testimony at the Court'. According to the Trial Chamber, the allegations of threats and witness intimidation submitted by the prosecution suggested that the testimonies and identities of prosecution witnesses had been revealed for witnesses whom the Chamber had granted protective measures to protect their identities. *The Prosecutor v. Jean-Pierre Bemba Gombo*, Doc. ICC-01/05-01/08/1789-Red, 'Public Redacted Version of 26 September 2011 Decision on the accused's application for provisional release in light of the Appeals Chamber's judgement of 19 August 2011', (27 September 2011), paras 29-30.

[129] 'The witness security issues are daunting, the incidents of witness tampering and interference unprecedented'. *The Prosecutor v. Francis Kirimi Muthaura and Uhuru Muigai Kenyatta*, Doc. ICC-01/09-02/11-437-Red2, 'Public Redacted Version of the Prosecution Response to 'Defence Application for (1) An Order prohibiting the Prosecution from contacting potential Defence witnesses without following the procedural safeguards stipulated in other cases before the ICC and (2) An Order to the Prosecution to disclose information on all contacts between the Prosecution and potential Defence witnesses'', (19 June 2012), para. 45.

[130] IBA consultation with the OTP, (21 February 2013) [notes on file with the IBA].

[131] 'Police identify eight Kenyans interfering with ICC witnesses', *The Star*, (20 March 2012), available at www.the-star.co.ke/news/article-25631/police-identify-eight-kenyans-interfering-icc-witnesses; 'ICC team investigates witness tampering', *The Star*, (17 April 2012), available at www.the-star.co.ke/news/article-22021/icc-team-investigates-witness-tampering.

several declined to testify on this basis'.[132] The present political environment in Kenya is reportedly such that even to be suspected as an ICC witnesses often live in fear of harassment and even death.[133]

Given that the Kenya cases are so closely connected, the persistence of the same pattern of problems (i.e., pressure on witnesses, and non-cooperation by the government) suggests to me that the remaining prosecutions against William Samoei Ruto and Joshua Arap Sang are now weaker; even if the Prosecutor maintains that developments in one trial have no effect on the others.

In the ICTY case against Vojislav Šešelj, a prosecution witness testified that 'half the town' where he lived knew of his plans to testify at the trial, even though he was a protected witness and his name had not been released.[134] The witness said that he was being pressured to change his testimony. Consequently, the ICTY launched proceedings against the defendant for having revealed the names of protected witnesses.[135] In an extraordinary but important decision, the Trial Chamber granted the Prosecution's Motion for Adjournment until such time as witnesses could testify freely and without intimidation.[136] The majority of the Court decided that the integrity of the proceedings would be compromised if the

---

[132] *The Prosecutor v. William Samoei Ruto and Joshua Arap Sang*, Doc. ICC-01/09-01/11-446, 'Prosecution Motion Regarding the Scope of Witness Preparation', (13 August 2012), para. 17; *The Prosecutor v. Francis Kirimi Muthaura and Uhuru Muigai Kenyatta*, Doc. ICC-01/09-02/11-462, 'Prosecution Motion Regarding the Scope of Witness Preparation', (13 August 2012), para. 17.

[133] 'Joseph', (a pseudonym for a Nairobi-based journalist), 'Being named an ICC witness has left me fearing death', *Radio Netherlands Worldwide*, (12 December 2013) available at www.rnw.nl/africa/node/901271. However, Steven Kay QC claims that allegations of witness harassment and fear are used as a 'frequent excuse' and that there has been no independent investigation to determine if there is any truth to such allegations. Discussion with Steven Kay QC, Defence Counsel for Uhuru Kenyatta (30 March 2014).

[134] Simon Jennings, 'Could Imposing Counsel on Šešelj Backfire?', *Institute for War and Peace Reporting*, (20 October 2008), available at http://iwpr.net/report-news/could-imposing-counsel-seselj-backfire.

[135] 'Šešelj Accused of Contempt of Court', *B92 News*, (21 October 2008), available at http://www.b92.net/eng/news/crimes-article.php?yyyy=2008&mm=10&dd=21&nav_id=54391.

[136] *See The Prosecutor v. Vojislav Šešelj,* Case No. IT-03-67-T, 'Decision on Prosecution Motion for Adjournment with Dissenting Opinion of Judge Antonetti in Annex', (11 February 2009).

Chamber were to hear further testimony from witnesses who were allegedly subjected to a campaign of intimidation.

The ICTY also faced major setbacks in its case against Kosovo's former Prime Minister, Ramush Haradinaj. The prosecution's case was considerably weakened because witnesses refused to testify. Of one hundred witnesses, thirty-four had their identities concealed, eighteen had to be forced by the Court to appear, and a number of witnesses simply refused to testify once they arrived at Court.[137] In the end, the defendant was acquitted. The judgement in the *Haradinaj* case reveals a disturbing picture of witness intimidation, which undoubtedly influenced the Court's decision to find the defendant not guilty because the Prosecutor failed to prove his case. The Court admitted to encountering 'significant difficulties in securing the testimony of a large number of witnesses'.[138]

In general, many witnesses lacked confidence in the Court's ability to protect them. Even when facing contempt of court charges for non-cooperation, more than twenty percent of the subpoenaed witnesses refused to testify.[139] One witness said he was threatened despite being identified only by a pseudonym and having his image and voice distorted. Another witness stated 'I don't want protective measures because such measures do not exist in reality; they only exist within the boundaries of this courtroom, not outside it'.[140] Other prosecution witnesses experienced extreme emotional distress and were excused from testifying. Even the Prosecutor admitted a 'chilling effect on witnesses [which deterred] potential witnesses from speaking to investigators.[141] Two ethnic Albanians from Kosovo were found guilty of contempt for interfering with a witness. The Court found:

[137] *The Prosecutor v. Ramush Haradinaj, Idriz Balaj and Lahi Brahimaj*, Case No. IT-04-84-T, 'Judgement', (3 April 2008), para. 22.
[138] *Ibid.*, para. 6.
[139] M. Simons, 'Former Leader in Kosovo Acquitted of War Crimes', *New York Times*, (4 April 2008), available at
http://www.nytimes.com/2008/04/04/world/europe/04kosovo.html?_r=0.
[140] Harry de Quetteville, 'Ramush: Kosovan hero or war criminal?', *The Telegraph*, (2 April 2008) available at
http://blogs.telegraph.co.uk/news/harrydequetteville/3693661/Ramush_Kosovan_hero_or_war_criminal/.
[141] Lucia Kubosova, 'Hague court rules Kosovar ex-leader innocent', *EU Observer*, (4 April 2008), available at http://euobserver.com/foreign/25923.

> [I]t was clear that Bajrush Morina's words were intended and could only be understood as a strong and unequivocal call on Witness 2 to refrain from testifying in the Haradinaj et al. case. In the Trial Chamber's view, such behaviour constituted intimidation.[142]

The efficacy and fairness of the entire trial was compromised by witness intimidation and fear.

With the ICTY, breaches of confidentiality orders have been common. In one case, the names of twenty protected witnesses appeared in the local newspaper and on at least two occasions, the defence referred to a protected witness by name during a public trial.[143]

Not surprisingly, the same plethora of witness problems has haunted Rwanda. There is compelling evidence that a number of victims and witnesses appearing in local courts were harassed, threatened, and some even killed.[144] Threats have included psychological intimidation and humiliation. One frequently employed threat involves lobbing stones onto the corrugated tin roofs of victim and witness houses. Not only does this frighten and unnerve the targeted victim, but sends a village-wide message of intimidation.

Sri Lanka is another recent example of a failing to protect witnesses and thus undermining domestic prosecutions. A recent final report published in February 2014, by the Office of the High Commissioner for Human Rights (OHCHR),[145] concluded that the steps taken by Sri Lanka towards recovery had not satisfied the requirements for an independent and credible investigation into allegations of serious human rights violations.[146] In particular, it noted that victims did not have faith in the

---

[142] *The Prosecutor v. Astrit Haraqija and Bajrush Morina*, Case No. IT-04-84-R77.4, 'Judgement on Allegations of Contempt', (17 December 2008), para. 60.

[143] Jennifer Llewellyn and Sandra Raponi, 'The Protection of Human Rights Through International Criminal Law: A Conversation with Madam Justice Louise Arbour, Chief Prosecutor for the International Criminal Tribunals for the former Yugoslavia and Rwanda', (1999) 57 *University of Toronto Faculty of Law Review* 83, 89.

[144] I serve on the board of directors for the International Legal Assistance Consortium (ILAC). ILAC conducted an assessment of justice in Rwanda in November 2007.

[145] *See* UNGA, 'Promoting reconciliation and accountability in Sri Lanka', UN Doc. A/HRC/25/23, (24 February 2014).

[146] *Ibid.*, para. 65.

independence or transparency of the process, which adversely affected the willingness of victims to come forward.[147] Equally damning was the finding that the draft legislation on the assistance and protection of witnesses fell below international standards.[148] Thus, it was impossible for Sri Lanka to conduct a domestic inquiry consistent with the complimentary principle.

Judicial and non-judicial protections are valuable only if a court effectively enforces them. States must formulate a protection policy that uses financial resources responsibly. Since there will be competing demands for funds, domestic war crimes courts must prioritise the establishment of an effective and comprehensive protection strategy.[149] Prosecutors from the world's international courts have recognised the failure of witness protection schemes and have issued an unprecedented joint statement imploring governments to increase measures for witness safety and to provide 'residual mechanisms' for supporting victims and witnesses.[150]

International law mandates the protection of witnesses. The principle of complementarity further requires domestic courts to ensure that their criminal procedure codes meet international standards, including witness protection. Domestic courts will also have to strike a balance between the rights of witnesses and the rights of the defendant.[151]

---

[147] *Ibid.*, para. 68.

[148] *Ibid.*, paras 69-70.

[149] *See* Laura Miller, United States Institute for Peace (USIP), 'Building the Iraqi Special Tribunal: Lessons from Experiences in International Criminal Justice', (13 June 2004), p. 6, available at http://www.usip.org/publications/building-the-iraqi-special-tribunal-lessons-experiences-in-international-criminal.

[150] Special Court for Sierra Leone-Office of the Prosecutor, 'Sixth Colloquium of International Prosecutors – Joint Statement', (15 May 2011), p. 2, available at http://www.sc-sl.org/LinkClick.aspx?fileticket=TwFuqmhQvS4%3D&tabid=53.

[151] In balancing the interests of the witness against those of the accused when the two are in conflict, courts should place greater weight on the latter according to the requirements of the ICCPR and the European Convention of Human Rights (ECHR), but they should afford witnesses greater protection than they would receive in a domestic tribunal. *See* David Tolbert and Frederick Swinnen, 'The Protection of, and Assistance to, Witnesses at the International Criminal Tribunal for the former Yugoslavia (ICTY)', in Hirad Abtahi and Gideon Boas (eds.), *The Dynamics of International Criminal Justice: Essays in Honour of Sir Richard May*, (Leiden: Martinus Nijhoff Publishers, 2006), pp. 204-206.

B. Defence Rights

The second crucial issue fundamental to the requirement that trial proceedings are fair and impartial is defence rights. Under the principle of complementarity, domestic war crimes courts must adhere to international legal standards concerning the rights of a defendant. A state's failure to conduct fair trials consistent with international standards will necessitate the imposition of international jurisdiction, either through the ICC or other legal mechanisms.

Too often defence issues fall to the bottom of the priority list. It is astounding that the defence is addressed in a relatively superficial way in most of the Statutes of current *ad hoc* and mixed courts.[152] While there is a strong focus on the role of judges and prosecutors, little attention is given to legal assistance for the defence.[153] Defence teams tend to be under funded and short-staffed.[154] The presumption of innocence is often absent in court statutes.[155]

Equally disturbing is the fact that defence attorneys often face the wrath of government officials for simply doing their job.[156] In one of the newest domestic war crimes courts – the International Crimes Tribunal in

---

[152] Mikhail Wladimiroff, 'Defending Individuals Accused of Genocide', (2007-2009) 40 *Case Western Reserve Journal of International Law*, 271, 274.

[153] *See* Colette Rausch (ed.), *Combating Serious Crimes in Post Conflict Societies: A Handbook for Policymakers and Practitioners,* (Washington: United States Institute for Peace, 2006).

[154] *See* Michael A. Newton, 'Evolving Equality: The Development of the International Defence Bar', (2011) 47 *Stanford Journal of International Law*, 379, 391 (repeating information gathered from David Wippman, *The Costs of International Prosecution*, (2006) 100 *American Journal of International Law*, 861, 872).

[155] For example, in Bangladesh International Crimes (Tribunal) Act of 1973, the accused does not have the right to counsel in the pre-trial stage of the proceedings, nor does the accused have a right to remain silent so as not to incriminate himself. International Crimes (Tribunals) Act 1973, Act No. XIX of 1973, (20 July 1973) (Bangladesh) (hereinafter Bangladesh Act of 1973), available at http://www.internationallawbureau.com/wp-content/uploads/2010/07/The-International-Crimes-Tribunals-Act-1973.pdf.

[156] *See, e.g.*, Tom Odula, 'Rwandan Police asked to release US Attorney', *UT San Diego*, (29 May 2010), available at http://www.signonsandiego.com/news/2010/may/29/rwandan-police-asked-to-release-us-attorney/.

Bangladesh – defence lawyers are already facing harassment, threats of violence and arrests.[157] Even the international defence lawyers have been harassed.[158] This opens the court to criticism of 'victors' justice'.

The resources available to defendants, both to prepare for and during a trial, are fundamental to justice through due process.[159] Without some measure of equality between the prosecution and defence, the trial cannot be regarded as fair. International law is clear on this point.[160]

Equality of arms, however, does not necessarily refer to equality of means. Equality of arms simply requires that the defence never be placed at a 'substantial disadvantage' vis-à-vis the prosecution in terms of its ability to present its case.[161] This would go beyond procedural equality between the parties. It would entail an obligation on the court to 'provide

---

157 *See* Human Rights Watch, 'Bangladesh: Stop Harassment of Defense at War Tribunal' (2 November 2011), available at http://www.hrw.org/news/2011/11/02/bangladesh-stop-harassment-defense-war-tribunal.

158 British lawyers Toby Cadman, Steven Kay QC, and John Cammegh, the defence counsel for five men detained by the International Crimes Tribunal Bangladesh (ICTB), were denied entry into Bangladesh on 6 August 2011 after a deputy secretary of the Bangladesh Home Ministry sent a letter to the immigration office requesting they deny entry visas. Curiously, the actual secretary in charge at the ministry denies any knowledge of such a letter. Obviously this raises quite a few issues, among them executive interference, right to counsel, etc. *See* 'ICT Accused UK Lawyer 'Banned' From Entering Bangladesh' *The New Age*, (11 August 2011), available at http://tobycadman.com/index/view/ict_accused_uk_lawyer_banned_from_entering_bangladesh.

159 Gideon Boas, a former senior legal officer of the ICTY, argues that '[t]he issue of resources is a crucial aspect of ensuring equality of arms between the parties'. *See* Gideon Boas, *The Milošević Trial: Lessons for the Conduct of Complex International Criminal Proceedings* (New York: Cambridge University Press, 2007), p. 263.

160 *See* International Covenant on Civil and Political Rights, 16 December 1966, in force 23 March 1976, GA Res. 2200A (XXI), 21 UN GAOR Supp. (No. 16) at 52, UN Doc. A/6316 (1966); 999 UNTS 171; 6 ILM 368 (1967), (hereinafter ICCPR), Article 14.

161 For example, the Court in *The Prosecutor v. Naser Oric* stated: '[a]t a minimum, equity of arms obligates a judicial body to ensure that neither party is put at a disadvantage when presenting its case'. *The Prosecutor v. Naser Oric*, Case No. IT-03-68-AR73.2, 'Interlocutory Decision on Length of Defence Case, (20 July 2005), paras 7–8.

every practicable facility it is capable of granting . . . when faced with a request by a party for assistance in presenting its case'.[162] Despite general acknowledgement that 'equality of arms' is fundamental, defence provisions—even in international courts—have often been an afterthought.[163]

Drawn from common law tradition, the equality of arms principle is well understood in adversarial proceedings, where significant disparity between the parties is likely to disadvantage the accused. In the ICTY *Tadić* case, the Court suggested that it could be more strictly observed, noting that 'it must be given a more liberal interpretation than that normally upheld with regard to proceedings before domestic courts', due to the added difficulties in tracing and gaining access to evidence.[164] Thus, one could argue that the equality of arms principle in regard to national war crimes courts must be more strictly interpreted, allowing for greater equality between the parties.

Even in international prosecutions, it is often 'a foregone conclusion that [the defendants] are responsible for terrible atrocities and will be convicted'.[165] Conviction is virtually certain after an indictment is served:

---

[162] *The Prosecutor v. Duško Tadić*, Case No. IT-94-1-A, 'Judgement', (15 July 1999), para. 52.

[163] *See* Rupert Skilbeck's criticism relating to the establishment of the Defence Office at the Special Court for Sierra Leone:

> The Defence Office . . . was only introduced at a late stage in the construction of the Court . . . The requirement in Article 19 of the Agreement that staff are 'phased in' with the chronological process of justice means that the Defence were the last to arrive, with the head of the Defence Office only arriving a week before the grand opening of the Court. Unfortunately, this reflects an historical trend that has previously caused huge difficulties in providing for effective representation and has led to significant inequalities between the prosecution and the defence.

Rupert Skilbeck, 'Building the Fourth Pillar: Defence Rights at the Special Court for Sierra Leone', (2004) 1 *Essex Human Rights Review*, 66, 71. *See also* Vincent O. Nmehielle, 'The Defense Office of the Special Court for Sierra Leone: A Watershed in Realizing the Rights of Accused Persons in International Criminal Justice' in Charles C. Jalloh (ed.), *The Sierra Leone Special Court and its Legacy: The Impact for Africa and International Criminal Law*, (New York: Cambridge University Press, 2014).

[164] *The Prosecutor v. Duško Tadić*, Case No. IT-94-1-A, 'Judgement', para. 52.

[165] William A. Schabas, 'Independence and Impartiality of the International Judiciary: Some Lessons Learned, and Some Ignored', in Edel Hughes, William Schabas and Ramesh Thakur (eds.), *Atrocities and International Accountability:*

'[t]he Prosecutor obtains rates of conviction before the international tribunals comparable to those in Burma or China, but that are unheard of in credible national justice systems'.[166] To this should be added the presumption of guilt widely held by government organisations, media and the public at large, which flies in the face of any legal presumption of innocence. Some commentators have suggested that the construction and operation of international courts reflects a compulsion to convict, with little regard for defence rights, and thus leads to an 'impartiality deficit' in international criminal proceedings.[167]

It is striking that neither the ICTY nor the ICTR created a formal structure to support the defence, despite the fact that both courts are the products of UN Security Council resolutions. Mikhail Wladimiroff, one of the first defence attorneys to appear at the ICTY, called attention to this problem when he stated:

> [I]nternational prosecutions have not primarily emerged from the need to administer justice, but rather from the firm belief that we should prosecute the perpetrators of those crimes we believe are the most heinous. The eagerness of the media, politicians and some nongovernmental organisations to achieve convictions, not merely fair proceedings, puts pressure on international trials. The popular perception is that an acquittal is a failure. This is the reason why international prosecutors may well be inclined to play a creative game in order to secure convictions, rather than assisting the court in finding the truth.[168]

The same concerns were addressed in a major report on defence issues:

> Defence is frequently overlooked in the early stages of planning for international trials. The International Criminal Tribunal for the former Yugoslavia (ICTY) in its early stages made no proper provision for defence, and in the preliminary months of its first case was employing only one defence lawyer, who was prepared on an *ad hoc* basis to waive his usual hefty fees for a payment capped at US $200 per day. The Special Panels for Serious Crimes in East Timor were planned without any regard to the need for defence, and began their operation with only one junior

---

Beyond Transitional Justice, (Tokyo: United Nations University Press, 2007), p. 182.

166 *Ibid.* p. 183.

167 Diane M. Amann, 'Impartiality Deficit and International Criminal Judging', in Hughes, Schabas and Thakur (eds.), *Atrocities and International Accountability: Beyond Transitional Justice*, pp. 209-211.

168 Wladimiroff, 'Defending Individuals Accused of Genocide', 274.

> overseas lawyer acting as a public defender, along with newly qualified national public defenders. The spectacle of nervous newly qualified lawyers facing up to experienced international prosecutors before the Special Panels in East Timor was not an edifying one. Although attempts have been made to improve the situation, there has never been any real recovery from this position.[169]

Justice Richard J. Goldstone, the first prosecutor for the ICTY and ICTR, took important steps to move the courts away from this position. I approached Justice Goldstone while working as Executive Director of the American Bar Association's Central and East European Law Initiative (CEELI). I wanted to offer CEELI's assistance to his office in the Court's first trial—the *Tadić* case. After an hour-long conversation, Justice Goldstone asked if CEELI could direct its assistance not to the prosecution but to the defence! Justice Goldstone was concerned that the defence did not have sufficient resources, and that the defence attorneys, who were from the civil law country of the Netherlands, did not have sufficient experience in common law trial proceedings (e.g., cross examining witnesses). I agreed, and at the conclusion of the trial Justice Goldstone stated 'without the support of CEELI, the first defendant, Duško Tadić, would not have had a fair trial'.[170] It is a credit to Justice Goldstone that as prosecutor, his interest included ensuring that the defence had sufficient support and resources.

Some courts are beginning to recognise the need to assist the defence. In Kosovo, authorities established the Criminal Defence Resource Centre[171] to provide legal advice on international crimes and provide counsel with access to a library and training in international human rights and criminal law.

The Extraordinary Chambers in the Courts of Cambodia (ECCC) also decided to create the Defence Support Section (DSS) to counterbalance the Office of the Prosecutor and ensure quality representation by the defence.

---

[169] Sylvia de Bertodano, *Report on Defence Provision for the Special Court of Sierra Leone* (No Peace Without Justice, 28 February 2003), *cited* in Charles C. Jalloh and Simon M. Meisenberg (eds.), 2 vols, *The Law Reports of the Special Court for Sierra Leone* (Leiden: Martinus Nijhoff Publishers, 2012), vol. 1, p. 480.

[170] Richard J. Goldstone, *For Humanity: Reflections of a War Crimes Investigator* (Yale University Press, 2000), p. 118.

[171] Organisation for Security and Cooperation in Europe, 'Kosovo Criminal Defence Resource Centre opens its doors', *Pristina,* (26 September 2001), available at http://www.osce.org/kosovo/53842.

The DSS creates and maintains a list of qualified counsel for the accused, puts together the defence teams, oversees legal aid, and provides administrative, logistical, and legal support to defence teams.[172]

When the Special Court for Sierra Leone (SCSL) was created, an Office of the Principal Defender (OPD) was also created to assist defence on all aspects of the judicial process, including providing duty counsel and legal assistance to indigent accused.[173] Although under the authority of the Registrar, the Office of the Principal Defender does possess a significant degree of independence. The SCSL Principal Defender, Vincent Nmehielle calls the OPD 'a watershed in the history of the Defence vis-à-vis the rights of accused persons in international criminal tribunals'.[174]

Despite these positive changes in selected courts, defence needs still tend to be ignored. Attorneys appearing before the ICC have sarcastically noted that in the first ten years of the Court's existence, there has never been court literature explaining the function of the defence. In contrast, the Court has created glossy brochures explaining the roles of the prosecutor, the Registry, and the Court.[175] It wasn't until 2010 that the Registry, with significant support and encouragement of the International Bar Association, created an 'informational flyer' explaining the role of the defence within the structure of the ICC.

With such inequality even in the international courts, there is legitimate concern that domestic war crimes courts will continue to ignore the needs of the defence. The consequence for those courts will be that they fail the 'complementarity test' and find themselves bound by the edicts of either the ICC or other international judicial mechanisms.

---

[172] *See* Extraordinary Chambers in the Courts of Cambodia (ECCC), 'Approved ECCC Budget 2010-2011', (5 April 2010), para. 82, available at http://www.eccc.gov.kh/sites/default/files/2010-2011_Budget_Document.pdf.

[173] Rules of Procedure and Evidence of the Special Court for Sierra Leone, 16 January 2002, as amended 31 May 2012, (hereinafter SCSL Rules of Procedure and Evidence), Rule 45, available at http://www.sc-sl.org/LinkClick.aspx?fileticket=Psp%2bFh0%2bwSI%3d&tabid=176.

[174] Vincent O. Nmehielle, 'The Office Counsel for the Defence at the International Criminal Court: Sharing the Experience of the Office of the Principal Defender of the Special Court for Sierra Leone', Paper delivered at the Seminar on Defence Counsel Issues at the International Criminal Court, The Hague, The Netherlands, (31 May 2006) [paper on file with author].

[175] *See* IBA, 'Responses of the International Criminal Bar to the Registry's Draft Strategy Paper on Relations with the Counsel' (8 April 2008) [on file with author].

As was the case in Iraq, the lack of security in Libya constrains lawyers' ability to represent defendants. Amnesty International observed that few lawyers are willing to represent alleged 'Gaddafi loyalists' based on fear of reprisal.[176]

During an assessment trip to Libya in January 2013, I interviewed the Deputy Minister of Justice and the President of the Libyan Bar Association.[177] The President informed me that the Bar was unable to secure qualified attorneys to represent Saif Al-Islam Gaddafi. He was doubtful that any Libyan attorney would step up to represent him. However, the President agreed that allowing international lawyers to join on the defence team would assist in increasing the credibility of the judicial process.

In the end, this was one of the main reasons that the ICC Pre-Trial Chamber rejected Libya's latest admissibility challenge.[178] The Court concluded that Libya was 'unable genuinely to carry out the investigation or prosecution',[179] because of its failure to obtain defence counsel for Mr Gaddafi and other members of the former regime, even after extended dealings with the Libyan Law Society and the Popular Lawyers' Office[180] and reaching out to Bar Associations in Libya and Tunisia.[181]

If the Court does take jurisdiction over a case based on an Article 17 admissibility test, it will face one of its most glaring challenges - enforcing its orders and decisions. As stated earlier, the ICC has no police force and must rely on states and the international community to affect the arrest and surrender of the accused, and to enforce all other decisions of the Court. However, as discussed in the next Chapter, the international community,

---

[176] Amnesty International, 'Libya must seek justice not revenge in case of former al-Gaddafi intelligence chief', (18 October 2012), available at http://www.amnesty.org/en/news/libya-must-seek-justice-not-revenge-case-former-al-gaddafi-intelligence-chief-2012-10-18.

[177] Interview with Deputy Minister of Justice and the President of the Libyan Bar Association, (Tripoli, January 2013). *See also* ILAC, 'ILAC Rule of Law Assessment Report: Libya 2013', (9 May 2013), available at http://www.ilac.se/2013/05/09/ilac-assessment-report-libya-2013/.

[178] *The Prosecutor v. Said Al-Islam Gaddafi and Abdullah Al-Senussi*, Doc. ICC-01/11-01/11-344-Red, 'Decision on the admissibility of the case against Saif Al-Islam Gaddafi', (31 May 2013), p. 91.

[179] *Ibid.*, para. 138.

[180] *Ibid.*, paras 212-214.

[181] *Ibid.*, para. 213.

in particular the UN, has been reluctant to create effective enforcement mechanisms to assist the Court.

CHAPTER FOUR

THE PRINCIPLE OF COMPLEMENTARITY AND THE ISSUE OF ENFORCEMENT

Introduction

For complementarity to be applied meaningfully, the ICC must be seen as a competent body able to prosecute indictments and enforce Court orders in cases over which it has jurisdiction. The delicate balance between the ICC and domestic courts is strengthened when the ICC is effective. If the Court were impotent in enforcing its decisions, states would have no incentive to cooperate with and abide by the orders of the ICC. The Pre-Trial Chamber expressed this very concern when it referred Chad to the UN Security Council for failing to abide by the Court's orders:

> …it is expected that the Council would respond by way of taking such measures, which are considered appropriate, if there is an apparent failure on the part of the relevant State Party to the Statute to cooperate in fulfilling the Court's mandate entrusted to it by the Council. Otherwise, if there is no follow up action on the part of the Security Council, any referral by the Council to the ICC under Chapter VII would never achieve its ultimate goal, namely, to put an end to impunity. Accordingly, any such referral would become futile.[1]

The Court's position is easy to comprehend. The fact is that the ICC has no police force and must rely on states and the international community to affect the arrest and surrender of the accused, and to enforce all other decisions of the Court.

Part IX of the Rome Statute places a general obligation on States Parties to fully assist the ICC in the investigation and prosecution of

---

[1] *The Prosecutor v. Omar Hassan Ahmad Al Bashir*, Doc. ICC-02/05-01/09-151, 'Decision on the Non-compliance of the Republic of Chad with the Cooperation Requests Issued by the Court Regarding the Arrest and Surrender of Omar Hassan Ahmad Al Bashir', (26 March 2013), para. 22.

crimes within its jurisdiction. Any organ of the Court may request cooperation and assistance, and under Article 87(7) of the Rome Statute, failure of a State Party to comply with a request may result in a finding of non-cooperation and referral to the Assembly of States Parties (ASP) or, if the case was referred to the Court by the UN Security Council, then referral to the Council. Article 87(7) of the Rome Statute reads:

> Where a State Party fails to comply with a request to cooperate by the Court contrary to the provisions of this Statute, thereby preventing the Court from exercising its functions and powers under this Statute the Court may make a finding to that effect and refer the matter to the Assembly of States Parties, or, where the Security Council referred the matter to the Court, to the Security Council.[2]

A functioning relationship between the Security Council and the Court, especially in terms of enforcement, is vital. As some states recognised during the early stages of creating the ICC, the Court must rely on 'the constructive cooperation of the permanent members of the Security Council', who in turn would 'guarantee' the Court's jurisdiction in judging crimes against humanity, *while 'ensuring follow-up to the Court's recommendations on post-crisis situations*[3] [emphasis added]. In a 2013 report, the Court noted that:

> A referral of a situation to the Court is crucial to ensure accountability, but without the necessary follow-up in terms of ensuring cooperation, and in particular arrest and surrender of the individuals identified by the Prosecutor, justice will not be done. On the contrary, a perception of inactivity or reticence from the Council to take further measures to ensure the cases can be brought to the courtroom and the Court is not isolated, would only undermine the Court's credibility and legitimacy and *"could be seen by the international community as a lack on the Council's part of the necessary commitment to uphold the rule of law generally and accountability in particular"*.[4]

---

[2] Rome Statute of the International Criminal Court, Rome, opened for signature 17 July 1988, 2187 UNTS 90 (entered into force 1 July 2002) UN Doc. A/CONF.183/9 (hereinafter, ICC Statute or Rome Statute), Article 87(7).

[3] Contribution of H.E. Mr Paskal Milo, Albanian Minister for Foreign Affairs: United Nations Diplomatic Conference of Plenipotentiaries on the Establishment of an International Criminal Court, 'Summary Record of the 4th Plenary Meeting', UN Doc. A/CONF.183/SR.4, (16 June 1998), p. 82, para. 14.

[4] ICC-ASP, 'Report of the Court on the status of ongoing cooperation between the International Criminal Court and the United Nations, including in the field', Doc. ICC-ASP/12/42, (14 October 2013), para. 55 [emphasis added].

It is important to stress that beyond the referral provision of Article 87(7), the Court's Statute does not specify any powers or sanctions available to the ASP or the Security Council to be used against a non-cooperative state. For instance, there are no treaty provisions, policy documents, or memoranda that deal with the procedure to be followed by the Security Council when the Court refers a non-cooperative State Party. With respect to the Court, the general powers of the Security Council are derived from Chapter VII of the UN Charter. The Rome Statute itself gives Chapter VII as the source of the Security Council's authority both to refer situations to the Court, and to defer ICC investigation or prosecution of a situation for twelve months.[5] As mentioned in Chapter 1, the broad effect of Chapter VII is to confer upon the Security Council the power to take measures in response to any threat to the peace, breach of the peace, or act of aggression.[6] The measures available to the Council include but are not limited to the complete or partial interruption of economic relations (i.e., sanctions) and the severance of diplomatic relations.[7]

However, despite three Article 87(7) referrals to the Security Council, there has been **no** action taken, to date, by the Security Council against an offending state. A review of the three referrals confirms that the Security Council failed to issue even an informal or soft condemnation of the offending state.

I. A Case History: the UNSC and the ASP on the Arrest of Omar Al Bashir

The ICC has made three judicial findings of non-cooperation[8] and six referrals to the ASP and the Security Council. These include Chad (2010,

---

[5] Charter of the United Nations, (24 October 1945) 1 UNTS XVI (hereinafter UN Charter) , Articles 13(a)(b) and 16 respectively.
[6] *Ibid.*, Article 39.
[7] *Ibid.*, Article 41.
[8] The wording of Article 87(7) provides a straightforward process for the Court to make a finding of non-cooperation and then refer the matter to the ASP, or to the Security Council (if the case concerns a situation referred by a Security Council resolution). In practice, the Court has interpreted Article 87(7) as providing two different referral approaches: a referral without a formal finding of non-cooperation, and a formal finding of non-cooperation with a referral. For instance, when reviewing the case against Sudanese President Omar Al Bashir, which has clearly posed the most significant cooperation challenge before the ICC, the Court interestingly decided to inform the ASP and the Security Council of events without

2011 and 2013), Djibouti (2011), Kenya (2010), and Malawi (2011). All six referrals related to the Sudanese President Omar Al Bashir, and the failure of states to arrest him while on their territory.

The Court's first referral of non-compliance of Chad to the ASP and Security Council concerned a visit made by Al Bashir in July 2010 to Chad. The Court decided that it was 'appropriate to inform the Security Council of the United Nations as well as the Assembly of States Parties to the Rome Statute about the recent visit of Omar Al Bashir to the Republic of Chad, in order for them to take any action they may deem appropriate'.[9] There were no sanctions imposed on Chad by the ASP or UNSC.

The ICC also referred Djibouti and Kenya for failing to arrest Al Bashir when travelling in those countries.[10] In both instances the Court asked the ASP and UNSC to take whatever action they deemed appropriate, and again, no sanctions were imposed upon Djibouti or Kenya.

---

reference to a formal finding of non-cooperation. The Court simply asked the ASP and the Security Council 'to take any measure they may deem appropriate'. *See The Prosecutor v. Omar Hassan Ahmad Al Bashir,* Doc. ICC-02/05-01/09-109, 'Decision informing the United Nations Security Council and the Assembly of the States Parties to the Rome Statute about Omar Al Bashir's recent visit to the Republic of Chad', (27 August 2010); *The Prosecutor v. Omar Hassan Ahmad Al Bashir*, Doc. ICC-02/05-01/09-107, 'Decision informing the United Nations Security Council and the Assembly of the States Parties to the Rome Statute about Omar Al Bashir's presence in the territory of the Republic of Kenya', (27 August 2010); *The Prosecutor v. Omar Hassan Ahmad Al Bashir*, Doc. ICC-02/05-01/09-129, 'Decision informing the United Nations Security Council and the Assembly of the States Parties to the Rome Statute about Omar Al Bashir's recent visit to Djibouti', (12 May 2011).

[9] *See The Prosecutor v. Omar Hassan Ahmad Al Bashir,* ICC-02/05-01/09-109, 'Decision informing the United Nations Security Council and the Assembly of the States Parties to the Rome Statute about Omar Al Bashir's recent visit to the Republic of Chad', (27 August 2010).

[10] *See The Prosecutor v. Omar Hassan Ahmad Al Bashir*, Doc. ICC-02/05-01/09-107, 'Decision informing the United Nations Security Council and the Assembly of the States Parties to the Rome Statute about Omar Al Bashir's presence in the territory of the Republic of Kenya', (27 August 2010); *The Prosecutor v. Omar Hassan Ahmad Al Bashir*, Doc. ICC-02/05-01/09-129, 'Decision informing the United Nations Security Council and the Assembly of the States Parties to the Rome Statute about Omar Al Bashir's recent visit to Djibouti', (12 May 2011).

As the Court began to receive reports of Al Bashir's various state visits, the ASP, if not the Security Council, started to comprehend the seriousness of non-cooperation. The Assembly adopted the *Assembly Procedures relating to non-cooperation* ('*Procedures*') at its Tenth Session.[11] The *Procedures* provide for both a formal and informal response to non-cooperative states.[12]

In the second referral to the ASP and the Security Council against Chad, Pre-Trial Chamber I found that Al Bashir visited Chad without being arrested, despite an active ICC Warrant of Arrest against him.[13] Chad's excuse was that it was abiding by the 'common position adopted by the African Union',[14] arguing that Heads of State of non-States Parties are immune to prosecution by the Court even where such situations have been referred by the UNSC.[15] From a legal jurisprudence perspective Chad's argument was baseless. The Security Council's referral of the Sudan situation brought Al Bashir under ICC jurisdiction. Not surprisingly, the Court was aggressive in reasserting its pre-eminent position in interpreting international law. The Chamber stated forcefully that 'the Republic of Chad did not respect the sole authority of the Court to decide whether immunities are applicable in a particular case'.[16] The

[11] ICC-ASP, 'Strengthening the International Court and the Assembly of States Parties', (21 December 2011), Doc. ICC-ASP/10/Res.5, Annex, pp. 38-41.

[12] *Ibid.*, pp. 40-41. A formal response procedure must be triggered by a Court decision and enables the President of the Assembly and the Bureau to undertake specific steps to address the issue. An informal response procedure can be triggered without a Court referral of non-cooperation to the ASP.

[13] *The Prosecutor v. Omar Hassan Ahmad Al Bashir*, Doc. ICC-02/05-01/09-140-tENG, 'Decision Pursuant to Article 87(7) of the Rome Statute on the Failure by the Republic of Chad to Comply with the Cooperation Requests Issued by the Court with Respect to the Arrest and Surrender of Omar Hassan Ahmad Al Bashir' (13 December 2011), para. 2. *See also*, *The Prosecutor v. Omar Hassan Ahmad Al Bashir*, Doc. ICC-02/05-01/09-1, 'Warrant of Arrest for Omar Ahmad Al Bashir', (4 March 2009); *The Prosecutor v. Omar Hassan Ahmad Al Bashir*, Doc. ICC-02/05-01/09-95, 'Second Warrant of Arrest for Omar Hassan Ahmad Al Bashir', (12 July 2010).

[14] *The Prosecutor v. Omar Hassan Ahmad Al Bashir*, Doc. ICC-02/05-01/09-140-tENG, 'Decision Pursuant to Article 87(7) of the Rome Statute on the Failure by the Republic of Chad to Comply with the Cooperation Requests Issued by the Court with Respect to the Arrest and Surrender of Omar Hassan Ahmad Al Bashir' (13 December 2011), para. 7.

[15] *Ibid.*, para. 13.

[16] *Ibid.*, para. 10.

Court's exasperation with Chad was all too apparent. This time, it made a judicial finding of non-cooperation and immediately ordered Chad's referral to both the UNSC and the ASP.[17] However, again nothing resulted in the referral process.

In the Malawi referral, Pre-Trial Chamber I made a judicial finding that Malawi was in non-compliance for failing to arrest Al Bashir while he was in Malawi to attend an economic summit.[18] The Court referred this non-compliance to the Security Council and to the ASP. There were strong legal grounds to do so as the Security Council itself had asked the Court to assume jurisdiction over the situation in Sudan. Furthermore, the Council's request came under UNSC Resolution 1593,[19] which urged all states and regional and international organisations to cooperate with the ICC. Thus, there was no legal ambiguity that Malawi, a State Party to the Rome Statute, was under an obligation to abide by UNSC Resolution 1593.

The ICC's third referral of Chad to the UNSC and the ASP arose from a subsequent visit to Chad by Al Bashir on 16 February 2013.[20] Chad again disregarded the two Warrants of Arrest and welcomed Mr Al Bashir back to the country. The Court once again found no justification for Chad's failure to arrest Al Bashir, and Chad was again held to be in non-compliance and referred to the ASP and the UNSC.[21] No action was taken by either entity.

---

[17] *Ibid.*, para. 14.

[18] *The Prosecutor v. Omar Hassan Ahmad Al Bashir*, Doc. ICC-02/05-01/09-139, 'Decision Pursuant to Article 87(7) of the Rome Statute on the Failure by the Republic of Malawi to Comply with the Cooperation Requests Issued by the Court with Respect to the Arrest and Surrender of Omar Hassan Ahmad Al Bashir', (12 December 2011), p. 21.

[19] UN Security Council, UN Doc. S/RES/1593 (2005), (31 March 2005). The Resolution reads: 'that the Government of Sudan and all other parties to the conflict in Darfur, shall cooperate fully with and provide any necessary assistance to the Court and the Prosecutor pursuant to this resolution and, while recognizing that States not party to the Rome Statute have no obligation under the Statute, urges all States and concerned regional and other international organizations to cooperate fully'.

[20] *The Prosecutor v. Omar Hassan Ahmad Al Bashir*, Doc. ICC-02/05-01/09-151, 'Decision on the Non-compliance of the Republic of Chad with the Cooperation Requests Issued by the Court Regarding the Arrest and Surrender of Omar Hassan Ahmad Al Bashir', (26 March 2013), para. 10.

[21] *Ibid.*, para. 23.

The ICC also issued a non-cooperation decision concerning Nigeria's failure to execute the arrest warrant for Al Bashir. In this instance, the ICC decided the matter did not warrant referral to the ASP or UNSC, but reiterated Nigeria's obligations under the Rome Statute.[22]

Since the adoption of the *Procedures*, all subsequent Court decisions issued under Article 87(7) have taken the form of express judicial findings of non-cooperation. Thus, when the Court received a report of a suspect visiting a State Party, without being arrested, then the state was 'invited' to make a submission of explanation before the Court. The Court then made its decision as to whether there had been non-cooperation. This procedure has been used, to date, on four occasions: Chad (twice), Malawi, and Nigeria. All of these non-cooperation instances related to visits by Al Bashir to a State Party who refused to arrest him while on its territory. Three of these findings were also referred to the ASP or the Security Council. But why the change in procedure? I would argue that it was because the response form the Security Council on issues of non-cooperation had been dismal. As shown in the assessment above, the Security Council was negligently silent on the first three non-cooperation referrals by the Court regarding the Al Bashir matter.

Yet, under the *Procedures*, even judicial findings of non-cooperation triggering a formal response procedure have resulted in only a fairly timid response from the Assembly.[23] Practically speaking, this merely means

---

[22] *The Prosecutor v. Omar Hassan Ahmad Al Bashir*, Doc. ICC-02/05-01/09-159, 'Decision on the Cooperation of the Federal Republic of Nigeria Regarding Omar Al Bashir's Arrest and Surrender to the Court, (5 September 2013), p. 6.

[23] *Ibid.*, para. 14. 'Subsequent to the Court decision, several steps could be undertaken to address the issue, bearing in mind that the good offices by the President of the Assembly may also continue as described below:

(a) Emergency Bureau meeting: where the matter is such that urgent action by the Assembly may still bring about cooperation, a meeting of the Bureau could be convened at short notice. The meeting would be an opportunity to receive the oral report from the President on any action taken, and to decide on what further action would be required.

(b) Open letter from the President of the Assembly, on behalf of the Bureau, to the State concerned, reminding that State of the obligation to cooperate and requesting its views on the matter within a specified time limit of no more than two weeks.7 The President of the Assembly could send a copy of the letter to all States Parties, encouraging them to raise the matter in bilateral contacts with the requested State, where appropriate.

engaging in dialogue with the offending state and calling upon State Parties and stakeholders to apply pressure on the offending state. This is hardly adequate to persuade a state to abide by Court decisions. For instance, in the Malawi and Chad response procedure, the Assembly's measures against the two countries focused exclusively on reports, letters, and meetings with the countries' representatives.[24] Thus, while noting that

---

(c) Upon expiration of the time limit or upon receipt of a written response, a meeting of the Bureau could be held (at the ambassadorial level), at which a representative of the State concerned would be invited to present its views on how it would cooperate with the Court in the future.

(d) Subsequently, and provided the next session of the Assembly is scheduled to take place more than three months after the Bureau meeting referred to under (c), the Bureau could request the New York Working Group to hold a public meeting on the matter to allow for an open dialogue with the requested State. This would include the participation of States Parties, observers and civil society representatives as currently provided under the Rules of Procedure of the Assembly of States Parties.

(e) Subsequently, a Bureau report on the outcome of this dialogue could be submitted to the next (or ongoing) session of the Assembly, including a recommendation as to whether the matter requires action by the Assembly.

(f) At the next (or ongoing) session of the Assembly, the report could be discussed in plenary session of the Assembly under the agenda item on cooperation. Furthermore, the Bureau could, if necessary, appoint a dedicated facilitator to consult on a draft resolution containing concrete recommendations on the matter'.

[24] ICC-ASP, 'Report of the Bureau on non-cooperation', Doc. ICC-ASP/11/29, (1 November 2012), paras 3-11. The President of the Assembly sent letters to Chad and Malawi in accordance with paragraph 14(b) of the *Procedures*. A dialogue was developed between Malawi and the President. Malawi reaffirmed its commitment to its obligations under the Rome Statute and subsequently declined to host President Al Bashir for an African Union summit. After difficulty establishing a dialogue with Chad, the President met with its Permanent Representative to the UN, who noted:

> 'that Chad was in full compliance with international law and was cooperating with the Court. He had also referred to the decisions of the African Union on this matter, especially the decision that African Union members would not cooperate with the Court pursuant to the provisions of article 98 of the Rome Statute of the ICC relating to immunities, for the arrest and surrender of President Omar El Bashir of Sudan'.

The Bureau convened a 'special meeting to consider the two instances of non-cooperation'. The President subsequently called upon all States Parties to 'raise the decision of the Pre-Trial Chamber I in their bilateral contacts with the authorities of Chad'. The President raised the issue of non-cooperation in July 2012 with those State Parties who were currently represented in the UNSC, and again understood that no UNSC action would be forthcoming.

the formal procedure of the ASP had elicited a positive response from Malawi, the Bureau of the Assembly recognised that it had no effect on Chad.[25] On top of this, the President of the Assembly admitted that the Security Council was unlikely to take any action against the two countries.[26]

The result is that a non-cooperative state, if not sanctioned, can and will continue along a belligerent path. For example, when Al Bashir visited Nairobi in 2010, the Kenyan government failed to arrest him. Assistant Foreign Minister Richard Onyonka defended the decision, explaining that arresting Al Bashir would risk the peace in neighbouring Sudan, where 'stability is vitally linked to Kenya's continued peace and well being'.[27] The ICC referred the visit to the ASP and UNSC, but no sanctions were imposed on Kenya, despite it being a State Party to the Rome Statute and additionally obligated to cooperate by way of UNSC Resolution 1593, which originally referred the Sudan situation to the ICC.[28] In 2012 and 2013, Mr Al Bashir visited Chad three times and also visited Nigeria, a State Party to the Rome Statute.[29] The ASP response was faint-hearted.[30]

---

[25] *Ibid.*, para. 16-17.

[26] *Ibid.*, para. 11.

[27] Richard Onyonka, a Kenyan assistant foreign minister, *quoted* in 'Kenya defends failure to arrest Sudan's president Omar Al Bashir in Nairobi', *The Guardian*, (29 August 2010), available at http://www.guardian.co.uk/world/2010/aug/29/kenya-omar-al-bashir-arrest-failure.

[28] UN Security Council, UN Doc. S/RES/1593 (2005), (31 March 2005).

[29] The Court investigated Mr Al Bashir's visit to Nigeria in light of Nigerian authorities' explanations and concluded that a referral to the ASP or UNSC was not warranted, but reminded Nigeria of its obligations and requested that Nigeria immediately arrest Mr Al Bashir if a similar situation arose again. *See The Prosecutor v. Omar Hassan Ahmad Al Bashir*, Doc. ICC-02/05-01/09-159, 'Decision on the Cooperation of the Federal Republic of Nigeria Regarding Omar Al Bashir's Arrest and Surrender to the Court, (5 September 2013), p. 6.

[30] ICC-ASP, 'Report of the Bureau on non-cooperation', Doc. ICC-ASP/12/34, (7 November 2013), paras 9-16. The President of the Assembly notified States Parties, Observer States and civil society organisations upon learning of the planned visits of Mr Al Bashir and Mr Hussein, encouraging them to join the efforts to prevent non-cooperation. The President issued press releases regarding the instances of non-cooperation in Chad and Nigeria. The President wrote to and met with representatives of the requested States to discuss non-cooperation. After Mr Al Bashir's third visit to Chad, the New York Working Group met to informally discuss non-cooperation, with many delegates urging Chad to avoid

Most recently, in February 2014, Al Bashir visited the Democratic Republic of Congo (DRC) to attend a conference of the Common Market for Eastern and Southern Africa (COMESA).[31] The DRC is a State Party to the Rome Statute and is also bound to comply with the ICC in relation to the Sudan situation pursuant to UNSC Resolution 1593.[32]

The only response the President of the ASP could muster was to deplore the visit and call upon the government of the DRC to execute the outstanding arrest warrant, reminding DRC of its obligations under the Rome Statute.[33] In an almost desperate act, the President repeated calls for States Parties to join efforts to prevent non-cooperation, and reminded States Parties of Assembly Resolution ICC-ASP/12/Res.3,[34] passed at the Assembly's Twelfth session in 2013, which requires States Parties to avoid contact with fugitives 'when such contacts undermine the objectives of the Rome Statute'.[35] In short, the best that the ASP could do is to implore its own Member States to abide by the obligations of the Rome Statue, a treaty that they freely signed.

Permanent Members of the Security Council have been similarly reluctant to assist the ICC, despite having supported referral of the Sudan situation to the Court. Chinese authorities failed to arrest Al Bashir when he visited Beijing in June 2011. Foreign Ministry spokesperson, Hong Lei, said that China was 'reserving' its opinion on the ICC prosecution of Al Bashir.[36] Commentators have suggested that China's reticence may be tied to the fact that China is a 'key arms supplier' to Sudan and its 'biggest

further repetition. The Bureau continued to discuss the issue of non-cooperation and was kept informed by the President.

[31] Human Rights Watch, 'Sudan President in DR Congo' (25 February 2014), available at http://www.hrw.org/news/2014/02/25/sudan-president-dr-congo.

[32] UN Security Council, UN Doc. S/RES/1593 (2005), (31 March 2005).

[33] ICC, 'Press Release: President of the Assembly calls upon the Government of the Democratic Republic of the Congo to respect its obligations under the Rome Statute', Doc. ICC-ASP-20140226-PR984, (26 February 2014).

[34] *See* ICC-ASP, Resolution ICC-ASP/12/Res.3, (27 November 2013).

[35] ICC, 'Press Release: President of the Assembly calls upon the Government of the Democratic Republic of the Congo to respect its obligations under the Rome Statute', Doc. ICC-ASP-20140226-PR984, (26 February 2014).

[36] 'UN Criticises China's Failure to Arrest Sudan's Bashir', *Voice of America*, (30 June 2011), available at http://www.voanews.com/english/news/africa/east/UN-Criticizes-Chinas-Failure-to-Arrest-Sudans-Bashir---124771729.html.

purchaser of oil'.[37] The continued lack of response, however, only emboldened Sudan to ignore the ICC.

To date, the Security Council has been deaf to the Court's concerns about enforcement. While its inaction is not surprising given the political dynamics that dominate the Security Council, it is particularly frustrating in cases (i.e., Sudan) where the ICC's jurisdiction originated from a Security Council referral. So long as the Security Council fails to act on ICC referrals, the Court will remain shackled in its dealings with non-cooperative states. This dynamic, unfortunately, weakens the principle of complementarity. If states do not believe that the Court has power to enforce its own decisions, they will neither fear the consequences of inaction, nor have incentives to work with the ICC in carrying out domestic prosecutions.

The UN Security Council's complete inertia towards referred instances of non-cooperation is alarming for another reason. States Parties are obligated to cooperate with the ICC under Article 87(7) of the Rome Statute, which they have signed and ratified. Furthermore, **all** UN Member States are obligated to cooperate with the ICC in relation to the Sudan situation under the terms of UNSC Resolution 1593. Thus, a state's non-cooperation constitutes a breach of international law, whether by treaty for States Parties, or by resolution for UN Member States. By disregarding all findings of non-cooperation to date, the Security Council is effectively sanctioning these sane breaches of international law.[38]

II. *Ad hoc* Tribunals: the ICTY and ICTR

The struggle to secure support from the UN Security Council against non-cooperative states is not limited to the ICC. The Security Council's

---

[37] *Ibid.*

[38] This breach has only recently been recognised by the international community. In November 2013, the EU Council Working Group on Public International Law (COJUR) published a note to delegations on the EU's response to third states' non-compliance with the ICC, wherein the COJUR-ICC Working Party observed that '[n]on-cooperation by a Rome Statute State Party not only undermines the Court but also constitutes a breach of a legal obligation' and that non-States Parties would also be under a legal obligation where UNSC referred a situation to the ICC and requested cooperation. *See* Council of the European Union, 'Note from International Criminal Court Sub-area of the Public International Law Working Group (COJUR-ICC) to Delegations', Doc. 16993/13, (27 November 2013).

apathetic stance toward international war crimes courts started with the ICTY and ICTR.

A. ICTY

Just like the ICC or any other international court, the ICTY depends on state cooperation to fulfil its mandate. It has no police force or enforcement body, and must rely upon states to execute Court orders, including arrest warrants. However, by the authority of the UN Charter, state cooperation is binding upon all UN Member States since the ICTY was established through Chapter VII.[39] States are required to cooperate with the Tribunal 'without undue delay with any request for assistance…'.[40] This mandate is much stronger than the treaty-based obligations of State parties to the ICC. The Security Council obligates **all** states to cooperate with the Tribunal. Thus, if a state fails to comply with an ICTY order, the Court can directly and immediately notify the Security Council and request action.[41]

Yet, the ICTY's Statute and Rules of Procedure and Evidence do not mandate the Security Council to take action or employ sanctions against uncooperative states. Not surprisingly, the history of the Council in this regard is one of inaction.

Despite the fact that all 161 indicted suspects have now been arrested, the ICTY faced considerable hurdles in its early years. The Court's history is largely defined by the obstructionism of Republika Srpska, Serbia and

---

[39] UN Security Council, UN Doc. S/RES/827 (1993), (25 May 1993).

[40] Statute of the International Tribunal for the Prosecution of Persons Responsible for Serious Violations of International Humanitarian Law Committed in the Territory of the former Yugoslavia since 1991, UN Doc. S/RES/827(1993) (hereinafter ICTY Statute), Article 29, reads, in part:

1. 'States shall co-operate with the International Tribunal in the investigation and prosecution of persons accused of committing serious violations of international humanitarian law.

2. States shall comply without undue delay with any request for assistance or an order issued by a Trial Chamber, including, but not limited to:

(a) the identification and location of persons;

(b) the taking of testimony and the production of evidence;

(c) the service of documents;

(d) the arrest or detention of persons;

(e) the surrender or the transfer of the accused to the International Tribunal'.

[41] ICTY Rules of Procedure and Evidence, Rule 7*bis*.

Croatia.[42] By 1997, four years after its creation, the Court had only eight individuals in custody.[43] These numbers hint at the challenges the Court faced in dealing with the newly formed states of the former Yugoslavia.[44] The General Assembly was well aware of the pervasive uncooperative policies taken by Croatia, Republika Srpska, and Serbia.[45] The Court's President, Fausto Pocar, described as a key problem 'systematic obstruction' by the army of Serbia and Montenegro with regard to documents sought by the ICTY Office of the Prosecutor, including the missing wartime archives of Republika Srpska, allegedly hidden or moved to Serbia.[46]

In 2008 Serge Brammertz, the ICTY Prosecutor at the time, called on the Security Council to endorse his call for full state cooperation, including and especially states of the former Yugoslavia, to bring to justice the remaining fugitives hiding in Serbian territory.[47]

On multiple occasions the ICTY reported acts of non-cooperation to the Security Council, with limited Council response.[48] The only course of

---

[42] ICC-ASP, 'Arresting Fugitives from International Justice and Other Aspects of State Cooperation: Insights from ICTY Experience, address given by Serge Brammertz to the International Criminal Court Assembly of State Parties', (16 November 2012), (hereinafter 'Arresting Fugitives: Address by Serge Brammertz'), p. 4, available at http://www.icc-cpi.int/iccdocs/asp_docs/ASP11/ICC-ASP11-COOP-Keynote_Remarks-Brammertz-ENG.pdf.

[43] ICTY, 'The Fugitives', (2014), available at http://www.icty.org/sid/10010.

[44] ICC-ASP, 'Arresting Fugitives: Address by Serge Brammertz', p. 4.

[45] United States, 'Statement before the UN General Assembly', UN Doc. A/52/PV.44, (4 November 1997), p. 16.

[46] UN Security Council, UN Doc. S/2005/781, 'Letter dated 30 November 2005 from the President of the International Tribunal for the Prosecution of Persons Responsible for Serious Violations of International Humanitarian Law Committed in the Territory of the former Yugoslavia since 1991, addressed to the President of the Security Council', (14 December 2005), paras 25-26.

[47] *See* UN Security Council, UN Doc. SC/9347, 'Mandate of Former Yugoslavia Tribunal Will Not Be Fully Achieved Without Arrest, Trial of Four Remaining Fugitives, Could Told', (4 June 2008).

[48] *See* UN Security Council, UN Doc. S/1999/1117, 'Letter dated 2 November 1999 from the President of the International Tribunal for the Prosecution of Persons Responsible for Serious Violations of International Humanitarian Law Committed in the Territory of the former Yugoslavia since 1991, addressed to the President of the Security Council' (2 November 1999). ICTY President Gabrielle Kirk McDonald, addressed continued State non-cooperation. Attached to the letter

action taken by Security Council was to adopt resolutions or release statements urging states to cooperate with the Court.[49] The Council did not take any new action, even in response to pressing ICTY notifications of state non-cooperation. In a remarkable admission, Serge Brammertz admitted that his office had reluctantly decided not to even bother with Rule 7 *bis* referrals to the Security Council because they simply were not a reliable way to achieve cooperation from states and had failed to produce any positive outcomes.[50]

B. ICTR

The ICTR was created by a UNSC Chapter VII resolution,[51] and its Statute contains provisions almost identical to the ICTY's regarding judicial cooperation and non-compliance.[52] However, unlike the ICTY, the

---

is a table detailing all Presidential letters to UNSC reporting non-cooperation, states concerned, and UNSC action in response.

[49] *See* e.g. UN Security Council, UN Doc. S/RES/1503 (2003) (28 August 2003); UN Security Council, UN Doc. S/RES/1534 (2004) (26 March 2004); UN Security Council, UN Doc. S/RES/1966 (2010) (22 December 2010); UN Security Council, UN Doc. S/PRST/1996/23 (8 May 1996); UN Security Council, UN Doc. S/PRST/1996/34 (8 August 1996); UN Security Council, UN Doc. S/PRST/1996/39 (20 September 1996); UN Security Council, UN Doc. S/PRST/2002/39 (18 December 2002).

[50] ICC-ASP, 'Arresting Fugitives: Address by Serge Brammertz', p. 2-3.

[51] UN Security Council, UN Doc. S/RES/955 (1994) (6 November 1994).

[52] Statute of the International Criminal Tribunal for Rwanda, UN Doc. S/RES/955 (1994) (6 November 1994) (hereinafter ICTR Statute).

> **'Article 28: Cooperation and Judicial Assistance**
>
> 1. States shall cooperate with the International Tribunal for Rwanda in the investigation and prosecution of persons accused of committing serious violations of international humanitarian law.
>
> 2. States shall comply without undue delay with any request for assistance or an order issued by a Trial Chamber, including but not limited to:
>
> (a) The identification and location of persons;
> (b) The taking of testimony and the production of evidence;
> (c) The service of documents;
> (d) The arrest or detention of persons;
> (e) The surrender or the transfer of the accused to the International Tribunal for Rwanda'.

Rules of Procedure and Evidence of the International Criminal Tribunal for Rwanda, Revision 19, (10 April 2013), UN Doc. ITR/3/Rev. 19 (2013), (hereinafter ICTR Rules of Procedure and Evidence):

ICTR has rarely referred a non-cooperation situation to the UNSC pursuant to Rule 7 *bis*,[53] despite numerous opportunities to do so.[54] For instance, Rwanda suspended its cooperation with ICTR on several occasions.[55] Still, the Court rarely turned to the Security Council with a referral. When there was a referral, the UNSC simply reaffirmed its support for the ICTR and recalled Rwanda's mandatory obligation to

---

'**Rule 7 *bis*: Non Compliance with Obligations**

(A) Except in cases to which Rules 11, 13, 59 or 61 applies, where a Trial Chamber or a Judge is satisfied that a State has failed to comply with an obligation under Article 28 of the Statute relating to any proceedings before that Chamber or Judge, the Chamber or Judge may request the President to report the matter to the Security Council.

(B) If the Prosecutor satisfies the President that a State has failed to comply with an obligation under Article 28 of the Statute in respect of a request by the Prosecutor under Rules 8 or 40, the President shall notify the Security Council thereof'.

[53] *See* UN Security Council, 'Letter dated 26 July 2002 from the President of the International Tribunal for the Prosecution of Persons Responsible for Serious Violations of International Humanitarian Law Committed in the Territory of Rwanda and Rwandan Citizens Responsible for Genocide and Other Such Violations Committed in the Territory of Neighbouring States between 1 January and 31 December 1994 addressed to the President of the Security Council', UN Doc. S/2002/847, (29 July 2002). *See also* UN Security Council, 'Letter dated 28 May 2010 from the President of the International Criminal Tribunal for Rwanda addressed to the President of the Security Council', UN Doc. S/2010/259, (28 May 2010) para. 69, which references another report of non-cooperation.

[54] *See* Victor Peskin, *International Justice in Rwanda and the Balkans: Virtual Trials in the Struggle for State Cooperation*, (Cambridge: Cambridge University Press, 2009), pp. 151-153; Lars Waldorf, '"A Mere Pretence of Justice": Complementarity, Sham Trials, and Victor's Justice at the Rwanda Tribunal', (2011) 33 *Fordham International Law Journal* 1221, 1228-1238.

[55] *See* e.g. 'Rwanda was right to suspend cooperation, says its envoy to UN court', *Hirondelle News Agency*, (18 January 2000), available at http://www.hirondellenews.com/ictr-rwanda/407-collaboration-with-states/collaboration-with-states-rwanda/17400-en-en-rwanda-was-right-to-suspend-cooperation-says-its-envoy-to-un-court64516451. *See also*, Waldorf, 'A Mere Pretense of Justice', 1230; Martin Ngoga, 'The Institutionalisation of Impunity: A Judicial Perspective on the Rwandan Genocide' in Phil Clark and Zachary D. Kaufman (eds.), *After Genocide: Transitional Justice, Post-Conflict Reconstruction and Reconciliation in Rwanda and Beyond*, (Columbia: Columbia University Press, 2009), pp. 328-322; Thierry Cruvellier, *Court of Remorse: Inside the International Criminal Tribunal for Rwanda*, (Madison: The University of Wisconsin Press, 2010), pp. 102-114; Peskin, *International Justice in Rwanda and the Balkans*, pp. 170-185.

cooperate[56] based on a Memorandum of Understanding with the UN signed in 1999,[57] and on a 2010 restatement of its commitment to cooperate with the ICTR.[58] In 2010, in response to a formal report of Kenya's non-cooperation regarding the fugitive Felicien Kabuga, the Security Council issued Resolution 1932 calling on all states to intensify cooperation with the ICTR in order to bring Kabuga to justice.[59] Four years later Kabuga remains at large.

III. International Pressure

As discussed in Chapter 2, the most effective way to bring to account those who commit international crimes is by securing the cooperation of nation states; this is the essence of complementarity. In this context, the importance of *political will* cannot be overstated. Complementarity is intended categorically to ensure that justice is perfected at the national level **or** through an international court. However, when domestic political will falters, international pressure is essential. But what type of international pressure is needed and what forms of political pressure have worked or failed?

In the case of the ICTY and the ICTR international pressure never materialised from the Security Council. As stated earlier, although both Courts' Statutes prescribe referral to the Council for uncooperative states, the experience of these courts shows that such a prescription was ultimately ineffective; referrals resulted in either no response at all, or in the adoption of useless resolutions and statements urging state cooperation. Either way, they had no effect in eliciting state cooperation.

Another type of international pressure does seem to be effective. Absent sufficient political will, pressure from other states, from regional organisations such as the European Union or North Atlantic Treaty

---

[56] UN Security Council, UN Doc. S/PRST/2002/39 (18 December 2002).

[57] 'Memorandum of Understanding between the United Nations and the Republic of Rwanda to Regulate Matters of Mutual Concern Relating to the Office in Rwanda of the International Tribunal for Rwanda', (3 June 1999), available at http://www.unictr.org/Portals/0/English/agreements/rwanda090603.pdf.

[58] ICTY, UN Doc. ICTR/INFO-9-2-645.EN, 'Rwanda and the ICTR Reaffirm their Cooperation', (30 June 2010), available at http://www.unictr.org/tabid/155/Default.aspx?id=1147.

[59] UN Security Council, UN Doc. S/RES/1932 (2010) (29 June 2010).

Organisation (NATO), or from NGOs can influence state cooperation in bringing perpetrators to account for their crimes.

Simple *realpolitik* based on state self-interest has proved most effective in achieving compliance. For example, in June 2012, Malawi's new President, Joyce Banda, refused to host the Sudanese President at a scheduled African Union (AU) Summit. The AU subsequently selected another host country. Malawi was concerned that if it welcomed Al Bashir, the international community might cut off badly needed economic aid.[60] The tactic worked. Britain agreed to work directly with the Reserve Bank of Malawi and pledged £20 million to help stabilise the economy. Earlier in June 2012, the International Monetary Fund (IMF) agreed to a $157 million aid package.[61]

The role that other forms of international pressure played in forcing states to cooperate with the ICTY is the strongest indication that a coordinated international approach to enforcement can work. The ambivalence of key entities, such as NATO, stymied the progress in creating the ICTY and revealed an unwillingness to pursue war crimes suspects.[62] For more than a decade, Radovan Karadžić and General Ratko Mladić—both indicted for their roles in the Srebrenica massacre—avoided capture and were protected by the Serbian government.[63] The international community bore some responsibility for this injustice. The NATO-led Implementation Force in Bosnia-Herzegovina (IFOR) was initially not allowed to pursue indicted war criminals. As Justice Richard J. Goldstone

---

[60] 'Malawi Cancels AU Summit Hosting over Sudan's Invite', *Al Jazeera,* (9 June 2012) available at http://www.aljazeera.com/news/africa/2012/06/20126974132905285.html.

[61] International Monetary Fund (IMF), 'IMF Mission and Malawi Authorities Reach Staff-Level Understandings on a New ECF-Supported Program', Press Release No. 12/205, (6 June 2012), available at http://www.imf.org/external/np/sec/pr/2012/pr12205.htm; Raphael Tenthani, 'Malawi Says No to Sudanese Leader, AU Says No to Summit', *Associated Press* (8 June 2012) available at http://www.alamogordonews.com/alamogordo-news/ci_20812516/malawi-says-no-sudanese-leader-au-says-no.

[62] *See* Mark S. Ellis, 'Combating Impunity and Enforcing Accountability as a Way To Promote Peace and Stability – The Role of International War Crimes Tribunals' (2006) 2 *Journal of National Security Law & Policy*, 111, 142-143.

[63] *See* David Rhode and Nicholas Wood, '10 Years Later, Tormenting Memories of Srebrenica', *New York Times* (8 July 2005) available at http://query.nytimes.com/gst/fullpage.html?res=9C03E0DB153DF933A25754C0A9639C8B63.

noted, 'NATO failed in 1995 and 1996 to apprehend the two men—there was no *international political will* to do it'.[64] The failure to bring these men to justice caused a rift in the local community, destabilised Bosnia, weakened the ICTY's mandate, and hindered the restoration of peace and security in the region.[65] Only later was IFOR given authority to make arrests.

However, international pressure once applied led to the eventual arrests of Radovan Karadžić, Ratko Mladić, and Goran Hadžić, the last remaining ICTY fugitives. It is true that the arrest of Mr Karadžić occurred two weeks after a new pro-European Government was formed in Belgrade.[66] This supports the argument that political will is a critically important factor in achieving accountability. However, there is no doubt that incentives and threatened sanctions by the European Union helped induce Serbia to make the arrests. Serbia's accession to the EU was expressly conditioned on full cooperation, with the Council of Europe concluding that the best proof of such would be the arrest of the remaining fugitives.[67] Serge Brammertz, ICTY Prosecutor, reported to the EU on Serbia's cooperation with the ICTY in order for the EU to evaluate progress in meeting that condition.[68] EU Member States also applied pressure. Although Serbia initialled a Stabilisation and Accession Agreement in 2007, some EU Member States refused to ratify the SAA until full cooperation was established.[69] The European Parliament postponed

---

[64] Telephone Interview with Justice Richard J. Goldstone, former Chief Prosecutor for the ICTY and the ICTR (6 August 2004) [emphasis added].

[65] *Ibid.*

[66] *See* a discussion on Serbia's views on the ICTY in Diane F. Orentlicher, *Shrinking the Space for Denial: The Impact on the ICTY in Serbia* (Open Society Justice Initiative, 2008).

[67] Expressly stated to be a condition of the 'Stabilisation and Association Agreement between the European Communities and its Members States and the Republic of Serbia', ECS No. 1(2010) (29 April 2008) and the 'Interim Agreement on Trade and Trade-related matters between the European Community and the Republic of Serbia' (30 January 2012) 28 *Official Journal of the European Union*. *See* e.g. Council of the European Union, 'Conclusions on Serbia', (25 October 2012) available at
http://www.eutrio.be/files/bveu/media/source1854/documents/Lien/10-25_Conclusion_Serbia_EN.pdf.

[68] ICC-ASP, 'Arresting Fugitives: Address by Serge Brammertz', p. 15.

[69] *See* in particular the expressed positions of the United Kingdom (United Kingdom Parliament), 'EU and Serbia', (3 November 2010), available at

ratification of an Interim Trade Agreement until full cooperation was achieved. The United States also suspended aid to Serbia in 2005 because of its failure to cooperate with the ICTY.[70]

In the week prior to Mladić's arrest, the ICTY Prosecutor submitted a report to the Security Council noting that Serbia's efforts to apprehend him had been inadequate, and that Mladić's capture was Serbia's 'most critical outstanding obligation' to date.[71] This report was issued at a time when neighbouring Croatia was poised to conclude its own EU membership talks. NGOs, such as Human Rights Watch, called on the EU to maintain pressure on Serbia to fully cooperate with the ICTY.[72] Following the Mladić arrest, the EU Commissioner for Enlargement, Štefan Füle, stated, '[a] great obstacle on the Serbian road to the EU has

---

http://www.publications.parliament.uk/pa/cm201011/cmselect/cmeuleg/428-vi/428vi13.htm); the Netherlands ('Dutch block EU-Serbia trade deal', *BBC News*, (16 September 2008), available at http://news.bbc.co.uk/1/hi/7618275.stm); and Belgium ('Belgium vows to block EU shift on Serbia', *Reuters*, (28 February 2007), available at http://www.reuters.com/article/2007/02/28/us-serbia-belgium-idUSL2746615720070228).

[70] *See* International Crisis Group, 'Update Briefing: Serbia: Spinning its Wheels', Europe Briefing No. 39, (23 May 2005), p. 1, available at http://www.crisisgroup.org/~/media/Files/europe/b039_serbia___spinning_its_wheels.pdf.

[71] UN Security Council, UN Doc. S/2011/316, 'Letter dated 12 May 2011 from the President of the International Tribunal for the Prosecution of Persons Responsible for Serious Violations of International Humanitarian Law Committed in the Territory of the former Yugoslavia since 1991, addressed to the President of the Security Council', (18 May 2011), para. 44.

[72] *See* Human Rights Watch, 'Concern Over EU Approach to Serbia's Cooperation With ICTY', (27 March 2007), available at http://www.hrw.org/news/2007/03/26/concern-over-eu-approach-serbia-s-cooperation-icty; Human Rights Watch, 'Council of Europe: Require Serbia to Turn Over Fugitives', (4 May 2007), available at http://www.hrw.org/news/2007/05/03/council-europe-require-serbia-turn-over-fugitives; Human Rights Watch 'Council of Europe: Hold Serbia to Account', (7 May 2007), available at http://www.hrw.org/news/2007/05/06/council-europe-hold-serbia-account; *see also* Amnesty International, 'Amnesty International's concerns and Serbia and Montenegro's commitments to the Council of Europe', (3 March 2004), available at http://www.amnesty.org/en/library/asset/EUR70/002/2004/en/ea2cda42-d63d-11dd-ab95-a13b602c0642/eur700022004en.html.

been removed'.[73] Then, in response to the Hadžić arrest, the ICTY Prosecutor commented that the two arrests 'mark a long-awaited step forward in Serbia's cooperation with the Tribunal. Serbia has now produced visible evidence that cooperation with the Tribunal is not an empty promise but a genuine commitment . . .'.[74] With these final two arrests, the ICTY had achieved the arrest of all 161 indicted persons, and notably, the Serbian authorities captured the last four ICTY fugitives – Radovan Karadžić, Stojan Župljanin, Ratko Mladić, and Goran Hadžić.[75] International pressure had an effect on Serbia, where the government finally overcame perceptions of indifference to impunity and facilitated the arrest of these high-level suspects.[76] Shortly thereafter, the European Commission recommended Serbia for candidate status.[77]

International pressure was also brought to bear against Croatia. Croatia's keen desire to join the EU was signalled by its willingness to negotiate a Stabilisation and Association Agreement as the first step toward EU membership. The EU Commission made it clear, however, that accession was conditioned on Croatia's full cooperation with the ICTY. As EU Enlargement Commissioner Olli Rehn stated:

> The Commission has delivered its part of the job in timely fashion. Now it is up to the Croatian authorities to prove that they fully cooperate with the tribunal in The Hague. If the Commission were to give its recommendation on the basis of today's information, I could not recommend opening negotiations with Croatia. I trust the Croatian government will take this message seriously. There is no shortcut to Europe, just the regular road, which means the respect of the rule of law.[78]

---

[73] European Commission, 'Statement by Commissioner Štefan Füle following the arrest of the former Bosnian Serb General Ratko Mladić', (26 May 2011), available at http://ec.europa.eu/commission_2010-2014/fule/headlines/news/2011/05/20110526_en.htm.

[74] ICTY, 'Statement of the Office of the Prosecutor of ICTY on the arrest of Goran Hadžić' (20 July 2011), available at http://www.icty.org/sid/10734.

[75] *See* ICTY, 'The Fugitives'.

[76] *See* Ellis, 'Combating Impunity and Enforcing Accountability', 145–146.

[77] The Delegation of the European Union to the Republic of Serbia, 'Serbia and the European Union', (2014) available at http://www.europa.rs/en/srbija-i-evropska-unija.html. *See also* ICC-ASP, 'Arresting Fugitives: Address by Serge Brammertz', p. 15.

[78] European Commission, 'Croatia - One Step Closer to the EU, Provided There Is Full Cooperation with ICTY', (31 January 2005), available at http://europa.eu/rapid/press-release_IP-05-110_en.htm?locale=en.

The then ICTY Prosecutor, Carla Del Ponte, sought to link accession talks to the extradition of Ante Gotovina.[79] Gotovina was Croatia's most wanted war crimes suspect and had been on the run for nearly four years. Like Mladić and Karadžić in Serbia, Gotovina was hailed in Croatia as a war hero. Four out of five Croats viewed his wartime activities as those of a patriot.[80] The EU, however, stood firm in its position that Gotovina must be handed over to the ICTY if Croatia wanted EU membership. Luxembourg's Foreign Minister, Jean Asselborn, whose country held the EU presidency, issued a warning to Croatia: '[w]e are in a crucial moment . . . [W]e need to see that Croatia is cooperating fully with the international court, that's a very clear and unambiguous message'.[81] EU Enlargement Commissioner Olli Rehn added, '[i]f there is no progress from the Croatian side, we are ready to postpone the start of talks'.[82]

The Croatian government had long maintained that it had no information regarding the whereabouts of ICTY indictees within its borders.[83] As a result of Croatia's continued indifference toward the ICTY, the EU refused even to *begin* accession talks.[84] It is interesting to note that the United States was not enthusiastic about conditioning EU accession on the arrest of Gotovina. In a cable revealed by Wikileaks, the US urged the EU to 'make Croatia's ICTY cooperation a *closing* rather than *opening* benchmark' for EU accession.[85] The US had a greater interest in protecting

---

[79] *See* Jamie Sterling, 'ICTY Prosecutor calls for EU pressure on Croatia, Serbia on war crimes suspects', *Jurist* (1 September 2005), available at http://jurist.law.pitt.edu/paperchase/2005/09/icty-prosecutor-calls-for-eu-pressure.php.

[80] *See* Ian Traynor, 'EU tells Croatia to find fugitive general, or forget about joining', *Taipei Times* (12 March 2005), at 9, available at http://www.taipeitimes.com/News/editorials/archives/2005/03/12/2003245943.

[81] 'EU renews pressure on Croatia over fugitive general', *EU Business* (21 February 2005), available at http://www.eubusiness.com/Croatia/050221115811.gv563lv4.

[82] *Ibid.*

[83] Dora Rotar, 'Croatian Accession to the EU: Political Battles and Legal Challenges', *Jurist*, (16 May 2012) available at http://jurist.org/dateline/2012/05/dora-rotar-croatia-eu.php.

[84] *See* EU-Croatia Portal, 'EU-Croatia', (2014) available at http://www.eu-croatia.org/eu-croatia.

[85] Ivan Carpio, '2009 Wikileaks Cable Reveals US Support of Croatia's EU Bid Despite ICTY Opposition', (2011) 18 *Human Rights Brief*, 51 [emphasis added].

the Croatian government and was eager to see the country move successfully towards accession.[86]

Fortunately, pressure by the EU prevailed and the Croatian Government slowly yielded. On 3 October 2005, the then ICTY Prosecutor, Carla Del Ponte, reported that 'Croatia [was] responding in a satisfactory manner to all [her] requests'.[87] She admitted, however, that 'Croatia and Serbia and Montenegro . . . [had] been cooperating with the tribunal only thanks to the international pressure'.[88] The clearest evidence that outside political pressure is essential to reversing a government's policy of impunity was provided by the actual arrest of Ante Gotovina, on 7 December 2005, by Croatian authorities.[89]

With regards to the ICC, States Parties often lack the resources to effect enforcement. For instance, Joseph Kony was indicted on 8 July 2005. However, he has continued to evade capture. African states have identified that the lack of aircraft is one of the 'major obstacles' in the search for Kony and other LRA leaders. In a recent effort to assist the Ugandan government, the United States announced the deployment of military aircraft and more special forces.[90] Given that the ICC has no police force nor is it an actual enforcement body, international pressure is critical to ensuring that fugitives are arrested and surrendered to the Court.

---

[86] *Ibid.*

[87] ICTY-Office of the Prosecutor, 'Assessment by the Prosecutor of the Co-operation Provided by Croatia', (3 October 2005), available at http://www.icty.org/sid/8535.

[88] Emma Thomasson, 'EU Must Push Serbia, Croatia on Suspects—Del Ponte', *RedOrbit* (1 September 2005), available at http://www.redorbit.com/news/international/227022/eu_must_push_serbia_croatia_on_suspectsdel_ponte/index.html; *see also* 'Balkan war crimes pressure on EU', *BBC News* (1 September 2005), available at http://news.bbc.co.uk/2/hi/europe/4206730.stm; James Kanter, 'EU Threatens to Freeze Talks with Serbia, Ministers Demand Arrest of Mladic', *International Herald Tribune* (28 February 2006).

[89] *See* 'Croatian fugitive general seized', *BBC News* (8 December 2005), available at http://news.bbc.co.uk/2/hi/europe/4510122.stm; *see also* Nicholas Wood, 'Croats Case Offers Guide to Finding Bosnian Serb Fugitives', *New York Times* (2 January 2006), available at http://www.nytimes.com/2006/01/02/international/europe/02croatia.html?_r=0.

[90] 'Joseph Kony: US military planes to hunt LRA leader', *BBC News* (24 March 2014) available at http://www.bbc.co.uk/news/world-africa-26712774.

Liberia is another example of how international pressure can play a positive role in ensuring accountability. For more than three years, the deposed Liberian dictator Charles Taylor, accused of war crimes and crimes against humanity, lived in exile in Nigeria, avoiding extradition to the UN-backed Special War Crimes Court for Sierra Leone. He remained free because of an internationally brokered deal to offer him refuge in hopes of ending Liberia's long civil war. Despite an arrest warrant from the Special Court of Sierra Leone, then Nigerian President Olusegun Obasanjo refused to comply with the extradition request.[91]

When Ellen Johnson Sirleaf was elected Liberia's new President in 2006, she initially refused Taylor's extradition because of her fear of violence and her view that the issue was of 'low priority'.[92] However, under intense international political pressure, including a threat by the US Congress to withhold aid to Liberia and to pressure Nigeria, President Johnson Sirleaf finally requested, and Nigeria agreed to, Taylor's extradition.[93]

International pressure can also be exerted when there is an international presence in the state in question. This was the case in Kosovo where the European Union created the European Union Rule of Law Mission in Kosovo (EULEX).[94] EULEX is the largest civilian mission ever launched

---

[91] *See* Lydia Polgreen and Marc Lacey, 'Nigeria Will End Asylum for Warlord', *New York Times* (26 March 2006), available at http://www.nytimes.com/2006/03/26/international/africa/26taylor.html.

[92] *See* Lydia Polgreen, 'Nigeria Says Ex-President of Liberia Has Disappeared', *New York Times*, (29 March 2006), available at http://www.nytimes.com/2006/03/29/international/africa/29liberia.html.

[93] *Ibid.*

[94] *See* the website for the European Union Rule of Law Mission (EULEX) Kosovo, available at http://www.eulex-kosovo.eu/en/front/. The legal basis for EULEX under European Law is the Council Joint Action 2008/124/CFSP of 4 February 2008 on the European Union Rule of Law Mission in Kosovo, OJ 2008 L No. 42 92. The joint action has been amended three times: Council Joint Action 2009/445/CFSP of 9 June 2009 amending Joint Action 2008/124/CFSP on the European Union Rule of Law Mission in Kosovo, OJ 2009 L No. 148 33; Council Decision 2010/322/CFSP of 8 June 2010 Amending and Extending Joint Action 2008/124/CFSP, OJ 2010 L No. 145; and Council Decision 2012/291/CFSP of 5 June 2012 amending an extending Joint Action 2008/124/CFSP on the European Union Rule of Law Mission in Kosovo, OJ 2012 L No. 146 46. Ultimately, however, EULEX has its mandate from UN Security Council Resolution 1244 (1999), which established the UN Interim Administration Mission in Kosovo

under the Common Security and Defence Policy. It is present to assist the Kosovo authorities in maintaining the rule of law through support of the police and judiciary. To this end it has its own police and judicial arms and comprises more than three thousand staff. The policing arm of EULEX exists to offer technical support to the Kosovo authorities (through monitoring, mentoring, and advising) in addition to *ensuring the arrest of persons guilty of war crimes in Kosovo*. According to its mandate, EULEX becomes directly involved only as a matter of strict necessity when the Kosovo authorities have failed to, or are unable to, act.

EULEX made its mark earlier in the process. EULEX immediately arrested nine alleged war criminals in March 2011 for their part in the 1998-1999 war in Kosovo.[95] By November 2013, fifteen more people were indicted for war crimes by EULEX prosecutors.[96] In addition, EULEX issued an arrest warrant for Fatmir Limaj, a former member of the KLA, who has claimed immunity from arrest based on his position as Deputy in the Kosovo Assembly.[97] EULEX had also actively pushed the Kosovo Assembly to clarify the immunity question in order to clear the way for Limaj's prosecution.[98] In a clear sign of domestic support for accountability, Kosovo's Constitutional Court ruled that government officials '[did] not enjoy immunity from prosecution for actions and decisions taken outside the scope of their responsibilities'.[99] Although Fatmir Limaj was later

---

(UNMIK). Since its creation, EULEX has subsumed most of UNMIK's roles, most notably those relating to civil law and order under paragraphs 9(d) and 11(i)–(k) of UN Security Council Resolution 1244. *See* UN Security Council, UN Doc. S/RES/1244 (1999) (10 June 1999).

[95] *See* EULEX Kosovo, 'EULEX Makes Arrests in War Crime Case' (16 March 2011), available at http://www.eulex-kosovo.eu/en/pressreleases/0125.php

[96] 'EULEX Kosovo prosecutor indicts 15 people for war crimes', *Jurist*, (8 November 2013) available at http://jurist.org/paperchase/2013/11/sprk-indicts-15-for-war-crimes-at-kla-detention-center-in-1998.php.

[97] *See* EULEX Kosovo, 'Statement on War Crimes Arrests' (17 March 2011), available at http://www.eulex-kosovo.eu/en/pressreleases/0126.php.

[98] *See* P. Collaku and A. Mustafa, 'EULEX Urges Limaj to Face War Crimes Trial', *Balkan Insight*, (15 July 2011) available at http://www.balkaninsight.com/en/article/eulex-asked-limaj-to-resign-and-face-war-crime-trial.

[99] M. Brajshori, 'Fatmir Limaj under house arrest after Kosovo court ruled on immunity', *SE Times*, (24 September 2011), available at http://www.setimes.com/cocoon/setimes/xhtml/en_GB/features/setimes/features/2011/09/24/feature-02.

acquitted,[100] the immunity issue pressed by the EULEX was well established. In January 2014, a politician handed himself over voluntarily and was arrested on suspicion of war crimes against ethnic Albanians.[101]

EULEX's overall impact on ensuring accountability in Kosovo has been impressive. According to Bernd Borchardt, EULEX Head of Mission, EULEX inherited 1200 war crimes cases from the previous UN mission project in Kosovo (UN Interim Administration Mission in Kosovo). A number of the cases were closed or dismissed due to lack of evidence. However, EULEX initiated fifty-one new war crimes cases, including investigations into cases where acts of sexual violence or rape have been assessed as war crimes. Currently, Kosovo and EULEX prosecutors are investigating more than one hundred war-crimes cases, with a number of ongoing war crimes trials.[102]

The Kosovo example, like Malawi, Serbia, Croatia, and Liberia, underscores the importance of international political pressure. The current international legal framework, strengthened by the principle of complementarity, is a necessary but insufficient basis for achieving accountability for war crimes. The international community must also play a role in enforcing Court orders, including arrest warrants, and be willing to use incentives and sanctions as needed in cases of non-compliance.

---

[100] 'Kosovo politician again acquitted of war crimes charges', *Jurist,* (18 September 2013) available at http://jurist.org/paperchase/2013/09/kosovo-politician-again-acquitted-of-war-crimes-charges.php.

[101] 'Kosovo Serb politician Oliver Ivanovic arrested over war crimes' *BBC News*, (23 January 2014) available at http://www.bbc.co.uk/news/world-europe-25933153.

[102] EULEX, 'EULEX and War Crimes', (14 June 2013) available at http://www.eeas.europa.eu/csdp/missions-and-operations/eulex-kosovo/news/20130614_en.htm.

CHAPTER FIVE

ADMISSIBILITY CHALLENGES

Introduction

As discussed earlier, under the Rome Statute, the ICC is charged with determining a state's willingness and ability to undertake domestic war crimes prosecutions. Article 19 also sets forth circumstances in which states may challenge the admissibility of a case to the Court.[1]

It is often noted that the Rome Statute falls short on the question of who bears the burden of proof in admissibility decisions.[2] Commentators point to the Rules of Procedure and Evidence, which merely provide that '[a] request or application made under Article 19 shall be in writing and contain the basis for it'.[3] However, recent Court decisions suggest that the **state** bears the burden of proof to demonstrate *inadmissibility* to the ICC.[4]

---

[1] Rome Statute of the International Criminal Court, Rome, opened for signature 17 July 1988, 2187 UNTS 90 (entered into force 1 July 2002) UN Doc. A/CONF.183/9 (hereinafter ICC Statute or Rome Statute). Article 19 reads: 'Challenges to the admissibility of a case on the grounds referred to in Article 17 or challenges to the jurisdiction of the Court may be made by:

(a) An accused or a person for whom a warrant of arrest or a summons to appear has been issued under Article 58;
(b) A State which has jurisdiction over a case, on the ground that it is investigating or prosecuting the case or has investigated or prosecuted; or
(c) A State from which acceptance of jurisdiction is required under Article 12'.

[2] *The Prosecutor v. Jean-Pierre Bemba Gombo*, Doc. ICC-01/05-01/08-802, 'Decision on the Admissibility and Abuse of Process Challenges' (24 June 2010), para. 201; *See* Claire Brighton, 'Avoiding Unwillingness: Addressing the Political Pitfalls Inherent in the Complementarity Regime of the International Criminal Court', (2012) 12 *International Criminal Law Review*, 629, 651.

[3] ICC, 'Rules of Procedures and Evidence', Doc. ICC-ASP/1/3 (Part.II-A) (hereinafter 'ICC Rules of Procedure and Evidence'), Rule 58(1).

[4] This is undisputed and discussed further below. *See* e.g., ICC Rules of Procedure and Evidence, Rule 58(1), requiring challenging parties to 'provide a basis for an admissibility challenge'. *See also The Prosecutor v. William Samoei Ruto, Henry*

In the *Jean-Pierre Bemba Gombo* case, relating to the situation in the DRC, the Trial Chamber specified that the challenging party bears the burden of proof to 'establish the facts and other relevant matters'.[5] The legal argument is interesting here because it draws a parallel between admissibility challenges and claims of abuse of process, since both seek to end the proceedings.[6] The Court reasoned that 'applying different burdens and standards of proof to concurrent and broadly similar arguments that have a common or overlapping factual foundation' would be 'absurd'.[7]

The Trial Chamber in *Bemba* also determined that standard of proof in admissibility hearings should be a 'balance of probabilities'.[8] The Chamber reasoned, in part, that the overwhelming majority of judicial systems impose a 'civil standard' of proof (i.e., balance of probabilities). The Chamber further reasoned that it would be unjust to impose 'a variable standard of proof on the accused'.[9] Most interesting is the fact

---

Kiprono Kosgey and Joshua Arap Sang, Doc. ICC-01/09-01/11-307, 'Judgment on the Appeal of the Republic of Kenya against the Decision of Pre-Trial Chamber II of 30 May 2011 entitled 'Decision on the Application by the Government of Kenya Challenging the Admissibility of the Case Pursuant to Article 19(2)(b) of the Statute'', (30 August 2011), (hereafter 'Appeal Chamber Admissibility Decision'), para. 62. *The Prosecutor v. Said Al-Islam Gaddafi and Abdullah Al-Senussi*, Doc. ICC-01/11-01/11-344-Red, 'Decision on the admissibility of the case against Saif Al-Islam Gaddafi', (31 May 2013), para. 220. In response to Libya's admissibility challenge, the Defence strategically highlighted the burden of proof on Libya, refuting Libya's presumption of favour for state investigations under the Rome Statute's scheme of national priority. *See* IBA, 'Interoffice Memorandum on ICC case: The Prosecutor v. Saif Al-Islam Gaddafi and Abdullah Al-Senussi: Admissibility Challenge from Libya before Pre-Trial Chamber I' (9 October 2012) [on file with author].

5 *The Prosecutor v. Jean-Pierre Bemba Gombo*, Doc. ICC-01/05-01/08-802, 'Decision on the Admissibility and Abuse of Process Challenges' (24 June 2010), para. 201.

6 *Ibid.,* paras 201, 203; Brighton, 'Avoiding Unwillingness: Addressing the Political Pitfalls', 651.

7 *Ibid.,* para. 201. 'In both situations, the accused is arguing that the proposed trial before the ICC should not occur. There is no logical or legal basis for suggesting that the burden of establishing the relevant facts rests with the accused for one argument (e.g. abuse—as suggested by the defence) but with the prosecution for the other. In each instance the Court is seized of an application to halt the proceedings before the Chamber considering the matter, with, potentially, identical consequences for the accused, the witnesses and victims'.

8 *Ibid.*, para. 203.

9 *Ibid.*

that the Court made its decision to support a higher standard of proof being found in 'academic commentary' rather than the text of the Rome Statute itself.[10] Finding no reason to assign a different standard, the Court concluded that:

> It would be unjust to impose a variable standard of proof on the accused, depending on the seriousness of the application that he is making. His ability to defend himself should not be made more difficult simply because he is challenging the prosecution's right to continue with the prosecution at this Court.[11]

The Court's decision is not without its critics. Claire Brighton harshly calls the Court's reasoning illogical.[12] She charges that the Court failed to appropriately distinguish between an admissibility challenge, which is designed to recognise a state's prosecutorial sovereignty, and an application of abuse of process, the aim of which is to ensure legitimacy.[13] Brighton also contends that the burden of proof is seldom placed on the defendant in a criminal trial.[14]

In *The Prosecutor v. Germain Katanga and Mathieu Ngudjolo Chui,* also regarding the DRC, the Appeals Chamber held that the challenging state 'bears the burden of proof to show that the case is inadmissible' and that, to discharge this burden, 'the State must provide the Court with evidence of a sufficient degree of specificity and probative value that demonstrates that it is indeed investigating the case'.[15]

In *The Prosecutor v. Saif Al-Islam Gaddafi*, the Pre-Trial Chamber clarified the burden by emphasising that a state must 'provide concrete, tangible and pertinent evidence that proper investigations are currently

---

[10] *Ibid.*

[11] *Ibid.*

[12] Brighton, 'Avoiding Unwillingness: Addressing the Political Pitfalls', 652-53.

[13] *Ibid.*, quoting *The Prosecutor v. Jean-Pierre Bemba Gombo*, Doc. ICC-01/05-01/08-802, 'Decision on the Admissibility and Abuse of Process Challenges' (24 June 2010), para. 146.

[14] Brighton, 'Avoiding Unwillingness: Addressing the Political Pitfalls', 652.

[15] *The Prosecutor v. Francis Kirimi Muthaura, Uhuru Muigai Kenyatta and Mohammed Hussein Ali*, Doc. ICC-01/09-02/11-274, 'Judgment on the Appeal of the Republic of Kenya against the decision of Pre-Trial Chamber II of 30 May 2011 entitled 'Decision on the Application by the Government of Kenya Challenging the Admissibility of the Case Pursuant to Article 19(2)(b) of the Statute'', (30 August 2011) (hereinafter 'Kenya Admissibility Decision'), para. 61.

ongoing'.[16] A state must, therefore, do more than proclaim it is investigating; there must be evidence of probative value.[17] In the context of an admissibility challenge, 'evidence' does not merely mean samples of evidence in the national case, but may include documents such as directions, orders, decisions, reports and updates that demonstrate that government authorities are taking concrete steps to ascertain whether the suspect is responsible for the conduct underlying the Court's warrant of arrest.[18]

As to the meaning of 'sufficient degree' mentioned in the *Katanga* case, the Court in the *Gaddafi* admissibility challenges has given the (limited) guidance that 'the challenging State is required to substantiate all aspects of its allegations *to the extent required by the concrete circumstances of the case*'[19] [emphasis added]. The Court hence sought evidence from Libya which addressed its particular doubts about the genuineness and scope of the national investigation into Mr Gaddafi's alleged crimes, finding on the whole the evidence adduced by Libya to be of too general a level, or irrelevant, in establishing the contours of the domestic case against him.[20]

It is likely that the two Chambers reached different conclusions because in the *Bemba* case, the admissibility challenge was brought by *the accused* and in the *Gaddafi* case, the challenge was brought by the state. In

---

[16] *The Prosecutor v. Saif Al-Islam Gaddafi and Abdullah Al-Senussi*, Doc. ICC-01/11-01/11-239, 'Decision Requesting Further Submissions on Issues Related to the Admissibility of the Case Against Saif Al-Islam Gaddafi', (7 December 2012), para. 8; *The Prosecutor v. Said Al-Islam Gaddafi and Abdullah Al-Senussi*, Doc. ICC-01/11-01/11-344-Red, 'Decision on the admissibility of the case against Saif Al-Islam Gaddafi', (31 May 2013), paras 54-55, quoting *The Prosecutor v. Francis Kirimi Muthaura, Uhuru Muigai Kenyatta and Mohammed Hussein Ali*, Doc. ICC-01/09-02/11-274, 'Kenya Admissibility Decision', para. 61.

[17] *The Prosecutor v. William Samoei Ruto, Henry Kiprono Kosgey and Joshua Arap Sang*, ICC-01/09-01/11-307, 'Appeal Chamber Admissibility Decision', paras 62-63.

[18] *The Prosecutor v. Saif Al-Islam Gaddafi and Abdullah Al-Senussi*, Doc. ICC-01/11-01/11-239, 'Decision Requesting Further Submissions on Issues Related to the Admissibility of the Case Against Saif Al-Islam Gaddafi', (7 December 2012), paras 10-12.

[19] *The Prosecutor v. Said Al-Islam Gaddafi and Abdullah Al-Senussi*, Doc. ICC-01/11-01/11-344-Red, 'Decision on the admissibility of the case against Saif Al-Islam Gaddafi', (31 May 2013), para. 52.

[20] *Ibid. See* e.g. paras 115-117, 123-124, 135.

the former situation, the Court would be particularly concerned with preserving the accused's procedural rights and thus might impose a less demanding burden.

In the *Gaddafi* case, the Court **rejected** the argument made by the Kenyan and Libyan governments that Article 17 does not require the challenging state to give details of an investigation and that statements by the challenging state should be respected, presumed accurate, and made in good faith unless there is '*compelling evidence* to the contrary'.[21] Consistent with the Kenyan decision, the Court required tangible proof and evidence with probative value that demonstrate the existence and genuineness of a national investigation or prosecution. While this standard could be seen as a flexible formulation, it is arguably no more susceptible to interpretation than 'balance of probabilities' or 'beyond reasonable doubt'. However, this standard provides procedural clarity to states in their submissions to the Court; it reinforces the state's obligation to genuinely investigate and prosecute alleged crimes and, when called upon, to thoroughly document compliance with the Statute.

In the Libyan situation before the Court, the Libyan government also argued that there is a second step in bringing admissibility challenges where the burden of proof lies with the Court (i.e., the OPCD, OTP or the OPCV).[22] Libya claimed that the burden of proof lies with the party (whether OPCD, OTP, or the OPCV) alleging that the state is unwilling or unable to genuinely carry out investigations. The standard to be applied, as argued by Libya, should be the 'beyond a reasonable doubt' standard of proof. The reason is that finding that a state lacks genuineness to prosecute

---

[21] *The Prosecutor v. Francis Kirimi Muthaura, Uhuru Muigai Kenyatta and Mohammed Hussein Ali*, Doc. ICC-01/09-02/11-274, 'Kenya Admissibility Decision', para. 62.

[22] The argument is based on the relevant jurisprudence of the Appeals Chamber in the case *The Prosecutor v. Germain Katanga and Mathieu Ngudjolo Chui*, in the context of an admissibility proceeding the Chamber shall address (i) whether, at the time of the proceedings in respect of an admissibility challenge, there is an ongoing investigation or prosecution of the case at the national level, and, in case of the affirmative, (ii) whether the State is unwilling or unable to genuinely carry out such investigation or prosecution (*The Prosecutor v. Germain Katanga and Mathieu Ngudjolo Chui*, Doc. ICC-01/04-01/07-1497, 'Judgment on the Appeal of Mr Germain Katanga against the Oral Decision of Trial Chamber II of 12 June 2009 on the Admissibility of the Case', (25 September 2009), para. 1).

is a finding of exceptional gravity and should require an exacting standard of review.[23]

Not surprisingly, the OTP argued that Libya had the burden to prove both elements of the admissibility test. The OTP's position was that not only is the challenging state in the best position to provide relevant evidence, but this allocation of the burden of proof is consistent with the underlying rationale of complementarity.[24] This is indeed a strong argument supported by the simple proposition that states are in a better position to establish the existence of national investigations and their ability and willingness to carry out genuine proceedings. Of course, states would have to submit 'clear and convincing evidence' that they can meet the standard of proof. The Court would have to find the case inadmissible without being persuaded that the case is genuinely pursued at the national level.[25]

In the end, the Pre-Trial Chamber rejected Libya's arguments and maintained that (a) the challenging State bears the burden of proof, and (b) this applies to *both limbs* of Article 17(1)(a). The Court categorically insisted that the challenging state fully substantiate its claim.[26]

---

[23] *The Prosecutor v. Saif Al-Islam Gaddafi and Abdullah Al-Senussi*, Doc. ICC-01/11-01/11-258-Red2, 'Libyan Government's Further Submissions on Issues Related to the Admissibility of the Case Against Saif Al-Islam Gaddafi', (23 January 2013), para. 25.

[24] *The Prosecutor v. Saif Al-Islam Gaddafi and Abdullah Al-Senussi*, Doc. ICC-01/11-01/11-276-Red2, 'Prosecution's response to 'Libyan Government's Further Submissions on Issues Related to the Admissibility of the Case Against Saif Al-Islam Gaddafi', (11 February 2013), para. 23. *See also The Prosecutor v. Saif Al-Islam Gaddafi and Abdullah Al-Senussi*, Doc. ICC-01/11-01/11-279, 'OPCV's Observations on 'Libyan Government's Further Submissions on Issues Related to the Admissibility of the Case Against Saif Al-Islam Gaddafi'', (18 February 2013), para. 38.

[25] *The Prosecutor v. Saif Al-Islam Gaddafi and Abdullah Al-Senussi*, Doc. ICC-01/11-01/11-279, 'OPCV's Observations on 'Libyan Government's Further Submissions on Issues Related to the Admissibility of the Case Against Saif Al-Islam Gaddafi'', (18 February 2013), paras 36 and 37.

[26] *The Prosecutor v. Said Al-Islam Gaddafi and Abdullah Al-Senussi*, Doc. ICC-01/11-01/11-344-Red, 'Decision on the admissibility of the case against Saif Al-Islam Gaddafi', (31 May 2013), para. 52.

I. Timing of Admissibility Challenges

What is more controversial in terms of applying the principle of complementarity is the question of *when* states can challenge admissibility. Under Article 19(4), any state with jurisdiction may challenge the ICC only once and only, save in exceptional circumstances, 'prior to or at the commencement of the trial'.[27] Pursuant to Article 19(7), if a state challenges admissibility to the ICC, the Prosecutor must cease his investigation until the matter is adjudicated. Moreover, '[w]here there is an admissibility challenge under consideration by the Court…the requested State may postpone the execution of a request…pending a determination by the Court'.[28] This includes postponing requests to surrender persons.[29]

Importantly, as discussed in Chapter 1, the Prosecutor does not acquire jurisdiction simply upon referral or request for an investigation.[30] Before initiating an investigation, the Prosecutor must, pursuant to Article 53 of the Rome Statute, determine that there is a reasonable basis to believe a crime has been committed, that the case would be admissible under Article 17, and that it would serve the interests of justice.[31]

However, once the decision is made to initiate an investigation, the Prosecutor must notify all relevant parties of the decision to investigate.[32] This is an essential point because the Rome Statute and the Rules of Procedure and Evidence do not plainly describe at what stage the Court's jurisdiction takes effect. It is reasonable to infer that the Court's jurisdiction takes effect at this very early stage, i.e., notification of the parties regarding the investigation.

---

[27] ICC Statute, Article 19(4).
[28] *Ibid.*, Article 95.
[29] *Ibid.*, Articles 89 and 95. Surrender is included because both articles are within Part IX.
[30] The Prosecutor has noted: 'neither referrals nor private communications automatically 'trigger' the powers of the Prosecutor'. *See* ICC-OTP, 'Annex to the 'Paper on Some Policy Issues Before the Office of the Prosecutor'', (September 2003), p. 1, available at http://www.icc-cpi.int/NR/rdonlyres/278614ED-A8CA-4835-B91D-DB7FA7639E02/143706/policy_annex_final_210404.pdf.
[31] ICC Statute, Articles 53(1)(a)-(c). *See* Chapter 2 for an in-depth discussion of these two elements of admissibility.
[32] ICC-OTP, 'Annex to the 'Paper on Some Policy Issues', p. 2.

The Rome Statute is clear that states with possible jurisdiction must 'make a challenge at the earliest opportunity'.[33] Since states are given notice of proceedings under the requirements of Article 18/Rule 52, this seems a logical time to bring a challenge. Beyond this point, there would have to be significant new developments to justify any subsequent delay in proceedings.

It is worth assessing what might happen if an admissibility challenge is not possible at this early stage. In such a circumstance, a state may be justified in challenging the admissibility of the case closer to the start of the trial. Insight on this can be gleaned from the early stages of the Rome Statute, when the 1994 ILC Draft actually addressed this issue. Draft Article 35 required that challenges to admissibility be made 'prior to the commencement of the trial'.[34] The related Commentary explains that '[i]ssues arising under Article 35 should normally be dealt with as soon as possible after they are made. After the commencement of a trial they can only be dealt with on the Court's own motion, on the basis that there will usually be no point in questioning at that time the exercise of a jurisdiction that has already begun to be exercised'.[35]

The timing of admissibility challenges was discussed further during the 1996 Preparatory Committee discussions where 'it was generally agreed that it should be prior to, or at the beginning of the trial and not later'.[36]

The Rome Statute, as promulgated, seems to limit the possibility of late challenges by requiring that they be raised 'at the *commencement of a trial*, or subsequently with the leave of the Court, [and] may be based *only* on [A]rticle 17, paragraph 1(c)' [emphasis added].[37] This is the *ne bis in*

---

[33] ICC Statute, Article 19(5).
[34] 'Report of the International Law Commission on the Work of Its Forty-Sixth Session', UN Doc. A/49/10 (1994), *reprinted in* (1994) 2 *Year Book of the International Law Commission*, 52.
[35] 'Report of the International Law Commission to the General Assembly on the Work of Its Forty-Sixth Session', UN Doc. A/CN.4/SER.A/1994/Add.l (Part 2), *reprinted in* (1994) 2 (II) *Year Book of the International Law Commission.*
[36] Christopher K. Hall, 'Article 19; Challenges to the Jurisdiction of the Court or the Admissibility of a Case', in Otto Triffterer (ed.), *Commentary on the Rome Statute of the International Criminal Court: Observers' Notes, Article by Article,* 2nd edn (München: CH Beck, Hart and Nomos, 2008), p. 657 (*quoting* the 1996 Preparatory Committee I, p. 39).
[37] Article 19(4) of the ICC Statute reads '[t]he admissibility of a case or the jurisdiction of the Court may be challenged only once by any person or State

idem provision of the Statute where the suspect has already been tried by a domestic court for a crime that was subject to the Court's jurisdiction. Therefore, a late admissibility challenge may only be made in circumstances where a state concluded an investigation and/or prosecution and obtained a final judgment.[38] Absent this exceptional circumstance, the requirement that states challenge admissibility 'at the earliest opportunity' would still hold. And although the Statute sheds no further light on the issue, the Court would certainly have the jurisdictional capacity to determine whether the challenge could have been made at an earlier opportunity.

However, as seen in the *Gaddafi* decision, the Court is open to expanding the timetable for admissibility challenges.[39] The decision reaffirmed that a state may bring an admissibility challenge only once. But the Court emphasised that in accordance with Article 19(4) of the Statute, a state may file a further challenge only 'in exceptional circumstances', at a 'time later than the commencement of the trial'.[40] Even the OTP has suggested that states emerging from conflict may not be immediately able to undertake investigations and prosecutions despite being 'willing' to do so.[41] In such a situation, 'the case would be admissible before the Court *until* such time as Article 17 requirements are met'.[42]

---

referred to in paragraph 2. The challenge shall take place prior to or at the commencement of the trial. In exceptional circumstances, the Court may grant leave for a challenge to be brought more than once or at a time later than the commencement of the trial. Challenges to the admissibility of a case, at the commencement of a trial, or subsequently with the leave of the Court, may be based only on article 17, paragraph 1 (c)'.

[38] Hall, 'Article 19; Challenges to the Jurisdiction of the Court or the Admissibility of a Case', p. 656.

[39] *The Prosecutor v. Said Al-Islam Gaddafi and Abdullah Al-Senussi*, Doc. ICC-01/11-01/11-344-Red, 'Decision on the admissibility of the case against Saif Al-Islam Gaddafi', (31 May 2013), para. 32.

[40] ICC Statute, Article 19(4).

[41] *The Prosecutor v. Saif Al-Islam Gaddafi and Abdullah Al-Senussi*, Doc. ICC-01/11-01/11-384-Red, 'Prosecution Response to the 'Document in Support of the Government of Libya's Appeal Against the Decision on the Admissibility of the Case Against Saif Al-Islam Gaddafi'', (22 July 2013), para. 182.

[42] *Ibid.*

A. Uganda

The Court's ruling in *The Prosecutor v. Joseph Kony et al.* also granted flexibility in the timing of an admissibility challenge.[43] Acknowledging that 'no State has, to date, challenged the admissibility of the case',[44] the Prosecutor did not argue that the government of Uganda forfeited its right to challenge admissibility by not doing so early on. The Prosecutor seemed to accept that a later challenge was possible if a State Party invoked complementarity, even if such an appeal caused the investigation to be deferred. The Prosecutor's willingness to extend the admissibility challenge timeframe seemed to sway the Court. The Pre-Trial Chamber ruled that:

> [T]he determination of admissibility is meant to be an ongoing process throughout the pre-trial phase, the outcome of which is subject to review depending on the evolution of the relevant factual scenario. Otherwise stated, the Statute as a whole enshrines the idea that a change in circumstances allows (or even, in some scenarios, compels) the Court to determine admissibility anew.[45]

Although the Court stopped short of extending the timeframe to the point of trial, its decision articulated a more flexible approach regarding when a challenge is permissible.

This makes sense in light of the fact that the Prosecutor has wide latitude in requesting the Court to reassess its decision to support a State's argument on admissibility. Article 19(10) reads:

> If the Court has decided that a case is inadmissible under Article 17, the Prosecutor may submit a request for a review of the decision when he or

[43] *See The Prosecutor v. Joseph Kony, Vincent Otti, Okot Odhiambo, Dominic Ongwen*, Doc. ICC-02/04-01/05-377, 'Decision on the admissibility of the case under article 19(1) of the Statute', (10 March 2009).

[44] *The Prosecutor v. Joseph Kony, Vincent Otti, Okot Odhiambo, Dominic Ongwen*, Doc. ICC-02/04-01/05-352, 'Prosecution's Observations regarding the Admissibility of the Case against Joseph Kony, Vincent Otti, Okot Odhiambo and Dominic Ongwen', (18 November 2008), para. 8.

[45] *The Prosecutor v. Joseph Kony, Vincent Otti, Okot Odhiambo, Dominic Ongwen*, Doc. ICC-02/04-01/05-377, 'Decision on the admissibility of the case under article 19(1) of the Statute', (10 March 2009), para. 28.

> she is fully satisfied that new facts have arisen, which negate the basis on which the case had previously been found inadmissible under Article 17.[46]

The Uganda situation is a good example of how, because of complementarity, admissibility decisions can be challenged and reassessed over time. On 16 December 2003, after failing to arrest members of the Lord's Resistance Army (LRA) accused of massacres, sexual enslavement, and the enlistment of child soldiers, the Ugandan government itself referred its situation to the ICC.[47] The Court made the referral public on 29 January 2004 pursuant to Article 14 of the Rome Statute.[48] Subsequently, the ICC Prosecutor announced an investigation into crimes against humanity and war crimes committed in the region since 1 July 2002.[49] Arrest warrants followed in October 2005.[50]

Uganda stated in its correspondence that it was unable to arrest those most responsible for war crimes, and believed the perpetrators to be either in the Democratic Republic of Congo or South Sudan. When the ICC issued its arrest warrants, it noted the earlier written referral by the Ugandan government, which stated that Uganda had been:

---

[46] ICC Statute, Article 19(10).

[47] *See* ICC, 'President of Uganda refers situation concerning the Lord's Resistance Army (LRA) to the ICC', Doc. ICC-20040129-44, (29 January 2004).

[48] ICC Statute, Article 14(1) reads, in part: '[a] State Party may refer to the Prosecutor a situation in which one or more crimes within the jurisdiction of the Court appear to have been committed requesting the Prosecutor to investigate the situation for the purpose of determining whether one or more specific persons should be charged with the commission of such crimes'.

[49] ICC-OTP, 'Prosecutor of the International Criminal Court opens an investigation into Northern Uganda', Doc. ICC-OTP-20040729-65, (29 July 2004).

[50] The indictment alleges, among other things, that the Lord's Resistance Army (LRA) leader Joseph Kony issued specific orders in mid-2002 and late 2003 to attack, loot, and abduct civilians. The five ICC-issued warrants were executed in 2005 and include LRA leader Joseph Kony and LRA senior members Vincent Otti, Okot Odhiambo, Raska Lukwiya, and Dominic Ongwen. Lukwiya was killed in 2006, and Otti was reportedly killed in 2007. *See Situation in Uganda*, Doc. ICC-02/04-01/05-53, 'Warrant of Arrest for Joseph Kony Issued on 8 July 2005 as Amended on 27 September 2005', (27 September 2005); *Situation in Uganda*, Doc. ICC-02/04-01/05-54, 'Warrant of Arrest for Vincent Otti', (8 July 2005); *Situation in Uganda*, Doc. ICC-02/04-01/05-55, 'Warrant of Arrest for Raska Lukwiya', (8 July 2005); *Situation in Uganda*, Doc. ICC-02/04-01/05-56, 'Warrant of Arrest for Okot Odhiambo', (8 July 2005); *Situation in Uganda*, Doc. ICC-02/04-01/05-57, 'Warrant of Arrest for Dominic Ongwen', (8 July 2005).

> unable to arrest...persons who bear the 'greatest responsibility' [and that] the ICC is the most appropriate and effective forum for the investigation and prosecution of those bearing the greatest responsibility for those crimes; [furthermore, Uganda] has not conducted and does not intend to conduct national proceedings in relation to the persons most responsible.[51]

However, as part of the government's effort to broker a deal with the LRA during peace talks, which began in July 2006, the government of Uganda and the Lord's Resistance Army (LRA) agreed in July 2008 to establish a domestic War Crimes Division to prosecute high-ranking officials accused of committing crimes against humanity during Uganda's civil war. Those accused of lesser crimes would be tried though northern Uganda's traditional justice system, known as *mato oput* ('drinking the bitter root'). In March 2010, Uganda passed the International Criminal Court Act, which undoubtedly was put forth for the purpose of circumscribing ICC jurisdiction.

The Agreement on Accountability and Reconciliation, agreed to by the government and the LRA on 29 June 2007, was conditioned on the government convincing the ICC to drop its indictments against LRA rebels, including LRA leader Joseph Kony.[52] In addition, an Annex to the Agreement signed in February 2008 stipulated that those responsible for 'serious crimes' would be tried by Uganda's formal domestic court system (a special War Crimes Division of the High Court of Uganda).[53] The Agreement also established a special investigative unit under Uganda's director of Public Prosecutions and a registry to assist in protecting victims and witnesses.[54] For other individuals, traditional justice mechanisms would be used.

---

[51] *Situation in Uganda,* Doc. ICC-02/04-01/05-53, 'Warrant of Arrest for Joseph Kony', para. 37.

[52] *See* 'Agreement on Accountability and Reconciliation between the Government of the Republic of Uganda and the Lord's Resistance Army/Movement', (29 June 2007), available at http://www.amicc.org/docs/Agreement_on_Accountability_and_Reconciliation.pdf.

[53] 'Annexure to the Agreement on Accountability and Reconciliation between the Government of the Republic of Uganda and the Lord's Resistance Army/Movement', (19 February 2008), para. 7, available at http://www.iccnow.org/documents/Annexure_to_agreement_on_Accountability_signed_today.pdf.

[54] *Ibid.*, para. 8.

The ICC responded aggressively. Indictments for the leaders of Uganda's LRA would remain in effect despite the Reconciliation Agreement and creation of the War Crimes Division of the High Court. The Prosecutor refused to meet with an LRA delegation to discuss the ICC indictments.[55] Uganda's government, of course, saw this decision as contradicting the core principle of complementarity. Consequently, lawyers for the Ugandan government filed an application for the withdrawal of the ICC indictments. The ICC Prosecutor responded that:

> Should the LRA indictees through their representatives wish to challenge the admissibility of the Prosecutor's case against Joseph Kony and the three other commanders, they can do so by making an application to the judges. Any LRA legal representative would have to follow the judicial procedures and file applications before the Pre-Trial chamber. The process is clear and does not involve the OTP.[56]

From the Prosecutor's perspective, the creation of a domestic war crimes court (i.e., Division) was simply a ruse to grant impunity to the LRA rebels. Indeed, there is wide speculation that the domestic war crimes court was created simply to persuade the ICC to drop its arrest warrants.[57] Moreover, a final peace accord was never signed by the LRA, and the Prosecutor argued that Kony's claims of peace talks were an international distraction:

> These attacks all follow a similar method with markets surrounded and looted, students abducted from school, properties burned and dozens of civilians killed, including several local chiefs. Tens of thousands have now been displaced ... Kony—just as he has many times in the past—uses the peace talks to gain time and support, to rearm and attack again. The price paid today by civilians is high. The criminals remain at large and continue

---

[55] The LRA delegation did meet the ICC's Registry's Head of the Legal Advisory Services Section and Head of the Victims and Counsels Division. *See* ICC, 'ICC officials discuss the role of the Registry in proceedings before the Court with the Lord's Resistance Army delegation', Doc. ICC-CPI-20080310-PR295, (10 October 2008).

[56] ICC-OTP, 'Statement of the Office of the Prosecutor on Uganda', (4 March 2008), available at http://www.icc-cpi.int/NR/rdonlyres/945119F8-7107-4FC1-8026-CD03ECCA5BB1/0/ICCOTPST20080304ENG.pdf.

[57] Devin Montgomery, 'Uganda Establishes Special War Crimes Court to try LRA Rebels', *Jurist*, (27 May 2008), available at http://jurist.law.pitt.edu/paperchase/2008/05/uganda-establishes-special-war-crimes.php.

> to commit crimes and they are threatening the entire region. Arrest is long overdue.[58]

The Prosecutor continued to submit that if Uganda had not investigated or prosecuted the LRA rebel leaders, there was no need to investigate the legitimacy of hypothetical proceedings.[59]

The Pre-Trial Chamber upheld the Prosecutor's position.[60] In its decision, the Court analysed whether the situation in Uganda remained admissible and whether Uganda was able to unilaterally withdraw the referral. The Court focused on the fact that 'measures undertaken to implement the provisions of the [Peace] Agreement and the Annexure [were] 'in the initial stages'' and 'a lot [was] yet to be done'.[61] The Court held that it was 'premature and therefore inappropriate to assess the features envisaged for the Special Division and its legal framework'.[62]

On the question of whether Uganda could withdraw the referral on its own initiative, the Chamber ruled that 'it is for the Court, and not for Uganda, to make such determination'.[63] In conclusion, the Court judged that despite the potential for domestic proceedings, the circumstances of admissibility had not changed, and so the case remained admissible. The decision was upheld on appeal.[64]

---

[58] *See* Devin Montgomery, 'ICC Prosecutor Urges Arrest of Uganda War Crimes Suspect after New Attacks', *Jurist*, (6 October 2008) *quoting* ICC, 'Prosecutor Calls for Renewed Efforts to Arrest LRA leader Kony in wake of new attacks', Doc. ICC-OTP-20081006-PR359 (6 October 2010).

[59] *The Prosecutor v. Joseph Kony, Vincent Otti, Okot Odhiambo, Dominic Ongwen*, Doc. ICC-02/04-01/05-352, 'Prosecution's Observations regarding the Admissibility of the Case against Joseph Kony, Vincent Otti, Okot Odhiambo and Dominic Ongwen', (18 November 2008), paras 9, 11.

[60] *The Prosecutor v. Joseph Kony, Vincent Otti, Okot Odhiambo, Dominic Ongwen*, Doc. ICC-02/04-01/05-377, 'Decision on the admissibility of the case under article 19(1) of the Statute', (10 March 2009), para. 50.

[61] *Ibid.*, para. 49.

[62] *Ibid.*, para. 51.

[63] *Ibid.*

[64] *See The Prosecutor v. Joseph Kony, Vincent Otti, Okot Odhiambo, Dominic Ongwen*, Doc. No. ICC-02/04-01/05-408, 'Judgment on the Appeal of the Defence Against the 'Decision on the Admissibility of the Case under Article 19(1) of the Statute' of March 10, 2009', (16 September 2009).

II. Self-referral and Withdrawal

The drafting history of the Rome Statute suggests that it was never considered likely that a State Party would refer itself to the ICC.[65] The term 'self-referral' does not appear in the Rome Statute, and there is scant discussion of this scenario.[66] Nonetheless, four of the six situations referred to the ICC Prosecutor, including Uganda, were triggered in this way.[67] Darfur is the only situation referred by a party other than the state with territorial jurisdiction (i.e., the state in which the alleged crimes took place).

The ability of a state to refer itself to the Court may come to be regarded as a mistake. Had this been foreseen and discussed when the

---

[65] As noted by William A. Schabas: '[s]elf-referral' flows from a creative interpretation of Article 14 of the Rome Statute that was not seriously contemplated by the 1998 Diplomatic Conference and during the prior negotiations. The 1994 draft statute submitted to the General Assembly by the International Law Commission included the concept of 'state-party referral', but described the source of the referral as a 'complainant state'. A State Party could lodge a 'complaint.... The language makes it clear enough that what was contemplated was a 'complainant State' 'lodg[ing] a complaint' against another state. *See* William A. Schabas, 'Complementarity in Practice: Some Uncomplimentary Thoughts', (2008) 19 *Criminal Law Forum*, 5, 12. Mahnoush Arsanjani and W. Michael Reisman also have noted that both '[b]efore and during the Rome negotiations, no one—neither states that were initially sceptical about the viability of an international criminal court nor states that supported it—assumed that governments would want to invite the future court to investigate and prosecute crimes that had occurred in their territory'. *See* Mahnoush Arsanjani and W. Michael Reisman, 'The Law-in-Action of the International Criminal Court' (2005) 99, *American Journal of International Law*, 385, 386–387.

[66] However, in 1995, the *Ad Hoc* Committee suggested that it should be possible for a state to voluntarily allow the ICC to take jurisdiction over a situation. *See* Mohamed M. El Zeidy, *The Principle of Complementarity in International Criminal Law; Origin, Development and Practice* (Leiden: Martin Nijhoff Publishers, 2008), p. 213.

[67] ICC, 'President of Uganda Refers Situation Concerning the Lord's Resistance Army (LRA) to the ICC', Doc. ICC-CPI-20040129-43, (29 January 2004). *See also* ICC, 'Prosecutor receives referral of the situation in the Democratic Republic of Congo', Doc. ICC-OTP-20040419-50, (19 April 2004); ICC, 'Prosecutor receives referral concerning Central African Republic', Doc. ICC-OTP-20050107-86, (7 January 2005); 'Referral Letter from the Government of Mali to the ICC', (13 July 2012), available at http://www.icc-cpi.int/NR/rdonlyres/A245A47F-BFD1-45B6-891C-3BCB5B173F57/0/ReferralLetterMali130712.pdf.

Rome Statute was drafted, it likely would have been regulated to avoid confusion. As it happened, self-referral was raised only tangentially in a discussion about a state 'waiver of complementarity'. Mohamed M. El Zeidy, President of the ICC Assembly of State Parties, described the controversy over potential state waivers: '[w]hile it has been proposed that the Statute should permit a situation where a State might 'voluntarily decide to relinquish its jurisdiction in favour' of the ICC, the proposal did not gain support from some delegations'.[68] The provision was not included in any draft of the Rome Statute.

Critics have noted that there is scope for 'self-referral' to be manipulated by states seeking to leverage the Court's authority to consolidate political gains.[69] As Professor William Schabas has noted, there are multiple examples of states using the courts to prosecute rebels and political opponents, and this becomes an inherent risk of self-referral.[70]

However, there is a clear and positive reason for the self-referral option to exist within the ICC structure. It promises accountability for states that may be legally capable but politically incapable of undertaking domestic war crimes trials. In a post-conflict environment, for instance, prosecuting a former head of state through a domestic war crimes court may entail significant if not impossible hurdles. One can imagine the difficulties of a country such as Zimbabwe bringing a criminal action against President Robert Mugabe for crimes against humanity. The ICC provides the necessary judicial platform for a state to 'self-refer' to a neutral court.

The more pressing issue is what happens when a state decides to *withdraw* its original referral request? What happens if a state is able to show that it has gained the capacity and willingness to undertake prosecutions despite initially referring the situation to the ICC?

---

[68] 'Report of the *Ad hoc* Committee on the Establishment of an International Criminal Court', UN Doc. A/50/22, (1995), para. 47; Mohamed M. El Zeidy, 'The Ugandan Government Triggers the First Test of the Complementarity Principle: An Assessment of the First State's Party Referral to the ICC', (2005) 5 *International Criminal Law Review,* 83, 100.

[69] *See, e.g.*, Arsanjani and Reisman, 'The Law-in-Action of the International Criminal Court', 392.

[70] Schabas, 'Complementarity in Practice', 33.

The primary tool for interpreting the Rome Statute is the text itself,[71] and this does not provide great insight into how a state might withdraw a referral.[72] The omission is not unexpected. As noted, the Statute's drafters did not anticipate self-referral as a trigger mechanism for jurisdiction; it is not surprising that discussion never turned to whether a referral could subsequently be withdrawn.

Amnesty International, among others, noted the omission when it reacted angrily to President Museveni's attempt to withdraw the Uganda referral in 2004. It said: '[t]here is not a scrap of evidence in the drafting history or in commentaries by leading international law experts on the Rome Statute suggesting that once a state party has referred a situation that

---

[71] Article 21 of the ICC Statute provides a description of applicable law for the interpretation and application of the ICC Statute. It provides:

1. The Court shall apply:

(a) In the first place, this Statute, Elements of Crimes and its Rules of Procedure and Evidence;

(b) In the second place, where appropriate, applicable treaties and the principles and rules of international law, including the established principles of the international law of armed conflict;

(c) Failing that, general principles of law derived by the Court from national laws of legal systems of the world including, as appropriate, the national laws of States that would normally exercise jurisdiction over the crime, provided that those principles are not inconsistent with this Statute and with international law and internationally recognized norms and standards.

2. The Court may apply principles and rules of law as interpreted in its previous decisions.

3. The application and interpretation of law pursuant to this article must be consistent with internationally recognized human rights, and be without any adverse distinction founded on grounds such as gender as defined in article 7, paragraph 3, age, race, colour, language, religion or belief, political or other opinion, national, ethnic or social origin, wealth, birth or other status.

[72] Michael P. Scharf and Patrick Dowd, 'No Way Out? The Question of Unilateral Withdrawals or Referrals to the ICC and Other Human Rights Courts', (2008-2009) 9 *Chicago Journal of International Law*, 573, 574; Arsanjani and Reisman, 'The Law-in-Action of the International Criminal Court', 395-397. For drafting history of the referral process, see also Antonio Marchesi, 'Article 14: Referral of a Situation by a State Party', in Otto Triffterer (ed.), *Commentary on the Rome Statute of the International Criminal Court: Observers' Notes, Article by Article*, 2nd edn (München: CH Beck, Hart and Nomos, 2008), pp. 575-579.

it can 'withdraw' the referral'.[73] It has been noted that drafters of the Rome Statute may have expected that a State Party would have had little interest in withdrawing a referral from the Court.[74]

For some scholars, the absence of any provision within the Statute, while not conclusive, 'strongly suggests that the Statute simply does not allow a self-referral to be withdrawn'.[75] The argument is that the text of the Rome Statute focuses on how the Prosecutor or Pre-Trial Chamber considers issues of admissibility and jurisdiction post-referral, 'convey[ing] the impression that once a referral has been made and the Court has exercised its jurisdiction, control and power over the referral lies entirely in the hands of the Court'.[76] This seems to be consistent with the *The Prosecutor v. Joseph Kony et al.* decision.[77]

Furthermore, since the referring state voluntarily waives its right to jurisdiction, the ICC could have sufficient legal basis to 'deprive that State of the right to re-obtain control over the situation, even if it has initiated domestic investigations into the situation'.[78] Some scholars argue that the Court should reject the state's request to reverse the initial referral even without hearing the merits of the arguments.[79] Assuming the Court has taken steps to exercise jurisdiction, the withdrawal of the referral is a unilateral removal of the situation from the jurisdiction of the Court.[80] As the Court determines its own jurisdiction, a State Party may not supersede this authority by unilaterally withdrawing a referral.[81]

---

[73] Amnesty International, 'Uganda: Government Cannot Prevent the International Criminal Court from Investigating Crimes', (16 November 2004), p. 2, available at http://www.amnesty.org/en/library/asset/AFR59/008/2004/en/db815a8b-fa9d-11dd-999c-47605d4edc46/afr590082004en.pdf.

[74] Scharf and Dowd, 'No Way Out? The Question of Unilateral Withdrawals or Referrals to the ICC', 582.

[75] *Ibid.*, 586.

[76] *Ibid.*

[77] *The Prosecutor v. Joseph Kony, Vincent Otti, Okot Odhiambo, Dominic Ongwen*, Doc. ICC-02/04-01/05-320, 'Decision initiating proceedings under article 19, requesting observations and appointing counsel for the Defence', (21 October 2008), p. 8.

[78] El Zeidy, *The Principle of Complementarity in International Criminal Law*, p. 279.

[79] *Ibid.*

[80] Scharf and Dowd, 'No Way Out? The Question of Unilateral Withdrawals or Referrals to the ICC', 588.

[81] *Ibid.*

An additional argument against withdrawal would be that if a referral could be reversed, it would politicise the entire complementarity process; there would be no limitations on the reasons to withdraw a case. A state could withdraw the referral because it disagreed with a charge or with a person being investigated, resulting in the state dictating to the ICC who the accused should be and what charges are acceptable.

However, these views seem harsh in relation to the aims and objectives embodied in the principle of complementarity. Complementarity is designed to promote domestic accountability; thus, the international community should remain flexible regarding a state's request to withdraw a referral based on new evidence and good faith cooperation.

It seems draconian to suggest that a state could never seek to reverse a referral to the ICC. The prominence of the complementarity principle within the Rome Statute suggests that states with genuinely changed circumstances should be able to petition for domestic proceedings. Article 19 of the Statute supports this position.[82] Even with arrest warrants issued, complementarity remains valid through each stage of the ICC proceedings.

This is essentially the Ugandan government's position in arguing that, even after an arrest warrant has been issued, it should be able to steer the course of justice on its own. The Ugandan government has stated that:

> We can save [Kony] because we are the ones who sought assistance from the ICC. Because he was not under our jurisdiction, we sought assistance from the ICC. If he signs the peace agreement and returns to our jurisdiction, it becomes our responsibility, not any other party's, including the ICC.[83]

---

[82] ICC Statute, Article 19(4) reads, in part: '[t]he admissibility of a case or the jurisdiction of the Court may be challenged only once by any person or State referred to in paragraph 2. The challenge shall take place prior to or at the commencement of the trial. In exceptional circumstances, the Court may grant leave for a challenge to be brought more than once or at a time later than the commencement of the trial. Challenges to the admissibility of a case, at the commencement of a trial, or subsequently with the leave of the Court, may be based only on article 17, paragraph 1 (c)'.

[83] Statement by President Yoweri Museveni *quoted* in 'Uganda: Optimism Prevails, Despite Setback in Peace Talks', *IRIN News*, (18 April 2008), available at http://www.irinnews.org/report.aspx?reportid=77823.

Many have argued that the Ugandan judiciary is one of the 'most proficient and robust in Africa' and is 'unquestionably able and willing' to prosecute crimes committed by the LRA.[84] The Open Society Institute, for example, has praised the country's investigators, prosecutors, and judges. A recent report found that '[t]here are no shortcomings in judicial or penal infrastructure that would prevent complementarity'.[85] Supporters of the Ugandan judiciary point to the Parliament's passing of the International Criminal Court Act and the establishment of the War Crimes Division (WCD) within the High Court allowing for prosecution according to domestic criminal law and the Geneva Conventions. They also argue that, in keeping with complementarity, the ICC Prosecutor should encourage Uganda to fulfil its obligations and, where possible, prosecute those individuals alleged to have committed serious crimes.

In failing to reconsider the genuine attempt to prosecute domestically those most responsible for atrocities, and in light of the admissibility requirements of Article 17, 'the Prosecutor's actions seem inconsistent with his profession of faith in the importance of national justice'.[86] As Wes Rist notes:

> By creating a special war crimes division in the Ugandan High Court, the government is taking the steps that the ICC was created to promote. This is not a failure for [ICC Prosecutor] Ocampo or the ICC. In fact, this is the result that the ICC should be hoping for. The outstanding indictments against Joseph Kony, Vincent Otti, Okot Odhiambo, and Dominic Ongwen have been a persistent bar to the attempts by both sides to reach a permanent peace agreement. In addition, there seem to be substantial

[84] Phil Clark, 'Law, Politics and Pragmatism: The ICC and Case Selection in the Democratic Republic of Congo and Uganda', in Nicholas Waddell and Phil Clark (eds.), *Courting Conflict? Justice, Peace and the ICC in Africa* (Royal African Society, 2008), p. 43. In 2008, the OHCHR reported that 'High Court judges are experienced judges who act with professionalism and court proceedings usually respect fair trial requirements'. However, commentators have raised questions over judicial independence and note that political interference has been recorded in some high-profile cases. *See* Open Society Foundations, *Putting Complementarity into Practice: Domestic Justice for International Crimes in Democratic Republic of Congo, Uganda, and Kenya*, (New York: Open Society Foundations, 2011), pp. 73-74.

[85] Open Society Foundations, *Putting Complementarity into Practice*, p. 7.

[86] Schabas, 'Complementarity in Practice', 23.

> reports that the population of Uganda wishes to see these individuals face justice in their own country and not at the ICC.[87]

Of course, under the principle of complementarity those domestic trials must be credible, independent, and impartial. They must adhere to international fair standards and impose penalties that are appropriate given the gravity of the crimes committed.

In the DRC *Lubanga* case, the Court seemed to recognise a situation where the capacity and willingness of a national judicial system has changed for the positive. The Court stated that:

> [T]he Prosecution's general statement that the DRC national judicial system continues to be unable in the sense of Article 17(1)(a) to (c) and (3), of the Statute does not wholly correspond to the reality any longer.[88]

In this situation, the Court established a fairly narrow test for admissibility challenges. If there is any chance of 'taking back' a case based on the principle of complementarity the national proceedings 'must encompass both the person and the conduct which is the subject of the case before the Court'[89] (this admissibility concept was discussed in Chapter 2). This condition, of course, seems reasonable. However, there is now a legal basis to argue that a state, under the principle of complementarity, could pursue at least a temporary deferral of the ICC's case if it can show the undertaking of the actual prosecution.

III. Non-States Parties: the Libya Situation

The right to challenge admissibility to the ICC extends to a non-State Party if a situation is referred by the UN Security Council under Chapter VII powers of the UN Charter. The state's obligations to comply with the ICC extends from obligations under the UN Charter, which supersede

[87] Wes Rist, 'Why Uganda's New War Crimes Court Is a Victory for the ICC', *Jurist*, (29 May 2008), available at http://jurist.law.pitt.edu/forumy/2008/05/why-ugandas-new-war-crimes-court-is.php.

[88] *The Prosecutor v. Thomas Lubanga Dyilo*, Doc. ICC-01-04-01/06-8-US-Corr, 'Decision concerning Pre-Trial Chamber I's Decision of 10 February 2006 and the Incorporation of Documents into the Record of the Case against Mr Thomas Lubanga Dyilo', (24 February 2006), para. 36.

[89] *The Prosecutor v. Thomas Lubanga Dyilo*, Doc. ICC-01/04-01/06-8-US-Corr, 'Annex I: Decision on the Prosecutor's Application for a warrant of arrest, Article 58', (10 February 2006), para. 31.

other treaty obligations or the state's prior decision *not* to be a signatory to the Rome Statute.[90]

UN Security Council referrals impose **the same** obligations on non-States Parties as those placed on States Parties through the Rome Statute. For example, neither Sudan nor Libya is a signatory to the Rome Statute.[91] Yet, Security Council resolutions specify that Libya and Sudan are obligated to 'cooperate fully' with the ICC, and their obligations mirror those of States Parties under the Rome Statute.[92] The relevant language adopted by the UN Security Council in referring those situations to the ICC (UNSC Resolution 1593[93] and UNSC Resolution 1970[94] respectively) is virtually identical. In both resolutions, the Council decided that the respective governments 'shall cooperate fully with and provide any necessary assistance to the Court and the Prosecutor pursuant to this resolution'.[95]

It is important to stress that to date the UN Security Council is of the view that its referral power under Article 13(b) of the Statute limits its authority to *obligate* **other** non-States Parties to cooperate with the ICC or submit to the Court's jurisdiction. This position was also reflected in UN Security Resolution 1970 regarding Libya, which reads in part: 'while

---

[90] ICC Statute, Article 13; Charter of the United Nations, (24 October 1945) 1 UNTS XVI (hereinafter UN Charter), Article 103 specifies superior duties to the UN Charter above other international treaties which includes Security Council resolutions. *See Questions of Interpretation and Application of the 1971 Montreal Convention Arising from the Aerial Incident at Lockerbie (Libyan Arab Jamahiriya v. United Kingdom)*, Provisional Measures, Order of 14 April 1992, ICJ Reports 1992, p. 3, para. 39. *See also* Dapo Akande, 'The Effect of Security Council Resolutions and Domestic Proceedings on State Obligations to Cooperate with the ICC' (2012) 10 *Journal of International Criminal Justice*, 299, 305-06.

[91] UN Treaty Collection, 'Status of the Rome Statute of the International Criminal Court', (29 January 2014) available at http://treaties.un.org/pages/ViewDetails.aspx?src=TREATY&mtdsg_no=XVIII-10&chapter=18&lang=en#8.

[92] *See* UN Security Council, UN Doc. S/RES/1970 (2011), (26 February 2011); UN Security Council, UN Doc. S/RES/1593 (2005), (31 March 2005); ICC Statute, Article 86. *See also* Akande, 'The Effect of Security Council Resolutions and Domestic Proceedings on State Obligations to Cooperate with the ICC', 305.

[93] UN Security Council, UN Doc. S/RES/1593 (2005), (31 March 2005).

[94] UN Security Council, UN Doc. S/RES/1970 (2011), (26 February 2011).

[95] *Ibid.*, para. 5; UN Security Council, UN Doc. S/RES/1593 (2005), (31 March 2005), p. 1.

recognising that States not party to the Rome Statute have no obligation under the Statute, [the Security Council] urges all States and concerned regional and other international organisations to cooperate fully with the Court and the Prosecutor'.[96]

Paragraph 6 of the same Resolution goes further. It states, in part, that:

> nationals, current or former officials or personnel from a State outside the Libyan Arab Jamahiriya which is not a party to the Rome Statute of the International Criminal Court shall be subject to the exclusive jurisdiction of that State for all alleged acts or omissions arising out of or related to operations in the Libyan Arab Jamahiriya established or authorized by the Council, unless such exclusive jurisdiction has been expressly waived by the State.[97]

The media originally interpreted this article as directed toward foreign mercenaries hired by the Libyan regime. In fact, this paragraph of the Resolution was motivated by the United States, which fought strongly against the prosecution of US nationals by the ICC, and generally against the prosecution of nationals of non-States Parties. As a non-State Party to the Rome Statute, the United States has signed more than one hundred bilateral 'Article 98' agreements to ensure that states do not surrender US nationals to the ICC but rather surrender them to the United States.[98] In reality, these Article 98 agreements have the same effect as state immunities.[99]

---

[96] UN Security Council, UN Doc. S/RES/1970 (2011), (26 February 2011), para. 5.
[97] *Ibid.,* para. 6.
[98] CICC, 'Status of US Bilateral Immunity Agreements', (11 December 2006), available at http://www.iccnow.org/documents/CICCFS_BIAstatus_current.pdf.
[99] International agreements made *after* the entry into force of the Rome Statute have been subject to much analysis and criticism and some critics argue that such agreements have no effect. For instance, Ilias Bantekas and Susan Nash have submitted that such agreements are a violation of the Rome Statute, which demands that States Parties cooperate with the Court in the investigation and prosecution of alleged offenders. Bantekas and Nash also note that such an agreement is a conflicting obligation agreed subsequent in time to the commitments accepted under the Rome Statute. They argue that '[a] state is not permitted to absolve its existing obligations by entering into a new conflicting treaty without the prior treaty having been terminated by the express consent of all relevant parties'. As a result, such agreements should have no binding effect. *See* Ilias Bantekas and Susan Nash (eds.), *International Criminal Law*, 3rd edn (London: Routledge and Cavendish, 2007) pp. 539–542; *see also* Claus Kreβ and Kimberly Prost in Otto Triffterer (ed.), *Commentary on the Rome Statute of the*

By the unanimously endorsed Security Council Resolution 1970 of 26 February 2011, the UN Security Council referred 'the situation in the Libyan Arab Jamahiriya since 15 February 2011 to the Prosecutor of the International Criminal Court (ICC)'.[100] The Council noted that 'the widespread and systematic attacks currently taking place in the Libyan Arab Jamahiriya against the civilian population may amount to crimes against humanity'.[101]

Following the Security Council's referral, Libya's National Transitional Council (NTC) began an investigation into financial crimes and corruption allegations against Saif Al-Islam Gaddafi; this was later extended to include alleged 'crimes against the person' under Libyan law in Decision Number 102. An investigation into serious crimes allegedly committed by Gaddafi during the revolution, including murder and rape, was launched on 8 January 2012.

On 3 March 2011, following a preliminary examination of available information, the ICC Prosecutor concluded that there was a reasonable basis to believe that crimes under the ICC's jurisdiction had been committed in Libya from 15 February 2011 onwards.[102] The preliminary investigation by the Prosecutor concluded that no 'genuine national

---

International Criminal Court: Observers' Notes, Article by Article, 2nd edn (München: CH Beck, Hart and Nomos, 2008), p. 1618. However, other commentators have taken a different view. *See* James Crawford, Philippe Sands and Ralph Wilde, 'Joint Opinion in the Matter of the Statute of the International Criminal Court and In the Matter of Bilateral Agreements Sought by the United States under Article 98(2) of the Statute', (5 June 2003), para. 38, available at http://www.amicc.org/docs/Art98-14une03FINAL.pdf. *See also* Salvatore Zappalà, 'The reaction of the US to the Entry into Force of the ICC Statute: Comments on UN SC Resolution 1422 (2002) and Article 98 Agreements', (2003) 1 *Journal of International Criminal Justice* 114.; *See also The Prosecutor v. Saif Al-Islam Gaddafi and Abdullah Al-Senussi,* Doc. ICC-01/11-01/11-130-AnxC, 'Report by Prosecutor General as to Scope of Investigation of Saif Al-Islam Gaddafi and Libyan Criminal Procedure', (1 May 2012).

[100] *See* UN Security Council, UN Doc. S/RES/1970 (2011), (26 February 2011), para. 4-8.

[101] *Ibid.,* p. 1.

[102] ICC, 'Situations and Cases: Libya', (2014) available at http://www.icc-cpi.int/en_menus/icc/situations%20and%20cases/Pages/situations%20and%20cases.aspx; ICC, 'ICC Prosecution to open an investigation in Libya', (2 March 2011), available at http://www.icc-cpi.int/en_menus/icc/situations%20and%20cases/situations/icc0111/press%20releases/Pages/statement%20020311.aspx.

investigation or prosecution'[103] was taking place. Regarding the Libyan admissibility challenge that followed, Prosecutor Moreno-Ocampo reaffirmed that the 'admissibility analysis' is an 'assessment as to whether or not the national authorities have investigated or prosecuted, or are investigating or prosecuting genuinely the cases selected by the Office [of the Prosecutor]'[104] which entails a continuous 'evaluation of Libya's efforts in order to ensure that Justice is done in Libya'.[105] A similar investigation into crimes allegedly committed by Al-Senussi commenced on 9 April 2012.[106]

Additionally, in February 2012, the NTC introduced the Transitional Justice Law, which established a National Fact-Finding and Reconciliation Commission mandated to investigate crimes and human rights violations committed since 1 September 1969. These new transitional laws 'would allow fact-finding reparations and trials in relation to the grievances suffered by the Libyan people during the tyranny of Gaddafi and other sufferings and injustices during the transitional period, as well as trials without compromising international standards'.[107] The Transitional Justice Law (TJL) was adopted on 22 September 2013[108] and promulgated by the General National Congress in December 2013[109]. The law requires that,

---

[103] ICC-OTP, 'Report on Preliminary Examination Activities', (13 December 2011), para. 118, available at http://www.icc-cpi.int/NR/rdonlyres/63682F4E-49C8-445D-8C13-F310A4F3AEC2/284116/OTPReportonPreliminaryExaminations13December2011.pdf.

[104] ICC-OTP, 'Third Report of the Prosecutor of the International Criminal Court to the UN Security Council Pursuant to UNSCR 1970 (2011), (16 May 2012), para. 61, available at http://www.icc-cpi.int/NR/rdonlyres/D313B617-6A86-4D64-88AD-A89375C18FB9/0/UNSCreportLibyaMay2012Eng.pdf.

[105] *Ibid.*, para. 62.

[106] *The Prosecutor v. Saif Al-Islam Gadaffi and Abdullah Al-Senussi*, Doc. ICC-01/11-01/11-466-Red, 'Decision on the Admissibility of the Case Against Abdullah Al-Senussi', (11 October 2013), para. 15.

[107] Human Rights Watch, 'Statement by Justice Minister of Libya Salah Marghani about Libya Chapter of World Report 2013', (6 February 2013), p. 2, available at http://www.hrw.org/sites/default/files/related_material/2013_Libya_Worldreport.pdf.

[108] United National Support Mission in Libya (UNSMIL), 'United Nations Welcomes Adoption of Transitional Justice Law', (25 September 2013), available at http://unsmil.unmissions.org/Default.aspx?ctl=Details&tabid=3543&mid=6187&ItemID=1735515.

[109] I have sourced conflicting dates for promulgation; the GNC website seems to indicate 2 December 2013 (General National Congress, 'Legislation', (2014), available at http://www.gnc.gov.ly/legislation_page.aspx), while a report from Lawyers for Justice in Libya states 8 December 2013 (Lawyers for Justice in

within 90 days of promulgation, all conflict-related detainees should be released or referred to the public prosecutor.[110] On 7 December 2013 four senior members of the Social Council of the Warfallah Tribes were released from Zawiya after a year's detention without trial.[111] To date, however, there is no information regarding implementation of the law nor any information as to progress with fact-finding reparations and trials.

The Fact-Finding and Reconciliation Commission seems to be a quasi-judicial instrument in which victims' rights are mentioned only with regard to compensation. The members of the Commission are all senior judges.[112] The current transitional justice law does not include criminal justice or institutional reform law, nor does it contain definitions of terms like 'victims'.[113] Furthermore, the Commission does not seem to be active in either truth seeking or reconciliation.

While recognised by the UN Human Rights Council as constituting a necessary positive step toward achieving justice and accountability in

---

Libya, 'An Eye on Human Rights in Libya – International Human Rights day 2013', (10 December 2013), available at http://www.libyanjustice.org/news/news/post/112-international-human-rights-day-2013---an-eye-on-human-rights-in-libya). An UNSMIL article dated 8 December 2013 refers to an event of 7 December 2013 occurring 'in the week in which the Law on Transitional Justice was promulgated by the General National Congress' (UNSMIL, 'Zawiya Releases, Transitional Justice Law Important Steps in Path Towards Justice and Reconciliation', (8 December 2013), available at http://unsmilunmissions.org/Default.aspx?ctl=Details&tabid=3543&mid=6187&ItemID=1773847).

[110] UNSMIL and OHCHR, 'Torture and Deaths in Detention in Libya', (October 2013) available at http://www.ohchr.org/Documents/Countries/LY/TortureDeathsDetentionLibya.pdf.

[111] UNSMIL, 'Zawiya Releases, Transitional Justice Law Important Steps in Path Towards Justice and Reconciliation'.

[112] UNSMIL, 'Transitional Justice – Foundation for a new Libya', (17 September 2012), p. 2, available at http://unsmil.unmissions.org/LinkClick.aspx?fileticket=8XrRUO-sXBs%3d&tabid=3543&language=en-US.

[113] UNSMIL, 'Recommendations of the Conference on Truth and Reconciliation', (12 December 2012), available at http://unsmil.unmissions.org/Default.aspx?tabid=5292&ctl=Details&mid=9097&ItemID=807652&language=en-US. *See also* Law No. 29 of 2013 Regarding Transitional Justice, available (in Arabic) at http://www.gnc.gov.ly/legislation_files/635246105701443979.pdf.

Libya, the Commission was criticised for lacking an independent and impartial process of membership appointment.[114]

Subsequently, the ICC Prosecutor requested arrest warrants for Libya's leader Muammar Gaddafi, along with his two closest associates, son Saif Al-Islam and Head of the Intelligence Abdullah Al-Senussi, for crimes against humanity committed since February 2011.[115] The application to the Pre-Trial Chamber I claimed direct evidence that Gaddafi maintained a 'systematic policy of suppressing any challenge to his authority', according to which he ordered abductions, mass arrests, torture, and killing of civilians, which were variously carried out by Al-Islam and Al-Senussi.[116] Substantial cooperation from eleven states enabled the Prosecutor to gather extensive evidence of crimes and Gaddafi's connection to them in just three months.[117] On 27 June 2011, ICC Pre-Trial Chamber I issued warrants for Muammar Gaddafi,[118] Abdullah Al-Senussi,[119] and Saif Al-Islam Gaddafi[120] for alleged crimes against humanity.

---

[114] UNHRC, 'Report of the International Commission of Inquiry on Libya', UN Doc. A/HRC/19/68, (8 March 2012), para. 114.

[115] *See Situation in the Libyan Arab Jamahiriya*, Doc. ICC-01/11-01/11-2, 'Warrant of Arrest for Muammar Mohammed Abu Minyar Gaddafi', (27 June 2011); *Situation in the Libyan Arab Jamahiriya*, Doc. ICC-01/11-01/11-4, 'Warrant of Arrest for Abdullah Al-Senussi', (27 June 2011); *Situation in the Libyan Arab Jamahiriya*, Doc. ICC-01/11-01/11-14, 'Warrant of Arrest for Saif Al-Islam Gaddafi', (27 June 2011).

[116] *Situation in the Libyan Arab Jamahiriya*, Doc. ICC-01/11-4-Red, 'Prosecutor's Application Pursuant to Article 58 as to Muammar Mohammed Abu Minyar Gaddafi, Saif Al-Islam Gaddafi and Abdullah Al-Senussi', (16 May 2011), para. 5.

[117] ICC, 'Questions and Answers on the ICC proceedings in the Libya situation following the Prosecutor's request for three arrest warrants', Doc. ICC-PIDS-Q&A-LIB-00-002/11_Eng, (16 May 2011), p. 2.

[118] *Situation in the Libyan Arab Jamahiriya*, Doc. ICC-01/11-01/11-2, 'Warrant of Arrest for Muammar Mohammed Abu Minyar Gaddafi', (27 June 2011). On 22 November 2011, Pre-Trial Chamber I decided to terminate the case against Muammar Gaddafi following his death. *See The Prosecutor v. Muammar Mohammed Abu Minyar Gaddafi, Saif Al-Islam Gaddafi and Abdullah Al-Senussi*, Doc. ICC-01/11-01/11-28, 'Decision to Terminate the Case Against Muammar Mohammed Abu Minyar Gaddafi', (22 November 2011).

[119] *Situation in the Libyan Arab Jamahiriya*, Doc. ICC-01/11-01/11-4, 'Warrant of Arrest for Abdullah Al-Senussi', (27 June 2011).

[120] *Situation in the Libyan Arab Jamahiriya*, Doc. ICC-01/11-01/11-14, 'Warrant of Arrest for Saif Al-Islam Gaddafi', (27 June 2011).

The Prosecutor also indicated his intention to investigate the role of NATO, opposition forces, and pro-Gaddafi troops in alleged war crimes during the Libya conflict.[121] This is appropriate because the Prosecutor and the Court are not bound by the material characterisation of the Security Council's initial referral. Article 13(a) of the ICC Statute gives the Security Council the power to refer a 'situation' to the Court, which is 'generally defined in terms of temporal, territorial and in some cases, personal parameters',[122] and not in material parameters. Furthermore, the ICC Statute makes clear that the Prosecutor decides independently on the specific 'cases' and charges arising out of a situation.

With the Libya situation, the Court faces the most aggressive attack launched on the complementarity principle in its history. The current legal struggle is straightforward but reflects the enduring conflict between states and the ICC regarding jurisdiction. The Libyan government argues that it is actively prosecuting Saif Al-Islam Gaddafi and, thus, under Article 17 of the Rome Statute and the complementarity principle, the ICC simply does *not* have jurisdiction.[123]

The admissibility hearing has focused on the independence and impartiality of investigations and prospective proceedings in Libya. An OPCD visit to Libya in March 2012 yielded considerable concern about Gaddafi's ability to 'effectively participate in his defence' as a result of threats to his personal security[124] and warned of the 'distorting effect' that 'personal revenge' can have on achieving a fair trial.[125] Gaddafi himself has stated that his case cannot be called a trial and that an execution based on such a trial would amount to murder.[126] Libya, however, has argued

---

[121] ICC-OTP, 'Statement to the United Nations Security Council on the situation in Libya, pursuant to UNSCR 1970 (2011)', (2 November 2011), available at http://www.icc-cpi.int:80/NR/rdonlyres/AC6273F2-B27D-4BA5-B6A4-A23856FAC887/283927/StatementICCProsecutorLibyaReporttoUNSC021113.pdf.

[122] *Situation in the DRC,* Doc. ICC-01/04-101-tEN-Corr, 'Decision on the Application for Participation in the Proceedings of VPRS1, VPRS2, VPRS3, VPRS4, VPRS5 and VPRS6', (17 January 2006), para. 65.

[123] The question of admissibility is separate from the question of jurisdiction, which was established by UN Security Council Resolution 1970.

[124] *The Prosecutor v. Saif Al-Islam Gaddafi and Abdullah Al-Senussi*, Doc. ICC-01/11-01/11-70-Red2, 'Second Public Redacted Version of the 'Addendum to the Urgent Report Concerning the Visit to Libya'', (5 March 2012), para. 58.

[125] *Ibid.*, para. 53.

[126] *The Prosecutor v. Saif Al-Islam Gaddafi and Abdullah Al-Senussi*, Doc. ICC-01/11-01/11-190-Corr-Red, 'Public Redacted Version of the Corrigendum to the

that 'to deny the Libyan people this historic opportunity to eradicate the long-standing culture of impunity would be manifestly inconsistent with the object and purpose of the Rome Statute, which accords primacy to national judicial systems'.[127]

The admissibility issue has been made more complex by the fact that ICC personnel have themselves put out contradictory statements. The former ICC Prosecutor remarked that the Libyan judicial system was capable of conducting a fair trial. Despite strong calls to the contrary from human rights groups,[128] the Prosecutor reiterated his 'firm view that the strength of the Rome system lies in the possibility for shared responsibility and complementary actions between the Court and Libyan national judicial institutions'.[129]

Even the US War Crimes Chief, Stephen Rapp, expressed his preference for Libya to serve as the trial forum: '[w]e certainly would like to see the Libyans provide a fair and appropriate justice at the national level. It won't be the same thing that happens in The Hague but The Hague is only for a relative handful of cases and the international system

---

'Defence Response to the Application on behalf of the Government of Libya pursuant to Article 19 of the ICC Statute'', (31 July 2012), (hereinafter 'Corrigendum to the 'Defence Response to the Application on behalf of the Government of Libya''), para. 8.

[127] *The Prosecutor v. Saif Al-Islam Gaddafi and Abdullah Al-Senussi*, Doc. ICC-01/11-01/11-130-Red, 'Application on behalf of the Government of Libya pursuant to Article 19 of the ICC Statute', (1 May 2012), para. 2. *See also* John Bellinger who argued that the decision on where to try Saif Al-Islam and Al-Senussi should be left to the Libyans. This argument is also supported by the NTC. As one NTC official stated: 'local justice is the rule and international justice is the exception'. *See* John Bellinger, 'Regime trials belong in Libya's courts', *Washington Post*, (23 November 2011) available at http://www.washingtonpost.com/opinions/trials-of-moammar-gaddafis-favored-few-belong-in-libyas-courts/2011/11/22/gIQANU4WmN_story.html.

[128] Human Rights Watch, 'Libya: Surrender Saif Al-Islam Gaddafi to ICC', (19 November 2011), available at http://www.hrw.org/news/2011/11/19/libya-surrender-saif-al-islam-gaddafi-icc; *See* Francois Murphy, 'ICC Prosecutor happy for Libya to try Gaddafi son', *Reuters*, (23 November 2011), available at http://www.reuters.com/article/2011/11/23/us-libya-icc-saif-idUSTRE7AM13H20111123.

[129] ICC-OTP, 'Fifth Report of the Prosecutor of the International Criminal Court to the UN Security Council Pursuant to UNSCR 1970', para. 11, (8 May 2013), available at http://www.icc-cpi.int/iccdocs/doc/Fifth-Report-Prosecutor-to-UNSC-pursuant-UNSCR-1970-2011-ENG.pdf.

we see developing is one where countries do these cases themselves with international assistance, sometimes with international participation'.[130]

The Libyan government 'regards the trial of Mr Gaddafi and Mr Al-Senussi as a matter of the highest national importance, not only in bringing justice for the Libyan people but also in demonstrating that the Libyan justice system is capable of proper investigation and prosecution, and that it can conduct fair trials (that meet all applicable international standards)'.[131]

A. Saif Al-Islam Gaddafi

Initially, Libya requested postponing Gaddafi's surrender under Article 94 whereby the execution of Court requests may be postponed if execution would interfere with unrelated ongoing domestic investigations or prosecutions. The Court, however, denied the request, ruling that Article 94 applies only to cooperation requests and not requests to surrender persons.[132] Subsequently, Libya notified the Court of its intention to submit an admissibility challenge: 'Libya also hereby notifies Pre-Trial Chamber I of its intention to challenge the admissibility of the case concerning Saif Al-Islam Gaddafi pursuant to Articles 19(2)(b), 19(5), and 19(6) of the ICC Statute. The challenge will be made on the grounds that

---

[130] *See* Chris McGreal, 'US Backs Libya in Dispute over Trial Location for Saif Al-Islam Gaddafi', *The Guardian,* (6 June 2012), available at http://www.guardian.co.uk/world/2012/jun/06/us-libya-saif-al-islam-gaddafi-trial.

[131] *The Prosecutor v. Saif Al-Islam Gaddafi and Abdullah Al-Senussi*, Doc. ICC-01/11-01/11-130-Red, 'Application on behalf of the Government of Libya pursuant to Article 19 of the ICC Statute', (1 May 2012), para. 11.

[132] *The Prosecutor v. Saif Al-Islam Gaddafi and Abdullah Al-Senussi*, Doc. ICC-01/11-01/11-72, 'Decision on Libya's Submissions Regarding the Arrest of Saif Al-Islam Gaddafi', (7 March 2012), paras 13-16. 'Given that the present cooperation request is a surrender request, the Chamber finds that Libya is not entitled to seek any relief pursuant to article 94(1) of the Statute. The Postponement Request must therefore be dismissed'. Akande also discusses obligations under Article 94 of the ICC Statute. *See* Akande, 'The Effect of Security Council Resolutions and Domestic Proceedings on State Obligations to Cooperate with the ICC', 321-324. 'Libya can only suspend the obligation to surrender by actually making an admissibility challenge. Libya may not suspend this obligation simply by relying on Article 94, which permits the postponement of the execution of a request for cooperation where the immediate execution of the request would interfere with an ongoing national investigation or prosecution' (*Ibid.*, 323).

Libya is investigating Saif Al-Islam Gaddafi before its national judicial system'.[133]

Libya made a second postponement request under Article 95, which provides that states may postpone the execution of Court requests when there is an admissibility challenge under consideration, pending a decision from the Court. The Pre-Trial Chamber denied the request, holding that postponement under Article 95 requires a formal admissibility challenge.

> [Article 95] may be invoked only *'where there is an admissibility challenge under consideration by the Court* pursuant to article 18 or 19' [emphasis added].... Though Libya has announced that an admissibility challenge is forthcoming, there is currently no such challenge before the Chamber. Therefore, the Chamber holds that article 95 of the Statute cannot serve as a legal basis for Libya's Second Postponement Request. Consequently, the Second Postponement Request presented by the Government of Libya must be rejected. At this time, the Chamber does not consider it necessary to determine whether article 95 of the Statute applies to surrender requests.[134]

The Court again requested that Libya 'proceed immediately with the surrender of Mr Gaddafi to the Court'.[135]

In May 2012, Libya formally challenged admissibility of the cases against Saif Al-Islam Gaddafi and Abdullah Al-Senussi.[136] The Pre-Trial

---

[133] *The Prosecutor v. Saif Al-Islam Gaddafi and Abdullah Al-Senussi*, Doc. ICC-01/11-01/11-82, 'Notification and Request by the Government of Libya in response to 'Decision on Libya's Submissions Regarding the Arrest of Saif Al-Islam Gaddafi'', (22 March 2012), para. 2. *See also*, Carsten Stahn, 'Libya, the International Criminal Court and Complementarity: A Test for Shared Responsibility', (2012) 10 *Journal of International Criminal Justice* 325, 332 (noting '[t]he situation in Libya is particular since domestic authorities refused to surrender Saif Al-Islam Gaddafi after arrest, without making an immediate admissibility challenge').

[134] *The Prosecutor v. Saif Al-Islam Gaddafi and Abdullah Al-Senussi*, Doc. ICC-01/11-01/11-100, 'Decision Regarding the Second Request by the Government of Libya for Postponement of the Surrender of Saif Al-Islam Gaddafi', (4 April 2012), para. 18.

[135] *Ibid.,* p. 9. *See also* Carsten Stahn, 'Libya, the International Criminal Court and Complementarity', (surrender, complementarity, admissibility in context of Libya).

[136] *See The Prosecutor v. Saif Al-Islam Gaddafi and Abdullah Al-Senussi*, Doc. ICC-01/11-01/11-130-Red, 'Application on behalf of the Government of Libya pursuant to Article 19 of the ICC Statute', (1 May 2012).

Chamber determined that Article 95 exceptions to cooperation also applied to requests to surrender, unlike Article 94.[137] The Court then granted Libya's request to postpone surrender pursuant to Article 95, pending the Court's decision on admissibility: '[w]ithout entering into the discussion of whether the case is admissible, the Chamber considers that Libya's Admissibility Challenge has been properly made within the terms of Article 19(2) of the Statute and Rule 58(1) of the Rules. Accordingly, the request for arrest and surrender for Mr Gaddafi may be postponed'.[138]

In October 2012, Pre-Trial Chamber I heard oral arguments to determine whether Libya was actually investigating the case and whether Libya was 'willing and able' to do so genuinely.[139] In summary, the Court questioned the status of Libya's investigation, methods of procuring evidence, legal basis for monitoring domestic cases, ability to prosecute under Libyan law, application of Libyan criminal procedural rights to Gaddafi's case, and the potential for continuance without custody of the accused. Notably, the Court stressed Libya's burden to 'provide concrete, tangible and pertinent evidence... that proper investigations are currently ongoing and proper and concrete preparations for the trial are ongoing'.[140]

The government counter-argued that the National Transitional Council's *raison d'être* is to 'ensure justice for the victims of State-sponsored human rights abuses'[141] and that 'Libya is *genuinely* investigating allegations of crimes against humanity, consistent with an

---

[137] *The Prosecutor v. Saif Al-Islam Gaddafi and Abdullah Al-Senussi*, Doc. ICC-01/11-01/11-163, 'Decision on the Postponement of the Execution of the Request for Surrender of Saif Al-Islam Gaddafi Pursuant to Article 95 of the Rome Statute', (1 June 2012), para. 37. '[T]he Chamber concludes that article 95 of the Statute is applicable to requests for arrest and surrender, pending determination of an admissibility challenge brought before the Court'.

[138] *Ibid.*, para. 39.

[139] *The Prosecutor v. Saif Al-Islam Gaddafi and Abdullah Al-Senussi*, Doc. ICC-01/11-01/11-T-2-Red-ENG, 'Hearing Transcript', (9 October 2012), at 4:17-23.

[140] *The Prosecutor v. Saif Al-Islam Gaddafi and Abdullah Al-Senussi*, Doc. ICC-01/11-01/11-T-3-Red-ENG, 'Hearing Transcript', (10 October 2012) (hereinafter '10 October Transcript'), at 64:20-22. Such evidence is 'really very important for the outcome of these proceedings' (*Ibid.*, at 64:25 – 65:1).

[141] *The Prosecutor v. Saif Al-Islam Gaddafi and Abdullah Al-Senussi*, Doc. ICC-01/11-01/11-130-Red, 'Application on behalf of the Government of Libya pursuant to Article 19 of the ICC Statute', (1 May 2012), para. 93.

intention and willingness to bring the concerned persons to justice within the meaning of Article 17(2) of the Statute'.[142]

The Libyan government, waiting for Gaddafi's transfer to Tripoli, has stressed that trials *in absentia* are not possible if '[the defendant] is present and the location of his presence is known on the Libyan territory'.[143] Although the government has affirmed its ability to 'obtain the accused or the necessary evidence and testimony',[144] the unresolved custody issue may prove damaging to Libya's admissibility challenge.

Alleged repeated violations of Gaddafi's rights are said to demonstrate an institutional lack of understanding of 'basic human rights or the role of the Defence'.[145] The UN International Commission of Inquiry in Libya reported that few officials demonstrate 'a real understanding of basic legal and human rights standards'.[146] The OPCD also pointed to admissions by government officials that 'Libyan authorities [do] not yet have the ability to properly gather evidence or present a case'[147] and more specifically, prosecuting authorities 'do not appear to have the capacity to verify or assess the credibility of witnesses'.[148]

---

[142] *Ibid.*

[143] *The Prosecutor v. Saif Al-Islam Gaddafi and Abdullah Al-Senussi*, Doc. ICC-01/11-01/11-T-3-Red-ENG, '10 October Transcript' at 62:11-14. *See also*, ICC Statute, Article 17(3) states: 'unable to obtain the accused' caused by 'total or substantial collapse or unavailability of its national judicial system' as grounds for 'inability'.

[144] *The Prosecutor v. Saif Al-Islam Gaddafi and Abdullah Al-Senussi*, Doc. ICC-01/11-01/11-130-Red, 'Application on behalf of the Government of Libya pursuant to Article 19 of the ICC Statute', (1 May 2012), para. 96.

[145] *The Prosecutor v. Saif Al-Islam Gaddafi and Abdullah Al-Senussi*, Doc. ICC-01/11-01/11-190-Corr-Red, 'Corrigendum to the 'Defence Response to the Application on behalf of the Government of Libya'', para. 369

[146] UNHRC, 'Report of the International Commission of Inquiry on Libya', UN Doc. A/HRC/19/68, (8 March 2012), para. 12.

[147] *The Prosecutor v. Saif Al-Islam Gaddafi and Abdullah Al-Senussi*, Doc. ICC-01/11-01/11-190-Corr-Red, 'Corrigendum to the 'Defence Response to the Application on behalf of the Government of Libya'', para. 373, *quoting* NTC official Fathi Baji interviewed in D. Kirkpatrick and M. Simons, 'Libya Resists International Court's Claim on War Crimes Case', *New York Times*, (21 March 2012).

[148] *Ibid.*, para. 369.

Ultimately, the Pre-Trial Chamber ruled against the Libyan government and held that the case is admissible to the ICC.[149] One of the Court's main findings was that Libya's domestic investigation was not demonstrably the same as the ICC's. The Court ruled that the Libyan case would not need to cover 'exactly the same acts…constituting instances of Mr Gaddafi's alleged course of conduct', but would need to show that the domestic case covered at least 'the same conduct underlying the Warrant of Arrest'.[150] The Court also found that many of the documents provided contained no relevant information for the determination.[151] The evidence did not allow the Chamber to discern sufficient detail about the national case against Mr Gaddafi[152] and was, therefore, insufficient to demonstrate that Libya was investigating the same case as that before the Court.[153]

In my opinion, the Libyan government's application was strong and the Pre-Trial Chamber's decision was harsh. The government put forward an account by the Libyan Prosecutor-General that emphasised the extensive nature of the investigation and compliance with domestic law. Specifically, it affirmed that both individuals (Gaddafi and Al-Senussi) were being actively investigated in respect of the same allegations of murder and persecution that form the basis for the ICC arrest warrants—which is to say that the domestic investigations covered 'substantially the same conduct' as the ICC indictments and for the same period in question.[154] The range of charges included: 'murder, complicity in incitement to rape, plunder, sabotage, embezzlement of public funds, and acts harmful to national unity'.[155] The fact that these acts are to be charged as 'ordinary crimes' pursuant to the relevant articles of the Libyan

---

[149] *The Prosecutor v. Said Al-Islam Gaddafi and Abdullah Al-Senussi*, Doc. ICC-01/11-01/11-344-Red, 'Decision on the admissibility of the case against Saif Al-Islam Gaddafi', (31 May 2013), p. 91.
[150] *Ibid.*, para. 83.
[151] *Ibid.*, para. 106, *citing* a number of documents provided by Libya.
[152] *Ibid.*, para. 135.
[153] *Ibid.*, para. 134.
[154] *The Prosecutor v. Saif Al-Islam Gaddafi and Abdullah Al-Senussi*, Doc. ICC-01/11-01/11-130-Red, 'Application on behalf of the Government of Libya pursuant to Article 19 of the ICC Statute', (1 May 2012), para. 83.
[155] Youssef Ba, 'Libya court indicts Kadhafi aides over 2011 uprising', *AFP*, (24 October 2013), available at
http://www.globalpost.com/dispatch/news/afp/131024/libya-court-indicts-kadhafi-aides-2011-uprising-charges.

Criminal Code 1953 to me is irrelevant.[156] My position is supported by a number of jurists who have argued that the prosecution of international crimes using ordinary domestic law would satisfy a state's obligations under the Rome Statute.[157]

The Libyan government appealed the Pre-Trial Chamber's ruling.[158] In a broad attack against the Court's interpretation of the complementarity principle, Libya argued that in 'fail[ing] to implement a procedure that reflected the dynamic nature of the complementarity assessment', the Court 'erred procedurally, or acted unfairly'.[159] These failings, it argued,

---

[156] *The Prosecutor v. Saif Al-Islam Gaddafi and Abdullah Al-Senussi*, Doc. ICC-01/11-01/11-130-Red, 'Application on behalf of the Government of Libya pursuant to Article 19 of the ICC Statute', (1 May 2012), para. 75.

[157] Ward Ferdinandusse has explored several cases where grave breaches of the Geneva Conventions have been prosecuted using ordinary criminal provisions, demonstrating that international law allows states to fulfil their obligations on the basis of ordinary criminal law, and points to an ICTY ruling, that there is no rule, either in customary or in positive international law, which obligates states to prosecute acts which can be characterised as war crimes solely on the basis of international humanitarian law, completely setting aside any characterisations of their national criminal law. *See The Prosecutor v. Hadžihasanović and Kubura,* Case No. IT-01-47-T, 'Judgment', (15 March 2006), para. 206. Ferdinandusse considered that the complementarity regime of the ICC appears to regard prosecutions of international crimes on the basis of ordinary criminal law as a sufficient response, which precludes the ICC from exercising jurisdiction. Ward Ferdinandusse, 'The Prosecution of Grave Breaches in National Courts', (2009) 7 *Journal of International Criminal Justice* 723, 729; *see* Morten Bergsmo, Mads Harlem and Nobuo Hayashi (eds.), 'Importing Core International Crimes into National Criminal Law', *Forum for International Criminal Justice and Conflict*, Publications No. 1, (Oslo: International Peace Research Institute, 2007), p. 12; *see also* Liu Daqun, 'Should the Principle of *Ne Bis in Idem* also Be Taken into Consideration? A Response to Yarwood and Dold', (2007) 6 *Chinese Journal of International Law*, 789. 'The ICC Statute adopts a very pragmatic approach. So long as the perpetrators are brought to justice and the proceedings are not in violation of Article 20(3)(a) and (b), it does not matter whether the acts are prosecuted or convicted as domestic crimes or international crimes, and the aim of the Statute is reached' (*Ibid.*, 792).

[158] *See The Prosecutor v. Saif Al-Islam Gaddafi and Abdullah Al-Senussi*, Doc. ICC-01/11-01/11-370-Red3, 'Document in Support of the Government of Libya's Appeal against the 'Decision on the Admissibility of the Case against Saif Al-Islam Gaddafi'', (24 June 2013).

[159] *Ibid.*, paras 120 and 125.

led to 'a Decision that was so unfair and unreasonable as to constitute an abuse of discretion'.[160]

The core of Libya's argument was that in requiring the Libyan government 'to provide additional proof of the 'actual contours' and 'precise scope' of its domestic investigation',[161] the Pre-Trial Chamber applied a legal standard which required it to investigate more than *substantially* the same conduct, in order for the case to be found inadmissible: in other words, that the standard of evidence required by the Chamber suggested that it was then applying a stricter admissibility test.

Secondly, Libya argued that this standard 'necessarily and erroneously requires the domestic criminal process to encompass nearly all aspects – or at least more than 'certain aspects' of the ICC case'.[162] It submitted that a national investigation should cover 'some but not all aspects of the ICC case'.[163]

Libya maintained that the Court's interpretation of Article 17(1)(a) was 'overly exacting and narrow' and is 'inconsistent with the Statute's presumption in favour of national jurisdictions'.[164] This argument is particularly relevant, in my opinion, to overall focus on the principle of complementarity, as I have argued in this book. If the Court holds on too tightly to its own perceived worth, it will destroy the principle of complementarity.

In Chapter 3, we discussed in detail the admissibility standard regarding a state's 'inability' to conduct national criminal proceedings. Article 17(3) of the Statute provides that:

> [i]n order to determine inability in a particular case, the Court shall consider whether, due to a total or substantial collapse or unavailability of its national judicial system, the State is unable to obtain the accused or the necessary evidence and testimony or otherwise unable to carry out its proceedings.[165]

---

[160] *Ibid.*, para. 141.
[161] *Ibid.*, paras 53, 59 and 63.
[162] *Ibid.,* para. 53.
[163] *See* e.g. *Ibid.*, para. 74.
[164] *Ibid.*, paras 46(b), 55-56.
[165] ICC Statute, Article 17(3).

In its argument, Libya believes that the Court has to articulate its reasoning beyond making general statements about the shortcomings of the Libyan judicial system.[166] I also believe this position is correct, despite the specific language found in Article 17(3) that focuses on the overall 'national judicial system'. Again, consistent with the spirit of the principle of complementarity, the interpretation of this article should be a more exacting, narrow and stringent one, which would have led to a finding of inadmissibility.

The OTP,[167] OPCV,[168] and the Defence all oppose the substance of Libya's Appeal and have each submitted a formal response.[169] The OPCV described the Court's interpretation and application of the law as 'reasonable' and its procedure as 'unimpeachable'.[170] The Defence urged the Appeals Chamber to summarily dismiss the Appeal.[171]

B. Abdullah Al-Senussi

Whereas the ICC has been adamant about trying Saif Al-Islam Gaddafi in The Hague, it turned 180 degrees on the admissibility challenge to the

[166] *The Prosecutor v. Saif Al-Islam Gaddafi and Abdullah Al-Senussi*, Doc. ICC-01/11-01/11-370-Red3, 'Document in Support of the Government of Libya's Appeal against the 'Decision on the Admissibility of the Case against Saif Al-Islam Gaddafi'', (24 June 2013), paras 148-149.

[167] *See The Prosecutor v. Saif Al-Islam Gaddafi and Abdullah Al-Senussi*, Doc. ICC-01/11-01/11-384-Red, 'Prosecution Response to the 'Document in Support of the Government of Libya's Appeal Against the Decision on the Admissibility of the Case Against Saif Al-Islam Gaddafi'', (22 July 2013).

[168] *See The Prosecutor v. Saif Al-Islam Gaddafi and Abdullah Al-Senussi*, Doc. ICC-01/11-01/11-411-Red, 'Observations on behalf of victims on the Government of Libya's appeal against the decision of Pre-Trial Chamber I entitled 'Decision on the Admissibility of the Case Against Saif Al-Islam Gaddafi', (21 August 2013), (hereinafter 'OPCV Response on the Government of Libya's Appeal').

[169] *See The Prosecutor v. Saif Al-Islam Gaddafi and Abdullah Al-Senussi*, Doc. ICC-01/11-01/11-386-Red, 'Defence Response to the 'Document in Support of the Government of Libya's Appeal Against the Decision on the Admissibility of the Case Against Saif Al-Islam Gaddafi', (18 July 2013) (hereinafter 'Defence Response on the Government of Libya's Appeal').

[170] *The Prosecutor v. Saif Al-Islam Gaddafi and Abdullah Al-Senussi*, Doc. ICC-01/11-01/11-411-Red, 'OPCV Response on the Government of Libya's Appeal', para. 18.

[171] *The Prosecutor v. Saif Al-Islam Gaddafi and Abdullah Al-Senussi*, Doc. ICC-01/11-01/11-386-Red, 'Defence Response on the Government of Libya's Appeal', para. 6.

case of *Abdullah Al-Senussi*.[172] The *Gaddafi* decision was completely antithetical to the *Al-Senussi* decision. On 11 October 2013, Pre-Trial Chamber I determined that the case of Abdullah Al-Senussi was inadmissible before the ICC.[173] The decision marks the first time the Court has found in favour of a challenging State in an admissibility decision.[174]

The initial question analysed by the Court in admissibility challenges is whether the challenging state can demonstrate that (a) concrete and progressive steps are being undertaken (b) to investigate the same person and 'substantially the same case' as that which is subject to the ICC Warrant of Arrest.[175]

As in the *Gaddafi* case, the OPCV and the Defence both argued that Libya had not submitted evidence 'of sufficient degree of specificity and probative value' (being the evidentiary standard previously articulated by the Court) to demonstrate that the scope of its domestic investigation covered the same underlying conduct cited by the Court.[176] The Defence described the materials submitted by Libya as 'general, vague, and lacking in sufficient detail'.[177] The OPCV said 'substantially the same conduct'

[172] The accused was Muammar Gaddafi's head of Military Intelligence, and bore the rank of colonel. The ICC issued its Warrant of Arrest against him on 27 June 2011. Mr Al-Senussi is charged with two counts of crimes against humanity (murder and persecution) as an indirect perpetrator. *See Situation in the Libyan Arab Jamahiriya*, Doc. ICC-01/11-01/11-4, 'Warrant of Arrest for Abdullah Al-Senussi', (27 June 2011).

[173] *See The Prosecutor v. Saif Al-Islam Gadaffi and Abdullah Al-Senussi*, Doc. ICC-01/11-01/11-466-Red, 'Decision on the Admissibility of the Case Against Abdullah Al-Senussi', (11 October 2013).

[174] 'Gaddafi-era spy chief al-Senussi to be tried in Libya', *BBC News*, (11 October 2013), available at www.bbc.co.uk/news/world-africa-24493885.

[175] The scope of the ICC case, as expressed in *Situation in the Libyan Arab Jamahiriya*, Doc. ICC-01/11-01/11-4, 'Warrant of Arrest for Abdullah Al-Senussi', (27 June 2011), is given in *The Prosecutor v. Saif Al-Islam Gadaffi and Abdullah Al-Senussi*, Doc. ICC-01/11-01/11-466-Red, 'Decision on the Admissibility of the Case Against Abdullah Al-Senussi', (11 October 2013), para. 70.

[176] *See The Prosecutor v. Saif Al-Islam Gadaffi and Abdullah Al-Senussi*, Doc. ICC-01/11-01/11-466-Red, 'Decision on the Admissibility of the Case Against Abdullah Al-Senussi', (11 October 2013), paras 41 and 51.

[177] *The Prosecutor v. Saif Al-Islam Gadaffi and Abdullah Al-Senussi*, Doc. ICC-01/11-01/11-356, 'Defence Response on behalf of Mr Abdullah Al-Senussi to 'Application on behalf of the Government of Libya relating to Abdullah Al-Senussi pursuant to Article 19 of the ICC Statute', (14 June 2013), para. 27.

means the 'overwhelming majority of incidents [referred to in the ICC Warrant of Arrest]',[178] and Libya demonstrated only that it was investigating 'a limited number of acts'.[179]

By contrast, the Prosecutor argued that Libya was able to demonstrate 'that it is investigating Mr Al-Senussi for the same case that is before the Court'.[180] The Prosecutor maintained the same position as in the *Gaddafi* case. Acknowledging that the evidence did not prove Libya to be investigating all incidents, he argued that any such shortcomings or evidentiary gaps were 'not substantial' and therefore did 'not affect the substantial identity between the two cases'.[181]

In the end, the Court agreed with the Prosecutor.[182] While finding much of the material inadequate or irrelevant in demonstrating the scope of Libya's domestic investigation,[183] the Court found other items of evidence directly relevant to the scope and progress of the case. It attached particular probative weight to witness accounts going to Mr Al-Senussi's authority over the security forces,[184] to his written orders,[185] and to medical reports describing injuries suffered by regime opponents.[186]

---

[178] *The Prosecutor v. Saif Al-Islam Gadaffi and Abdullah Al-Senussi*, Doc. ICC-01/11-01/11-353-Red, 'Observations on behalf of victims on Response on the 'Application on behalf of the Government of Libya relating to Abdullah Al-Senussi pursuant to Article 19 of the ICC Statute'', (17 June 2013), para. 36.

[179] *The Prosecutor v. Saif Al-Islam Gadaffi and Abdullah Al-Senussi*, Doc. ICC-01/11-01/11-466-Red, 'Decision on the Admissibility of the Case Against Abdullah Al-Senussi', (11 October 2013), para. 56.

[180] *Ibid.,* para. 43. *See also The Prosecutor v. Saif Al-Islam Gadaffi and Abdullah Al-Senussi*, Doc. ICC-01/11-01/11-321-Red, 'Prosecution's Response to 'Application on behalf of the Government of Libya relating to Abdullah Al-Senussi pursuant to Article 19 of the ICC Statute'', (2 May 2013), para. 86.

[181] *Ibid.,* para. 50. *See also The Prosecutor v. Saif Al-Islam Gadaffi and Abdullah Al-Senussi*, Doc. ICC-01/11-01/11-321-Red, 'Prosecution's Response to Application on behalf of the Government of Libya relating to Abdullah Al-Senussi', para. 78.

[182] *Ibid.,* paras 160-162 and 167-168.

[183] *Ibid.* The material included bare summaries of witness statements (paras 84-87); letters by local authorities describing the outline of the investigation (paras 88-99); and witness statements concerning Saif Gaddafi (para. 110).

[184] *Ibid.,* para. 118.

[185] *Ibid.,* paras 144-145.

[186] *Ibid.,* para. 143.

The real controversy of this decision relates to the second part of the admissibility assessment: whether Libya was willing and able to provide Mr Al-Senussi a genuine trial. Factual evidence was required in support of two key questions: (1) does Libya have the capacity to conduct a fair trial, and (2) what impact might the unstable security environment have on an investigation and trial?

What was interesting about the Court's decision was that it focused on procedural irregularities in Mr Al-Senussi's domestic trial, such as his lack of defence counsel throughout the investigative stage. However, the Court ruled that this did 'not indicate Libya's unwillingness or inability to carry out the proceedings against Mr Al-Senussi'.[187]

There are arguable weaknesses, or at least points of reasonable contention, in the Court's findings as to the legal consequences of Mr Al-Senussi's lack of representation. In its Decision, the Court repeatedly emphasises the need for Libya (as for all parties) to properly substantiate its assertions.[188] Libya stated that a number of local lawyers expressed a willingness to represent Mr Al-Senussi.[189] The Prosecutor also said 'there is no impediment or defect that would render the future appointment of counsel impossible'.[190] The Court acceded, although Libya appears to have provided no substantiating documentation or evidence in support of this claim.[191]

---

[187] *Ibid.,* para. 242.

[188] *Ibid.,* paras 27, 207, 208 and 221. *See* para. 239, as the Chamber reprimands the Defence for making 'generic assertions without any tangible proof' and for not making 'concrete information' available to the Court.

[189] *See also The Prosecutor v. Saif Al-Islam Gadaffi and Abdullah Al-Senussi*, Doc. ICC-01/11-01/11-455, 'Government's Submissions and Response to Defence 'Filing on behalf of Mr Abdullah Al-Senussi pursuant to 'Decision on additional submissions in the proceedings related to Libya's challenge to the admissibility of the case against Abdullah Al-Senussi' of 19 September 2013' and 'Addendum' filed on 5 September 2013'', (26 September 2013), para. 27.

[190] *The Prosecutor v. Saif Al-Islam Gadaffi and Abdullah Al-Senussi*, Doc. ICC-01/11-01/11-466-Red, 'Decision on the Admissibility of the Case Against Abdullah Al-Senussi', (11 October 2013), para. 194.

[191] *Ibid.,* para. 239: 'the Chamber considers that the above submissions by the Defence amount to generic assertions without any tangible proof, and that no concrete information in this regard is made available to the Chamber'.

The Court's rationale seems to have focused on the case's political sensitivity and the country's security situation.[192] The Court's finding of 'ability' is remarkable since these impediments are almost certain to be ongoing difficulties.

Equally surprising is the fact that the Court did not consider the relevance (if any) of Article 21(3) or Article 17. As discussed earlier, Article 21(3) 'makes the interpretation as well as the application of the law relevant under the Statute subject to internationally recognised human rights'.[193] The Court's finding also made no reference to the statements by the Appeals Chamber in the *Lubanga* case, which categorically confirmed the applicability of these principles to jurisdictional disputes. Finally, there was no discussion of the ICC's basic fair trial expectations in admissibility proceedings under Article 17.[194]

In assessing Libya's ability to prosecute under Article 17(3), the Court's reasoning was nothing if not convoluted. It stated that Libya is 'not unable to otherwise carry out the proceedings against Mr Al-Senussi due to a total or substantial collapse or unavailability of its national judicial system'.[195] The Court concluded that 'the domestic proceedings…have so far not been prejudiced by…security challenges'[196] and, as to future proceedings, 'the Chamber cannot conclude at this point in time that the situation is such that [his] case will be impeded from proceeding further' by reason of poor security.[197] This last statement is striking considering that the security situation in Libya continues to unravel. However, the Court seemed to be making a distinction between the generic insecurity that might exist in any post-conflict environment and specific security issues attached to a particular trial.

---

[192] *Ibid.*, paras 232, 306 and 307.

[193] *The Prosecutor v. Thomas Lubanga Dyilo*, Doc. ICC-01/04-01/06-772, 'Judgment on the Appeal of Mr Thomas Lubanga Dyilo against the Decision on the Defence Challenge to the Jurisdiction of the Court pursuant to article 19(2)(a) of the Statute of 3 October 2006', (14 December 2006), para. 36.

[194] *Ibid.*, e.g. para. 37: '[a] fair trial is the only means to do justice. If no fair trial can be held, the object of the judicial process is frustrated and the process must be stopped'.

[195] *The Prosecutor v. Saif Al-Islam Gadaffi and Abdullah Al-Senussi*, Doc. ICC-01/11-01/11-466-Red, 'Decision on the Admissibility of the Case Against Abdullah Al-Senussi', (11 October 2013), para. 309.

[196] *Ibid.*, para. 299.

[197] *Ibid.*, para. 308.

In its decision, the Court emphasised that 'the existence of certain constraints under which a national system may be acting does not *per se* render the State unwilling or unable genuinely to carry out proceedings'[198] and that:

> More precisely, in relation to inability under article 17(3) of the Statute … not simply any 'security challenge' would amount to the unavailability or a total or substantial collapse of the national judicial system.[199]

The Court accepted Libya's assurance that security for Mr Al-Senussi was 'tight and effective, with local shops being asked to close for the duration of the hearing'.[200]

The Court also cites the conduct of one domestic hearing on 19 September 2013 as 'further confirmation' of Libya's ability to address its 'ongoing security difficulties'.[201] However, in a clear omission, the Court did not pause to consider the significance of the abduction of the Libyan Prime Minister, which took place the day before it issued its decision. The Court even dismissed the abduction and abuse of Taha Bara, Deputy Prosecutor to Mr Al-Senussi's case.[202] The Court found that there was no proof linking the abduction to the proceedings against Mr Al-Senussi.[203] While the Court acknowledged other threats or incidents of violence on judicial authorities, it did not believe they were to the extent where Libya could not carry out the proceedings.[204] The Court will likely point to the recent 24 October 2013 hearing at the Tripoli Criminal Court as another example of Libya's ability to undertake domestic trials. Gaddafi, Al-Senussi and roughly thirty other aides to former Libyan dictator Muammar Gaddafi were officially ordered to stand trial.[205]

The Court also focused on witness protection, which, as discussed in Chapter 2, is crucial to showing a country's ability to prosecute. The Court recognised that Libya did **not** have the capacity to ensure protective

---

[198] *Ibid.,* para. 261.
[199] *Ibid.*
[200] *Ibid.*, para. 215.
[201] *Ibid.,* para. 303.
[202] *Ibid.*, para. 275.
[203] *Ibid.*
[204] *Ibid.,* para. 281.
[205] Youssef Ba, 'Libya court indicts Kadhafi aides over 2011 uprising', *AFP*.

measures for witnesses.[206] Yet again, the Court ignored its initial instinct. The Court decided that Libya **did** have the capacity to ensure protective measures.

The Court recalled the *Gaddafi* Admissibility Decision,[207] wherein Libya had not provided 'evidence about specific protection programme that may exist under domestic law'[208] and the Court was thus 'not persuaded by the assertion that the Libyan authorities currently have the capacity to ensure protective measures'.[209] In the *Al-Senussi* decision, the Court noted that 'Libya has provided no new submissions intended to demonstrate the existence and effective functioning of a witness protection programme in the country'.[210] Where this had been compelling for the Chamber in the *Gaddafi* decision, the Chamber in the *Al-Senussi* decision considered it in the context of the 'considerable'[211] evidence provided by Libya, noting that it had provided more evidence than in *Gaddafi*, and finding 'no indication that collection of evidence and testimony has ceased or will cease because of unaddressed security concerns for witnesses in the case against Mr Al-Senussi'.[212] The Chamber also opined that these security concerns did not appear to have affected the progress of domestic judicial proceedings. In the context of these 'concrete circumstances',[213] the Court found that the absence of evidence showing Libya's capacity to ensure witness protection did not result in a genuine inability to carry out domestic proceedings.

Despite the dubious reasoning behind the Court's decision to find the case of Abdullah Al-Senussi inadmissible, there are factual differences between the *Gaddafi* and *Al-Senussi* cases that could merit the different outcomes. For one, Al-Senussi is in official custody before the Libyan

[206] *The Prosecutor v. Saif Al-Islam Gadaffi and Abdullah Al-Senussi*, Doc. ICC-01/11-01/11-466-Red, 'Decision on the Admissibility of the Case Against Abdullah Al-Senussi', (11 October 2013), para. 283.
[207] *See The Prosecutor v. Said Al-Islam Gaddafi and Abdullah Al-Senussi*, Doc. ICC-01/11-01/11-344-Red, 'Decision on the admissibility of the case against Saif Al-Islam Gaddafi', (31 May 2013).
[208] *Ibid*, para. 211.
[209] *Ibid.*
[210] *The Prosecutor v. Saif Al-Islam Gadaffi and Abdullah Al-Senussi*, Doc. ICC-01/11-01/11-466-Red, 'Decision on the Admissibility of the Case Against Abdullah Al-Senussi', (11 October 2013), para. 287.
[211] *Ibid.*, para. 298.
[212] *Ibid.*
[213] *Ibid.*, para. 301.

Accusation Chamber and under the Tripoli Criminal Court; Gaddafi has been held by a militia group in the town of Zintan since his capture in November 2011. To date Saif Al-Islam Gaddafi has appeared five times in court in the Libyan town of Zintan.[214] The next hearing is scheduled in the near future.[215] Clearly, a solution needs to be found whereby the Libyan government takes jurisdiction over the case and custody over Gaddafi. However, until that time, the ICC should not have inferred that the Libyan government was failing its obligation to bring Gaddafi to justice.

In the *Al-Senussi* hearing, the ICC also gave the Libyan government and other parties an opportunity to submit additional updated evidence concerning the domestic investigation. The Court's varying and **inconsistent** rulings on legal issues common to both cases (e.g., the lack of defence counsel and effective witness protection programme, and the country's poor security environment) worked in favour of Al-Senussi.

For example, in the area of witness protection, the Court in the *Gaddafi* case expressed numerous concerns about the existence of effective witness protection programs in Libya, including the welfare of detainees and witness immunity.[216] In the *Al-Senussi* decision, the Court's concerns about the (established) mistreatment and torture of individuals in detention, and the clear potential of these practices to affect testimony, were not accorded anywhere near the same weight.[217] The Court ruled that

---

[214] 'Gaddafi's Son Appears in Court; Case Postponed', *The Daily Star*, (2 May 2013) available at http://www.dailystar.com.lb/News/Middle-East/2013/May-02/215757-gaddafis-son-saif-al-islam-to-appear-in-court.ashx#axzz2S9Fj9uIE. His first appearance took place on 17 January 2013, *see* 'Saif al-Islam Gaddafi Appears in Libya Court', *BBC News*, (17 January 2013) available at http://www.bbc.co.uk/news/world-africa-21066567. Additional appearances occurred on 19 September 2013 ('Gaddafi's son Saif appears in Libyan court', *Al Jazeera*, (19 September 2013) available at http://www.aljazeera.com/news/africa/2013/09/2013918202644378938.html), 12 December 2013, ('Trial of Gaddafi Son Adjourned', *Press TV*, (13 December 2013), available at http://www.presstv.com/detail/2013/12/13/339709/trial-of-gaddafi-son-adjourned/).

[215] *See* 'Trial of Gaddafi Son Adjourned', *Press TV*, (13 December 2013).

[216] *The Prosecutor v. Said Al-Islam Gaddafi and Abdullah Al-Senussi*, Doc. ICC-01/11-01/11-344-Red, 'Decision on the admissibility of the case against Saif Al-Islam Gaddafi', (31 May 2013), paras 209-211.

[217] *The Prosecutor v. Saif Al-Islam Gadaffi and Abdullah Al-Senussi*, Doc. ICC-01/11-01/11-466-Red, 'Decision on the Admissibility of the Case Against Abdullah Al-Senussi', (11 October 2013), paras 297-301.

Libya's witness protection programs 'in the concrete circumstances of the present case, [do] not result in Libya's inability genuinely to carry out its proceedings'.[218]

Perhaps mindful of comparisons with the *Gaddafi* case, the Court in the *Al-Senussi* decision stressed the need to look at admissibility issues on a case-by-case basis. The Court repeatedly mentioned the importance of assessing each case on its own particular facts.[219]

I think the Court was equivocal as to how the evidence provided by the Libyan government in the *Al-Senussi* case was any stronger than its admissions in the *Gaddafi* case. In the *Gaddafi* case, the Court concluded that Libya failed to demonstrate 'whether and how it will overcome the existing difficulties in securing a lawyer for the suspect',[220] owing to 'the security situation in Libya and the risk faced by lawyers who act for associates of the former regime'.[221] Yet, surely these same concerns still exist for any domestic trial against Al-Senussi. A recent report by Human Rights Watch (HRW) supports this claim. For instance, HRW reports that Libya failed to grant basic due process rights, found in domestic and international law, to **both** defendants.[222] For example, neither Gaddafi nor Al-Senussi have had access to a lawyer and they were interrogated without a lawyer. They were also denied the right to remain silent, the right to know the identity of their interrogators, and the opportunity to review the evidence against them.[223] These findings do not support a claim that the two cases are markedly different for the purpose of an Article 17 admissibility test.

In the end, the key issue is a country's willingness and ability to prosecute. Judicial 'action' taken by the Libyan government would seem to satisfy the requirements of Article 17(1)(a) of the ICC Statute. This is supported by the usual submissions on the independence of the Libyan

---

[218] *Ibid.,* para. 301.
[219] *Ibid.,* paras 27, 66, 208, and 301.
[220] *The Prosecutor v. Said Al-Islam Gaddafi and Abdullah Al-Senussi*, Doc. ICC-01/11-01/11-344-Red, 'Decision on the admissibility of the case against Saif Al-Islam Gaddafi', (31 May 2013), para. 215.
[221] *Ibid.,* para. 212.
[222] Human Rights Watch, 'Libya: Gaddafi Son, Ex-Officials, Held Without Due Process', (13 February 2014), available at http://www.hrw.org/news/2014/02/13 /libya-gaddafi-son-ex-officials-held-without-due-process.
[223] *Ibid.*

judiciary and domestic guarantees of due process; Libya is meeting the requirements of due process 'in accordance with international standards'; and the domestic investigation has been 'prioritised', in spite of resource constraints, to ensure that 'justice is not only done, but also seen to be done'.[224]

Libya's position is consistent with UN Security Council Resolution 1970 which referred the situation to the ICC. The Resolution is clear in conferring and affirming the exclusive jurisdiction of non-States Parties to the ICC over nationals alleged to have committed criminal acts, **unless** that State waives its exclusive jurisdiction (e.g. in favour of another State, or the ICC or another tribunal). The specific language states:

> The Security Council … [d]ecides that nationals, current or former officials or personnel from a State outside the Libyan Arab Jamahiriya which is not a party to the Rome Statute of the International Criminal Court shall be subject to the exclusive jurisdiction of that State for all alleged acts or omissions arising out of or related to operations in the Libyan Arab Jamahiriya established or authorized by the Council, unless such exclusive jurisdiction has been expressly waived by the State.[225]

IV. Sudan

Unlike the situation in Libya, the Court's decision of the admissibility of Sudan's President Al Bashir is unencumbered with any admissibility complexities. Sudan has refused to cooperate with the ICC, arguing that it has the capacity to undertake domestic trials and, thus, making the ICC indictments inadmissible under the principle of complementarity. One day after the ICC Prosecutor initiated an investigation, the Sudanese government established a new Special Criminal Court for events in Darfur as a 'Substitute to the International Criminal Court'.[226] The government went even further by establishing additional seats for the new court and extending its jurisdiction. A specialised Prosecution of Crimes against

---

[224] *The Prosecutor v. Saif Al-Islam Gaddafi and Abdullah Al-Senussi*, Doc. ICC-01/11-01/11-130-Red, 'Application on behalf of the Government of Libya pursuant to Article 19 of the ICC Statute', (1 May 2012), para. 94.

[225] UN Security Council, UN Doc. S/RES/1970 (2011), (26 February 2011), para. 6.

[226] 'Sudan: Judiciary challenges ICC over Darfur Cases', *IRIN News*, (24 June 2005), available at http://www.irinnews.org/report.aspx?reportid=55068.

Humanity Office was also established, as well as several special investigative committees.[227]

However, despite these developments there has been no genuine progress by the Sudanese government towards ending impunities for those responsible for atrocities. And certainly there is no political will to undertake genuine domestic trials.

V. Article 16

Due to the continued stalemate between Libya and the ICC, the international community may have its first opportunity to pioneer the use of Article 16 of the Rome Statute in determining where and how to try Saif Al-Islam Gaddafi.

Under Article 16, the UN Security Council is entitled to defer proceedings for a period of twelve months, at the end of which it may choose to renew the deferral. Nine of the fifteen Security Council members must agree, and there can be no veto by a permanent member. The Security Council's authority to defer a case comes under Chapter VII of the UN Charter, which requires the deferral to be premised on 'maintain[ing] or restor[ing] international peace and security'.[228] However, it is not the UN Charter that makes Article 16 legally binding; it is the ICC Statute.

Article 16 was one of the most contentious issues during the negotiations of the Rome Statute. It was introduced as a compromise between states that wanted to reduce the ICC's prosecutorial autonomy by giving the Security Council more control, and states that preferred that the Security Council exercise less control.[229] Article 16 provided a middle

---

[227] *See* OCHCR, 'Second Periodic Report of the United Nations High Commissioner for Human Rights on the Human Rights Situation in Sudan', (27 January 2006), pp. 29-30, available at http://www.ohchr.org/Documents/Countries/sudanjanuary06.pdf.

[228] Charter of the United Nations, (24 October 1945) 1 UNTS XVI (hereinafter UN Charter), Chapter VII, Article 39.

[229] In fact, the 1994 draft of the International Law Commission stated that no prosecution would be commenced under the Statute arising from a situation being handled by the Security Council, 'unless the Security Council otherwise decides'. *See* 'Report of the International Law Commission on the Work of its Forty-Sixth

position, granting the Security Council the power to defer proceedings in the instance of a situation referred by a State Party, a non-State Party, or the Prosecutor herself. As Luigi Condorelli and Santiago Villalpando rightly noted, the final text of Article 16 'overcomes the evil consequences of the permanent members' power to veto within the Security Council'.[230]

Paradoxically, Article 16 allows a political body to intervene in an independent judicial process. It allows the Security Council to set aside the interests of justice and prioritise the requirements of international peace and security.

However, because Article 16 has never been executed, there remains confusion as to how a country can take advantage of it. Kenya, after a failed attempt to change trial venues from The Hague to either Kenya or Tanzania, launched a campaign to discontinue ICC proceedings.[231] Kenya's Ambassador to the UN, Mr Macharia Kamau, lodged a petition to the Security Council asking for the 'immediate termination' of the trials. His letter reportedly cites the threat of renewed instability in Kenya, states that the ICC process is 'neither impartial nor independent', and refers to Kenyan sovereignty and the preference for a 'home-grown solution', while suggesting that the ICC Prosecutor's case was 'falling apart in the face of lack of evidence…and incompetent prosecution'.[232] The letter also charged that forcing Kenyatta and Ruto to leave Kenya to attend trial in The Hague would result in internal unrest that could even 'spill over to neighbouring countries'.[233] He noted that Kenya had the capacity for a domestic solution without ICC interference.[234]

However, the Rome Statute does not give the Security Council power to dismiss or terminate a case. The Ambassador's request for an

---

Session, Draft Statute for an International Criminal Court', UN Doc. A/49/355, (1 September 1994), Article 23(3).

[230] Luigi Condorelli and Santiago Villalpando, 'Referral and Deferral by the Security Council', in A. Cassese, P. Gaeta, J. Jones (eds.) *The Rome Statute of the International Criminal Court: A Commentary*, 2 vols. (Oxford: Oxford University Press, 2002), vol. 1, p. 646.

[231] ICC, 'Ruto and Sang case: Trial to open in The Hague', Doc. ICC-CPI-20130715-PR931, (15 July 2013).

[232] 'Kenya Asks UN to Halt ICC Charges Against Kenyatta', *BBC News*, (9 May 2013), available at www.bbc.co.uk/news/world-africa-22472242.

[233] *Ibid.*

[234] *Ibid.*

'immediate *termination* of the case in The Hague without much further ado' is wrong.[235]

Since Kenya is not currently a member of the Security Council, it could not request the deferral of proceedings on its own initiative. But because there was a consensus among African Union States that proceedings should be delayed,[236] Rwanda, Togo and Morocco, who were non-permanent members of the Security Council, at that time, initiated a vote within the Council, urging it to adopt a resolution to delay proceedings.[237] In the end, the Security Council rejected the resolution.[238]

Notwithstanding the Kenya situation, Article 16, if implemented properly, could nonetheless play an important role in ensuring accountability. As one prominent scholar argues, Article 16 'represents one way in which the tension between the search for peace and the demands for justice may be mediated'.[239] It is not uncommon for states to reach negotiated peace settlements by offering amnesties and other guarantees to belligerents, insurgents, and rebels. In such a context, Article 16 could be used if and only if an ICC investigation posed a *threat* to peace and security. The suspension of proceedings would be temporary. In

[235] Mark Kersten, 'A Bizarre Snowball's Chance in Hell: Kenya Asks Security Council to Terminate Kenyatta Case at the ICC', *Justice in Conflict*, (13 May 2013), available at http://justiceinconflict.org/2013/05/13/a-bizarre-snowballs-chance-in-hell-kenya-asks-security-council-to-terminate-kenyatta-case-at-the-icc/ [emphasis added].

[236] 'African Union urges ICC to defer Uhuru Kenyatta case', *BBC News*, (12 October 2013), available at http://www.bbc.co.uk/news/world-africa-24506006. *See also* African Union, 'Africa to Request Deferment of Indictments against Kenyan President and Vice President', (11 October 2013), available at http://www.au.int/en/content/extraordinary-session-assembly-african-union.

[237] 'Africans push deferral of Kenya trials with UN draft resolution', *Reuters*, (1 November 2013), available at http://uk.reuters.com/article/2013/11/01/uk-kenya-icc-un-idUKBRE9A012O20131101.

[238] Seven Security Council members voted in favour of the resolution, while eight members abstained from voting. Consequently, the Council lacked the nine affirmative votes needed to adopt the resolution. UNSC, Doc. SC/11176, 'UN Security Council to vote this week on delay of Kenya trials: Rwanda', (15 November 2013), available at http://www.un.org/News/Press/docs/2013/sc11176.doc.htm.

[239] Dapo Akande, Max du Plessis, Charles Chernor Jalloh, 'An African expert study on the AU concerns about article 16 of the Rome Statute of the ICC', (South Africa: Institute for Security Studies, 2010), p. 5.

the *Gaddafi* case, there is no trade-off between peace and justice. Invoking Article 16 would be solely for the purpose of providing extra time to determine how and where best to prosecute Gaddafi.

One important consideration is whether an Article 16 deferral can occur only at the **initial stage** of an investigation. It is reasonable to argue that the deferral provision was not intended for use late in the proceedings when suspects have been named and arrest warrants issued; it certainly does not exist merely to delay trial proceedings.

A Security Council decision to defer a case late in the proceedings would constitute significant interference with the Court. At this stage, both the Prosecutor and the Court will have invested significant time and resources in the case. While the principle of complementarity should arguably not be weighed against court costs, commentators have rightly noted that '[a] withdrawal in these circumstances would incur a considerable loss of credibility for the Court and would...represent a defeat for the policy against impunity, the principle that animates the very idea of the Court'.[240]

It is important to note that the language of Article 16 does not explicitly **exclude** the possibility of a Security Council deferral after proceedings have commenced. Indeed, the deliberate choice of the words 'investigation or prosecution' in the Article suggests that a late stage deferral is possible.

There also exists ambiguity regarding whether Article 16 allows the Security Council to target its deferral demand to a particular individual or situation. Certainly this is what the Sudanese government is hoping in relation to the indictment against President Al Bashir. When the ICC Prosecutor opened an investigation into the situation in Darfur following referral by the Security Council, he eventually brought indictments against four individuals. However, it is the Al Bashir indictment that the Sudanese government has sought to defer. The failure of the Security Council to decide on the matter induced the African Union to call for non-cooperation with the ICC.[241] Its members, including some states that are party to the

---

[240] Arsanjani and Reisman, 'The Law-in-Action of the International Criminal Court', 397.

[241] *See* Africa Union, 'Decision on the Meeting of African States Parties to the Rome Statute of the International Criminal Court (ICC)', (14 July 2009), available

Rome Statute, resolved not to cooperate with the arrest warrant against Al Bashir.[242]

VI. Article 127, Withdraw

In addition to an Article 16 deferral by the UN Security Council, the Rome Statute permits a State Party to withdraw itself from the jurisdiction of the Court. Article 127(1) of the Rome Statute states:

> A State Party may, by written notification addressed to the Secretary-General of the United Nations, withdraw from this Statute. The withdrawal shall take effect one year after the date of receipt of the notification, unless the notification specifies a later date.[243]

Because such a withdrawal would only take place a year or more after state notification to the UN, it would not apply to any proceedings currently before the Court.[244] As soon as the withdrawal came into effect, however, it would preclude investigation and prosecution by the ICC.[245]

Until that time, a State Party that notifies the Security Council of its intention to withdraw from the Rome Statute will not be discharged from its obligations under the Statute. This includes any financial obligations to the Court and the ongoing duty to cooperate fully on any matter already under consideration of the Court.[246]

During the one-year period, the ICC Prosecutor could still bring additional proceedings and the state would have a duty to cooperate fully with the Court.[247] Of course, the problem for the ICC with any state

---

at http://www.africa-union.org/root/au/Conferences/2009/july/Press%20Release %20-%20ICC.doc.

242 Amnesty International, 'African Union Refuses to Cooperate with Bashir Arrest Warrant', (6 July 2009), available at http://www.amnesty.org/en/news-and-updates/african-union-refuses-cooperate-bashir-arrest-warrant-20090706.

243 ICC Statute, Article 127(1).

244 Article 127(2) of the ICC Statute states that a State Party is not 'discharged, by reason of its withdrawal, from the obligations arising from the Statute while it was a Party to the Statute'.

245 *Ibid.*

246 *Ibid.*

247 Charles C. Jalloh, 'Kenya Should Reconsider Proposed Withdrawal from the ICC', *Jurist,* (13 September 2013), available at http://jurist.org/forum/2013/09/charles-jalloh-kenya-icc.php.

withdrawal is that the Court has little, if any, power to enforce compliance. If a state fails to cooperate, the Court could refer the issue to the Assembly of States Parties (ASP). Article 112(2)(g) allows the ASP to '[p]erform any other function consistent with' the Statute.[248] Thus, the ASP could potentially urge a non-cooperating state to act, or press for negotiation, arbitration, or other methods of mediation.[249] However, as demonstrated in Chapter 5, this power is very limited.

Kenya's recent declaration that it would withdraw from the Rome Statute makes it the first State Party to take such action.[250] This occurred even though the ICC Prosecutor has hinted that the Court might assist Kenya in the prosecution of those responsible for the Nairobi Westgate Shopping Mall attack in September 2013.[251]

Taking into account Article 127, the Prosecutor could initiate an investigation into the crimes committed at Westgate if they are believed to be within the Court's jurisdiction. If the Prosecutor undertook a *proprio motu* investigation, then Kenya would still be legally obligated to cooperate with the Court, despite its announcement to withdraw from the Statute.

---

[248] ICC Statute, Article 112(2)(g) reads '[t]he Assembly shall: . . . (g) Perform any other function consistent with this Statute of the Rules of Procedure and Evidence'.

[249] Jalloh, 'Kenya Should Reconsider Proposed Withdrawal from the ICC'.

[250] 'Kenya MPs Vote to Withdraw from ICC', *BBC News*, (5 September 2013) available at http://www.bbc.co.uk/news/world-africa-23969316.

[251] ICC-OTP, 'Statement of ICC Prosecutor Fatou Bensouda in relation to the Westgate Mall attack, Nairobi, Kenya', (24 September 2013), available at http://www.icc-cpi.int/en_menus/icc/press%20and%20media/press%20releases/Pages/otp-statement-24-09-2013.aspx. The Prosecutor stated that: '[s]uch attacks by armed groups upon innocent civilians are contrary to international law and may constitute a crime under the Rome Statute, to which Kenya is a State Party. In expressing her solidarity with the victims, their families and the people of Kenya, and with full respect for the primacy of jurisdiction of the Republic of Kenya, the Prosecutor stands ready to work with the international community and the Government of Kenya to ensure that those responsible for these crimes are brought to justice'.

VII. Creating a Third Party to Determine a State's 'Unwillingness' and 'Inability' to Investigate

The Libya situation perfectly illustrates the subjectivity involved in determining unwillingness or inability to prosecute. The struggle between the Court and Libya makes clear the need for more objective mechanisms in assessing domestic legal and judicial capabilities; this is paramount to creating a more balanced collaboration between the Court and domestic actors.

A number of states have expressed concern over the ICC's power to determine unilaterally whether a state has the capacity to undertake national prosecutions.[252] Not unlike Rwanda's distrust of the ICTR, there is some dissatisfaction with how the ICC wields its decision-making authority.[253]

Concerns were raised as early as 1996 at the Preparatory Committee when states argued for more stringent and objective criteria in assessing national judicial proceedings.[254] Some scholars argue that a determination of inability cannot come fully into play until national proceedings are 'underway or have been initiated'.[255] However, it makes no sense to begin a review at this late stage. Assessing a state's ability to prosecute occurs more naturally at an early stage, when the Court has been informed by the relevant state that it intends to investigate and prosecute under the complementarity principle.

During the Rome Conference, several states expressed concern that the Court possesses too much discretion in determining admissibility.[256] States were concerned about not being able to prevent the Court from exercising jurisdiction over crimes committed on their territory or over their own

---

[252] *See* Mark S. Ellis, 'The International Criminal Court and its Implication for Domestic Law and National Capacity Building', (2002) 15 *Florida Journal of International Law*, 215, 240.

[253] *Ibid.*

[254] Report of the *Ad hoc* Committee on the Establishment of an International Criminal Court, UN Doc. A/50/22, (1995), para. 166.

[255] El Zeidy, *The Principle of Complementarity in International Criminal Law*, p. 230.

[256] Jann K. Kleffner, *Complementarity in the Rome Statute and National Criminal Jurisdiction*, (Oxford: Oxford University Press, 2008), p. 90.

citizens.[257] Some were also uncomfortable with the ICC passing judgment on their own national courts.

As mentioned, Libya is a good example of the current dilemma. The new Transitional Government wanted to try, before his death, former Libyan leader Muammar Gaddafi, despite the ICC's indictment against him: '[i]f we caught him, we are not going to give him to anyone. We would just take him to trial—a fair trial—under Libyan laws'.[258] The government has taken the same position in regards to Saif Al-Islam Gaddafi. It has argued forcefully that Gaddafi would receive a fair trial in Libya.[259]

The result is a standoff between the ICC and a sovereign nation. As discussed earlier, the Libyan government has formally challenged the ICC's right to try Saif Al-Islam Gadaffi, arguing that it is willing and able to hold a domestic trial, even if it requires support from the international community.[260]

The tension reached unprecedented levels with the arrest of ICC staffers who were attempting to meet with Gaddafi. The staffers, including Registry attorney Melinda Taylor, were jailed for twenty-five days. Part of Taylor's task while visiting Libya was to gather evidence on whether Libya would be an appropriate venue for Gaddafi's trial. Taylor was accused of endangering Libya's security by passing coded letters to Gadaffi and smuggling in a hidden camera and recording device. Remarkably, the ICC did not denounce the arrests, and it used 'cautious

---

[257] John T. Holmes, 'Complementarity: National Courts *versus* the ICC' in A. Cassese, P. Gaeta, J. Jones (eds.) *The Rome Statute of the International Criminal Court: A Commentary*, 2 vols. (Oxford: Oxford University Press, 2002), vol. 1, pp. 672-674.

[258] Statement by Emhemmed Ghula, a leader of the Tripoli rebel underground, *quoted* in David D. Kirkpatrick and Steven L. Myers, 'After Uprising, Rebels Face a Struggle for Unity', *New York Times*, (22 August 2011).

[259] *See* Ashley Hileman, 'Libya Prime Minister Assures Fair Trial Success for Gaddafi Son', *Jurist,* (22 November 2011), available at http://jurist.org/paperchase/2011/11/libya-prime-minister-assures-fair-trial-for-Gaddafi-son.php.

[260] *The Prosecutor v. Saif Al-Islam Gaddafi and Abdullah Al-Senussi*, Doc. ICC-01/11-01/11-130-Red, 'Application on behalf of the Government of Libya pursuant to Article 19 of the ICC Statute', (1 May 2012), para. 14.

language in its handling of the crisis'.[261] ICC president Sang-Hyun Song apologised to the Libyan authorities for the 'difficulties' caused by the mission.[262]

As IBA director, I released two harshly worded press statements arguing that, 'detaining ICC staff members on an official visit was a violation of the privileges and immunities accorded to ICC staff members under international law'.[263] To date, however, the Court has provided no credible account of what happened during Ms Taylor's visit. In my discussions with Libyan officials, they were adamant that Ms Taylor had violated both international and Libyan law during her mission to Libya.

The Kenya situation has also generated significant hostility toward the Court. According to Steven Kay QC, thc Court has 'attempted to fit Kenya into its jurisdiction', which exacerbated hostility and created a lack of respect for the Court.[264] At a recent summit in Addis Ababa, African Union (AU) Chairman Hailemariam Desalegn said that the AU opposed an ICC trial of Kenyan President Uhuru Kenyatta, and that the cases against Kenyatta and his Deputy President William Ruto should be referred to domestic courts.[265] Hailemariam, who is also Ethiopia's Prime Minister, had the backing of other African leaders who supported a referral back to Kenyan courts.[266] The AU claimed that referring the cases back to Kenya

---

[261] Vivienne Walt, 'Libya Releases ICC Lawyer, but Will Justice Follow?', *TIME World,* (3 July 2012), available at http://world.time.com/2012/07/03/libya-releases-icc-lawyer-but-will-justice-follow/#ixzz1zfetXHzj.

[262] 'Libya: ICC Staff Held in Zintan Released', *BBC News,* (2 July 2012) available at http://www.bbc.co.uk/ news/world-africa-18671454.

[263] *See* Mark S. Ellis *quoted* in IBAHRI, 'Release of ICC Staff in Libya Welcomed by IBAHRI', (3 July 2012) available at http://www.ibanet.org/Article/Detail.aspx?ArticleUid=e32869cd-17ac-4f5e-aa53-0a29ada63d05. *See also* IBA, 'IBAHRI calls for immediate release of four ICC staff detained in Libya', (12 June 2012), available at http://www.ibanet.org/Article/Detail.aspx?ArticleUid=4EA2B9BB-8E35-4A2C-B06F-8802F6B5EF1E.

[264] Discussion with with Steven Kay QC, Defence Counsel for Uhuru Kenyatta (27 March 2014).

[265] 'African Union Accuses ICC of 'Hunting' Africans', *BBC News*, (27 May 2013), available at www.bbc.co.uk/news/world-africa-22681894.

[266] W. Davidson, 'African Union Summit Backs Return of Kenyan ICC Cases, *Bloomberg*, (27 May 2013), available at http://www.bloomberg.com/news/2013-05-27/african-leaders-set-to-back-return-of-kenyan-icc-cases.html.

would engage 'national mechanisms to investigate and prosecute the cases under a reformed judiciary …to prevent the resumption of conflict and violence in Kenya'.[267] This was echoed by Macharia Kamau, Kenya's Ambassador to the UN, who wrote to the UN Security Council requesting that the trials be halted; he claimed that the ICC was neither impartial nor independent, and prosecution of Kenyatta and Ruto could throw the country into turmoil.[268]

Not long after, the AU went a step further and unanimously held that African Heads of State should be immune from prosecution by the ICC.[269] The AU alleges that the EU uses ICC prosecution to leverage political power in Africa.[270]

Hailemariam's statement reflects an underlying hostility between many African countries and the ICC. Currently, all ICC cases focus on crimes committed in Africa,[271] and many Africans feel they are being unfairly targeted.[272] Hailemariam claimed that the ICC process had degenerated into 'race hunting'[273] and objected to a 'flawed' process whereby '99%' of those indicted by the ICC were African.[274] This hostility also led to a motion in the Kenyan Parliament to withdraw from the ICC.[275]

---

267 'Africa backs Kenya Call for Hague Court to Drop Kenyatta Case', *Thomson Reuters Foundation*, (24 May 2013), available at http://www.trust.org/item/20130524103940-oe9c4/.

268 'African Union Accuses ICC of 'Hunting' Africans', *BBC News*, (27 May 2013), available at www.bbc.co.uk/news/world-africa-22681894.

269 'Africa leaders should be immune from ICC prosecution: AU', *Jurist*, (15 October 2013), available at http://jurist.org/paperchase/2013/10/africa-leaders-should-be-immune-from-icc-prosecution-au.php

270 *Ibid.*

271 The ICC currently has ongoing cases in: Kenya, Uganda, Democratic Republic of Congo, Sudan, Central African Republic, Côte d'Ivoire, Libya and Mali. *See* ICC-OTP, 'Situations and Cases', (2014), available at http://www.icc-cpi.int/en_menus/icc/situations%20and%20cases/Pages/situations%20and%20cases.aspx.

272 'Africa backs Kenya Call for Hague Court to Drop Kenyatta Case', *Thomson Reuters Foundation*, (24 May 2013).

273 'African Union Accuses ICC of 'Hunting' Africans', *BBC News*, (27 May 2013), available at www.bbc.co.uk/news/world-africa-22681894.

274 *Ibid.*

275 'Kenya MPs Vote to Withdraw from ICC', *BBC News*, (5 September 2013) available at http://www.bbc.co.uk/news/world-africa-23969316.

This strident position was recently re-asserted by the AU when its Member States issued an ultimatum to the President of the ICC, Sang Hyung Song.[276] Their concerns focused on four areas: (1) the evidentiary standard of the OTP, (2) court funding from NGOs, (3) alleged failure to safeguard the rights of accused and (4) the OTP's *proprio motu* power of initiation. The AU is demanding that it be informed of 'a pattern of concrete, satisfactory steps to remedy these four issues by 30 April 2014' or its Member States will cease all cooperation with the ICC.

The AU has already forced the ASP to adopt an exceptional amendment to the Court's Rules of Procedure and Evidence. The amended Rule ('Rule 134*quater*')[277] allows the accused, who are 'mandated to fulfil extraordinary public duties at the highest level' to be absent from trial.[278] Persons who qualify are able to apply for permission from the Court to be absent from trial. In making its decision, the Court must decide whether it is in the interests of justice to allow the accused to be absent.

Kenya's Vice President William Samoei Ruto has applied to be excused form his entire trial, based on the new amended Rule. The ICC Appeals Chamber had earlier overturned the Trial Chamber's decision to grant Ruto a 'blanket excusal' from his trial.[279] Mr Ruto's application will

---

276 'African Union letter to ICC President Sang Hyung Song attacking OTP', *Journalists for Justice*, (31 January 2014) available at http://www.jfjustice.net/african-union-letter-to-icc-president-sang-hyung-song-attacking-otp/. While this source reports the letter as a draft letter proposed by Kenya (*see also* 'Kenya pushes for AU's April ultimatum to ICC', *The Star*, (31 January 2014), available at http://www.the-star.co.ke/news/article-153152/kenya-pushes-aus-april-ultimatum-icc, which reports it as a draft letter proposed by Rwanda on behalf of Kenya), other sources (without the full text as reproduced here, but with corresponding quotations) do not qualify the letter as a draft. *See* e.g. Oliver Mathenge, 'Kenya: Reform or We Will Not Cooperate, AU Tells ICC', *The Star* (1 February 2014) available at http://allafrica.com/stories/201402030255.html; Olive Burrows, 'Africa warns Hague court over ties with NGOs, Capital News', *Capital News,* (31 January 2014) available at http://www.capitalfm.co.ke/news/2014/01/africa-warns-hague-court-over-ties-with-ngos/.

277 ICC-OTP, 'Amendments to the Rules of Procedure and Evidence', Doc. ICC-ASP/12/Res.7, (27 November 2013), p. 4.

278 *Ibid.*

279 *The Prosecutor v. William Samoei Ruto and Joshua Arap Sang*, Doc. ICC-01/09-01/11-1066, 'Judgment on the appeal of the Prosecutor against the decision

be the first test of Rule 134*quater*.[280]

It is difficult to predict how the Court will rule but it is unlikely that it will allow a high-ranking government official to be absent throughout the trial. To do so would be a paradigm shift in international criminal law and would permanently undermine the very foundation of the Rome Statute. Furthermore, as discussed in Chapter 1, the Court has never ruled a case inadmissible in the '*interests of justice*' as set forth in Article 17 of the ICC Statute. Thus, it is implausible that the Court would determine that this same '*interests of justice*' standard would permit a high-ranking government official to be absent from trial.

The Arab League also supported the resolution and refused to cooperate with the arrest warrant. Many African and Middle Eastern countries protested the indictment based on what they believed was unfair targeting of African countries, and argued that prosecution of Al Bashir would paralyse the peace process in Sudan.[281]

Rwanda too maintained an aggressive position vis-à-vis the ICTR. The government has long maintained that its judicial system is capable of undertaking domestic war crimes trials consistent with international standards. Yet, despite conducting more than thirty-five domestic genocide cases between 2006 and 2010,[282] the ICTR and a number of European countries rejected numerous extradition requests by Rwanda.

To avoid these protracted conflicts over jurisdiction, the international community should consider establishing an International Advisory Group to provide expertise and recommendations on domestic trial capacity. I have previously called upon the international community to create such a group to ensure that an objective, impartial, and non-political evaluation is

---

of Trial Chamber V(a) of 18 June 2013 entitled 'Decision on Mr Ruto's Request for Excusal from Continuous Presence at Trial', (25 October 2013), para 63.

[280] *See The Prosecutor v. William Samoei Ruto and Joshua Arap Sang*, Doc. ICC-01/09-01/11/11-1124, 'Defence request pursuant to Article 63(1)) of the Rome Statute and Rule134quater of the Rules of Procedure and Evidence to excuse Mr William Samoei Ruto from attendance at trial' (16 December 2013).

[281] Argaw Ashine, 'Sudan: AU Warns Over Bashir Warrant', *All Africa*, (19 July 2010), available at http://allafrica.com/stories/201007191955.html.

[282] *See The Prosecutor v. Jean-Bosco Uwinkindi*, Case No. ICTR-2001-75-R11*bis*, 'Republic of Rwanda's Response to 6 June 2011 Order to Provide Further Information Regarding 36 Genocide Cases at The High Court', (20 June 2011).

made regarding a state's willingness and ability to carry out judicial proceedings consistent with international standards and the principle of complementarity.[283] The focus of the evaluation would be on a state's *national judicial system* rather than all of the state's institutions. The assessment would also be focused on areas where there has been sufficient weakening of the judicial system so as to make it impossible to undertake investigations or prosecutions of war crimes. Such an evaluation would not be binding on the ICC but would offer guidance for the Court in rendering a fair and impartial decision regarding admissibility. An organisation such as the International Bar Association could oversee the Advisory Group.

The legal basis for such a group can be found in the Rome Statute. Article 54(3)(c) allows the ICC Prosecutor to '[s]eek the cooperation of any state or intergovernmental organisation or arrangement in accordance with its respective competence and/or mandate' during his investigations. Similarly, Article 15(2) allows the ICC Prosecutor, when initiating investigations *proprio motu*, to 'seek additional information from States, organs of the United Nations, intergovernmental or nongovernmental organisations, or other reliable sources that he or she deems appropriate'.[284] Finally, Article 42(1) of the Statute stipulates that the Prosecutor is 'responsible for receiving referrals and any substantiated information on crimes within the jurisdiction of the Court, for examining them and for conducting investigations and prosecutions before the Court'.[285] The authority granted under Articles 54, 42, and 15 is extraordinarily broad and would certainly allow the ICC to cooperate with an International Advisory Group.[286]

The procedural support mechanism is found within the Court's Jurisdiction, Cooperation and Complementarity Division (JCCD). The JCCD analyses information received by the OTP under Rome Statute Article 15, which authorises the Prosecutor to determine if 'there is a

---

[283] Ellis, 'The International Criminal Court and Its Implication for Domestic Law', 240.

[284] ICC Statute, Article 15(2).

[285] *Ibid.*, Article 42(1).

[286] *See* William W. Burke-White, 'Implementing a Policy of Positive Complementarity in the Rome System of Justice', (2008) 19 *Criminal Law Forum* 59, 81, *citing*, US Department of State, 'Country Reports on Human Rights Practices for 2001', (2002), available at http://www.state.gov/j/drl/rls/hrrpt/2001/eur/8227.htm.

reasonable basis to proceed with an investigation'.[287] The JCCD, consisting of lawyers, analysts, and international cooperation experts, advises the Prosecutor on the admissibility of individuals. The JCCD can seek additional information from states, organs of the United Nations, intergovernmental or non-governmental organisations, or other reliable sources that he or she deems appropriate.

The International Advisory Group would give legitimacy to the JCCD by making the process for determining admissibility less political and more objective. Comprised of legal experts and academics, the Group could interview ministers, government officials, prosecutors, judges, lawyers, and local civil society groups familiar with a state's domestic legal system. To ensure fair geographical representation, the selection of members could be modelled after the process by which non-permanent members are appointed to the Security Council. Firsthand and unbiased information about a state's judicial infrastructure would be essential in determining whether a state is able to conduct its own trial proceedings.

Questions that might be addressed by the Advisory Group include: Can the proceedings be conducted impartially and independently? Does the domestic court have extensive backlogs resulting in long pre-trial detention? Is there adequate security for court personnel? Does the state have a sufficient number of trained defence lawyers and an effective legal aid programme for indigent defendants? What is the level of court management? Are there undue delays in conducting trials? Are there sufficient guarantees against outside pressure on the judiciary? Is there unwarranted prosecutorial discretion in conducting investigations and trials? Does the state impose the death penalty? Can the court provide witnesses and victims with medical, psychological and material support during and after trial through a victim and witness support office? Can the court guarantee the security of these same witnesses and victims prior to, during, and after the trial? Is the country open to international assistance in criminal matters? Could political strife and repression hinder the judicial system? Does the state have detention facilities that meet international standards?

A full written evaluation of the legal system under review would be provided to the ICC and made public. The report would include the Group's finding as to whether the state is able to conduct a fair trial.

---

[287] ICC Statute, Article 15(3).

Dissenting opinions and unanimous findings would be so noted. If a trial proceeds in the domestic court, the Advisory Group would continue to monitor the proceedings to ensure their consistency with international norms.

It is important that an International Advisory Group not become another organ of the ICC. The independence and integrity of the Group is important in providing unbiased recommendations to the ICC. If designed correctly, the Group could significantly improve the often contentious and pestilent issues arising between the ICC and states. It could create a paradigm shift in how the Court interacts with states and lessen the inevitable tension that emerges when trying to determine if a state has the ability to carry out domestic investigations and prosecutions consistent with international standards.

CHAPTER SIX

INTERNATIONAL FINANCIAL AND PROFESSIONAL SUPPORT FOR DOMESTIC WAR CRIMES COURTS

Introduction

The absence of international assistance for post-conflict states willing to conduct domestic war crimes trials is a serious deficiency in the overall support for international justice. The international community witnessed this with the trial of Saddam Hussein in Iraq in 2005. The push for domestic war crimes trials against Saddam Hussein and his cohorts was a prime example of a trial process lacking in international due process standards. The international community, led by the United States, was fervent in wanting Iraq to undertake domestic trials. Prior to formation of the Iraqi War Crimes Court, I made this statement in an op-ed for the *International Herald Tribune*:

> I have long questioned the wisdom of Iraq undertaking its own domestic war crimes trials against Saddam and other members of his regime. Although I recognize that trials in Iraq, by Iraqis could be very cathartic, I have maintained strong reservations about whether Iraq is at a stage in its development where it can cope with such trials.[1]

Soon after Saddam's capture, the head of the US-led coalition authority's *Crimes Against Humanity Investigations Unit* said he believed that by giving Iraqis the power to conduct Saddam's trial, Iraq would be 'creating an experienced cadre of judges, lawyers and investigators steeped in international notions of due process. When their tribunal work

[1] Mark S. Ellis, 'Next, the Trial of Saddam', *International Herald Tribune*, (9 April 2005), available at http://www.nytimes.com/2005/04/08/opinion/08iht-edellis.html.

is finished, many will return to Iraq's still fragile legal system, where they will be able to pass their skills on to their compatriots'.[2]

In further support of the Iraqi Court, US President George W. Bush's spokesman, Scott McClellan, said that President Bush was 'pleased that Saddam Hussein and his regime leaders are going to be brought to justice by the Iraqi people in an Iraqi court for the atrocities his regime committed. This is an important step that will help the Iraqi people bring closure to the dark past of Saddam Hussein's brutal dictatorship'.[3] McClellan went on to say that '[j]ustice and the rule of law are part of the new Iraq with Saddam Hussein removed from power'.[4] Considering the role the United States was playing in the post-Saddam Iraq, it should not come as a surprise that the Iraqi government concurred with these international plaudits.

Of course, this stated optimism about the Iraqi judicial system ignored the need for having a cadre of experienced judges, prosecutors, and investigators for a trial of this magnitude. Bush's statement that the 'justice and the rule of law' were existent in Iraq was, to say the least, premature in light of the chaos and instability that defined the Iraqi legal system. However, the United States was willing to encourage a judicial process that relied on inexperienced judges, lawyers, and investigators who would be learning international notions of due process 'on the go'. This judicial weakness was exacerbated by the fact that with the exception of the United States, the international community, including the UN and the EU, was unwilling to assist Iraq, primarily because of Iraq's insistence on upholding the death penalty.[5] In the end, it was actually the International Bar Association that intervened with significant assistance to the new Iraqi War Crimes Court. The international community simply did

---

[2] Tom Parker, 'Judgment at Baghdad', *International Herald Tribune*, (7 July 2004), available at http://www.nytimes.com/2004/07/07/opinion/judgment-at-baghdad.html.

[3] 'Bush 'Pleased' Saddam Being Tried', *Dawn*, (2 July 2004), available at http://archives.dawn.com/2004/07/02/int2.htm.

[4] *Ibid.*

[5] *See also* John Bellinger, 'Regime trials belong in Libya's courts', *Washington Post*, (23 November 2011) available at http://www.washingtonpost.com/opinions/trials-of-moammar-gaddafis-favored-few-belong-in-libyas-courts/2011/11/22/gIQANU4WmN_story.html. Bellinger stated '[t]his was a missed opportunity to assist in bringing justice for Saddam's human rights violations and developing the rule of law in Iraq. The international community should not repeat the same mistake in Libya'.

not engage with the Court. Eight years later, the international community is facing the same challenges in Libya.

The issue of trying suspected war criminals in Libya, rather than in The Hague at the ICC, again points directly at the crucial issue of international support for domestic trials under the principle of complementarity. As discussed in Chapter 3, in its admissibility hearing before the ICC, the Libyan government argued that a proper application of the principle of complementarity requires states that are able to carry out investigations and prosecutions to do so. That ability, the government argued, is strengthened by international cooperation and assistance, to carry out those investigations and prosecutions.[6]

In its submission to the Court, the Libyan government explained that it had requested assistance from the international organisations to train the judiciary and legal practitioners and argued that such support, 'including the Court, the UN, and civil society', would enable Libya to conduct proceedings 'in accordance with international standards'.[7] However, the government admitted that the international community has been slow to provide this type of assistance to Libya.

The UN Commission of Inquiry was more assertive in holding that the Libyan government 'will need considerable support from the United Nations and the international community' to improve the country's human rights situation.[8]

It is important to emphasise the role of the international community in assisting newly created domestic war crimes courts. Even for international courts, undertaking war crimes trials is an arduous and challenging

---

[6] *The Prosecutor v. Saif Al-Islam Gaddafi and Abdullah Al-Senussi*, Doc. ICC-01/11-01/11-130-Red, 'Application on behalf of the Government of Libya pursuant to Article 19 of the ICC Statute', (1 May 2012), para. 98. *See also* John Bellinger, 'Regime trials belong in Libya's courts', *Washington Post*, (23 November 2011) available at http://www.washingtonpost.com/opinions/trials-of-moammar-gaddafis-favored-few-belong-in-libyas-courts/2011/11/22/gIQANU4WmN_story.html. Bellinger argued that the international community, human rights groups and the ICC should provide technical and financial assistance to build the capacity for fair trials in Libya.

[7] *Ibid.*, para. 97.

[8] UNHRC, 'Report of the International Commission of Inquiry on Libya', UN Doc. A/HRC/19/68, (8 March 2012), para. 817.

endeavour. However, for post-conflict states, the process can be near impossible. These states face a myriad of problems, ranging from lack of resources, lack of political will, and absence of human capital, to corruption and politicised courts.

The ICC has recognised the need to provide assistance to states through *positive complementarity*, even though the Rome Statute does not directly recognise the concept. This concept is described as ensuring that 'national jurisdictions are strengthened and enabled to conduct genuine national investigations and trials of crimes included in the Rome Statute…'.[9] The Assembly of States Parties has also made clear the need to assist states:

> There is also an increasing awareness that building national capacity with regard to Rome Statute crimes requires a targeted approach providing the necessary expertise required in this area. Consequently, there would be a need to ensure that rule-of-law programmes take into account the specific needs of investigating and prosecuting such crimes and bringing the cases to a successful conclusion. In addition, it would over time, as experience grows, be possible to identify best practices with regard to investigations and prosecutions at the national level and how States can and should assist each other in building capacity in this area.[10]

A number of prominent scholars also support a policy of positive complementarity.[11] Some have argued that positive complementarity is a logical manifestation of the Prosecutor's mandate to encourage and assist

---

[9] ICC-ASP, 'Report of the Bureau on Stocktaking: Complementarity - Taking Stock of the Principle of Complementarity: Bridging the Impunity Gap', Doc. ICC-ASP/8/51, (18 March 2010), para. 16.

[10] ICC-ASP, 'Report of the Bureau on Complementarity', Doc. ICC-ASP/9/26, (17 November 2010), para. 9.

[11] For example *see*, Christopher K. Hall, 'Developing and Implementing an Effective Positive Complementarity Strategy', in Carsten Stahn and Göran Sluiter (eds.), *The Emerging Practice of the International Criminal Court* (Leiden: Koninklijke Brill NV, 2009), pp. 219-229; Jann K. Kleffner, *Complementarity in the Rome Statute and National Criminal Jurisdiction*, (Oxford: Oxford University Press, 2008); William W. Burke-White, 'Implementing a Policy of Positive Complementarity in the Rome System of Justice', (2008) 19 *Criminal Law Forum* 59; William W. Burke-White, 'Proactive Complementarity: The International Criminal Court and National Courts in the Rome System of Justice', (2008) 49 *Harvard International Law Journal* 53; Mohamed M. El Zeidy, 'The Principle of Complementarity; A New Machinery to Implement International Criminal Law', (2001-2002) 23 *Michigan Journal of International Law*, 869, 869-975.

the state to shoulder its responsibilities to prosecute, and that there are strong indications that the Rome Statute confers upon the Prosecutor an obligation to engage in this conception of complementarity.[12]

However, there is a major gap in this aspirational goal of positive complementarity. It is recognised that the ICC will *not* be involved with 'capacity building, financial support and technical assistance, but instead leaving these actions and activities for States, to assist each other on a voluntary basis'.[13]

At a recent meeting of the Assembly of States Parties, the Secretariat stated:

> Clearly the Court and the Assembly are not development cooperation agencies, and hence their role in the practical aspects of strengthening national jurisdictions will be very limited. This must be the responsibility of dedicated rule-of-law actors.[14]

At the Review Conference in Kampala in June 2010, the Bureau of the Assembly of States Parties passed a resolution that recognised 'the need for additional measures at the national level as required and for the enhancement of international assistance to effectively prosecute perpetrators of the most serious crimes of concern to the international community'.[15] However, the emphasis is on the voluntary nature of assistance among states. The resolution asks for '[s]tates to assist each other in strengthening domestic capacity to ensure that investigations and prosecutions of serious crimes of international concern can take place at the national level'.[16] It encourages 'the Court, States Parties and other stakeholders, including international organisations and civil society, to further explore ways in which to enhance the capacity of national jurisdictions to investigate and prosecute serious crimes of international concern…'.[17]

---

[12] Discussion with Wayne Jordash, Attorney for Abdullah Al-Senussi (*The Prosecutor v. Saif Al-Islam Gaddafi and Abdullah Al-Senussi*, Case No. ICC-01/11-01), (18 August 2013).
[13] ICC-ASP, 'Report of the Bureau on Stocktaking: Complementarity', Doc. ICC-ASP/8/51, para. 16.
[14] ICC-ASP, 'Report of the Bureau on Complementarity', Doc. ICC-ASP/9/26, para. 13.
[15] ICC, Resolution RC/Res.1, (8 June 2010), para. 3.
[16] *Ibid.*, para. 5.
[17] *Ibid.*, para. 8.

The Court has recognised that it should monitor the activities of national proceedings,[18] although the Court admits that it has no current procedures to do so.[19] However, there is no evidence to date that the Court has any intention to assist with domestic prosecutions under the principle of complementarity.

Consequently, to ensure a more equitable and successful outcome for future courts, the international community should create a cohesive and lasting assistance programme. There is evidence that the international community is already willing to undertake this type of programme. The Assembly of States Parties (ASP) lists a broad range of international NGOs, which provide advice to states on implementing the Statute; this advice can have both political and technical dimensions.[20] Research centres with specialist knowledge in international law have also provided advice on implementation to national governments, drawing on legal experts and staff of the ICC itself.[21] Examples of enacted legislation by country, and model laws drafted according to region or legal system, have also been made readily available.[22]

There exists today the Justice Rapid Response Initiative (JRR). The JRR is an intergovernmental stand-by facility to assist in cases where genocide, war crimes, crimes against humanity, or serious human rights violations may have occurred.[23] As noted by Burke-White, a number of

---

[18] *The Prosecutor v. Saif Al-Islam Gaddafi and Abdullah Al-Senussi*, Doc. ICC-01/11-01/11-T-3-Red-ENG, 'Hearing Transcript', (10 October 2012), at 64:10-65:1.

[19] *See* IBA, 'Interoffice Memorandum on ICC case, The Prosecutor v. Saif Al-Islam Gaddafi and Abdullah Al-Senussi: Admissibility Challenge from Libya before Pre-Trial Chamber I' (9 Oct 2012), [on file with author].

[20] ICC-ASP, 'Complementarity – Completed Projects'.

[21] *See* as an example University of Nottingham, 'International Criminal Justice Unit', (2014) available at www.nottingham.ac.uk/hrlc/abouthrlc/operationalunits/internationalcriminaljusticeunit.aspx.

[22] CICC, 'Implementation of the Rome Statute', (2014), available at www.iccnow.org/index.php?mod=romeimplementation.

[23] *See* Justice Rapid Response, available at http://www.justicerapidresponse.org. *See also* Jenia Iontcheva Turner, 'Transnational Networks and International Criminal Justice', (2007) 105 *Michigan Law Review* 985, 1011 *referring* to footnotes 121-125 and accompanying text: '[t]hese governments include Argentina, Brazil, Canada, France, Germany, Netherlands, Norway, Sweden, Switzerland, and the UK. Also involved in the planning stages of the JRR were the

governments have created special offices for the prosecution of international crimes, which also 'regularly provide assistance to other States'.[24] But as stated by the JRR itself, the aim of the programme is more passive than active. The JRR maintains a roster of individuals who have a broad range of expertise including forensic specialties, witness protection, military analysis, and human rights investigations.[25] However, the JRR to date has dispatched or deployed only a small number of experts to certain institutions or commissions (e.g., a gender-based violence investigator was deployed to the Independent International Commission of Inquiry on the Syrian Arab Republic) and engaged in several training programmes (e.g., the JRR co-hosted a training course on 'Investigating Cases of Sexual and Gender-based Violence as International Crimes' in Doha, Qatar, between 21 and 26 September 2013).[26]

I. International Technical Assistance Office

There needs to exist a much more robust and comprehensive assistance programme that will more effectively address the concerns of national level prosecutions. I believe this can be accomplished with the creation of a permanent International Technical Assistance Office (ITAO). I have previously called for, and written about, the creation of the ITAO.[27] The ITAO would be administered by an NGO, such as the International Bar Association (IBA) or a consortium of legal groups, such as the International Legal Assistance Consortium (ILAC), the International Center for

---

EU Commission, the ICC Office of the Prosecutor, and NGOs such as the Vera Institute for Justice, International Center for Transitional Justice, Coalition for an ICC, Argentine Anthropological Forensic Team, and International Institute for Criminal Investigations' *quoting* International Criminal Defence Attorneys Association, *Justice Rapid Response Initiative* (August 2004), p. 1, available at http://www.aiadicdaa.org/lnci/Justice%20Rapid%20Response%20Report%20Aug%2004.pdf.

[24] Burke-White, 'Implementing a Policy of Positive Complementarity', 81 *citing* US Department of State, 'Country Reports on Human Rights Practices for 2001'.

[25] *See* Justice Rapid Response, available at http://www.justicerapidresponse.org.

[26] *Ibid.*

[27] *See* Ellis, 'The International Criminal Court and Its Implication for Domestic Law'; Mark S. Ellis, 'International Justice and the Rule of Law: Strengthening the ICC through Domestic Prosecutions', (2009) 1 *Hague Journal on the Rule of Law*, 79, 81-82. There has recently been discussion of creating a judicial rapid response mechanism among states. However, the mechanism would be focused on efforts to investigate, prosecute, and bring to justice alleged perpetrators of genocide, crimes against humanity, and war crimes at the state level.

Transnational Justice (ICTJ) or the Open Society Justice Initiative (OSJI). The international community has gradually moved its perception of NGOs away from that of human rights 'advocates' concerned with protest, to that of a legitimate resource of knowledge and technical assistance. In part, this shift can be attributed to the indispensable technical legal assistance that NGOs have provided to international, mixed, and selected national courts.

However, the ITAO would not work in an isolated environment. It would work closely with international entities, including the UN Development Programme (UNDP), the High Commissioner for Human Rights (OHCHR), the UN Office on Drugs and Crime (UNODC), the Commonwealth Secretariat, the Department of Peacekeeping Operations (DPKO), the UN Rule of Law Unit, the UN Rule of Law Coordination and Resource Group, the European Union, the Assembly of States Parties, and other international and regional bodies, as well as national governments and the JRR.

The purpose of the ITAO would be to provide technical and unbiased assistance to domestic war crimes courts so as to strengthen their capacity to undertake trials. The Office would focus on establishing standards and best practices for domestic prosecutions of international crimes. The ITAO could direct its assistance to states willing to cooperate with the ICC by undertaking their own domestic war crimes trials. For instance, members of the African States Parties to the Rome Statute have called for a programme of international cooperation to enhance the capacity of Member States to undertake trials.[28]

The Office could also help in situations where the ICC, because of its initial investigation into a situation, has lost credibility with the offending state. For instance, when the ICC initiated arrest warrants in Sudan, the Sudanese government made it clear that Sudan would cease to cooperate with the Court.[29] In its eighth report to the UN Security Council, the OTP

[28] Assembly of the African Union, 'Decision on the Meeting of Africa States Parties to the Rome Statute of the International Criminal Court', Doc. Assembly/ AU/13(XIII) (July 1–3, 2009), para. 6.

[29] Shortly after the decision issuing the arrest warrant, President Al Bashir ordered the expulsion of a significant number of humanitarian aid workers from the country. *See* ICC-OTP, 'Eighth Report of the Prosecutor of the International Criminal Court to the UN Security Council Pursuant to UNSCR 1593 (2005)', (3 December 2010), para. 42, available at

noted that the Office tried to establish a working relationship with the Sudanese government in 2005, and that a level of cooperation was initially provided. However, following the issuance of the first arrest warrants against Ahmad Harun and Ali Kushayb in 2007, cooperation ceased.[30] Notably, the 2010 arrest warrant issued for the Sudanese President Ahmad Al Bashir for three counts of genocide did not improve the situation.

As discussed earlier, Kenya represents an example where international assistance could be beneficial. Kenya remains eager to establish a mechanism to try perpetrators of war crimes. Despite the ICC indictment against senior governmental officials who allegedly incited and organised violence, there are still others who should be brought to justice. The Truth, Justice and Reconciliation Commission (TJRC) has recently identified a significant number of additional suspects.[31] However, Kenya's own domestic judicial system remains relatively weak, and could certainly benefit from international support so as to create viable and independent domestic war crimes court proceedings.[32]

In July 2008, the government of Uganda created a special division of the High Court—the International Crimes Division (ICD)—to undertake trials against alleged war criminals. It is currently trying a Commander of the Lord's Resistance Army for war crimes.[33] However, this new war

---

http://www.icc-cpi.int/NR/rdonlyres/DCBF2658-4DBA-43EE-BCBC-FB2330FF7AD8/279075/8thUNSCreportsenttoUNENG1.pdf.

[30] *Ibid.*, para. 82.

[31] 'Uhuru Kenyatta and William Ruto named in Kenya TJRC report', *BBC News*. *See also* TJRC, 'Report of the Truth, Justice and Reconciliation Commission of Kenya', 6 vols, (Kenya: Truth, Justice and Reconciliation Commission, 2013). vol. 4, Appendices 1 and 2, pp. 128-180.

[32] In its recent report, the OSJI report that there are challenges in the lack of legal education relating to international criminal law, poor capacity among prosecutors to undertake serious criminal investigations, a lack of legal aid to provide for defence, a lack of capacity to protect witnesses and victims, and a recognised lack of judicial independence. *See* Open Society Foundations, *Putting Complementarity into Practice: Domestic Justice for International Crimes in Democratic Republic of Congo, Uganda, and Kenya*, (New York: Open Society Foundations, 2011), p. 7.

[33] The suspect is Thomas Kwoyelo and is charged with war crimes under Uganda's penal code and violations of Uganda's 1964 Geneva Conventions Act. *See* Human Rights Watch, 'Uganda: Q&A on the trial of Thomas Kwoyelo', (7 July 2011), available at http://www.hrw.org/news/2011/07/07/uganda-qa-trial-thomas-kwoyelo.

crimes court has publicly requested international assistance in capacity building, e.g., training judges, prosecutors and attorneys.[34] A 2012 Human Rights Watch report indicated that 'many trainings have been conducted in relation to the ICD's work, and [that] anyone working in a professional capacity with the division has participated in some form of training'.[35] However, the report concluded that the quality of the training and its intensity risked 'creating more confusion than understanding unless they are highly tailored to participants' particular responsibilities and the ICD's functioning'.[36]

In 2010, the Democratic Republic of Congo (DRC) created mobile courts in the eastern part of the country to prosecute persons who committed crimes under the ICC's jurisdiction, particularly crimes involving sexual violence. The mobile courts were created to address the lack of governmental authority in large swathes of the country. They travel to remote locations, stay there for a period of between one and two months and hear as many cases as possible during this period. Although initially they were established to deal with sexual violence, they are capable of hearing cases relating to other matters.

From the onset they have been supported by international NGOs. 'Organisations including the American Bar Association (ABA), the United Nations Development Programme (UNDP), and Lawyers Without Borders (ASF), channel funding into local bar associations to allow them to run the trials'.[37] The DRC, however, needs significantly more international assistance to ensure the long-term success of these innovative courts.

The UN High Commissioner for Human Rights has called for Haiti to try former president Jean-Claude Duvalier for serious violations of human rights during his rule. The High Commissioner's Office offered technical

---

[34] *See* Justice James Ogoola, Principle Judge, Uganda War Crimes Division *quoted* in 'Foreign Judges to be on war crimes court', *New Vision*, (26 January 2010), available at http://www.newvision.co.ug/D/8/13/708187.

[35] Human Rights Watch, 'Justice for Serious Crimes Before National Courts: Uganda's International Crimes Division', (2012), p. 26, available at http://www.hrw.org/sites/default/files/reports/uganda0112ForUpload_0.pdf.

[36] *Ibid.*

[37] Passy Mubalama and Simon Jennings 'Roving Courts in Eastern Congo', *Institute for War and Peace Reporting*, (13 February 2013), available at http://iwpr.net/report-news/roving-courts-eastern-congo.

assistance to Haiti's judiciary in order to undertake prosecutions.[38] Yet, the UNHCHR is not equipped nor was it designed to provide on-ground technical legal assistance in this area of law.

Côte d'Ivoire announced that it would establish its own commission to investigate alleged war crimes and crimes against humanity committed during post-election violence since November 2010. However, in my discussions with a number lawyers in the country it is clear to me that the country does not yet have the capacity to undertake credible investigations on its own.

There are already a number of examples of selected international training programmes aimed at domestic war crimes proceedings. The ICTJ organised training seminars for judges of the Special Court of Sierra Leone.[39] Trial observers immediately noted a marked improvement in the treatment of witnesses by the Court; judges also remarked on the helpfulness of the training.[40] The IBA trained judges and lawyers in the former Yugoslavia and Iraq on international human rights and humanitarian law.[41] No Peace Without Justice (NPWJ) established a Legal Profession Programme in Sierra Leone to promote and train domestic lawyers on international human rights standards and humanitarian law.[42] It also conducted training seminars for the Special Court defence counsel and provided international experts to discuss their own roles and responsibilities in bringing cases before international courts.[43]

---

[38] Kyung-wha Kang, UN Deputy High Commissioner for Human Rights, 'Statement by the United Nations Deputy High Commissioner for Human Rights, Kyung-wha Kang at the end of her mission to Haiti', (5 July 2011), available at http://www.ohchr.org/EN/NewsEvents/Pages/DisplayNews.aspx?NewsID=11209&LangID=E.

[39] ICTJ, 'Sierra Leone', (2014), available at http://ictj.org/our-work/regions-and-countries/sierra-leone.

[40] *Ibid.*

[41] *See* IBAHRI, 'IBAHRI Training Manuals', (2014), available at http://www.ibanet.org/Human_Rights_Institute/HRI_Publications/HRI_Training_Manuals_.aspx.

[42] No Peace Without Justice, 'Sierra Leone Program', (2014), available at http://www.npwj.org/ICC/Sierra-Leone-Program.html; No Peace Without Justice, 'Conflict Mapping in Sierra Leone; Violations of International Humanitarian Law from 1991 to 2002', (March 2004) available at http://www.npwj.org/ICC/Conflict-Mapping-Sierra-Leone-Violations-International-Humanitarian-Law-1991-2002.html.

[43] *See* No Peace Without Justice, 'Sierra Leone Program'.

The ABA provided training to Sudanese lawyers on how to defend cases brought before the ICC regarding the atrocities in Darfur. The programme provided participants with advocacy, interviewing, and cross-examination skills specific to international war crimes. Sudanese lawyers were also provided with an overview of the relationship between Sudanese courts and the government, as well as a general review of international, criminal, civil, and common law.[44]

Similarly, REDRESS, a human rights organisation, and the Sudan Organisation Against Torture (SOAT) partnered to produce a handbook for Sudanese lawyers on national and international remedies for torture. This handbook provided Sudanese lawyers with step-by-step guidance on how to gain justice for torture survivors, using both national and international legal institutions, including the ICC.[45]

Recently, the United Nations Support Mission in Libya (UNSMIL) provided Libyan judges and prosecutors with training. The training component was recognised by the ICC in the admissibility challenge by the Libyan government in the *Al-Senussi* case.[46] In ruling in favour of the Government's request to try Al-Senussi in Libya, the Court acknowledged the positive impact of the international assistance.[47]

The Commonwealth Secretariat has published a model law on the implementation of the Rome Statute.[48] It has also published a guidebook

---

[44] *See* American Bar Association, 'Darfur Legal Training Project', (30 September 2008), available at http://www.americanbar.org/groups/litigation/initiatives/good_works/darfur_project.html.

[45] *See* REDRESS and Sudan Organisation Against Torture, 'National and International Remedies for Torture: A Handbook for Sudanese Lawyers', (March 2005), available at http://www.redress.org/downloads/publications/Sudan05.PDF.

[46] *The Prosecutor v. Saif Al-Islam Gadaffi and Abdullah Al-Senussi*, Doc. ICC-01/11-01/11-466-Red, 'Decision on the Admissibility of the Case Against Abdullah Al-Senussi', (11 October 2013), para. 20.

[47] *Ibid.*, 20.

[48] Commonwealth Secretariat, 'Model Law to Implement the Rome Statute of the International Criminal Court', (2003), available at http://www.secretariat.thecommonwealth.org/document/181889/34293/35144/144060/model_law_on_rome_statute_text.htm. *See also* Revised version of the 'Model Law to Implement the Rome Statute of the International Criminal Court' in Commonwealth Secretariat, 'International Criminal Court (ICC) Statute and

for Commonwealth States on prosecuting international crimes, covering a number of topics, including doctrines of international criminal law.[49] Similarly, the ICTY launched a collaborative project to support and strengthen national courts in the former Yugoslavia. The programme is aimed at improving the Court's efficiencies, including providing training courses and materials.[50] This mirrors the programme recommended by Amnesty International through training sources for states that cover issues such as fair trial, non-use of the death penalty, the principle of criminal responsibility, nomination of judges, and victim reparations.[51]

The ITAO would consolidate these types of assorted and divergent efforts into a more structured, effective and financially supported technical assistance programme.

A. Fair, Impartial and Effective Trials

The ITAO could focus on several elements crucial to conducting fair, impartial, and effective domestic war crimes trials. First, the ITAO could provide direct assistance in the early stages of formulating a new domestic war crimes court. Through the ITAO, a panel of international experts would be convened to provide support to the court as needed. The panel would be comprised of jurists with wide-ranging, high-level experience in international criminal law. The panel would be geographically diverse and include different areas of legal expertise. For example, the panel might include judges, professors, and prosecutors from North America, Europe, and Africa where war crimes cases have been heard. Their combined skills and expertise would give the new court access to the very best in establishing a newly promulgated domestic court. In fact, the panel members would not have to be located in the affected country; they could work 'virtually' from their respective home jurisdictions.

---

implementation of the Geneva Conventions', (2011) 37 *Commonwealth Law Bulletin* 681.

[49] *See* Ben Brandon and Max du Plessis (eds.), *The Prosecution of International Crimes: A Practical Guide to Prosecuting ICC Crimes in Commonwealth States* (London: Commonwealth Secretariat, 2005).

[50] ICTY, 'Capacity Building', (2014) available at http://www.icty.org/sid/240.

[51] *See* Amnesty International, 'International Criminal Court: Updated Checklist for Effective Implementation' (2010), available at http://www.amnesty.org/en/library/asset/IOR53/009/2010/en/38132683-2e8e-41fc-a6b6-ec9f69482a29/ior530092010en.pdf.

The ITAO could help draft the court's statute and rules so that both conformed to international standards. Transparency in the drafting process would help legitimise the court and alleviate the distrust that can sometimes be associated with the establishment of war crimes courts.[52] Using international legal experts allows domestic actors an opportunity to discuss ideas and overcome problems in a cooperative, non-combative environment. Outside experts would have advantages over internal actors in being able to connect networks and build a space for effective political dialogue and development. One successful use of this model is a panel of experts that was convened under the auspices of IBA to work with and encourage Serbian leaders to accept amendments to its draft War Crimes Law.[53]

In 2003, there was clearly little public support for war crimes trials in Serbia, a perspective shared by many state actors, including the police.[54] Judge Theodor Meron, President of the ICTY, also expressed doubts about the ability of Serbia to hold credible war crimes trials.[55] Eventually, the Minister for Justice announced that he would support the drafting of a new law creating a special war crimes court. However, the draft law ended up being formulated hurriedly and contained several weaknesses. In response, I convened a group of experts to assist the Serbian government to review the draft law, and organised a workshop where areas of conflict could be discussed openly. The result was noteworthy; by the end of the workshop,

---

[52] *See* Human Rights Watch, 'Memorandum to the Iraqi Governing Council on 'The Statute of the Iraqi Special Tribunal'', (December 2003), available at http://www.hrw.org/legacy/backgrounder/mena/iraq121703.htm.

[53] *See* Mark S. Ellis, 'Coming to Terms with its Past - Serbia's New Court for the Prosecution of War Crimes', (2004) 22 *Berkeley Journal of International Law*, 165, 166-167.

[54] An overwhelming public feeling in Serbia was that the police would be a major impediment to conducting successful trials. This view recognised the fact that many police were involved in the crimes committed and were therefore reluctant to investigate such crimes effectively. *See* Ellis, 'Coming to Terms with its Past', 182.

[55] Judge Meron reported to the UN Security Council in 2004. *See* Mark S. Ellis, 'The Legacy of the ICTY: National and International Efforts in Capacity Building' in Richard H. Steinberg (ed.), *Assessing the Legacy of the ICTY* (Leiden/Boston: Martinus Nijhoff Publishers, 2011), p. 143. *See also* Dominic Raab, 'Evaluating the ICTY and its Completion Strategy: Efforts to Achieve Accountability for War Crimes and Their Tribunals' (2005) 3 *Journal of International Criminal Justice*, 82, 93-94.

the Serbian government had agreed to substantial changes to the draft law.[56]

B. Substantive Legal and Procedural Issues

Second, the ITAO could provide an international perspective on key legal substantive and procedural issues facing a new domestic war crimes court once it commenced proceedings.

Of course, it is important to recognise that the newly established court would rightfully want to control its own proceedings and maintain its independence; the new court would also face considerable pressure from local actors to do so. Thus, it is crucial that advice from the ITAO on substantive and procedural law not be seen as interfering in what is essentially a domestic legal process. The ITAO would establish a set of objectives and goals to **ensure** and maintain an appropriate balance between outside assistance and national autonomy. The ITAO would:

- Establish a good working relationship between the domestic court and the ITAO;
- Provide timely, accurate, and independent advice on international law issues;
- Guarantee that all advice be independent and impartial;
- Ensure that all facts relevant to the domestic court be examined and taken into account before legal advice would be given;
- Air any dissenting views from the ITAO;
- Help raise the understanding and appreciation of international law and legal precedents within the domestic war crimes court; and
- Help ensure that the decisions of the domestic war crimes court be consistent with those of international and mixed courts.

Achieving these objectives will go a long way in establishing an effective and efficient communication procedure between the domestic court and the ITAO. A five-step process for soliciting advice from the

---

[56] *Ibid.,* 167. In light of Judge Meron's initial doubts as to the ability of the domestic courts, it is interesting to note a number of cases have been transferred from the ICTY to the Serbian war crimes courts. *See* Erik Møse, 'The ICTR's Completion Strategy – Challenges and Possible Solutions', (2008) 6 *Journal of International Criminal Justice* 667, 672. *See also*, Ellis 'The Legacy of the ICTY', p. 142.

ITAO would supplement this approach: (1) the domestic court (through an international adviser or the Court President) could contact the ITAO and provide all relevant information on the legal issues identified by the domestic court, (2) the ITAO would arrange for the relevant information and any requests for legal advice to be translated into a working language (e.g., English), (3) the ITAO would prepare legal advice, (4) the legal advice would be translated into the local language, and (5) the translated legal advice (i.e., brief) would then be sent to the Court's contact.

The legal advice (or brief) could take the form of an *amicus curiae*; the domestic court would receive the brief as a 'friend of the court' and circulate it to all parties at the proceedings. Alternatively, the domestic court could treat the advice as 'confidential' and allow the judges to promulgate or ignore the advice given.

A similar, although truncated process, was initiated by the IBA while assisting the Iraqi war crimes court. After extensive consultations with the Court, I agreed that the IBA would provide analyses of crucial areas of law identified by the Iraqi judges. During a two-year period, we provided assessments on eight areas of law: (1) the principle sources for international standards on judicial independence, (2) the practice and decision of international courts in respect of multiple convictions and multiple sentences, (3) the sources of international law on the issue of joint criminal enterprise in cases of genocide, (4) international standards for providing transcripts of proceedings, (5) the issue of retroactivity of criminal offences, (6) the legality of the Iraqi War Crimes Court, (7) Head-of-State immunity, and (8) Joint Criminal Enterprise.[57] This process took place in an environment that promoted open dialogue and allowed the key Iraqi players to gain confidence for undertaking the trials.

The Iraqi Court's statute provided the basis for this programme and is a good model for future domestic war crimes courts. Following the Iraqi experience, future courts should adopt statutory language that allows for international legal advice. An example of language that could be adopted by future domestic war crimes courts would be the following:

---

[57] The programme was created through an agreement between the UK Government and the IBA. The panel of international experts appointed by the IBA included, Justice Richard J. Goldstone, Judge Patricia Wald, Judge David Hunt, and UK Barristers Stuart Alford and Brenda Hollis.

> The Court may appoint non-nationals to act in an advisory capacity to the Court. The role of the advisors shall be to provide assistance to the Court with respect to international law and the experience of international courts.

C. Trial Observations

Third, the ITAO could provide trial observers to review, assess, and evaluate each trial undertaken by the domestic war crimes court. Endemic to most post-conflict countries are judicial systems that can neither guarantee fair and politically unbiased judicial processes, nor try cases that are impartial and without ethnic bias.

As discussed in this book, to gain international recognition of its domestic war crimes trials, national governments would have to ensure that the trials meet international standards. Court proceedings would benefit from international and national observers—trained lawyers and judges—who can independently observe and report on the trial process. There could be trial observers present throughout each trial, including pre-trial proceedings.

A trial observer programme should be a 'partnership' between the ITAO and domestic judicial personnel. This would require a 'buy-in' from domestic war crimes courts based on the understanding that the role of international trial observers is to *assist* the new court. Regular meetings with court personnel for the purpose of reviewing the progress of the trial would take place so as to improve the court proceedings.

However, it is important to note that the monitoring aspect of the proposed ITAO would gain support from the ICC itself. Under Article 18(5) of the Rome Statute, the OTP may request that the '[s]tate concerned periodically inform the Prosecutor of the progress of its investigations and any subsequent prosecutions'.[58] As noted earlier, Article 53 further requires that the Prosecutor continue to evaluate any national proceedings.[59]

---

[58] Rome Statute of the International Criminal Court, Rome, opened for signature 17 July 1988, 2187 UNTS 90 (entered into force 1 July 2002) UN Doc. A/CONF.183/9 (hereinafter, ICC Statute or Rome Statute), Article 18(5).

[59] *Ibid.*, Article 53(4), which reads, in part: '[t]he Prosecutor may, at any time, reconsider a decision whether to initiate an investigation or prosecution based on new facts or information'.

Thus, the OTP is required to monitor any ongoing domestic proceeding throughout its duration to ensure that the trial continues to meet the requirements of Article 17.[60] Any targeted ITAO assistance, and its impact upon the ongoing viability of the domestic proceedings, could be monitored through this type of program.[61]

The observers could also monitor trial proceedings during closed sessions to preserve a higher degree of transparency when the court determines it best to protect the identity of a witness. Trial observers would need to be given authority by the domestic war crimes court, notwithstanding any procedural law or regulation to the contrary, to attend and observe the trials. The easiest way of ensuring this is to encourage newly created domestic war crimes courts to include statutory language permitting international observers to monitor due process standards. At the conclusion of each trial, the trial observers could hold separate meetings with the relevant judges, prosecutors, and defence counsel to review the trial and make recommendations. In the end, the trial observers would offer a 'check' on the court proceedings, monitoring standards of efficiency, due process and competency. The ITAO could seek assistance from regional organisations. For example, a trial observation team in Africa could include representatives from the African Commission on Human Rights and Peoples or the Southern African Litigation Centre (SALC).

Trial observations have been successfully utilised in international and mixed courts. For example, the IBA launched its own ICC monitoring programme. The programme monitors the proceedings of the Court and focuses on issues affecting fair trials, the rights of the accused, and the implementation of the Statute and Rules of Procedure and Evidence. To achieve these objectives, the IBA employs a full-time representative in

---

[60] Markus Benzing, 'The Complementarity Regime of the International Criminal Court: International Criminal Justice between State Sovereignty and the Fight against Impunity', (2003) 7 *Max Planck Yearbook of United Nations Law* 591, 632.

[61] *See* Burke-White, 'Implementing a Policy of Positive Complementarity', 74, footnote 36: noting for example, 'the Organisation on Security and Cooperation in Europe (OSCE) has taken primary responsibility for monitoring 11*bis* trials before the State Court of Bosnia and Herzegovina and transmits reports on the quality of the proceedings to the Prosecutor of the ICTY. […] Human Rights Watch, Amnesty International and the International Center for Transitional Justice have all issued reports on the quality of proceedings before various national courts'.

The Hague to regularly monitor court proceedings and to liaise with other interested parties. The programme also includes evaluations of legal, administrative, and institutional issues that could potentially affect the impartiality of proceedings and the development of international justice.

NGOs have created similar monitoring programmes for the Special Court of Sierra Leone. The Sierra Leone Court Monitoring Programme (SLCMP) is an independent programme comprised of Sierra Leonean lawyers and civil society members. Collaborating with the Sierra Leonean Coalition for Justice and Accountability, the SLCMP monitors proceedings at the Special Court in order to provide a fair, independent, and critical assessment of the Court for local and international communities, as well as for the Court itself. In addition to hosting a radio programme, the SLCMP issues reports, articles, newsletters, and commentaries on both the procedural and substantive work of the Special Court. Moreover, the SLCMP aims to increase local capacity for monitoring efforts.[62]

For the ICTY, the Institute for War and Peace Reporting (IWPR) has conducted comprehensive analyses of the Court through a weekly regional report covering an expanse of issues. In a unique format, the IWPR documents the proceedings of trials in a 'Tribunal Update', which carries features and commentary on the wider issues surrounding war crimes. The IWPR is at the leading edge in this field, as it is the only specialist agency to have reported in-depth since the ICTY's very formation.

D. Judicial Nominations

Fourth, the ITAO could play a central role in overseeing and certifying the nomination and selection process for judges through an independent and transparent judicial appointments committee. Even in circumstances of a collapsed state power vacuum, evident in many post-conflict states, it is still possible to re-establish limited judicial authority and select judges, using a model that preserves national integrity and ensures that appointees are qualified and able to uphold principles of independence and impartiality.

---

[62] Sierra Leone Court Monitoring Programme, 'Court Monitoring Training Manual', (11 September 2009), pp. 1-3, available at http://www.carl-sl.org/home/images/stories/docs/SLCMPTraining_manual.pdf.

A judicial appointments committee is 'not an 'off-the-shelf' product which can be adopted wholesale, but rather a system that must be constructed to accommodate the particular legal, political and cultural considerations of the country'.[63] Nevertheless, if introduced with due consideration, such a committee could deliver significant benefit:

> The rationale for the establishment of a[n] [appointments] commission must be that it will guarantee the independence of the system from inappropriate politicisation, strengthen the quality of the appointments made, enhance the fairness of the selection process, promote diversity in the composition of the judiciary and so rebuild public confidence in the system.[64]

The ITAO could also play a role in this process by establishing a committee composed of independent experts and judges, experts from international bar associations, domestic NGOs, and academic institutions to assist the new court. This approach is based on the effectiveness of engaging broad aspects of the legal profession as well as civil society in helping to add legitimacy to the court's work.

The ITAO committee would use its position to give an independent evaluation of each candidate and state whether he or she fulfils the qualifications established in criminal and international law set out in the court's statute. The ITAO could institutionalise a system of independent review and transparency in the nominations process. A similar process has recently been used by the United Nations for the selection of judges for its internal court. The IBA was asked by the United Nations to assist in assessing the qualifications of those judges nominated.

E. Training

Fifth, the ITAO could provide specific training to judges involved with domestic war crimes trials. The need for continuing legal education in this area is all too apparent. Even for international war crimes courts, a significant number of jurists do not have the requisite trial experience to undertake high profile trials.[65] The issue is even more acute for domestic

---

[63] Kate Malleson, 'Creating a Judicial Appointments Commission: Which Model Works Best?', (2004) 1 *Public Law*, 102, 103.
[64] *Ibid.*
[65] *See* generally Patricia M. Wald, 'The International Criminal Tribunal for the former Yugoslavia Comes of Age: Some Observations on Day-To-Day Dilemmas of an International Court', (2001) 5 *Washington University Journal of Law and*

courts. Although most jurists in post-conflict countries will have formal university-level training, they will not have practiced before war crimes courts, nor will they have specific knowledge of international criminal law. The training could be conducted separately for judges, prosecutors, and lawyers and, when appropriate, jointly on issues relevant to members of all three groups. The ITAO could coordinate with other international training programmes to provide additional training assistance in domestic war crimes trials.

The ITAO team would also assist newly created domestic war crimes courts in adopting methods to ensure conformity to international standards of judicial conduct. These would include explicit rules to govern the conduct of judges and provide disciplinary measures in case of breach. Definitions of conduct giving rise to a breach should be clearly outlined in the statute. The ITAO team could assist in drafting precise rules governing the conduct of judges and devise appropriate mechanisms for enforcement, including a monitoring body (external or internal) to discipline any breaches of judicial conduct. Decisions calling for the suspension, removal, or disciplining of a judge could be subject to independent review, although not of the government.

Rwanda is a good model in preparing for the transfer of cases from the ICTR. Rwanda has initiated a number of positive changes to its domestic laws to strengthen its judicial independence. For instance, judges can **only** be removed for reasons of 'bad conduct, incompetence or serious professional misconduct'.[66] Moreover, all issues dealing with the discipline and evaluation of judges are handled by the judiciary's own independent High Council.[67] The Council is independent from the executive and legislative branches of the government.[68]

Another area where the ITAO would be useful is in assisting domestic war crimes courts to outline clear definitions of judicial misconduct and to establish a fair complaint and disciplinary procedure that addresses allegations of judicial misconduct. International and regional standards

---

Policy, 87, 94-95; Patricia M. Wald, *Tyrants on Trial – Keeping Order in the Courtroom*, (New York: Open Society Institute, 2009), p. 58.

[66] *The Prosecutor v. Bernard Munyagishari*, Case No. ICTR-2005-89-R11*bis*, 'Decision on the Prosecutor's Request for Referral of the case to the Republic of Rwanda', (6 June 2012), para. 190.

[67] *Ibid.*, para. 191.

[68] *Ibid.*

require that judges may only be removed from office for limited reasons. Provisions set out in the UN *Basic Principles* highlight the importance of procedures to govern the discipline and removal of judges.[69] Principle 18 states that: 'judges shall be subject to suspension or removal only for reasons of incapacity or behaviour that renders them unfit to discharge their duties'.[70] While the exact type of conduct that would subject a judge to disciplinary proceedings is absent from the *Basic Principles*, it does recognise that proceedings should be determined in accordance with 'established standards of judicial conduct'.[71]

The Principles and Guidelines on the Right to a Fair Trial and Legal Assistance in Africa provide that: '[j]udicial officials may only be removed or suspended from office for gross misconduct incompatible with judicial office, or for physical or mental incapacity that prevents them from undertaking their judicial duties'.[72] The Latimer House Guidelines provide: '[g]rounds for removal of a judge should be limited to: (A) inability to perform judicial duties; and (B) serious misconduct'.[73]

In cases of misconduct, many court statutes, including those governing the *ad hoc* international courts, are silent. For instance, in the case of the ICTY, Judge Karibi-Whyte famously fell asleep for extended periods, even being heard to 'breathe noisily' during the *Čelebići* trial.[74] However, the lack of disciplinary actions against him was problematic. Despite the fact that defence counsel tactfully challenged the judge's behaviour during the trial, the judge was not replaced.[75] When counsel for the accused later

[69] United Nations Basic Principles on the Independence of the Judiciary, UN Doc. A/CONF.121/22/Rev.1, p. 59 (1985), (hereinafter Basic Principles on the Independence of the Judiciary), Principles 17–20.
[70] *Ibid.*, Principle 18.
[71] *Ibid.*, Principle 19
[72] African Commission on Human and Peoples' Rights, 'Principles and Guidelines on the Right to a Fair Trial and Legal Assistance in Africa', Doc. ACHPR/Res.41(XXVI) 99 (1999), Principle 4(p).
[73] Commonwealth Secretariat, 'Commonwealth (Latimer House) Principles on the Three Branches of Government', (10 May 2004), VI(I)(a)(i), available at http://secretariat.thecommonwealth.org/document/181889/34293/35468/37744/latimerhouse.htm.
[74] Michael Bohlander (ed.), *International Criminal Justice: A Critical Analysis of Institutions and Procedures* (London: Cameron May, 2007), p. 387.
[75] Counsel for the accused, Landžo, was criticised on appeal for failing to raise the issue more forcefully at trial, when remedial measures may have been taken. Counsel had argued that to have done so would have been inappropriate and futile

raised Judge Karibi-Whyte's inattention as a ground for acquittal, the Appeals Chamber dismissed it.[76] In a rather absurd ruling, the Court concluded that the appeal was 'opportunistic'. This was in spite of acknowledging that '[t]he Extracts Tapes do demonstrate a recurring pattern of behaviour where Judge Karibi-Whyte appears not to have been fully conscious of the proceedings for short periods at a time. [...] On one occasion [...] the judge appeared to be asleep for approximately thirty minutes. [...] Judge Karibi-Whyte can also be heard to be breathing very noisily at times, but such times include occasions where he is obviously very fully conscious of the proceedings'.[77] The judge was not disciplined, nor dismissed.[78]

The issue of judicial misconduct has never been more acute than at the ECCC. Remarkably, the procedure for the recusal or disqualification of a judge from the ECCC does *not* include any past episodes of corruption or judicial misconduct that are unrelated to the case currently before the Court. For instance, in response to Ieng Sary's request to disqualify Judge Nil Nonn for his past acceptance of bribery[79], the Trial Chamber

because 'it would have alienated one of the three tiers of fact, causing irreparable harm' to their case. Instead, she mentioned it 'informally' to the Senior Legal Officer of the Trial Chamber (*The Prosecutor v. Zejnil Delalic, Zdravko Mucic, Hazim Delic and Esad Landžo*, Case No. IT-96-21-A, 'Judgement', (20 February 2001), (hereinafter *Čelebići* Appeals Judgement), para. 644.). It is also significant that at least one of the other judges was aware of the Judge's slumber. On appeal, it was noted that on 'occasion, Judge Jan leant over to touch Judge Karibi-Whyte when his head had dropped'. *See Čelebići* Appeals Judgement, para. 628.

[75] *Čelebići* Appeals Judgement, para. 628.

[76] *Ibid.*, para. 628.

[77] *Ibid.*, para. 628.

[78] However, the Appeal Judgement does criticise the inattention shown by the judge: '[i]t must be said, firmly, that Judge Karibi-Whyte's conduct cannot be accepted as appropriate conduct for a judge. Even if, as may well be the position, he had no control over his loss of attention, litigants are in general entitled to the full attention of the judges who have to decide their case' (*Ibid.*, para. 629). Judge Karibi-Whyte did not seek another term as ICTY Judge, instead returning to Nigeria after the end of the trial in November 1998. As a result, no further censure was possible. It is not clear if his decision not to seek re-election was caused by his inattention during the *Čelebići* trial.

[79] *See* Case No. 002/19-09-2007-ECCC/TC, 'Ieng Sary's Application to Disqualify Judge Nil Nonn Due to his Purported Admission that he has Accepted Bribes & Request for a Public Hearing or in the Alternative for Leave to Reply to any Submissions Presented by Judge Nil Nonn in Response to this Application' (14 January 2011).

responded that Internal Rule 34 provides judge disqualification for 'bias against a particular accused in relation to a particular case, and cannot be used to lodge a general complaint about the fitness of an individual to serve as a judge'.[80] Thus, the Court did not disqualify Judge Nil Nonn because the bribes he received in previous cases were not strictly relevant to his perception of the Khmer Rouge cases. Absurdly, even if judges exhibit bias or have engaged in misconduct in previous cases, it is still not enough to disqualify them from the case at hand. The Trial Chamber conceded that '[a] pattern of improper conduct … may call into question a person's qualifications to act as a judge at the ECCC, [but] [n]o relevant mechanisms are provided in the ECCC Law and Agreement'.[81] It is perhaps telling that the resignation of International Co-Investigating Judge Siegfried Blunk only materialised after significant political controversy, as described above.[82]

Iraq is another example of where a domestic court fell short of providing judicial conduct guidelines. The Iraqi War Crimes Court did not have an internal monitoring process for judicial misconduct. A committee of judges decides on disciplinary matters.[83] Decisions of the committee can be appealed if it decides to remove a judge.[84] According to the Iraqi Court's Statute, a judge will be removed if he is convicted of a non-political felony, gives false information, or fails to perform his duty without legitimate reason.[85] However, one of the most controversial sections of the Court's Statute is that it allows judges to be transferred from the Court '*for any reason*'[86] [emphasis added]. As mentioned earlier, this provision allowed the arbitrary removal of several judges from the Court and stands in clear violation of the UN *Basic Principles*, which recommends that judges should not be removed or sanctioned except for

---

[80] Case No. 002/19-09-2007-ECCC/TC, 'Decision on Ieng Sary's Application to Disqualify Judge Nil Nonn and Related Requests', (28 January 2011), para. 8.
[81] *Ibid.*, para. 9.
[82] Judge Blunk resigned from the ECCC due to 'political interference from the Cambodian government'. His resignation followed months of controversy, as the court failed to proceed with Case 003 and Case 004 (*See* Seth Mydans, 'Judge Quits Tribunal in Khmer Rouge Inquiry', *The New York Times*, (10 October 2011) available at http://www.nytimes.com/2011/10/11/world/asia/judge-quits-cambodia-tribunal.html?_r=0).
[83] Law of the Iraqi Higher Criminal Court, *Al-Waqa'I Al-Iraqiya* (The Official Gazette of Iraq), (18 October 2005), (hereinafter Iraq Statute), Article 6(1).
[84] *Ibid.*
[85] *Ibid.,* Article 4(5).
[86] *Ibid.*, Article 4(4).

reasons of incapacity or behaviour that renders them unfit to discharge their duties.[87]

F. Gender Diversity

Sixth, the ITAO would also assist war crimes courts in creating gender balance and its ethnic diversity in their composition. It is important that the composition of a domestic war crimes court reflect the make-up of society, as this can help it gain legitimacy and public confidence, particularly in post-conflict contexts where mistrust and ethnic divisions are still keenly felt.[88] Achieving a diverse judiciary is not easy but both international and domestic courts have made important contributions to reaching this goal.

The importance of gender balance is recognised in Article 38 of the Rome Statute, which requires States Parties, when selecting judges, to 'take into account the need, within the membership of the Court, for… [a] fair representation of female and male judges'.[89] During the ballot stages of voting, the agreed procedure provides that each State Party shall vote for a minimum number of candidates of each gender.[90] As of 2014, the ICC consisted of ten female and eight male judges.[91] Some have suggested that the quota system of the ICC undermines the principles of judicial selection, and may compromise the standard of the Court.[92] However, this can be avoided if gender balance is viewed as one factor among many in selecting judges, and thus may influence selection where a male and female candidate, who are otherwise equal in merit, are being considered.

---

[87] UN Basic Principles on the Independence of the Judiciary, Principle 18.

[88] Ruth Mackenzie, Kate Malleson, Penny Martin and Philippe Sands (eds.), *Selecting International Judges: Principle, Process and Politics*, (Oxford: Oxford University Press, 2010), pp. 137, 175.

[89] ICC Statute, Article 36(8)(a)(iii).

[90] ICC-ASP, 'Procedure for the Nomination and Election of the judges for the International Criminal Court', Doc. ICC-ASP/3/Res.6, (10 September 2004), para. 20(c).

[91] ICC, 'Biographical Notes', (2014), available at http://www.icc-cpi.int/en_menus/icc/structure%20of%20the%20court/chambers/the%20judges/Pages/the%20judges%20%20%20biographical%20notes.aspx.

[92] Mackenzie, Malleson, Martin and Sands (eds.), *Selecting International Judges: Principle, Process and Politics*, p. 49.

Diversity is an important consideration in the selection of judges in any judicial body, and a particular 'selection issue worthy of attention is the relatively low number of female judges'.[93] For example, one of the most glaring deficiencies in the ICTR was its dearth of female judges. In fact, the Court initially had only one female judge, Navanethem Pillay, who was largely responsible for the acknowledgment that widespread rape and sexual violence had occurred in Rwanda. The realisation of that gender inequity resulted in the inclusion of an article in the Rome Statute that provided for 'a fair representation of female and male judges'.[94]

The absence of women in international courts, in general, has been a cause for particular concern. For instance, as of 2013, only 110 (24.9%) of a total of 442 counsel registered to practice before the ICC were women, although it should be noted that this is a major improvement from only three years ago when seventeen percent (62) of List Counsel were women. Judge Navanethem Pillay, the first female judge at the ICTR, who went on to become the first female President of that Court, stated:

> Who interprets the law is at least as important as who makes the law, if not more so. I cannot stress how critical I consider it to be that women are represented and a gender perspective integrated at all levels of the investigation, prosecution, defence, witness protection and judiciary.[95]

Only after the ICC Registry and the IBA launched a campaign to reverse the under representation of women in the List of Counsel did the number improve. In launching the campaign, I stated the following:

> The Female Counsel Campaign is a unique opportunity to encourage qualified women lawyers to engage with the ICC in matters of international criminal justice. It is hoped that, through this campaign, there will emerge an increased awareness about the Rome Statute system in

[93] Ruth Mackenzie and Philippe Sands, 'International Courts and Tribunals and the Independence of the International Judge', (2003) 44 *Harvard International Law Journal* 271, 278.

[94] ICC Statute, Article 36(8)(a)(iii).

[95] Simone Monasebian, 'Sex Matters: The Invisibility of Women at the Iraqi Tribunal', in Michael P. Scharf and Gregory S. McNeal (eds.), *Saddam on Trial: Understanding and Debating the Iraqi High Tribunal* (Durham: Carolina Academic Press, 2006), p. 96. (Monasebian also notes that Judge Pillay, as the only woman judge at the ICTR at the time, worked hard to develop sexual violence and rape counts into international criminal prosecutions. As a result of such efforts, sexual violence counts are now recognised as capable of being classed as war crimes, crimes against humanity, or even genocide).

> general, the ICC List Counsel in particular, and ultimately the number of women lawyers on the List will rise. The ICC List Counsel provides a unique opportunity for women lawyers practicing at the national level to receive training and develop key legal skills and networking opportunities in the field of international criminal law and the ICC. This training can also be utilised at the national level. This is positive complementarity at work. Most important, by increasing the number of female lawyers appearing before the ICC, this campaign ensures that women's voices will be *heard* and that women will be *seen* as playing a necessary and crucial role in promoting international justice.[96]

The issue of gender balance has been the subject of several recommendations at the ECtHR. Resolution 1366,[97] amended by Resolutions 1426[98] and 1627,[99] emphasises the importance of achieving a gender balance on the ECtHR. These resolutions set out the Assembly's policy 'not to consider lists of candidates where … the list does not include at least one candidate of each sex, except when the candidates belong to the sex which is under-represented in the Court, that is to say, the sex to which less than 40% of the total number of judges belongs'.[100] However, this requirement is restricted to the gender representation as reflected in the judiciary of the country of origin, as opposed to the actual gender balance on the ECtHR.[101] However, it is interesting to note that

---

[96] IBA, 'IBA/ICC Press Conference to Launch Campaign Calling for Increased Number of African Female Lawyers at the ICC; Remarks from Mark S. Ellis, IBA Executive Director' (12 May 2010) [emphasis added], available at http://www.ibanet.org/Document/Default.aspx?DocumentUid=941CB046-8BBB-4022-A79E-F96175D54FFD.

[97] Parliamentary Assembly of the Council of Europe, Resolution 1366 (2004).

[98] Parliamentary Assembly of the Council of Europe, Resolution 1426 (2005).

[99] Parliamentary Assembly of the Council of Europe, Resolution 1627 (2008). *See also* Parliamentary Assembly of the Council of Europe, Resolution 1841 (2011).

[100] *See* Parliamentary Assembly of the Council of Europe, Resolution 1366 (2004) as amended by Parliamentary Assembly of the Council of Europe, Resolution 1426 (2006). *See also* European Court of Human Rights, 'Advisory Opinion on Certain Legal Questions Concerning the Lists of Candidates Submitted with a View to the Election of Judges to the European Court of Human Rights', (12 February 2008), paras 20, 26. Parliamentary Assembly of the Council of Europe, Resolution 1627 (2008) allows the Assembly to consider single-sex lists of candidates of the sex that is over-represented in the Court in exceptional circumstances.

[101] Parliamentary Assembly of the Council of Europe, Recommendation 1649 (2004), paras 17-18.

presently only 36.2% of the judges on the Court are women, [102] thus falling short of the minimum gender balance.

The diversity requirement obviously extends beyond gender to include additional considerations, particularly of ethnicity and nationality. Appointing judges who reflect different ethnic and national groups within a society should be seen in a similar light to gender diversity. Diversity of ethnic and national background among judges can encourage public faith in the court, without taking priority over the personal and experiential merits of candidates.

The importance of diversity in the judiciary is not to create a body that is representative in the sense used in relation to elected politicians. Instead, as argued by Kate Malleson, '[o]ne can hope that a more diverse judiciary may include a wider range of skills and experience which will enhance the quality of its decision-making in a general sense … [and] the primary rationale for wishing to appoint judges from more diverse backgrounds is to strengthen the legitimacy of the judiciary'.[103]

G. Victim and Witness Support

Seventh, the ITAO could assist domestic war crimes courts in establishing an administrative framework for long-term victim and witness support. This issue has been discussed in Chapter 2. Both international and mixed courts have consistently consolidated extrajudicial victim and witness protection concerns into one administrative unit, typically named the 'Victims and Witnesses Unit' or some derivation thereof. This practice has been relatively successful in providing appropriate protection and security.

Protective measures can vary widely based on the importance of the information that witnesses can offer and the nature and severity of the threat against them. Measures may be as simple as helping witnesses deal with the practical and psychological aspects of the trial, or as complex as helping them relocate and change their identity. Because war crimes courts are generally established in post-conflict environments, witness protection

[102] Parliamentary Assembly of the Council of Europe, 'Nomination of Candidates and Election of Judges to the European Court of Human Rights', Doc. 11767, (1 December 2008), para. 26.
[103] Kate Malleson, 'Creating a Judicial Appointments Commission', 106.

is critical to the success of the trial and can be critical to the safety of the individuals involved.

Working with local police or security units to detect the actual level of threat will be the first step for any court, and the basis upon which to determine the required elements of a witness protection programme. Once the police have identified the threat, the investigation can be tailored to include different methods for questioning witnesses.

The experience of Serbia's war crimes trials provides helpful insight for domestic courts. It was difficult to persuade people to come to Belgrade to testify. Non-Serbs simply did not trust the Serbian court. However, Nataša Kandić of the Humanitarian Law Centre provided crucial support for witnesses who appeared before the Court. Together with the Court's Victim and Witness Unit, the Centre met witnesses at the airport or train station, and also provided accommodation and general support to witnesses.[104]

Côte d'Ivoire is another country that lacks a system of witness protection 'in law or as a matter of practice' in domestic war crimes cases.[105] Victims are understandably hesitant to bring complaints and testify against those in power. The ITAO would be perfectly situated to assist the government to enact laws that would in the words of Human Rights Watch create 'a neutral witness protection unit …for all witnesses, [including] relocation agreements with third countries to protect witnesses in extreme circumstances'.[106]

It is inconceivable to think that newly created domestic war crimes courts in post-conflict countries could accomplish the task of creating a viable witness protection programme without international assistance. One of the main reasons that international support is needed involves the cost. Victim-witness protection comes at an enormous cost. The ICC budgets

---

[104] Human Rights Watch, 'Unfinished Business – Serbia's War Crimes Chamber', (June 2007), pp. 7-8, available at http://www.hrw.org/legacy/backgrounder/eca/serbia0607/serbia0607web.pdf.

[105] Human Rights Watch 'Turning Rhetoric into Reality: Accountability for Serious International Crimes in Côte d'Ivoire', (4 April 2013), p. 54, available at http://www.hrw.org/sites/default/files/reports/CDI0413_ForUpload.pdf.

[106] *Ibid.*, p. 7.

more than €6 million to its victims and witnesses unit.[107] The ITAO could also work with domestic war crimes courts to establish clear and definitive protocols regarding victim-witness examination as part of their statutory guidelines. By ensuring that witnesses are treated with respect, domestic war crimes courts will protect the psychological and emotional well being of witnesses, and thus promote witness candour and cooperation. In so doing, the courts create an atmosphere conducive to witness candour, which ultimately strengthens the court's legitimacy.[108] To achieve this goal, the newly formed courts should include provisions in their procedural rules that allow for stronger judicial control over victim-witness examination and cross-examination, as well as allowing greater flexibility for alternative methods of testifying. In addition, the courts should provide training for new judges covering judicial control over victim-witness testimony.[109] The local Bar could establish training for attorneys on the same issues.

It should be no surprise that at-risk witnesses are likely to need protection after their involvement with a case, both with regard to their physical safety and their psychological well being.[110] In fact, for many

---

[107] *See* ICC-ASP, 'Proposed Programme Budget for 2013 of the International Criminal Court', Doc. ICC-ASP/11/10, (16 August 2012), p. 122.

[108] *See generally* Laura Miller, United States Institute for Peace (USIP), 'Building the Iraqi Special Tribunal: Lessons from Experiences in International Criminal Justice', (13 June 2004), p. 6, available at http://www.usip.org/publications/building-the-iraqi-special-tribunal-lessons-experiences-in-international-criminal.pp. 9-10.

[109] Telephone Interview with David Tolbert, ICTY Deputy Prosecutor (4 December 2013).

[110] The experience of the previous courts indicates that the need for post-trial protection of witnesses was one that the international community realized through experience. The ICTY did not address this issue in its Statute or Rules of Procedure and Evidence, although it did supply some post-trial protection in practice. *See* Mikaela Heikkilä, *International Criminal Tribunals and Victims of Crimes*, (Turku: Åbo Akademi University, 2004), p. 134. Subsequent courts, however, explicitly charge their VWUs with protecting witnesses after trial. *See* Rules of Procedure and Evidence of the International Criminal Tribunal for Rwanda, Revision 19, (10 April 2013), UN Doc. ITR/3/Rev. 19 (2013), (hereinafter ICTR Rules of Procedure and Evidence), Rule 34(A)(iii) (commanding the VWU to '[d]evelop short term and long term plans for the protection of witnesses who have testified before the Tribunal and who fear a threat to their life, property, or family'); Rules of Procedure and Evidence of the Special Court for Sierra Leone, 16 January 2002, as amended 31 May 2012, (hereinafter SCSL Rules of Procedure and Evidence), Rule 34(ii) ('The Victims

victims and witnesses, the most serious safety concerns arise after the verdict is determined. While there may no longer be concern about the use of intimidation to affect witness testimony, the desire for revenge remains a significant concern. As discussed extensively in this book, a lesson for domestic courts is that there are greater difficulties in providing post-trial protection than protection before and during trial.[111] Although very few witnesses end up being relocated,[112] domestic war crimes courts must be capable of relocating witnesses and their families either within their own country or, if necessary, to another country.[113] Relocating within country will be particularly challenging for domestic war crimes courts. Witnesses often do not want to relocate, and the logistics required for relocating witnesses are enormous.[114]

The Special Court for Sierra Leone continues to implement measures for the protection of witnesses. Reportedly, though, these witnesses have a fairly significant chance of being located despite the Special Court's measures.[115] For instance, one witness who had testified as an 'insider' witness for the Special Court case *The Prosecutor v. Brima, Kamara and Kanu*, also known as the Armed Forces Revolutionary Council (AFRC) case,[116] had been relocated to a safe house by the Witness and Victim Services (WVS) after giving evidence. However, he was severely beaten

---

and Witnesses Section shall…develop short-term and long-term plans for [witnesses'] protection and support'); and ICC, 'Rules of Procedures and Evidence', Doc. ICC-ASP/1/3 (Part.II-A) (hereinafter 'ICC Rules of Procedure and Evidence'), Rule 17(2)(a)(i) (The Victims and Witnesses Section is responsible 'formulating long- and short-term plans for [witnesses'] protection').

[111] *See* e.g Nina Ban-Jensen, Tom Gjelten, Roy Gutman, Ivana Nizich, Diane F. Orentlicher and Thomas Warrick, 'Tribunal Justice: The Challenges, the Record and the Prospects', (1998) 13 *American University International Law Review* 1541, 1567.

[112] Interview with Richard Harten, ICTY VWS Protection Officer, and Olivia Debaveye, ICTY VWS Associate Legal Officer (7 December 2013).

[113] Interview with David Tolbert, ICTY Deputy Prosecutor (4 December 2013).

[114] Interview with Peter McCloskey, ICTY Attorney (7 December 2013).

[115] Human Rights Watch, 'Bringing Justice: The Special Court for Sierra Leone', (8 September 2004), p. 29, available at http://www.hrw.org/sites/default/files/reports/sierraleone0904.pdf.

[116] *See* The Special Court for Sierra Leone, 'Case 16: *The Prosecutor v. Brima, Kamara and Kanu* (AFRC Case)', (2014) available at http://www.sc-sl.org/CASES/ProsecutorvsBrimaKamaraandKanuAFRCCase/tabid/106/Default.aspx.

after he was recognised in the street. The witness had ignored advice by WVS staff to stay inside for his own protection.[117]

Uganda's ICD (International Crimes Division) faces similar problems. Although the government has taken significant steps to improve witness protection and support, the measures remain limited. However, the government has made it clear that it is open to international assistance.[118]

Bosnia-Herzegovina is an example of a country where witnesses come from small, closely-knit ethnic communities, and identification of witnesses is easy. If a witness participates in a case, the community knows. They will likely find out the nature of the testimony, persons whom the witness may have identified, and other pertinent information. Thus, having witnesses return to their own community can generate serious challenges for the court.[119] Their families too are in danger. In many instances, internal relocation will simply be impossible. Despite notable progress in improving protection for witness through the creation of the Witness Protection Unit, within the Bosnian State Investigation and Protection Agency, there is still 'no follow up for witnesses after they testify, and witnesses have recanted their testimony in some cases because of threats'.[120]

In Kosovo, for example, the close-knit Kosovan community makes relocation within Kosovo oftentimes useless.[121] In cases of continued

---

[117] Human Rights Watch, 'Bringing Justice', p. 31.
[118] Human Rights Watch, 'Justice for Serious Crimes Before National Courts', p. 21.
[119] Comments by David Schneiderman, Deputy Chief Prosecutor, War Crimes Court for Bosnia and Herzegovina, (The Hague, 15 January 2009). *See also* David Tolbert and Aleksandar Kontić, 'The International Tribunal for the former Yugoslavia ('ICTY') and the Transfer of Cases and Materials to National Judicial Authorities: Lessons in Complementarity' in Carsten Stahn and Mohamed M. El Zeidy (eds.) *The International Criminal Court and Complementarity From Theory to Practice*, 2 vols. (Cambridge: Cambridge University Press, 2011) vol. 2, p. 896.
[120] Human Rights Watch, 'Justice for Atrocity Crimes: Lessons of International Support for Trials before the State Court of Bosnia and Herzegovina', (March 2012), p. 29, available at http://www.hrw.org/sites/default/files/reports/bosnia0312_0.pdf.
[121] *See* EULEX Kosovo, 'Witness Security and Protection in Kosovo: Assessment and Recommendations', (November 2007), p. 8, available at http://www.eulex-kosovo.eu/training/justice/docs/OSCE-USoffice_witness-Security_and_Protection.pdf.

threat, protection measures may have to continue after the testimony. This could include continuing financial assistance, providing physical security and psychological support, and monitoring lines of communication.

Consequently, domestic courts need to structure international relocation agreements.[122] The ITAO could assist in this endeavour. States may find it necessary to enter into agreements with other states for the purpose of sending or receiving relocated witnesses who are unable to remain in their home countries. This cooperation can be achieved through regional and bilateral agreements, or special agreements concluded on a case-by-case basis directly between the controlling entities of the countries involved.[123] These agreements should be with as many countries as possible in order to create diversity of choice. These agreements should cover all logistical issues, including exit and entry permits, visas, travel documentation, safe transport arrangements, personal protection arrangements, and provisions for safe accommodation.[124] Domestic war crimes courts should secure these agreements as early as possible.[125] Arranging a relocation can often take a year or longer.[126] Courts need to ensure that relocation agreements are negotiated pre-trial, and executed and carried out immediately after the trial ends.

---

[122] Thierry Cruvellier and Marta Valiñas, 'Croatia: Selected Developments in Transitional Justice', ICTJ Occasional Paper Series (December 2006), pp. 23-24, available at
http://wcjp.unicri.it/proceedings/docs/ICTJ_Croatia%20developments%20tr%20justice_2006_eng.PDF.

[123] UN Office on Drugs and Crime (UNODC), 'Good Practices for Protection of Witnesses in Criminal Proceedings Involving Organised Crime', (2008), p. 82, available at http://www.unodc.org/documents/organized-crime/Witness-protection-manual-Feb08.pdf.

[124] *See* Ban-Jensen, Gjelten, Gutman, Nizich, Orentlicher and Warrick, 'Tribunal Justice: The Challenges, the Record and the Prospects', 1566.

[125] Similar recommendations have been made by other observers with regards to previous war crimes tribunals. *See* Ivana Nizich, 'International Law Weekend Proceedings: International Tribunals and their Ability to Provide Adequate Justice: Lessons from the Yugoslav Tribunal', (2001) 7 *Journal of International and Comparative Law*, 353, suggesting that witness relocation agreements should be negotiated before the start of investigations; and Stephanie K. Wood, 'A Woman Scorned for the 'Least Condemned' War Crime: Precedent and Problems with Prosecuting Rape as a Serious War Crime in the International Criminal Tribunal for Rwanda', (2004) 13 *Columbia Journal of Gender and Law* 274, (arguing that war crimes tribunals should be more proactive in negotiating more witness relocation agreements with third parties).

[126] Interview with Richard Harten and Olivia Debaveye (7 December 2013).

H. Post-Trial Sentencing

Eighth, the ITAO could work with new domestic war crimes courts to see that post-trial sentencing meets international standards. It is not sufficient to hold fair trials without ensuring that those found guilty are treated in a manner established by international law. Failure to do so will cast a long shadow over the proceedings. History has shown itself to be a harsh judge against states that fail in this regard. The Saddam trial was the most notorious example. Despite being judged as having met most of the conditions of a fair trial, Saddam's sentencing and execution were considered unqualified failures that tainted the trial process itself. [127] The ITAO could play an important role in ensuring that future domestic war crimes courts adhere to international standards in the post-trial phase of the proceedings.

I. Judicial Selection

Ninth, the ITAO could assist a newly created domestic court in selecting international judges, if they were disposed of accepting this type of judicial framework. One of the more direct ways that national war crimes proceedings can meet the conditions set forth in Article 17 is to incorporate international judges into the trial process. While one of the most obvious advantages of domestic courts is to ensure domestic 'buy-in' to the judicial process, the potential advantage of including international judges on the court's bench should not be dismissed. International judges can provide a significant skill-set, as they can offer experience in complex international criminal matters. The Iraqi War Crimes Court faced this dilemma.

The Iraqi Court's Statute required all of its judges to be Iraqi nationals.[128] It had originally been recommended that non-Iraqi judges sit in mixed panels in the Iraqi War Crimes Court.[129] A provision to allow a non-Iraqi judge with expertise to sit as a judge had appeared in the Court's Statute. It was felt that the involvement of international judges was needed

---

[127] *See* Mark S. Ellis, 'From the Saddam Trial, Vital Lessons', *International Herald Tribune* (4 August 2006).

[128] Iraq Statute, Article 28.

[129] Sonya Sceats, *The Trial of Saddam Hussein*, Chatham House Briefing Paper No. 05/02 (2005), pp. 5-7, available at http://www.chathamhouse.org/sites/default/files/public/Research/International%20 Law/bptrialhussein.pdf.

because few, if any, Iraqi judges had the experience required of judges for trials involving complex international crimes.[130] However, Iraqis found this provision to be offensive, as they felt that mandatory international assistance implied that Iraqis were ill equipped to manage the Court themselves.[131] Thus, the Court reverted back to requiring only nationals to play the role in adjudicating the crimes before the Court, unless a foreign state became a party to the proceedings, at which time the Court, with approval by the Council of Ministers, could appoint a non-Iraqi judge.[132]

I had made clear in an op-ed that this decision was a mistake.[133] Human Rights Watch too advocated for trying Saddam by a mixed bench of international and Iraqi jurists. Richard Dicker, Director of the International Justice Project at Human Rights Watch stated that:

> Up until now, the most complex trials in Iraq have lasted no more than a few days. The law should require that international judges with expertise trying serious human rights crimes sit on the bench alongside Iraqis. This would assist, not replace, Iraqi judges in ensuring justice for the horrific crimes committed.[134]

Justice Richard J. Goldstone, the first prosecutor at the ICTY, also recommended that the Court include international judges and prosecutors working alongside Iraqis.[135]

Perhaps to counter the rejection of international judges, there was a change in the Court's Rules of Procedure and Evidence that *required* the Court to appoint international advisers to the Trial Chambers, Appeals Panel, Investigative Judges and the Prosecutor to provide 'non-binding *ex*

---

[130] *Ibid.*
[131] *Ibid.*
[132] Iraq Statute, Article 3(5).
[133] *See* Mark S. Ellis, 'Can Saddam's Trial be Salvaged?', *International Herald Tribune*, (10 February 2006).
[134] Human Rights Watch, 'Iraq: Law Creating War Crimes Tribunal Flawed Protections for Legitimate, Credible Trials Needed', (11 December 2003), available at http://www.hrw.org/fr/news/2003/12/10/iraq-law-creating-war-crimes-tribunal-flawed.
[135] 'Saddam Trial on Hold until Iraq Stabilises', *The Scotsman*, (8 June 2004), available at http://www.scotsman.com/news/world/saddam-trial-on-hold-until-iraq-stabilises-1-534128.

parte advice and recommendations'.[136] However, there was confusion because the Court's Statute indicated that the Court had *the right* to appoint international advisers.[137] It was not mandatory. The Trial Chamber did, in fact, seek an international adviser through the IBA. We selected a highly qualified United Kingdom judge who worked with the Court for more than a year.

As in the Iraqi case, Kenya's attempt to create its own domestic war crimes court faced many similar challenges, including the perception that the Kenyan judiciary could be negatively affected by corruption and political interference.[138] Consequently, the Kenyan government took an extraordinary step by including in the new Court's draft Statute a provision that allowed international judges to serve on the new Court.[139]

In July 2008, the Ugandan government established the War Crimes Division of the High Court of Uganda. This new domestic court consists of five national judges, and the Court may also engage 'international advisers', similar to the Iraqi Court. However, there is now discussion that international judges, for instance, from African countries, should be added to the bench.[140] Considering Uganda's past tendency to appoint judges on

---

136 Rules of Procedure and Evidence of the Iraqi Special Tribunal, *Al-Waqa'I Al-Iraqiya* (The Official Gazette of Iraq), (18 October 2005), (hereinafter Iraq Rules of Procedure and Evidence), Rule 21(4).
137 Iraq Statute, Article 7(2).
138 ICTJ, *Kenya: Impact of the Rome Statute and the International Criminal Court*, (June 2010), p. 2, available at http://ictj.org/sites/default/files/ICTJ-Kenya-ICC-Impact-2010-English.pdf.
139 Draft of the Statute for the Special Tribunal for Kenya, (December 2008), (hereinafter Draft Statute for Special Tribunal for Kenya), available at http://www.iccnow.org/documents/STATUTE_OF_THE_SPECIAL_TRIBUNAL_FOR_KENYA.pdf. Articles 11(2) and 11(3) of the Draft Statute for Special Tribunal for Kenya state that in both the Trial Chamber and Appeals Chamber: 'two judges shall be non-Kenyans and shall be appointed by the President in consultation with the Prime Minister from a list of persons nominated by the Panel of Eminent Persons'.
140 ICTJ, *Uganda: Impact of the Rome Statute and the International Criminal Court* (May 2010), p. 3, available at http://ictj.org/sites/default/files/ICTJ-Uganda-Impact-ICC-2010-English.pdf. *See also* T. Bwambale 'Foreign Judges to be on War Crimes Court', *The New Vision*, (26 January 2010), available at http://www.newvision.co.ug/D/8/13/708187.

a purely political basis, it would serve Uganda well to include international judges on the bench.[141]

Rwanda is debating new legislation that provides for international judges to sit on war crimes cases referred by the ICTR:

> ...[i]n the interest of justice and for the purpose of consistency of the judgements rendered in Rwanda...judges from other countries [may] be sent to assist the Rwandan judges in trying cases whose referral to Rwanda is being sought...[142]

The War Crimes Chamber of the State Court of Bosnia and Herzegovina (BiH)[143] is a domestic court that does allow international judges to serve on its panel.[144] The Court presents a very interesting model. Although it is a domestic court, it has features of a mixed court, due to its inclusion of international judges. Additionally, there is a Special Department for War Crimes within the Prosecutor's Office staffed with domestic and international experts. The Court departs from the standard mixed model, however, in that its international judges are phased out over time, at the end leaving a purely domestic tribunal.[145]

---

141 *See* IBAHRI, 'Judicial Independence Undermined: A Report on Uganda', (September 2007), paras 4.58-4.59.

142 *See* Letter from the Republic of Rwanda National Public Prosecution Authority to the ICTR (19 August 2011) [on file with author].

143 The BiH War Crimes Chamber is fully integrated into the domestic Bosnian legal system and operates within the overall framework of the Criminal Division of the State Court of Bosnia-Herzegovina. The Chamber was created, in part, to take on some of the cases from the ICTY, allowing the international court to concentrate on prosecuting high-ranking criminals. The Chamber not only handles cases referred to it by the ICTY, but also tries the most sensitive cases brought at a national or local level. For more information, *see* the website of the State Court of Bosnia-Herzegovina, available at http://www.sudbih.gov.ba/?jezik=e.

144 OSCE, 'War Crimes Trials Before Domestic Courts of Bosnia and Herzegovina: Progress and Obstacles' (March 2005), p. 10, available at http://www.oscebih.org/documents/osce_bih_doc_2010122311024992eng.pdf.

145 War crimes cases are now allocated to panels composed of two Bosnian judges and one international judge. Though mixed feelings have been expressed to the pace of the transition from hybrid to a domestic model, the international judges have continued to play a role beyond their anticipated exit date in 2009 and remained throughout 2010. For views on the hybrid panels, *see* ICTJ, 'The War Crimes Chamber in Bosnia and Herzegovina: From Hybrid to Domestic Court' (1 January 2008), p. 11. For the current status of judicial panels, *see* the Court of Bosnia and Herzegovina, available at

The Bosnian model of domestic war crimes prosecutions is working. A study conducted by Human Rights Watch confirmed that international judges and prosecutors have encouraged faith in the impartiality and conduct of both institutions.[146] The presence of international staff helped insulate the court from political pressures and strengthened its independence.[147] In short, the BiH approach recognises the important role that international judges can play in domestic war crimes courts, providing much needed skills in human rights and humanitarian law as well as complex criminal law and procedure.

Moreover, the cooperation between national and international judges has resulted in the transfer of knowledge and skills necessary to conduct such complicated and sensitive trials. The entire structure of the criminal justice system in Bosnia has been overhauled the Court has received significant spill over benefits, which would probably not have occurred in the absence of such substantial transformation. Between 2002 and 2004, all of the courts in Bosnia-Herzegovina were restructured and a reappointment process for judges and prosecutors was initiated.[148] Prior to reappointment, judicial selection and promotion was based on ethnicity and patronage. These reforms were a response to serious concern that war crimes could not be tried impartially, independently and free of political, criminal influence, or ethnic bias.[149]

The selection process for the judges was conducted by the High Judicial and Prosecutorial Councils (HJPCs), which were composed of both national and international appointees.[150] The HJPCs' task was to establish an appropriate balance of judges of different ethnicities. The process required that all judges currently serving end their tenure so that all posts could be advertised. Incumbents, as well as external applicants, were eligible to apply for the 'new' positions.[151] The re-appointment process has been celebrated as a truly comprehensive approach to evaluating the quality and competency of candidates.[152] However, as with any judicial selection procedure, merit must remain the priority for the

---

http://www.sudbih.gov.ba/?opcija=sadrzaj&kat=3&id=3&jezik=e.

[146] Human Rights Watch, 'Justice for Atrocity Crimes', p. 1.

[147] *Ibid.*

[148] ICTJ, 'The War Crimes Chamber in Bosnia and Herzegovina', p. 38.

[149] *Ibid.*, pp. 11, 16.

[150] *Ibid.*, pp. 13, 38.

[151] *Ibid.*

[152] *Ibid.*

selection of any candidate for judicial office. The diversification of the selection pool should enhance, rather than reduce competition and improve overall candidature.[153]

In order to ensure compliance with Article 17 of the Rome Statute, future domestic war crimes courts should consider the possibility of allowing the participation of international judges, at least in some capacity (e.g., as advisers). Working alongside their domestic counterparts, international judges would greatly contribute to the administration of justice, offering a broader perspective on international criminal law and thus ensuring credibility for the domestic war crimes courts that are invariably trying cases of international focus.[154] National courts could easily take advantage of their lack of such statutory encumbrances to create a role for international judges.

The ITAO could play a crucial role in helping to identify foreign judges and prosecutors to serve the Court. As recommended earlier, (see Chapter on judicial selection) newly established war crimes courts should seriously consider having international judges and prosecutors serve on the court in the same way hybrid courts (e.g., the BiH Court) operate.

J. Defence Attorneys

Tenth, the ITAO could work on creating a role for international defence lawyers. One of the most important issues faced by domestic war crimes courts is the paucity of trained defence attorneys. It is unlikely that most countries establishing war crimes courts will have had experience trying international crimes. The fact is that defending a client accused of war crimes is an arduous and challenging task. Defence counsel must have in-depth knowledge of international criminal law, including genocide, war crimes, and crimes against humanity. The attorney(s) must also be well-educated in legal principles unique to international prosecution such as command responsibility, rape as a war crime, superior orders, and the

[153] *See* Kate Malleson, 'The Judicial Appointments Commission in England and Wales: New Wine in New Bottles?', in Kate Malleson and Peter H. Russell (eds.), *Appointing Judges in an Age of Judicial Power: Critical Perspectives from Around the World,* (London: University of Toronto Press, 2006) pp. 39–55 (this conclusion is made in relation to the attempt to improve diversity in the English Judiciary).
[154] Human Rights Watch, 'Judging Dujail, The First Trial Before the Iraqi High Tribunal', (November 2006), p. 84-86, available at http://www.hrw.org/sites/default/files/reports/iraq1106webwcover.pdf.

limited defences relevant to international crimes. However, there is clear evidence that most attorneys in post-conflict developing countries have very little knowledge, if any, of international criminal law. This problem is compounded by the fact that local judges also lack this basic knowledge of international law.[155]

The example of Bosnia and Herzegovina is very encouraging. In 2005 the Criminal Defense Support Section (in Bosnian Odsjek krivicne odbrane, OKO) was created by the Registry of the court. The office employed an international director and a number of international law 'fellows'— young lawyers who had a legal background in international criminal law and human rights law.[156] The OKO then started a transitional phase where national lawyers assumed leadership of the office. Today all OKO staff members are Bosnian nationals.[157] The OKO model proved to be successful. As in the case of international judges, local defence lawyers obtain significant knowledge and skills in international human rights law, while international staff shield the office from accusations of national bias and also ensure adherence to international standards.

Consequently, domestic courts should permit international lawyers to represent defendants. International counsel can often provide a level of expertise in international criminal law that can benefit the defence. The trial against Saddam Hussein provides valuable insight to this issue. The Iraqi Court's Rules of Procedure and Evidence stipulate that no foreign defence attorney is permitted to appear before the Iraqi High Criminal Court unless he or she is a 'Palestinian living in Iraq'.[158] Foreign advisers and experts, however, are allowed to assist the Defence Office.[159]

It is interesting to note that the Iraqi Court, at first, permitted foreign defence counsel. In the *Dujail* trial, a number of foreign attorneys, including former US attorney general Ramsay Clark, joined the defence team for Saddam Hussein. Although they did not take an active role in the

---

[155] OSCE Office for the Democratic Institute and Human Rights, 'Supporting the Transition Process: Lessons Learned and Best Practices in Knowledge Transfer', (2009) available at http://www.osce.org/odihr/68108, p. 30.
[156] Human Rights Watch, 'Justice for Atrocity Crimes', p. 14.
[157] *Ibid.*
[158] Iraq High Criminal Court, The Law of Lawyers No. 173 of 1963 with All Its Amendments, Article 2(1), available at http://print.todayiraq.com/PDF/the-law-of-lawyers-no173.pdf.
[159] Iraq Rules of Procedure and Evidence, Rules 21(3), 21(4), 30(6).

actual trial proceedings—i.e., examining or cross-examining witnesses—they were given limited permission to address the Court.

However, during the second trial—the *Anfal* case—the Court decided that foreign defence attorneys would no longer be permitted to appear in Court. The Court's decision was one of the reasons Saddam's defence counsel boycotted the trial proceedings. The defence attorneys argued that because of the complexity of the trial, it was essential for the defence team to include both Iraqi and international attorneys. The Court, however, ruled that it was consistent with the Court's statute that foreign attorneys could only 'advise' the Iraqi attorneys and not take an active role in the trial itself. That role would be left for Iraqi attorneys and the Iraqi Bar Association. This may be a small distinction, but it has enormous consequences—consequences that domestic war crimes courts should avoid. Domestic war crimes courts should ensure that national and international attorneys have equal standing before the Court.

Cambodia offers a good example of the challenges involved when the Bar has undue authority over the qualifications of counsel. The Cambodian Bar Association (CBA) created a major crisis with the Extraordinary Chambers of the Court of Cambodia (ECCC) by insisting that the Bar had ultimate control over defence counsel appearing before the ECCC. Its position was that the Bar was the only body mandated to regulate legal professionals in Cambodia. It went so far as to state that the Defence Office of the ECCC was considered to be 'illegal' because it was outside the control of the Cambodian Bar.

The Bar also accused the IBA of violating Cambodian law by proposing a training programme for Cambodian defence attorneys without the Bar's approval. In the end, the IBA cancelled the programme. In a press release dated 24 November 2006, speaking on behalf of the IBA, I stated:

> The Cambodian Bar has issued instructions forbidding lawyers from attending a training programme planned by the International Bar Association (IBA) and the Office of the Extraordinary Chambers in the Courts of Cambodia (ECCC). The Bar's President, Ky Tech, has publicly threatened that 'measures' will be taken against any attendee, and against the IBA's international participants. The IBA has also refused to accept the Bar's demands for control of selection of participants and speakers. The prohibition by the Cambodian Bar is part of a wider scheme of opposition to obstruct the operation of the Tribunal. In consequence, the IBA has cancelled the programme.

> The Bar's actions represent a disturbing development in the functioning of international justice, placing obstacles in the path of bringing those accused of international crimes to trial. The IBA's programme was intended to improve the quality of legal services and the administration of justice in Cambodia, and help educate and inform the Cambodian public about international justice. It is unacceptable that the Cambodian Bar, which should share these objectives, is seeking to frustrate them in this way.[160]

Regarding the participation of foreign counsel, the language in the UN-Royal Government of Cambodia Agreement creating the Court suggested that foreign defence counsel *would* be admitted to appear before the Court.[161] However, the Law on Criminal Procedure of 1993 permits foreign defence counsel to practice in Cambodia after the appropriate authorisation, but it allows only Cambodian lawyers to act as advocates in court.[162] During a meeting between Court representatives and me, it was acknowledged that there was a discrepancy between the two regulations. In essence, the internal rules of procedure were muddled in terms of setting standards for international and Cambodian defence counsel to appear before the Court. The CBA argued that it retained the ability to prevent international attorneys from participating in the proceedings and that the 1993 law had to be amended for foreign defence attorneys to act as advocates for defendants in Court.[163]

---

[160] IBA, 'Press Release: Cambodian Bar issued instructions forbidding lawyers from attending a training programme planned by IBA and ECCC', (4 November 2006).

[161] United Nations, 'Agreement Between the United Nations and the Royal Government of Cambodia Concerning the Prosecution Under Cambodian Law of Crimes Committed During the Period of Democratic Kampuchea', (6 June 2003), Article 21(3), (making reference to 'Any counsel, whether of Cambodian or non-Cambodian nationality…'.) The agreement also guarantees the right of defendants to choose their defence counsel (Article 13(2)).

[162] *See* 'State of Cambodia Law on Criminal Procedure', adopted 28 January 1993 and promulgated by Decree No. 21 (3 August 1993). *See also* Cambodian Law on the Statutes of the Bar, (22 August 2005), Articles 5, 6, 31-34; Michael Bohlander, Roman Boed and Richard J. Wilson, *Defense in International Criminal Proceedings: Cases, Materials and Commentary*, (New York: Transnational Publishers, 2006), pp. 859-860.

[163] Sok Sam Ouen, Cambodian Defenders Project Executive, *referred* to in Prak Chan Thul and Erik Wasson, 'KR Judges Say They Still Need More Training', *The Cambodia Daily*, (17 May 2006), available at http://khmerrougetrial.blogspot.co.uk/2006/05/kr-judges-say-they-still-need-more.html.

The CBA maintained its position, indicating that only attorneys approved and licensed by the Bar should be permitted to appear before the war crimes court and that foreign lawyers would not have full rights to defend clients in court. National lawyers have the right to speak first in addressing the Court in all matters.[164] This mirrors a similar restriction set forth by the Iraqi Court. In the end, the Court's internal rules require that both national and foreign lawyers *must* be registered with the CBA.[165] This leads to even further problems.

The Cambodian Bar Association took the extraordinary position that foreign lawyers appearing before the new Court must pay a fee for the privilege. Under the Bar's proposal, foreign lawyers would have had to pay a $500 application fee to become a member of the Cambodian Bar. If selected to represent a client, the lawyer would have had to pay an additional $2,000 plus $200 a month in membership dues. All the fees would go to the Bar Association.[166]

The international judges on the Court rightfully concluded that the imposition of a fee was unacceptable and 'severely limits the rights of accused and victims to select counsel of their choice'.[167] In media interviews, I have stated:

> You need to ensure that foreign lawyers who have expertise in this area are able, with no barriers, to participate. This is absolutely consistent with international standards and should be something the CBA abides by.
>
> I become concerned when I see the CBA raise the issues they have. They are continuing to send out statements [that] are all signs of a Bar Association that is putting up barriers rather than finding ways to support this very important process of international justice. This is what a domestic bar should be doing—embracing the idea of accountability and justice, not attempting to impede it.
>
> The Bar could have used the fee issue as an opportunity to set high standards for an open trial process that does not restrict foreign lawyers

---

[164] Internal Rules of Extraordinary Chambers in the Courts of Cambodia (Rev. 8), as amended 12 August 2011, (hereinafter ECCC Internal Rules), Rule 22(2)(b).
[165] *Ibid.*, Rule 22(1)(a).
[166] Discussion with Cambodian Bar representatives, (November 2006).
[167] ECCC, 'Statement from the Review Committee of the ECCC', (16 March 2007), available at http://www.eccc.gov.kh/sites/default/files/media/16_Mar-Review_Committee_Statement.pdf.

> participating and that is committed to establishing a judicial process that meets international standards.
>
> I do not think that the CBA at this moment is playing a constructive role in setting standards that would be accepted and embraced by future courts.[168]

In the end, the CBA capitulated and instituted a flat registration fee of $500 for all international lawyers appearing before the Court.[169] Yet, such a fee is still unwelcome and should be shunned by domestic bar associations and courts.

The best scenario for domestic war crimes courts is to allow a combined defence team with both local attorneys and international attorneys. Local attorneys understand cultural issues and domestic law, whereas international attorneys can provide the necessary level of international legal experience. Foreign counsel can use their experience and expertise to ensure that international law is understood and correctly utilised in defence strategy. There should be active participation by foreign counsel. Justice is better served with their inclusion. Preventing international attorneys from participating in trials that deal with international crimes is short-sighted. In fact, I would argue that the exclusion of international lawyers on the defence team violates international standards of conducting a fair, impartial trial if local counsel lacks the necessary expertise in international law. The 'mixed' tribunals provide the best model for future domestic war crimes court because of their 'automatic' inclusion of international lawyers in 'partnership' with local attorneys.

Each defence team should have at least one attorney who has competence in criminal law and/or international criminal law/international humanitarian law/international human rights law. While there should not be a presumption that foreign attorneys are better than domestic attorneys, the international attorney brings expertise in international law and also improves the appearance of objectivity. When the defence team lacks experience in relevant international law, errors are made. Although domestic, national war crimes courts hear cases involving international

---

[168] 'Bar fees last KRT hurdle', *Phnom Penh Post*, (23 March 2007), available at http://www.phnompenhpost.com/national/bar-fees-last-krt-hurdle.

[169] *See* 'Cambodia Cuts Fees Threatening Khmer Rouge Trial', *Reuters*, (28 April 2007), available at http://in.reuters.com/article/2007/04/28/idINIndia-296029 20070428.

law. Thus, including international attorneys increases the perception of fairness and impartiality within the domestic war crimes court. The Sierra Leone Court accomplished this objective by appointing an international lawyer, a Sierra Leonean lawyer, a legal assistant, and an investigator to each defendant. Although a mixed court, the Sierra Leone Court is a good model for domestic courts.

Although some experts are sceptical about allowing foreign defence counsel to appear in domestic war crimes courts because of issues dealing with domestic regulations,[170] this should not be a reason for exclusion. In addition, if the court is located in a failed state (i.e., a state emerging from internal conflict where legal structures and personnel are absent), then international lawyers must be allowed to appear. There will simply be a dearth of qualified domestic defence attorneys. For instance, sixteen years after the Rwandan genocide, the country has only 280 lawyers in private practice.[171] Moreover, even countries emerging from conflict not considered 'failed' (e.g., Serbia), often lack defence lawyers who can act professionally and ethically. As reviled in a damning report by the Humanitarian Law Center in 2013, most of the defence lawyers focused on 'obstructing and delaying proceedings…[and] engaging in petty politics' rather than focusing on their clients.[172] Needless to say, such behaviour does not contribute to the quality of the proceedings nor to the interests of the accused.

The newest mixed Court—The Special Tribunal for Lebanon—permits both Lebanese and foreign attorneys to appear before the Court.[173] However, it is interesting to note that such an arrangement is not explicitly provided for in either the Statute of the Special Tribunal for Lebanon or in its Rules of Procedure and Evidence. However, such a right does arise from Rule 59(A) and 59(D) of the Rules of Procedure and Evidence in

---

[170] Interview with David Tolbert (4 December 2013).

[171] *The Prosecutor v. Gaspard Kanyarukiga*, Case No. ICTR-2002-78-R11*bis*, 'Decision on Prosecutor's Request for Referral to the Republic of Rwanda', (6 June 2008), para. 55.

[172] Humanitarian Law Center, 'Report on War Crimes Trials in Serbia in 2012' (January 2013), p. 11, available online at http://www.hlc-rdc.org/wp-content/uploads/2013/02/Report-on-war-crimes-trials-in-Serbia-in-2012-ENG-FF.pdf.

[173] *See* Article 8 of the 10 November 2010 Directive on the Assignment of Defence Counsel, available at http://www.stl-tsl.org/x/file/TheRegistry/Library/Background Documents/RulesRegulations/practice_directions/Directive%20on%20Assignment%20of%20Counsel%20_ENG_%20November2010.pdf.

connection with Article 8(D)(ii) of the Directive on the Appointment and Assignment of Defence Counsel.[174] Thus, once again, a mixed court has recognised the importance of including foreign defence counsel in the trial process.

K. Victim Compensation

Eleventh, the ITAO could assist in establishing an international compensation programme for victims. As earlier discussed, consistent with the guidelines found in the UN Basic Principles on Reparations, victims' reparations should be promoted in domestic courts to promote healing for both the victim and the community.[175] States are generally required under

---

[174] Special Tribunal for Lebanon, Rules of Procedure and Evidence, Revision 5, (20 February 2013), UN Doc. STL/BD/2009/01/Rev. 5, Rules 59(A) and 59(D) state;

'(A) Whenever the interests of justice so demand, the Head of Defence Office shall assign counsel to a suspect or an accused who lacks the means to remunerate such counsel. Such assignments shall be treated in accordance with the procedure established in the Directive on the Appointment and Assignment of Defence Counsel adopted by the Head of Defence Office and approved by the Plenary.

(D) A suspect or accused has the right to be represented by any counsel properly admitted to the list, except insofar as such representation would not ensure the combined language abilities required for fair and expeditious proceedings. A suspect or accused who has been denied his choice of counsel from the list may ask for a review of the decision by the President'.

STL, Directive on the Appointment and Assignment of Defence Counsel Article 8(C)(ii) of states:

> (C) The applicant shall, in addition to the application form, supply the Head of the Defence Office with the following:
>
> (ii) a certificate issued by the relevant authority of each State of which the person is a national or where the person is domiciled stating the existence, if any, of criminal convictions or ongoing criminal proceedings.

[175] 'Declaration of Basic Principles of Justice for Victims of Crime and Abuse of Power', UN Doc. A/RES/40/34 (29 November 1985); *see also* 'Basic Principles and Guidelines on the Right to a Remedy and Reparations for Victims of Gross Violations of International Human Rights Law and Serious Violations of International Humanitarian Law', UN Doc. A/RES/60/147 (21 March 2006); International Covenant on Civil and Political Rights, 16 December 1966, in force 23 March 1976, GA Res. 2200A (XXI), 21 UN GAOR Supp. (No. 16) at 52, UN Doc. A/6316 (1966); 999 UNTS 171; 6 ILM 368 (1967), (ICCPR), Article 2(3) and 14.

international law to provide 'effective remedies to victims of gross violations of human rights, including reparation'.[176]

International courts have argued that in order to bring about reconciliation and to ensure the restoration of peace, it is necessary that victims be compensated.[177] Domestic courts could easily make the same argument. In fact, it is even more important that newly created domestic war crimes courts be seen as being sensitive to, and supportive of, victims. However, post-conflict states are unlikely to have sufficient financial resources to create a comprehensive programme. Realistically, the international community will have to play a role in helping finance a victim compensation scheme in post-conflict countries willing to undertake domestic war crimes trials. And consistent with international law, the international community **should** assist countries in this way. Yet, the experience of the ICC does not bode well for domestic compensation schemes. The Court has collected only minimal voluntary contributions for its Trust Fund, significantly less than what is required.[178]

L. Other Issues

Finally, the ITAO could assist the Office of the Prosecutor in assessing a state's overall commitment to conducting fair trials. This is important because under the Rome Statute the Prosecutor can seek periodic updates regarding pending investigations, which states are required to provide without 'undue delay'.[179] Even after the domestic investigation and prosecution begins, the ICC Prosecutor can evaluate the proceedings and inform the Pre-Trial Chamber of progress. If the Prosecutor is not satisfied that a state is sufficiently investigating a case, he or she may submit a request to the Chambers for review of the decision on admissibility,

---

[176] *Ibid.*

[177] *See* UN Security Council, UN Doc. S/2009/589, 'Letter dated 12 November 2009 from the President of the International Tribunal for the Prosecution of Persons Responsible for Serious Violations of International Law Committed in the Territory of the former Yugoslavia since 1991, provided to the Security Council pursuant to paragraph 6 of Council resolution 1534 (2004), addressed to the President of the Security Council', (12 November 2009), para. 57.

[178] Conor McCarthy, *Reparations and Victim Support in the International Criminal Court*, (Cambridge: Cambridge University Press, 2012), p. 59.

[179] ICC Statute, Article 18(5) (authorizing the Prosecutor to request that the domestic court (the State) 'periodically inform the Prosecutor of the progress of its investigations and any subsequent prosecutions').

arguing that new facts have arisen negating the basis for which the case was previously found to be inadmissible.[180]

However, states can and will use the complementarity principle to assert a presumption of supremacy. If the ICC attempts to circumvent this presumption, a state can challenge the admissibility of a case to the ICC on grounds that it itself *is* investigating or prosecuting the case, or *has* investigated or prosecuted the case. In fact, as argued by Leila Sadat, it is perfectly acceptable for a state to *open* an investigation for the sole purpose of depriving the ICC of jurisdiction. The presumption of supremacy will be upheld so long as the state does not show an 'unwillingness' to prosecute.[181]

International support for a domestic war crimes court upholds the integrity of the institution by providing it with a strong mandate, ensuring financial support for the court and its staff, and establishing the efficiency of executive actions to enforce the court's rulings. Without the support of the international community to drive the objective of accountability over impunity, the success of any domestic war crimes proceeding will be muted and unsustainable. A state's ability to secure domestic political support can be significantly enhanced if the international community shows its commitment to actively assist in the reform process.

---

[180] *Ibid.*, Article 19(10).

[181] Leila N. Sadat and S. Richard Carden, 'The New International Court: An Uneasy Revolution', (2000) 88 *The Georgetown Law Journal*, 381, 418.

CONCLUSION

This book began by emphasizing the invidious nature of twentieth – and now twenty-first – century armed conflict, which continues to claim the lives of innocent children, women, and men. In the year 2012 alone, at least 92,600 people were killed or injured, and 3.5 million displaced.[1] International criminal justice is, and always should be, premised on the fact of this suffering; law is meant to ensure that crimes do not go unpunished and that perpetrators are held accountable.

Civilians have become the prime casualties of modern warfare. During World War I, civilian deaths were roughly one-tenth the number of soldier deaths. In World War II, civilian deaths were equal to the number of soldier deaths. In Vietnam, civilian deaths outnumbered soldier deaths 9 to 1. If one includes victims of repressive authoritarian regimes, the number of deaths between 1946 and 2008 could exceed 101 million.

Yet despite the growing proportion of civilian casualties, individuals responsible for war crimes and other atrocities are rarely prosecuted. The hearing of such cases in a court of law has been an 'historical anomaly'. Impunity, often presented as a precondition for peace, is devastatingly common. Survivors are asked to forget the past and move on. But impunity for those who perpetrate crimes is just another affront — both to the victim and to the concept of justice.

In July 1999, I had a very personal experience of the injustice we do to the victims and survivors of war and state repression. Standing on a dirt airfield outside Skopje, Macedonia, among a sea of 20,000 people, I listened to one harrowing story after another. I was in the Stenkovec refugee camp to record those stories and help set up a system for documenting atrocities committed in Kosovo.

---

[1] Kate Halff, 'Persons displaced internally by conflict and violence in 2012', in Stuart Casey-Maslen (ed.), *The War Report 2012* (Oxford: Oxford University Press, 2013), p. 272.

The summer heat was unbearable; swirling clay collected on my clothes and dried my mouth. Makeshift tents were scattered around; there were limited bathroom facilities and no showers. At Stenkovec there was a notable absence of men and boys; the Serbian military had forced women and girls across the Macedonian border – young men were kept behind, many of them never to be seen again.

During my weeklong visit, I watched busloads of new arrivals enter the camp. Each time a bus arrived, the entire camp would surround the incoming vehicle to see if a lost family member might disembark. I am still haunted by the sight of one young girl's face pressed to the window, her hollow eyes staring blankly. Her pain was palpable and I knew that history was being repeated.

While collecting accounts of rape, torture, and executions at the hands of Serbian troops, I was struck by the refugees' yearning for justice. In telling their stories, they hoped that those responsible would be held accountable, including the political leaders who orchestrated the savagery and continued to act with impunity.

My mind drifted back to the stories of Nuremberg, and to US Chief Prosecutor Robert H. Jackson's opening statement:

> The wrongs, which we seek to condemn and punish, have been so calculated, so malignant, and so devastating that civilisation cannot tolerate their being ignored, because it cannot survive their being repeated.[2]

Jackson expressed the hope that law might somehow redeem the next generation and prevent similar atrocities from being carried out. In 1945, when the international community said 'Never Again', law was to be the vehicle of conscience and justice. But as I looked out at the desperation in Skopje, I knew that the international community had failed the challenge.

The Nuremberg trials, having crystallised the notion that basic human rights inhere in individuals, spawned what is now known as the international human rights regime. For several decades, the Cold War

---

[2] Transcript of Robert Jackson's Opening Statement, (21 November 1945) in *Trial of the Major War Criminals before the International Military Tribunal, Nuremberg (14 November 1945 – 1 October 1946*, 42 vols., (Nuremberg: International Military Tribunal, 1947), vol. 2, pp. 98-99.

tipped the scales away from international enforcement. Human rights law became the exclusive domain of the sovereign state, and states were the only relevant actors. Moreover, sovereignty came to mean legally equal; no state could be held liable in the court of another state.

Things began to change, however, at the end of the Cold War. A paradigm shift in which individual human rights could 'trump' state sovereignty altered the international legal order.

In the 1990s, atrocities committed in the former Yugoslavia and Rwanda prompted an important development in international criminal justice. Under the UN Charter, the Security Council invoked Chapter VII powers to establish *ad hoc* criminal tribunals for the former Yugoslavia and Rwanda. While these courts got off to a slow start, their operation (still ongoing) paved the way for the Rome Treaty and the creation of the International Criminal Court. The ICC's Statute reflects a belief in accountability over impunity, and a determination that grave breaches of international humanitarian law should not go unpunished. Specifically created to investigate and prosecute egregious violations of international law – genocide, crimes against humanity, and war crimes – the ICC holds the promise of justice through effective enforcement.

By ending impunity, the Court was also conceived as a means to deter such crimes in the future. And because the most egregious crimes threaten the peace, security, and wellbeing of the world, the ICC embodies a hope that international law might play a role in maintaining or restoring peace and security.

But in pursuing the vision of justice, are we placing unreasonable demands on these tribunals? Since the creation of the ICC, the world has witnessed multiple conflicts characterised by egregious violations of international law. Much to the consternation of international human rights advocates, the role of the ICC as a deterrent to such crimes has been ineffective.

As this book demonstrates, the ICC is in trouble. The relationship between state sovereignty and international law has yet to be fully resolved, and a number of states have critically undermined the Court. For instance and as earlier indicated, the African Union has called upon all African countries to withdraw from the ICC *en masse*.

The US, Israel, Iran, Russia, China, India, Pakistan, and Turkey are not State Parties to the Rome Statute. Ten years on from the momentous achievement of creating the ICC, we must ask: Can there be a credible mechanism of international justice without the active participation of key states? Can the Court ensure uniformity in the exercise of jurisdiction over international crimes by domestic war crimes courts? The verdict is still out on these questions, but if the ICC is to succeed it must embrace the right and duty of nation states to bring to justice those who have committed international crimes. In a paradoxical way, international law must become less international and more domestic. To accomplish this, the ICC must adopt an uncompromising and steadfast reliance on the principle of *complementarity*. The future of international justice depends on the willingness and ability of nation states to effectively operate domestic war crimes courts consistent with international standards. If these standards are met, indigenous national criminal jurisdictions will become the 'accountability centres' for international crimes.

Several nation states have already assumed a major role in the universal duty to achieve judicial accountability. Bangladesh, Burundi, Colombia, Croatia, Ecuador, Guatemala, Haiti, Kenya, Serbia, Macedonia, Rwanda, Uganda, and Uruguay are examples of countries that have undertaken or are in the process of undertaking war crimes trials against citizens of their own states accused of gross violations of international law. For instance, in February 2014, the Bangladesh's International Crimes Tribunal (ICTB) indicted Syed Mohammad Qaisar, the former state minister for agriculture during the military rule of General HM Ershad, on sixteen charges of crimes against humanity and genocide committed during the 1971 Bangladesh Liberation War with Pakistan.[3] Qaisar was the seventeenth person trial before the ICTB.

Another recent example is Haiti. There has been an ongoing legal process to bring Jean-Claude Duvalier to account for alleged crimes against humanity committed during Duvalier's dictatorship in Haiti, which spanned from 1971 to 1986.[4] However, in January 2012, the investigating judge announced that the charges for crimes against humanity had been

[3] *See* 'SM Qaisar indicted', *The Daily Star*, (3 February 2014), available at http://www.thedailystar.net/sm-qaisar-indicted-9697.

[4] Rory Carroll, 'List of charges against Jean-Claude 'Baby Doc' Duvalier continues to grow', *The Guardian*, (21 January 2011), available at http://www.theguardian.com/world/2011/jan/21/baby-doc-duvalier-haiti-charges.

dropped because the limitations period had expired.[5] This was a misguided decision considering that there is no statute of limitations for these types of heinous crimes.

Fortunately, in February 2014, the appellate court reversed the previous decision, ruling that Duvalier could be charged with crimes against humanity.[6] A decision will now be made as to whether or not Duvalier will be tried domestically for crimes against humanity.[7] Considering the political challenges of bringing someone like Duvalier to justice, Haiti has taken an extraordinary step in support of the principle of complementarity to ensure that alleged perpetrators of international crimes are brought to justice.

For its part, the ICC cannot undermine national sovereignty nor interfere in judicial matters that naturally fall within the jurisdiction of states. The Court must be willing and able to actively support domestic prosecutions through the principle of complementarity. If the Court holds too tightly to a desire to gain jurisdiction over crucial cases, it will lose credibility.

The Court's decision in the *Gaddafi* case illustrates a troubling trend. Despite strong and compelling arguments by the Libyan government that it was willing and able to conduct a fair trial against Saif Al-Islam Gaddafi, the Court, in my opinion, erred in its decision and succumbed to a false sense of entitlement over the case. The Court then reversed itself in the *Abdullah Al-Senussi* case. Even though the factual situation was similar in both cases, the Court ruled that Libya appeared willing and able to carry out proceedings against Al-Senussi. The problem for the Court is that it is unclear how the evidence provided by Libya in the *Al-Senussi* case was any stronger than that provided in the *Gaddafi* case.

---

[5] 'Haiti court postpones decision on Duvalier trial', *Yahoo News*, (20 February 2014), available at http://news.yahoo.com/haiti-court-postpones-decision-duvalier-trial-193845018.html.

[6] Jacqueline Charles, 'Victims applaud Haitian court decision on Jean-Claude "Baby Doc" Duvalier', *Miami Herald*, (20 February 2014) available at: http://www.miamiherald.com/2014/02/20/3949021/haiti-appellate-court-paves-way.html.

[7] *Ibid.*

Embracing complementarity is important to due process, but also because evidence suggests a burgeoning trend away from the most robust elements of universal jurisdiction.

In the past, states were more accepting of the principle of *absolute* universal jurisdiction. According to most literal interpretation, this principle promotes jurisdiction by the forum state over offences committed abroad by the accused—in other words, the exercise of jurisdiction is not dependent on the accused being on the territory of the forum state. It is based solely on the nature of the crime without regard to where it was committed, the nationality of the accused, or any other connection to the forum state. Most importantly, the principle does not require an assessment of relevant 'personal jurisdiction'. Thus, any state has the authority to unilaterally pursue an action against an individual, regardless of that individual's nationality.[8] This fairly aggressive form of universal jurisdiction made it considerably more likely that persons responsible for atrocities would be brought to justice.

However, *absolute* universal jurisdiction has more recently been relegated to a limited number of crimes, namely those contained in the 1949 Geneva Conventions (and additional Protocol I of 1997) and the 1984 Convention Against Torture. Contracting Parties to the Convention must either prosecute or extradite persons suspected of committing 'grave breaches'[9] of the Conventions, regardless of those persons' nationalities or

---

[8] *See* Mark S. Ellis, 'Combating Impunity and Enforcing Accountability as a Way To Promote Peace and Stability – The Role of International War Crimes Tribunals' (2006) 2 *Journal of National Security Law & Policy*, 111, 116-117.

[9] 'Grave breaches' refers to a series of acts found in the four 1949 Geneva Conventions and in the Additional Protocol I, which represents the most serious violations of international humanitarian law. These would include wilful killing, torture, inhuman treatment of protected individuals, extensive destruction of property not justified by military necessity, and wilfully attacking civilians. *See* Geneva Convention for the Amelioration of the Conditions of the Wounded and Sick in Armed Forces in the Field, (12 August 1949), 6 UST 3114, 75 UNTS 31, (hereinafter Geneva Convention I), Article 50; Geneva Convention for the Amelioration of the Condition of the Wounded, Sick and Shipwrecked Members of Armed Forces at Sea, (12 August 1949), 6 UST 3217, 75 UNTS 85, (hereinafter Geneva Convention II), Article 51; Geneva Convention Relative to the Treatment of Prisoners of War, (12 August 1949), 6 UST 3316, 75 UNTS 135, (hereinafter Geneva Convention III), Article 130; Geneva Convention Relative to the Protection of Civilian Persons in Time of War, (12 August 1949), 6 UST 3516, 75 UNTS 287, (hereinafter Geneva Convention IV), Article 147; Protocol Additional

whether they are connected to the Contracting Party.[10] The ICJ, in the Advisory Opinion on the *Legality of the Threat or Use of Nuclear Weapons*, has held this principle to be part of customary international law.[11]

The Convention Against Torture[12] also obligates Contracting Parties to prosecute or extradite suspected torturers.

Even the 1948 Genocide Convention has not had the effect of compelling states to prosecute the crime of genocide. Although there are those who firmly argue in favour of universal jurisdiction,[13] the Convention does not specifically recognise universal jurisdiction over the crime of genocide.

---

to the Geneva Conventions of 12 August 1949, and relating to the Protection of Victims of International Armed Conflicts (Protocol I), (8 June 1977), 1125 UNTS 3, Articles 11 and 85.

[10] Geneva Convention I, Article 49; Geneva Convention II, Article 50; Geneva Convention III, Article 129; Geneva Convention IV, Article 147.

[11] *Legality of the Threat or Use of Nuclear Weapons,* Advisory Opinion, ICJ Reports (8 July 1996), p. 226.

[12] Convention Against Torture and Other Cruel, Inhuman or Degrading Treatment or Punishment, 10 December 1984, in force 26 June 1987, UN Doc. A/39/L.34/Add.1, 1465 UNTS 85, p. 197 (hereinafter Convention Against Torture).

[13] Although Article 1 of the 1948 Genocide Convention confirms that states shall undertake an obligation to prevent and punish genocide, Article 6 compels prosecution only in states where the genocide was committed or 'by such international penal tribunal as may have jurisdiction'. Convention on the Prevention and Punishment of the Crime of Genocide, 9 December 1948, in force 12 January 1951, GA RES 260/A (III), 78 UNTS 277, (hereinafter Genocide Convention), Articles 1 and 6. Proposals for an Optional Protocol that would give the Genocide Convention universal jurisdiction have been suggested by Sudhanshu Swaroop, who argues that the case to give genocide universal jurisdiction is compelling: '[w]hy should there be an *'aut dedere aut judicare'* provision in the Torture Convention, but not in the Genocide Convention?' *See* Sudhanshu Swaroop, 'Genocide and Universal Jurisdiction: A Proposal', Nick Donovan (ed.), *The Enforcement of International Criminal Law*, (Laxton: Aegis Trust, 2009), p. 25. International and domestic court decisions are in the process of creating a considerable body of state practice, *opinio juris*, that points to a growing acceptance of universal jurisdiction for genocide, despite the provisions of the Convention. *See* William A. Schabas, *Genocide in International Law: The Crimes of Crimes* (Cambridge: Cambridge University Press, 2000), pp. 361–67. Professor Theodor Meron has stated that 'it is increasingly recognized by leading commentators that the crime of genocide may also be cause for prosecution by any state'. *See* Theodor Meron, 'International Criminalization of Internal Atrocities', (1995) 89 *American Journal of International Law* 554, 569. Amnesty International

The reasons behind the more limited use of absolute universal jurisdiction are undoubtedly many. However, I believe that the fall-back on state sovereignty has led to a realisation that *absolute universal jurisdiction* can be disjointed and difficult to enforce. Unique challenges, such as trials *in absentia*, are created when a state attempts to prosecute crimes committed on foreign territory by nationals of another state.

Increasingly, states are embracing the principle of *conditional universal jurisdiction,* which requires a stronger link between a criminal act and the forum state.[14] Conditional universal jurisdiction is viewed as giving states extraterritorial jurisdiction so long as there is some connection between the crime and the forum state (e.g., the victim or the accused is a citizen or resident of the forum country). Conditional universal jurisdiction also tends to denote procedural limitations established by the state (e.g., requiring the Federal Prosecutor to approve

---

has stated that: '[i]t is now beyond doubt that every state, whether party to the Genocide Convention or not, is permitted to exercise universal jurisdiction over persons suspected of genocide. In addition, there is support for the view that states are also required to exercise such jurisdiction over persons suspected of genocide found in territory under their control, to extradite the person to a state able and willing to do so or surrender the suspects to an international criminal court'. *See* Amnesty International, 'Universal Jurisdiction: The duty of states to enact and implement legislation', (London: International Secretariat, 2001), pp. 10-11. The ICTR has also ruled that universal jurisdiction exists for the crime of genocide, as has the ICTY. *See The Prosecutor v. Bernard Ntuyahaga*, Case No. ICTR-98-40-T, 'Decision on the Prosecutor's Motion to Withdraw the Indictment' (18 March 1999). *The Prosecutor v. Duško Tadić,* Case No. IT-94-1-A, 'Decision on the Defence Motion for Interlocutory Appeal on Jurisdiction', (2 October 1995) para. 62. The European Court of Human Rights has ruled that the crime of genocide is subject to universal jurisdiction. *See Jorgic v. Germany*, (Application No. 74613/01) 2007-IX ECHR 583, (12 July 2007), paras 67–70. The Spanish Supreme Court, held in an 8-7 decision that Spain could not pursue universal jurisdiction over crimes of genocide in Guatemala because the Genocide Convention did not confer the principle of universal jurisdiction. *See* 'Sentencia del Tribunal Supremo sobre el caso Guatemala por genocidio' [Judgment of the Spanish Supreme Court Concerning the Guatemala Genocide Case], No. STC 327/2003 (25 February 2003) (Spain). However, the Spanish Constitutional Court overruled the earlier decision and found that Spain's universal jurisdiction statute applied to Spanish citizens who were the target of universal crimes and that the earlier decision was in fact a contradiction of the Genocide Convention. *See Guatemala Genocide Case*, Judgement No. STC 237/2005 (26 September 2005).

[14] Spain, the United Kingdom, France, Germany, Belgium, The Netherlands, Denmark, Sweden and Finland.

any prosecutions). However, by embracing this more restricted form of universal jurisdiction, states are actually making it more difficult to hold perpetrators accountable for their crimes.

Nevertheless, the shift regarding the principle of universal jurisdiction might actually strengthen the ICC. The trend among states to embrace conditional universal jurisdiction is consistent with the ICC's principle of complementarity. Both concepts reinforce state sovereignty. Because the ICC is treaty based, it offers a legal structure that is predictable and rational. The principle of complementarity within the Rome Statute allows for a more cooperative application of international criminal law. While the ICC stands as a centralised authority to ensure accountability for the worst atrocities, its authority is tempered by the principle of complementarity. In contrast to universal jurisdiction, the principle of complementarity brings predictability to the enforcement of international criminal law.

Prosecuting war crimes is arduous and challenging and states must ensure that their own judicial systems and trials are consistent with international standards of independence and fairness. If domestic courts do not meet these fundamental requirements, they will compromise not only the legal process but also the legitimacy of the proceedings. The importance of meeting international standards must not be underestimated. This will be a formidable undertaking; particularly since most domestic war crimes trials will take place in post-conflict environments. The international community must play an active role in assisting domestic courts. It would be hypocrisy to demand accountability at the domestic level without providing international support.

As discussed in this book, one of the fundamental tenets of an effective programme for prosecuting international crimes in domestic courts is the protection of witnesses and victims. Domestic courts will simply not pass the complementarity test without a witness protection programme that meets international standards; this is critical in the early development of any war crimes court. A court must have measures in place to protect witnesses prior to, during, and after trials. Beyond meeting the requirements of complementarity, an effective witness protection programme increases the likelihood that justice will be served, and helps to ensure confidence in the judicial process.

Another finding of this book is that confidentiality for witnesses and victims has been and remains problematic for war crimes courts. The challenge is heightened by the need to balance the fair trial rights of the accused with the need to protect witnesses and victims. Future domestic war crimes courts should adopt a balancing test to determine whether to impose confidentiality measures. The experience of existing international and mixed courts shows how difficult this process can be. Also, because domestic war crimes courts will inevitably have limited resources, they may be inclined to invoke less expensive, but more expansive, anonymity measures. This could easily undermine the rights of the defence.

The principle of complementarity also requires that judges operate in accordance with international standards of independence and impartiality. As discussed in Chapter 2, the selection of judges will be one of the most important factors in ensuring a fair and just trial. This becomes a crucible in post-conflict environments where often there is a dearth of judges available to staff domestic war crimes courts. Furthermore, in post-conflict states, major national actors are likely to have played some role, active or passive, in the conflict. Concerns over judicial impartiality therefore become critically important, necessitating full transparency throughout the appointment process.

The most important thing domestic courts can do to uphold judicial standards is to permit international judges to serve alongside national judges. Such cooperation and breadth of experience offers a wider perspective on international criminal law and adds credibility to the domestic court trying cases according to international standards.[15]

It is important to remember that accountability ultimately requires the *political will* to prosecute crimes and adhere to due process. This in turn requires *popular support,* without which there is real doubt about the long-term sustainability of the proceedings. Non-government organisations can play an important role in this area. As one legal expert has stated:

> Over the past fifteen years, every tribunal has needed the support of NGOs to push governments to cooperate on the apprehension and transfer of indicted persons, provide intelligence and other information necessary to criminal investigations and trials, and help secure financial resources. Without the involvement of supportive governments and NGOs, many of

[15] *See* Human Rights Watch, 'Judging Dujail, The First Trial Before the Iraqi High Tribunal', (November 2006), p. 84-86, available at http://www.hrw.org/sites/default/files/reports/iraq1106webwcover.pdf.

these tribunals would have languished without defendants to try or key evidence to present.[16]

The international community may also need to pressure national governments if there is insufficient political will to initiate or sustain a trial. Such an approach does work. The international community's active involvement made war crimes trials in Serbia possible. Remarkably, Serbia is currently conducting internationally accepted domestic war crimes trials directed at its **own** citizens. For example, in June 2012, the War Crimes Chamber of the Belgrade District Court convicted four Serbian national former police officers for war crimes committed during the Serbo-Croatian war.[17] By 2014, Serbia's War Crimes Court had convicted nine former 'Jackals', members of the Serbian armed forces, of killing over 120 ethnic Albanian civilians in the villages of Ćuška, Zahac, Pavlin, and Ljubenić during the 1999 Kosovo War.[18] The nine members were found guilty of breaching the Geneva Conventions and were specifically found to have 'committed murders, rapes and robberies in an extremely brutal way, with the main goal to spread fear among Albanian civilians in order to force them to leave their homes and flee to Albania'.[19]

The Serbian government has also taken the extraordinary step of apologising for crimes committed in Croatia and Bosnia during the 1991-1995 Balkan Wars.[20] The National Assembly of Serbia passed a declaration condemning crimes committed in Srebrenica in July 1995, when 8,000

---

[16] Telephone Interview with Nina Bang-Jensen, Former Director of the Coalition for International Justice (CIJ) (11 November 2013).

[17] 'Former Serbian Police Jailed over Croatia Crimes', *Radio Free Europe/Radio Liberty*, (19 June 2012), available at www.rferl.org/content/serbia-croatia-convicted/24619144.html. The Court convicted the four Serbian nationals on charges of killing at least six Croatian civilians in October 1991, in Beli Manastir of eastern Croatia. The victims included an entire family of four. The accused were also charged with illegal detention, violation of bodily integrity, intimidation, terror, torture and inhuman treatment of civilians.

[18] 'Serbs jailed for murder of over 100 ethnic Albanians, Agence France Press', *Arab News* (12 February 2014) available at http://www.arabnews.com/news/524541.

[19] Judgement of Judge Snezana Nikolic Garotic *quoted* in 'Serbian ex-paramilitaries guilty of Kosovo killings', *BBC News*, (11 February 2014), available at http://www.bbc.co.uk/news/world-europe-26146224.

[20] *See* Jay Carmella, 'Serbia president apologizes for Croatia war crimes', *Jurist* (11 May 2010), available at http://jurist.org/paperchase/2010/11/serbia-president-apologizes-for-croatia-war-crimes.php.

Muslim men and boys were murdered. Although the declaration did not admit to genocide, the Serbian government did apologise to the victims' families, stating that 'everything possible had not been done to prevent the tragedy'.[21] Serbia, through this declaration, also promised full support to the ICTY, including 'the detection and arrest of Ratko Mladić for the purpose of standing trial before the [ICTY]'.[22] Serbia fulfilled that promise.

Liberia too was pressured by the international community to seek the extradition of Charles Taylor to be tried for international crimes.

In instances of non-cooperation, the Court is clearly hampered by the Security Council's inaction. While the Court is not a UN institution, there is a clear argument for the Council to facilitate state cooperation when a situation falls within ICC jurisdiction. By remaining silent, despite receiving reports of non-cooperation from the ICC, the Security Council effectively undermines the ICC's ability to carry out its mandate.

Once a state decides to undertake a domestic prosecution of war crimes, the international community should provide the state with direct technical assistance. It is disingenuous for the international community to demand accountability without providing support as needed. As set forth in Chapter 6, the creation of an International Technical Assistance Office (ITAO) would be a worthy effort. To date, there is no comprehensive technical legal assistance programme to assist states undertaking domestic war crimes trials. The ITAO would fill this gap and play a crucial role in ensuring that the principle of complementarity is successfully embraced and implemented by states.

Despite the recurrence of some of the worst atrocities in twentieth-century history, neither the international community nor individual states have shown sufficient political will to countermand impunity. The emergence of modern international courts such as the ICTY, the ICTR, the ECCC, and the SCSL has been a step in the right direction. These courts have been pivotal in the development of international law, and the ICC was the crowning jewel. Unfortunately, in the twelve years of its existence, the ICC has been underwhelming. The Court has spent over $1

[21] 'Declaration of the National Assembly of the Republic of Serbia Condemning the Crimes in Srebrenica', *Official Gazette of the Republic of Serbia*, RS No. 6, (31 March 2010).
[22] *Ibid.*

billion to support thirty-four judges and over 700 staff.[23] The result has been two convictions. States have challenged its mandate and legitimacy while scholars have attacked its performance.

The Court's survival now lies in the principle of complementarity, arguably the most important concept in the Rome Statute. The Preamble clearly reminds states that it is their 'duty' to exercise 'criminal jurisdiction over those responsible for international crimes'.[24] Ironically, the principle of complementarity shifts the burden of accountability for *international* crimes to states. As Judge Fausto Pocar, former President of the International Criminal Tribunal for the former Yugoslavia (ICTY) (also former Chairman of the United Nations Human Rights Committee), stated: '[d]eveloping domestic capacity for the prosecution of international crimes and the application [by domestic judiciaries] of international law as clarified by international courts is… a primary objective to be achieved'.[25]

Ensuring accountability for heinous crimes is essential to the cause of international justice, and the international community has a duty to act on behalf of the voiceless victims of atrocities. The principle of complementarity elaborated in the Rome Statute offers the best means for achieving justice. It combines the responsibility and sovereign right of national jurisdiction with the force of an internationally-backed criminal court. While uncertainty and challenges remain, this dual system of international and domestic complementary jurisdiction is the best opportunity available to ensure that accountability trumps impunity.

---

[23] David Davenport, 'International Criminal Court: 12 Years, $1 Billion, 2 Convictions', Forbes.com, 12 March 2014, available at http://www.forbes.com/sites/daviddavenport/2014/03/12/international-criminal-court-12-years-1-billion--2-convictions-2.

[24] Rome Statute of the International Criminal Court, Rome, opened for signature 17 July 1988, 2187 UNTS 90 (entered into force 1 July 2002) UN Doc. A/CONF.183/9, Preamble.

[25] Judge Fausto Pocar, 'Dialogue with Member States on rule of law at the international level organised by the Rule of Law Unit: UN Approach to Transitional Justice', (2 December 2009), p. 2, available at www.unrol.org/files/TJ%20panel%20discssion%20-%20FP%20statement.pdf.

APPENDIX

Introduction

This appendix offers an overview of armed conflict data from the following sources: *The War Report 2012*;[1] the published findings of a broad study on conflict and international criminal justice edited by M. Cherif Bassiouni[2] (hereinafter *The Pursuit of International Criminal Justice*); and a November 2013 special report on conflict which appeared in *The Economist*.[3] Whereas *The War Report* addresses 2012 conflicts, *The Pursuit of International Criminal Justice* and *The Economist* assess conflicts from 1946 up to and including 2008 and 2012, respectively. Due to their prominence in the field and utilisation as data sources in the aforementioned publications, direct reference will also be made to the UCDP[4]/PRIO[5] datasets on conflict[6] (hereinafter 'UCDP/PRIO conflict

---

[1] Stuart Casey-Maslen (ed.), *The War Report 2012* (Oxford: Oxford University Press, 2013).

[2] M. Cherif Bassiouni (ed.), *The Pursuit of International Criminal Justice: A World Study on Conflicts, Victimization, and Post-Conflict Justice*, 2 vols. (Oxford: Intersentia, 2010).

[3] 'How to Stop the Fighting Sometimes', *The Economist*, (9 November 2013), available at http://www.economist.com/news/briefing/21589431-bringing-end-conflicts-within-states-vexatious-history-provides-guide; 'Defining Conflicts: What Makes a War', *The Economist*, (9 November 2013), available at http://www.economist.com/news/briefing/21589432-some-say-killing-25-people-year-enough-others-suggest-1000-what-makes-it-war.

[4] *See* website of the Uppsala Conflict Data Program (UCDP), Department of Peace and Conflict Research, Uppsala Universitet, available at www.ucdp.uu.se.

[5] *See* website of the Peace Research Institute Oslo (PRIO), available at http://www.prio.no/.

[6] UCDP/PRIO, 'UCDP/PRIO Armed Conflict Dataset v.4-2013, 1946 – 2012', (1 July 2013), available at http://www.pcr.uu.se/research/ucdp/datasets/ucdp_prio_armed_conflict_dataset/?languageId=1; UCDP/PRIO, 'UCDP/PRIO Armed Conflict Dataset Codebook v.4-2013', (1 July 2013), available at http://www.pcr.uu.se/digitalAssets/167/167198_codebook_ucdp_prio-armed-conflict-dataset-v4_2013.pdf. The data was first presented in Nils Petter Gleditsch, Peter Wallensteen, Mikael Eriksson, Margareta Sollenberg and Håvard Strand,

data'), UCDP datasets on battle-related deaths[7] (hereinafter 'UCDP victim data') and PRIO datasets on battle-related deaths[8] (hereinafter 'PRIO victim data').

I. Definitions and Sources

Each publication employs a different definition of the terms *armed conflict*, *victim*, and variations thereof. The definitions employed affect the parameters of data collection and presentation, so it is essential to understand these terms in their specific context.

A. Definition of 'Armed Conflict'

i. The War Report 2012

The War Report 2012 applies the standards recognised under international humanitarian law (IHL) and international criminal law (ICL). It defines international armed conflict (IAC) as the use of armed force between states; or the use of armed force 'by one state against another state, irrespective of whether the latter state fights back';[9] or the invasion and

---

'Armed Conflict 1946-2001: A New Dataset', (2002) 39 *Journal of Peace Research* 615-637. For the latest presentation of this data, *see* Lotta Themnér and Peter Wallensteen, 'Armed Conflicts, 1946-2012', (2013) 50 *Journal of Peace Research* 509-21.

[7] UCDP, 'UCDP Battle-Related Deaths Dataset v.5-2013, 1989-2012', (1 July 2013), available at http://www.pcr.uu.se/research/ucdp/datasets/ucdp_battle-related_deaths_dataset/; UCDP, 'UCDP Battle-Related Deaths Dataset Codebook v.5-2013', (1 July 2013), available at http://www.pcr.uu.se/digitalAssets/167/167154_codebook-ucdp-battle-related-deaths-dataset-v.5-2013.pdf. For the latest presentation of this data, *see* Ralph Sundberg, 'Collective Violence 2002 - 2007: Global and Regional Trends', in Lotta Harbom and Ralph Sundberg (eds.), *States in Armed Conflict* (Uppsala: Universitetstryckeriet, 2007).

[8] PRIO, 'PRIO Battle Deaths Dataset 3.0', (October 2009), available at http://www.prio.no/Data/Armed-Conflict/Battle-Deaths/The-Battle-Deaths-Dataset-version-30/; 'PRIO Battle Deaths Dataset 1946–2008 Codebook for Version 3.0', (September 2009), available at http://www.prio.no/Global/upload/CSCW/Data/PRIObd3.0_codebook.pdf. Data presented in Bethany Lacina and Nils Petter Gleditsch, 'Monitoring Trends in Global Combat: A New Dataset of Battle Deaths', (2005) 21 *European Journal of Population* 145–166.

[9] Casey-Maslen, *The War Report 2012*, p. 7.

occupation of one state by another state, even if there is no armed resistance.

It identifies two further possible forms of IAC without clarification as to whether these are included within the parameters of data collection:

> … when one State supports an armed non-state actor (ANSA) operating in another State when that support is so significant that the foreign state is deemed to have 'overall control' over the actions of the ANSA; [10]

> … where there is an armed conflict 'in which peoples are fighting against colonial domination and alien occupation and against racist regimes in the exercise of their right of self-determination'.[11]

The report defines non-international armed conflict (NIAC) as:

> a situation of regular and intense armed violence between the security forces of a state, especially the army, and one or more organised non-governmental armed groups;[12]

> and/or 'a situation of intense armed violence between two or more organised armed groups within a state';[13] and/or 'intense armed violence between two or more organised armed groups across an international border'.[14]

ii. The Pursuit of International Criminal Justice

This study defines armed conflicts as either:

> the clashing of interests (positional differences) over national values of some duration and magnitude between at least two parties (organized groups, states, groups of states, organizations) that are determined to pursue their interests and achieve their goals;[15]

---

[10] *Ibid.*
[11] *Ibid.*
[12] *Ibid.*, p. 9.
[13] *Ibid.*
[14] *Ibid.*
[15] Christopher Mullins, 'Conflict Victimization and Post-Conflict Justice 1945-2008' in Bassiouni, *The Pursuit of International Criminal Justice*, vol. 1, p. 75. *See also*, Heidelberg Institute for International Conflict Research, 'Conflict Barometer' (2013), available at http://www.hiik.de/en/konfliktbarometer/.

a protracted armed conflict between governmental authorities and organized armed groups or between such groups;[16]

a contested incompatibility that concerns government or territory or both where the use of armed force between two parties results in at least 25 battle-related deaths in a year.[17]

iii. The Economist

The Economist does not define or classify types of armed conflict.

iv. UCDP/PRIO conflict data

The UCDP/PRIO defines armed conflict as a contested incompatibility wherein the use of force between two parties results in at least 25 battle-related deaths per annum. At least one party must be the government of a state, and the incompatibility must arise over government, territory, or both.[18]

v. Analysis

The definitions used by *The War Report 2012* and *The Pursuit of International Criminal Justice* encompass armed conflict between two non-governmental parties, providing a broader definition of armed conflict than that used by UCDP. *The War Report 2012* offers the widest definition; because it does not require a minimum number of annual battle-related deaths, it would include minor conflicts.

While the UCDP definition includes an incompatibility component concerning government, territory or both, *The Pursuit of International Criminal Justice's* definition seems to be wider, encompassing clashes over positional differences 'over national values'. This may account for *The Pursuit of International Criminal Justice's* higher number of total conflicts.

---

[16] *Ibid.*
[17] *Ibid.*
[18] 'UCDP/PRIO Armed Conflict Dataset Codebook v.4-2013', Section 2(1). *See also* 'UCDP/PRIO Armed Conflict Dataset v.4-2013, 1946 – 2012';. Gleditsch, Wallensteen, Eriksson, Sollenberg and Strand, 'Armed Conflict 1946-2001: A New Dataset'; Themnér and Peter Wallensteen, 'Armed Conflicts, 1946-2012'.

B. Definition of 'Victim'

i. The War Report 2012

The War Report 2012 defines conflict-related casualties as deaths and injuries during, or directly related to, armed conflict and includes both civilians and combatants. It does not include victims of psychological trauma, mental torture, or sexual violence. In large part this is due to non-availability of data.

ii. The Pursuit of International Criminal Justice

The study defines victims as military or civilian casualties directly or indirectly attributable to violence, and does not include within its victimisation figures data on the injured or sick.

iii. The Economist

The Economist defines victims as persons killed in a battle involving government troops and/or troops of politically organised rebels.[19]

iv. UCDP victim data

UCDP victim data records all combat-related fatalities, both military and civilian.

v. PRIO victim data:

> The PRIO Battle Deaths Dataset defines battle deaths as deaths resulting directly from violence inflicted through the use of armed force by a party to an armed conflict during contested combat. ... Contested combat excludes the sustained destruction of soldiers or civilians outside of the context of any reciprocal threat of lethal force (e.g. execution of prisoners of war).[20]

---

[19] This is the definition attached to the info graphics used. However, the info graphics cite UCDP and PRIO victim data as their source, and UCDP and PRIO victim data definitions include civilian deaths.

[20] 'PRIO Battle Deaths Dataset 1946–2008 Codebook for Version 3.0', p. 3. *See also* 'PRIO Battle Deaths Dataset 3.0'; Lacina and Gleditsch, 'Monitoring Trends in Global Combat: A New Dataset of Battle Deaths'.

It includes deaths from wounds received in combat as well as deaths in combat.

II. Sources of Data

The War Report 2012 cites the UN and its agencies; other international organisations; governments reporting on casualties in other countries; governments of states experiencing conflict; international NGOs; national NGOs; media sources; academics; and sources that compile or analyse reporting.[21]

The Pursuit of International Criminal Justice's study cites established databases including UCDP/PRIO conflict data; IGO and NGO reports; and international media.[22]

The Economist cites UCDP/PRIO conflict data, UCDP victim data, and PRIO victim data.[23]

UCDP/PRIO conflict data cites media reports; case studies; journal articles; NGO reports; online databases; and regional experts.[24]

UCDP victim data cites news agencies; journals; research reports; documents produced by IOs, NGOs and multi-national organisations; documents of the warring parties where available; and global, regional and country-specific sources.[25]

---

[21] Casey-Maslen, *The War Report 2012*, pp. 15-16 for a more detailed list. Interestingly, *The War Report 2012* does not expressly cite UCDP/PRIO conflict data.
[22] Mullins, 'Conflict Victimization and Post Conflict Justice', pp. 73-74.
[23] 'How to Stop the Fighting Sometimes', *The Economist*; 'Defining Conflicts: What Makes a War', *The Economist*.
[24] 'UCDP/PRIO Armed Conflict Dataset v.4-2013, 1946 – 2012'; 'UCDP/PRIO Armed Conflict Dataset Codebook v.4-2013'. *See also* Gleditsch, Wallensteen, Eriksson, Sollenberg and Strand, 'Armed Conflict 1946-2001: A New Dataset'; Themnér and Peter Wallensteen, 'Armed Conflicts, 1946-2012'.
[25] 'UCDP Battle-Related Deaths Dataset Codebook v.5-2013', pp. 6-7. *See also* 'UCDP Battle-Related Deaths Dataset v.5-2013, 1989-2012'; Sundberg, 'Collective Violence 2002 - 2007: Global and Regional Trends'.

PRIO victim data does not specify its sources of data in the PRIO victim data codebook.[26]

A. Differences in Statistical Data

i. Differences in Statistical Data on Conflicts

The table below records the number of unique armed conflicts as identified by each source.

	The War Report 2012	***The Pursuit of International Criminal Justice***	***The Economist***	**UCDP/PRIO conflict datasets**
Armed conflicts in 2012	37	N/A	Not specified	32
Armed conflicts 1946 - 2008	N/A	313	Not specified	246*
Armed conflicts 1946 - 2012	N/A	N/A	416	253*

The Economist stated that 416 armed conflicts occurred in 1946-2012 and cited UCDP/PRIO conflict data as its source. The UCDP/PRIO conflict datasets listed a total of 253 unique armed conflicts occurring in 1946-2012. It was not possible to independently resolve the discrepancy between the two totals, and *The Economist* does not describe how it reached its total.

To examine the statistical differences in further detail, it is necessary to divide and compare data for different time periods:

[26] 'PRIO Battle Deaths Dataset 3.0'; 'PRIO Battle Deaths Dataset 1946–2008 Codebook for Version 3.0'. *See also* Lacina and Gleditsch, 'Monitoring Trends in Global Combat: A New Dataset of Battle Deaths'.

- 2012 (comparing *The War Report 2012* with UCDP/PRIO conflict data)
- 1946 – 2008 (comparing *The Pursuit of International Criminal Justice* with UCDP/PRIO conflict data)
- 2009 – 2011 (only UCDP/PRIO conflict data for this period)

UCDP/PRIO conflict data was utilised by both *The Pursuit of International Criminal Justice* and *The Economist*; armed conflicts occurring after 2008 are outside the temporal limits of *The Pursuit of International Criminal Justice's* work, but UCDP/PRIO data on armed conflicts during 1946-2012 is cited as the source for *The Economist* article. UCDP/PRIO conflict datasets allow for data analysis by year, and thus provide a point of comparison to *The War Report 2012*.

a. 2012

The table below records total armed conflicts in 2012 according to the two available sources.

	The War Report 2012	**UCDP/PRIO conflict data**
Armed conflicts in 2012	37	32

While there is disagreement as to the total number of conflicts, they commonly identify 12 distinct conflicts.

They commonly identify the following conflicts, but present them differently:

- Sudan v. Sudan Revolutionary Front (SRF) – identified as one unique conflict in UCDP/PRIO conflict data; presented as three distinct conflicts in *The War Report 2012* (Sudanese armed forces v. SPLM/A-North; v. JEM; v. SLA).
- Syria v. Free Syrian Army and al-Nusra – identified as one unique conflict in UCDP/PRIO conflict data; identified as two distinct conflicts in *The War Report 2012* (Syrian armed forces and Shabbiha v. Free Syrian Army; v. al-Nusra).
- Russia v. Caucasus – identified as one conflict in UCDP/PRIO conflict data; identified as two military occupations in *The War Report 2012* (with Russia partially occupying Georgia and Moldova)

The following entries are listed as armed conflicts by *The War Report 2012* but not by UCDP/PRIO:

- Military occupation of Cyprus by Turkey
- Military occupation of Eritrea by Ethiopia
- Military occupation of Lebanon by Israel
- Military occupation of Western Sahara by Morocco
- Afghanistan armed forces v. Haqqani Network[27]
- Afghanistan armed forces v. Hezb-e-Islami[28]
- Central African Republic armed forces and Ugandan People's Defence Forces v. Lord's Resistance Army
- Colombia v. ELN
- DRC armed forces v. Lord's Resistance Army
- DRC armed forces v. FDLR
- DRC armed forces v. ADF-NALU
- MLNA v. AQIM, Ansar Dine, and MOJWA (conflict located in Mali)
- Mexican army and police v. Sinaloa Cartel[29]

---

[27] *The War Report 2012* identifies this as a distinct conflict in its breakdown of the 37 total conflicts in 2012 (*see* Casey-Maslen, *The War Report 2012*, p. 14). However, in addressing armed conflict in Afghanistan in 2012, *The War Report 2012* states at pp. 68-69 that '[t]here are arguably separate NIACs against other non-state armed groups, particularly the Haqqani network and Hezb-e-Islami, although the *War Report* is not certain that direct combat between each of these groups and the Afghan government forces and/or ISAF is of sufficient frequency and intensity to amount to an NIAC'.

[28] *Ibid.*

[29] *The War Report 2012* identifies this as a distinct conflict in Mexico in its breakdown of the 37 total conflicts in 2012 (*see ibid.*). However in later addressing armed conflict in Mexico in 2012, *The War Report 2012*, p. 126 states: 'That this drug-related violence constitutes an armed conflict is controversial'. The UCDP has the following relevant entry in its FAQs:

> '**How does the UCDP deal with criminal violence, such as that in Mexico between drug cartels?** The UCDP does not apply any labels regarding the nature of organized violence. Violence is thus not categorized according to any possible 'political' as opposed to 'criminal' goals. There is little logic to claiming that cattle-rustling and land clashes in Kenya are political while battles over the drug market and urban turf in Mexico are criminal.
>
> Instead, the UCDP looks at whether or not those clashing are organized into identifiable groups. If this is the case, and clashes between two such actors cause 25 or more deaths in one calendar year, a non-state conflict is registered in UCDP data'.

- Mexican army and police v. Las Zetas gang[30]
- Sinaloa Cartel and Gulf Cartel v. Las Zetas gang (conflict located in Mexico)[31]
- Yemeni armed forces v. al-Houthi

The following entries are listed as unique armed conflicts occurring in 2012 by UCDP/PRIO but not by *The War Report 2012*:

- Algeria v. AQIM, MOJWA
- Ethiopia v. OLF
- Ethiopia v. ONLF
- India v. Kashmir Insurgents
- India v. CPI-Maoist
- India v. GNLA
- Iraq v. ISI
- Mali v. MLNA[32]
- Mali v. Ansar Dine, Red Berets[33]
- Nigeria v. Jama'atu Ahlis Sunna Lidda'awati wal-Jihad
- Pakistan v. BLA, BRA
- Pakistan v. TTP, TTP-TA, and Lakshar-e-Islam
- Philippines v. ASG, BIFM
- South Sudan v. SLMA

The different definitions of armed conflict are a significant factor in the above discrepancies. Unlike UCDP/PRIO, *The War Report 2012* does not include armed conflicts with fewer than 25 battle-related deaths. Thus, the following entries are not included in *The War Report 2012*:

- Military occupation of Cyprus by Turkey
- Military occupation of Eritrea by Ethiopia

See Uppsala Universtit, 'Frequently Asked Questions' (2014), available at http://www.pcr.uu.se/research/ucdp/faq/?languageId=1.

[30] *Ibid.*

[31] *Ibid.*

[32] *The War Report 2012* is uncertain as to whether this reached the threshold of armed conflict. 'If the armed violence between Malian armed groups and the Malian armed forces in early 2012 did reach the threshold of intensity ('protracted armed violence') to be considered an NIAC, this conflict appears to have effectively ended by April 2012' (*see* Casey-Maslen, *The War Report 2012*, pp. 117, 125).

[33] *Ibid.*

- Military occupation of Lebanon by Israel
- Military occupation of Western Sahara by Morocco

If the figures (each having <25 battle-related deaths) are considered reliable by UCDP, then these conflicts would not meet the criteria for UCDP conflict data.

A further distinction is that *The War Report 2012* presents conflict data by the country in which armed conflict occurs. Where it has identified multiple distinct conflicts in one country – such as Afghanistan, the Central African Republic, Colombia, the Democratic Republic of Congo, and Yemen – it presents total figures across all conflicts for that country. It is not possible to ascertain the annual battle-related deaths for each distinct conflict, and thus one reason as to why conflicts in the aforementioned countries are listed in *The War Report 2012* but not in UCDP/PRIO conflict data may be that those conflicts did not meet the minimum threshold of 25 battle-related deaths.

Thus, all of the entries listed in *The War Report 2012* – but not those included in UCDP/PRIO data – can be explained according to UCDP/PRIO's definition of armed conflict.

The Pursuit of International Criminal Justice's work is limited to 1946-2008. *The Economist* article is based on UCDP/PRIO conflict data, which is currently limited to 1946-2012. As UCDP/PRIO data can be reviewed by year, *The Pursuit of International Criminal Justice's* work will be compared against UCDP/PRIO conflict data for the corresponding period (1946-2008) only.

b. 1946 – 2008

- *The Pursuit of International Criminal Justice* identifies a total of 313 armed conflicts occurring during 1946-2008,[34] and breaks these down into the following subcategories:

[34] Mullins, 'Conflict Victimization and Post-Conflict Justice' p. 67.

Type of conflict	Number of cases	Number of victims
Internal conflict or state repression	65	64-69m
NIACs (most of which are civil wars)	152	17.6-21.7m
External wars	96 (5 ongoing)	8.2-11m
Total	*313*	*89.8-101.7m*

- UCDP/PRIO conflict data identifies a total of 246 unique armed conflicts occurring during 1946-2008.

This is broken down into the following subcategories of conflict:

Type of conflict	Number of cases
Extrasystemic armed conflict	21
Interstate armed conflict	45
Internal armed conflict	171
Internationalised internal armed conflict	48
Total	*285*[35]

There is a high volume of data for the 1946-2008 period provided by both *The Pursuit of International Criminal Justice* and UPCD/PRIO, and the different methods of presenting data make it difficult to accurately ascertain overlap and dissention.[36] Thus I will not provide a breakdown as I did for *The War Report 2012* and UPCD/PRIO conflict data, but will instead highlight selected entries to demonstrate differences that may contribute to the differences in total figures.

---

[35] This figure is greater than the number of unique armed conflicts. UCDP/PRIO conflict data identifies an armed conflict as a unique armed conflict irrespective of whether the type of conflict changes. An example of this is Iran v. KDPI, 1946-1993, which is recorded in UCDP/PRIO conflict data as both an internal armed conflict and internationalised internal armed conflict as the situation developed. Thus UCDP/PRIO conflict data records 246 unique armed conflicts during this period, but 285 separate incidents of different types of conflict.

[36] *The War Report 2012* is uncertain as to whether this reached the threshold of armed conflict. 'If the armed violence between Malian armed groups and the Malian armed forces in early 2012 did reach the threshold of intensity ('protracted armed violence') to be considered an NIAC, this conflict appears to have effectively ended by April 2012' (*see* Casey-Maslen, *The War Report 2012*, pp. 117, 125).

On close examination of where discrepancies lie, I noticed that where conflicts were resolved and later restarted, UCDP/PRIO sometimes recorded this as one unique conflict (while still recording the resolution) whereas *The Pursuit of International Criminal Justice* recorded these as distinct conflicts, increasing the total.

An example of this is the collected data on Peru, which is recorded by *The Pursuit of International Criminal Justice* as two distinct NIACs:

Date	Conflict	Type	Victimisation	PCJ
1965-1966	Peru	P	500	Yes: i
1980/1-2000	Peru	P	69,280	Yes: d, i

UCDP/PRIO conflict data notes one unique conflict in Peru, as illustrated by a reduced extract from the UCDP/PRIO conflict dataset[37]:

ID	SideA	SideB	SideBID	Year monitored	Start date	End date
95	Peru	ELN, MIR	1609, 1610	1965	1965-06-15	1965-12-31
95	Peru	Sendero Luminoso	1611	1982	1965-06-15	
95	Peru	Sendero Luminoso	1611	1983	1965-06-15	
95	Peru	Sendero Luminoso	1611	1984	1965-06-15	
95	Peru	Sendero Luminoso	1611	1985	1965-06-15	
95	Peru	Sendero Luminoso	1611	1986	1965-06-15	
95	Peru	Sendero Luminoso	1611	1987	1965-06-15	
95	Peru	Sendero Luminoso	1611	1988	1965-06-15	
95	Peru	MRTA, Sendero Luminoso	1612, 1611	1989	1965-06-15	
95	Peru	MRTA, Sendero Luminoso	1612, 1611	1990	1965-06-15	
95	Peru	MRTA, Sendero Luminoso	1612, 1611	1991	1965-06-15	
95	Peru	MRTA, Sendero Luminoso	1612, 1611	1992	1965-06-15	
95	Peru	MRTA, Sendero Luminoso	1612, 1611	1993	1965-06-15	
95	Peru	Sendero Luminoso	1611	1994	1965-06-15	

[37] UCDP/PRIO, 'UCDP/PRIO Armed Conflict Dataset v.4-2013, 1946 – 2012'.

95	Peru	Sendero Luminoso	1611	1995	1965-06-15	
95	Peru	Sendero Luminoso	1611	1996	1965-06-15	
95	Peru	Sendero Luminoso	1611	1997	1965-06-15	
95	Peru	Sendero Luminoso	1611	1998	1965-06-15	
95	Peru	Sendero Luminoso	1611	1999	1965-06-15	1999-12-31
95	Peru	Sendero Luminoso	1611	2007	1965-06-15	
95	Peru	Sendero Luminoso	1611	2008	1965-06-15	
95	Peru	Sendero Luminoso	1611	2009	1965-06-15	
95	Peru	Sendero Luminoso	1611	2010	1965-06-15	2010-12-30

The above demonstrates that while there are three recorded instances of armed conflict (as determined by start and end dates), and while they may have different secondary parties (identified by SideB and SideBID columns), UCDP/PRIO interprets this as one unique conflict (as determined by the issuance of one unique conflict ID number). In this regard, it is interesting to note that UCDP actually record more conflict in Peru than *The Pursuit of International Criminal Justice's* table, which does not include the conflict recorded by UCDP/PRIO between 2007-2010, despite *The Pursuit of International Criminal Justice's* broader definition of armed conflict. It seems that UCDP/PRIO assigns unique conflict ID numbers where a conflict arises out of a different incompatibility. Where conflicts occur between a primary party and different secondary parties, but arise out of the same incompatibility, they are not considered unique by UCDP/PRIO.

c. 2009 – 2011

Only UCDP/PRIO conflict data is available for 2009 – 2011. UCDP recorded 46 unique armed conflicts occurring in 2009-2011.

This is broken down into the following subcategories of conflict:

Type of conflict	**Number of cases**
Extrasystemic armed conflict	0
Interstate armed conflict	1
Internal armed conflict	36
Internationalised internal armed conflict	9
Total	*46*

ii. Differences in statistical data on victims

- *The War Report 2012* provides data on casualties and displaced populations as a result of armed conflict in 2012.
- *The Economist* does not provide a clear numeric casualty total.
- *The Pursuit of International Criminal Justice* provides data on victimisation during 1946-2008.
- UCDP victim data is available from 1989 – 2012.
- PRIO victim data is available from 1946 – 2008.

Both PRIO and UCDP victim data can be analysed by year, allowing for comparison of UCDP victim data for 2012 with *The War Report 2012*, and UCDP victim data with PRIO victim data for 1989-2008. *The Pursuit of International Criminal Justice's* victim data can be compared with PRIO victim data for 1946-2008.

	The War Report 2012	***The Pursuit of International Criminal Justice***	***The Economist***[38]	**UCDP victim data**	**PRIO victim data**
1946-2008	N/A	89.8-101.7m	N/A	N/A	7,739,848[39]
1989-2008	N/A	N/A	N/A	746,402[40]	938,301[41]
1989-2012	N/A	N/A	N/A	856,521[42]	N/A
2009-2012	N/A	N/A	N/A	110,119[43]	N/A
2012	92,662-104,414+[44]	N/A	N/A	37,941[45]	N/A

[38] *The Economist* did not state any figures for total victims during 1946-2012. It produced a graphic displaying the total number of victims, but in insufficient quality for an accurate reading. I have therefore chosen not to estimate *The Economist's* figures.

[39] Best estimate; low estimate 4,481,318, high estimate 19,715,413.

[40] Best estimate; low estimate 703,597, high estimate 1,047,293.

[41] Best estimate; low estimate 541,667, high estimate 2,523,456.

[42] Best estimate; low estimate 810,418, high estimate 1,200,801.

[43] Best estimate; low estimate 106,821, high estimate 153,508.

a. 2012

It is immediately clear that there is a significant discrepancy between *The War Report 2012* and UCDP estimates, as even the lower end of *The War Report's* calculation is significantly higher than UCDP's highest estimate. This could be attributable to two factors: the difference in their definitions of victims and conflicts. *The War Report 2012* defines casualties as death or injury to civilians or combatants resulting from armed conflict, while UCDP includes neither civilians nor injuries within its data collection. Furthermore, *The War Report 2012* provided a more expansive definition of armed conflict than UCDP, as detailed above in the armed conflicts section, which further widens its parameters for victim totals. This becomes clear on reviewing *The War Report 2012's* individual conflict victim totals; in the section addressing differences in statistical data regarding conflicts, I noted that *The War Report 2012's* definition of armed conflict does not contain a minimum number of battle-related deaths, and that it consequentially identifies armed conflicts where UCDP does not. This increases *The War Report 2012's* casualty total with the deaths and injuries it records from the additional conflicts.

b. 1989-2008

UCDP and PRIO victim datasets yield different best estimates and different low-high estimates. I cannot explain the discrepancy, as the PRIO victim data estimates are higher despite having a potentially more limited definition of victim. It is not possible to comment on whether the discrepancy can be attributed to different data sources, as the PRIO victim data codebook does not specify its sources. *The Pursuit of International Criminal Justice's* publication notes that UCDP relies only upon independently verified figures from three separate sources.[46]

c. 1946-2008

There is an enormous difference between *The Pursuit of International Criminal Justice* and PRIO victim data's casualty estimates. This may be affected by *The Pursuit of International Criminal Justice's* wider definition of victimisation, which includes indirect casualties as well as those directly attributed to armed conflict; this is the only substantial difference between the two definitions. Neither publication includes injuries or illness within its definition of casualty.

---

[44] Deaths and injuries. *The War Report 2012* also estimated 3,177,000+ new displacements for 2012.

[45] Best estimate; low estimate 37,175, high estimate 60,260.

[46] Mullins, 'Conflict Victimization and Post Conflict Justice', p. 74.

An example of discrepancies between victim data can be seen in the following data recorded for internal conflict in Pakistan in 1971.

	The Pursuit of International Criminal Justice	**PRIO victim data**
Victimisation	1,500,000	50,000-250,000[47]

A large factor behind the discrepancy is that *The Pursuit of International Criminal Justice's* data includes state repression and democide (murder by government) in the figures for internal conflict, while PRIO victim data either does not do so, or does so to a lesser extent e.g.:

	The Pursuit of International Criminal Justice	**PRIO victim data**
Conflict	USSR, 1946-1991	Russia (Soviet Union), 1946-50
Victimisation	22,000,000	25,145[48]

	The Pursuit of International Criminal Justice	**PRIO victim data**
Conflict	China 1949-1987-cont'd	N/A
Victimisation	35,236,000	N/A

This is a consequence of *The Pursuit of International Criminal Justice's* wider definition of armed conflict, which permits the inclusion of democide within its data collection parameters.

d. The Economist

No data from *The Economist* has been included in this section, as it does not provide total numbers of casualties. Instead, *The Economist* published an info graphic of the 100 deadliest conflicts, ranked according to number of deaths. The figures were entirely different from those

[47] No best estimate available.

[48] Best estimate; low estimate 5,175, high estimate 29,411.

contained in UCDP and PRIO victim data, which it cited as its sources. The following table demonstrates the difference

	Greece 1946-9	Kenya 1952-6	Algeria 1952-62	UK 1971-98
PRIO low estimate	24,000	4025	100,000	562
PRIO high estimate	160,000	15,000	443,453	3,149
PRIO best estimate	154,000	12,955	182,526	3,149
The Economist total	77,000	6,500	91,300	1,500

It is unconfirmed, but the above table suggests that *The Economist* reached its totals by halving PRIO's best estimate for victims in an armed conflict. It is not clear either in the info graphic or the article that this is the method used, or why this was deemed more reliable than the best estimates from PRIO, who had collected the data. Given the lack of explanation, I am reluctant to treat *The Economist's* victimisation totals as reliable. In addition, *The Economist* only produced victim totals for the 100 'deadliest conflicts' and thus it is not possible to produce an overall picture of victimisation since 1945 using their data.

B. Conclusions

i. Armed Conflicts

Some of the discrepancies in statistics may be attributed to different definitions of conflict, as discussed above. To reiterate, it appears that *The War Report 2012* had the broadest definition (albeit somewhat vague due to the possible inclusion of disputed definitions of IAC) and did not require a minimum number of battle-related deaths for conflict to be recorded.

Because of its definition of armed conflict, UCDP's conflict data is limited to incompatibilities concerning government, territory, or both, while *The Pursuit of International Criminal Justice's* definitions allow for other possibilities.

On examining the differences in statistical data between *The War Report 2012* and UCDP, it became clear that *The War Report 2012* and UCDP/PRIO interpreted some conflicts differently. As outlined above, UCDP listed Sudan v. SRF as one unique conflict, while *The War Report 2012* broke the SRF down into its components and recorded three unique conflicts. This also appeared in analysis and comparison of *The Pursuit of International Criminal Justice's* data with UCDP/PRIO conflict data, as discussed above, in relation to Peru.

A further difference is the primary mode of distinction between conflicts. *The Pursuit of International Criminal Justice's* data presentation begins by dividing all conflicts into subcategories (internal conflict or state repression; NIACs; external wars) and then records unique conflicts within those categories, while UCDP divides conflicts into subcategories *after* identifying unique armed conflicts. Thus where a situation of conflict moves from one subcategory to another – for example, from purely internal armed conflict to an NIAC or internationalised armed conflict – UCDP/PRIO conflict data records this as one unique conflict, while *The Pursuit of International Criminal Justice* might record this as multiple distinct conflicts; *The Pursuit of International Criminal Justice's* tables of collected data do not provide for a situation in which one unique armed conflict might take different forms. This is, however, difficult to confirm due to the limitations of *The Pursuit of International Criminal Justice's* data presentation method.[49]

Instances such as this may further account for UCDP recording a lower total of armed conflicts than *The Pursuit of International Criminal Justice* during the 1946-2008 period.

---

[49] Mullins, 'Conflict Victimization and Post Conflict Justice', pp. 88-107 contains tables of the collected data. Unfortunately these tables are simplified, identifying conflicts only by states that were party to the conflict or states in which the conflict predominantly took place. This makes identifying themes and features of *The Pursuit of International Criminal Justice's* data presentation for comparison with the more detailed UCDP/PRIO conflict data, which identifies secondary parties, difficult. For example, *The Pursuit of International Criminal Justice*'s data on purely internal conflicts and state repression records two entries for Burundi of the same type of armed conflict; the entries differ in their timespans and level of victimisation, but this does not include data on secondary parties to the conflict despite an acknowledgement that the method of classification of conflict typology allows for incidents involving dissident groups to be categorised as purely internal conflicts. For an explanation of classification of conflict typology, *see* Mullins, 'Conflict Victimization and Post Conflict Justice', pp. 76-77.

The method of analysis and presentation used in the UCDP/PRIO conflict datasets enables a more fluid and realistic presentation of armed conflicts, which can escalate to the extent of changing the type of conflict without the original conflict ceasing and becoming a 'new' conflict.

b. Victims

The War Report 2012 provides the most comprehensive definition of victim, providing data on total displacements for each conflict in 2012 in addition to both combatant and civilian deaths, in addition to including injury within the category of victimisation. This perhaps is a more accurate reflection of the impact of conflict on persons. Other datasets, such as UCDP victim data, PRIO victim data, and the *The Pursuit of International Criminal Justice* report, accounted only for deaths.

The datasets varied in their presentation of range and estimates; *The War Report 2012* frequently provided estimated figures or figures such as '100+'. It is thus impossible to ascertain the upper limits of the data. *The Pursuit of International Criminal Justice* typically provided range figures, while UCDP and PRIO provided ranges from which they deduced best estimates. As explained above, it is possible that different forms of data verification (e.g. UCDP victim data requiring independent verification in three different sources before data can be relied upon) may have influenced the discrepancies between figures.

The largest discrepancy between the datasets can be attributed to the differing definitions of armed conflict. *The Pursuit of International Criminal Justice's* data incorporates democide, which because it is not included in other datasets' definitions, increases *The Pursuit of International Criminal Justice's* total victim count significantly.

INDEX

ability, 22, 25, 36, 37, 62, 66, 69-71, 111, 113-115, 120, 123, 127, 130, 185, 190, 192, 196, 208, 209, 217, 218, 221, 229, 230, 235-237, 240, 251, 285, 289, 290, 297
  See also inability
accountability, 2, 3, 6, 9, 22, 24, 37, 76, 82, 85, 89, 90, 107, 129, 169, 174-176, 188, 195, 202, 256, 281, 285, 295-298
  International Criminal Court, 2, 12, 89, 90, 153, 192, 225, 288, 294
accountability centres, 2, 289
accountability mechanisms, 8, 9, 51-53, 76, 81-82
accused, *see also* defence rights
  rights of, 33, 129, 143, 144, 149, 255, 280, 295
  equality of arms, 33, 144-146
  due process, 7, 8, 9, 26, 53, 77, 90, 96, 107, 116, 145, 221, 222, 238, 239, 255, 291, 295
  presumption of innocence, 144, 147
ad hoc jurisdiction, 46, 48
admissibility, 8, 10, 33, 37, 42, 49, 55, 56, 58, 59, 62-71, 74, 81, 93, 96, 98, 109, 114, 196, 204-208, 210-214, 219-221, 229, 234-235, 240, 285
  admissibility test, 26, 37, 38, 53, 62, 74, 111, 112, 150, 216, 221
  balance of probabilities, 178, 181
  burden of proof, 177-182
  challenges to admissibility, 60, 127-130, 150, 177-183, 189, 197, 201, 206-210, 213-214, 249, 285
  inability, *see* inability
  inactivity, 63, 65, 153
  sufficient degree, 179, 180, 214
  timing, 183-190, 197
  unwillingness, *see* unwillingness
Afghanistan, 41, 75, 307, 309
African Charter on Human and Peoples Rights, 99
African Union, 10, 71, 156, 168, 225, 226, 230-233, 288
Al Bashir, Omar Hassan Ahmad, 36, 126, 154-161, 168, 222, 226, 227, 234, 246
Al-Senussi, Abdullah, 96, 203, 213-222, 249, 290
  admissibility, 96, 207, 213
  domestic trial, 5, 96, 206, 210, 216-221
  investigation, 201, 210, 215
American Bar Association, 148, 247
American Convention on Human Rights, 99
amicus curiae, 253
amnesty, 79, 89, 90, 225
Amnesty International, 7, 31, 52-54, 111, 132, 133, 150, 170, 193, 194, 227, 250, 255, 292, 293
Arab League, 234
Arap Sang, Joshua, 66, 140, 178, 180, 233, 234
Argentina, 6, 114, 115, 243
armed conflict, 1, 74, 114, 286, 299-318
  definition, 300-302

arrest warrants, 36, 41, 63, 158, 161, 163, 174-176, 187, 189, 195, 203, 210, 226, 227, 234, 245, 246
Assembly of States Parties (ASP), 46, 125, 126, 153-161, 192, 228, 241-245, 296
attorney, *see* lawyers
aut dedere aut judicare, 292

balance of probabilities, 177, 180
Bangladesh, 144, 145, 289
bar associations, 150, 247, 257-281
  Cambodian Bar Association, 278-281
Bassiouni, Cherif M., 1, 31, 299
Belgium, 13, 14, 91
Bensouda, Fatou, 41, 90, 136
Bosnia and Herzegovina, 132-134, 168, 169, 269, 275, 277, 294
  War Crimes Chamber of the State Court, 133, 274
budget, 133, 266
burden of proof, 177-182
Burma, 76, 146
Bush, George W., 239

Cambodia, 104-109, 148, 278-280
  See also Extraordinary Chambers in the Courts of Cambodia (ECCC)
Cambodian Bar Association (CBA), 278-281
Central African Republic (CAR), 41, 58, 307, 309
Chad, 126, 152-160
Chapter VII. *See* UN Charter.
China, 21, 147, 161, 289, 315
civilian population, 41, 80, 174, 189, 200, 203, 286, 296, 303, 314, 318
co-perpetration, 58
compliance, 9, 24, 30, 116, 138, 155, 157, 165, 168, 176, 181, 210, 228
  See also non-compliance
conduct, 21, 56, 60, 91, 117, 197, 210, 258
  same conduct, 65, 66, 68, 210, 212, 214
  judicial conduct, 258-261, 275
conflict, 72, 95, 113, 115, 117, 238, 241, 254, 256, 258, 265, 266, 277
  See also post-conflict environment, post-conflict states
Convention Against Torture, 91, 291, 292
compensation, 54, 202, 283, 284
complementarity,
  See principle of complementarity
Convention for the Prevention and Punishment of the Crime of Genocide, 121, 292
Côte d'Ivoire, 40-43, 248, 266
counsel, 22, 33, 69, 128, 148-150, 214, 220, 248, 255, 259, 263, 264, 276-283
  See also defence attorneys, lawyers
crimes against humanity, 2, 5, 39-41, 48, 52, 55, 56, 57, 79, 80, 83, 85, 119, 120, 153, 174, 176, 187, 188, 192, 200, 203, 222, 223, 238, 243, 248, 276, 288-290
Croatia, 132, 163, 164, 170-173, 176, 289, 296
customary international law, 89, 91, 115, 121, 124, 292

Darfur, 6, 33, 36, 191, 222, 224, 249
  See also Sudan
  defence attorneys, *See* counsel, lawyers
  foreign defence attorneys, 277-283
defence rights, 130, 144-151
deferral, 6, 26, 73, 78, 154, 186, 197, 223-227

Article 16, 223-227
Del Ponte, Carla, 172, 173
Democratic Republic of the Congo (DRC), 5, 75, 79, 95, 161, 178, 179, 187, 197, 247, 309
displaced persons, 1, 2, 80, 189, 286, 313
disqualification or recusal of judges, 100, 260, 261
domestic courts, 2, 3, 5, 8, 9, 18, 22, 23, 25, 26, 29, 36, 68, 78, 89, 100, 116, 121, 131, 134, 143, 146, 152, 185, 188, 231, 236, 237, 250, 252, 253, 257, 261, 262, 266, 268, 279-274, 277, 282-284, 294, 295
domestic jurisdiction, 4, 8, 9, 23, 25, 78
domestic war crimes courts, 2-12, 23-27, 36, 37, 74, 78, 89, 115, 129, 132, 143, 144, 149, 189, 192, 238-285, 289, 294-297
double jeopardy (*ne bis in idem*), 62, 184, 185
due process, 7, 8, 9, 26, 53, 77, 90, 96, 107, 116, 145, 221, 222, 238, 239, 255, 291, 295

Economist, The, 299-318
Egypt, 38, 39, 48
El Zeidy, Mohamed M., 18, 43, 77, 192
enforcement, 20, 24, 35-37, 63, 70, 78, 94, 112, 113, 133, 134, 151-153, 162, 163, 168, 173, 191, 194, 229, 241, 258, 269, 288, 294
equality of arms, 33, 145, 146
European Convention on Human Rights (ECHR), 96, 98, 99, 119
European Court and Commission of Human Rights (ECtHR), 91-96
European Parliament, 169
European Union (EU), 25, 83, 167-174, 232, 245
European Union Rule of Law Mission in Kosovo (EULEX), 174-176
evidence, 2, 4, 7, 23, 30, 32, 33, 50, 59, 68, 70, 82, 83, 91, 96, 100, 108-113, 115, 116, 119, 125, 127, 131-142, 146, 171, 173, 176, 179-182, 193, 195, 203, 208-224, 230, 243, 268, 277, 290, 291, 296
Extraordinary Chambers in the Courts of Cambodia (ECCC), 104-108, 148-149, 260-261, 278-279, 297
judicial independence, 105-109

fair trial, 7, 8, 19, 33, 34, 53, 66, 94-98, 113, 117-120, 127-131, 137, 144, 148, 204-206, 216, 217, 230, 236, 250, 255, 259, 271, 284, 290, 295
See also accused, defence rights
France, 13, 14, 17, 27, 29, 30, 91, 97, 98, 120, 121, 243, 293
formal response procedure, 156, 158, 213
See also informal response procedure
former Yugoslavia, 75, 78, 87, 117, 164, 248, 250, 288
See International Criminal Tribunal for the former Yugoslavia

gacaca, 51-54
Gaddafi, Muammar, 5, 110, 150, 201-204, 218, 230
Gaddafi, Saif Al-Islam, 5, 25, 38, 63-65, 69, 70, 93-96, 109, 110, 127, 150, 179-181, 185, 200, 203-221, 223, 226, 230, 290
Gaza, 45-48
Gbagbo, Laurent, 40, 43, 44
gender-based violence, 244
gender diversity, 105, 262-265

Geneva Conventions, 196, 211, 291, 292, 296
genocide, 2, 51, 52, 55, 76, 117, 119-123, 234, 243, 246, 253, 282, 288, 289, 297
Georgia, 30-35, 306
Goldstone, Richard J., 34, 88, 148, 168-169, 272
Gotovina, Ante, 172, 173
gravity, 37, 42, 49, 50, 55-62, 182, 197

Habré, Hissène, 91-92
Hadžić, Goran, 169, 171
Haradinaj, Ramush, 141-142
heads of State, 4, 17, 192,
immunity, 123, 125, 156, 232
human rights law, 84, 277, 282, 288
Human Rights Watch, 38, 101, 106, 170, 221, 247, 266, 272, 275
humanity, crimes against. *See* crimes against humanity,
hybrid or mixed courts or tribunals, 104, 115, 133, 144, 245, 252, 255, 265, 271-276, 281-283, 295
ICC. *See* International Criminal Court
ICJ. *See* International Court of Justice
ICTR. *See* International Criminal Tribunal for Rwanda
ICTY. *See* International Criminal Tribunal for the former Yugoslavia
ILC. *See* International Law Commission

immunities, 33, 89, 90, 108, 117, 123-125, 156, 175, 199, 220, 231-232, 253
impartiality, 53, 54, 69, 77, 84, 94-111, 115, 119, 126-144, 147, 197, 203, 204, 224, 232, 234-236, 250-252, 254, 256, 275, 281, 282, 295
See also judges
imprisonment, 79, 118
in absentia trials, 102, 108, 209, 293
inability, 6, 8, 9, 16, 17, 23, 26, 33, 63, 64, 65, 68, 69, 70, 74, 94, 112, 113, 115, 119, 121, 123, 126, 130, 132, 150, 175, 181, 187, 197, 212, 216-221, 229, 259
See also ability
independence, *See* judicial independence
indictments, 48, 90, 110, 146-147, 152, 188, 189, 196, 210, 222, 226, 230, 234, 246
informal response procedure, 156
See also formal response procedure
innocence, presumption of, 144, 147
intent, 59, 93, 94, 78, 87, 206, 209
interest of justice, 37, 49-55, 61, 62, 72, 183, 224, 233, 234
International Advisory Group, 234-237
International Bar Association (IBA), 34, 45, 67, 107, 109, 149, 231, 235, 239, 244, 248, 251-257, 263, 273, 278-279
International Bar Association's Human Rights Institute (IBAHRI), 67, 109, 231, 248, 274
International Court of Justice (ICJ), 28, 45, 91, 198, 292
International Covenant on Civil and Political Rights (ICCPR), 99, 131, 143, 145, 284
international crimes, 2-13, 23-26, 36-38, 67, 68, 74-76, 89, 127, 148, 167, 211, 244, 245, 250, 272, 276-281, 289, 290, 294, 297, 298
International Criminal Court (ICC), budget, 133, 266-267

creation and establishment of, 2, 13, 19, 20, 22, 28, 58, 65, 184, 192, 194, 223
complementarity, *See* principle of complementarity
enforcement, *See* enforcement
human rights body, 9-10
implementation, 5, 35, 113, 123-127, 225, 243, 249, 255
investigation, *See* investigation
jurisdiction, *See* jurisdiction
non-States Parties, to, 4-6, 27-34, 39-46, 156, 197-199, 222
referral, *See* referral
Rules of Procedure and Evidence, 43, 55, 59, 73, 100, 102, 177, 183, 233, 255, 272
withdrawl, *See* withdrawl
witness interference, 139-140
See also Office of the Prosecutor, Rome Statute of the International Criminal Court,
International Criminal Tribunal for Rwanda (ICTR), 22, 76, 91, 114, 117-123, 130, 147, 148, 162-168, 229, 234, 258, 263, 267, 274, 282, 293, 297
transfer to domestic courts, 117-123
International Criminal Tribunal for former Yugoslavia (ICTY), 3, 4, 7, 21-24, 87, 88, 95, 117, 130, 131, 140-142, 146-148, 162-173, 250, 251, 256, 259, 272, 297, 298
international judges. *See* judges
international jurisdiction, 4, 35, 144
See also universal jurisdiction
International Law Commission (ILC), 20-25, 28, 184, 191, 223, 284
International Monetary Fund (IMF), 168
international pressure, 167-176
International Technical Assistance Office (ITAO), 244-285
assistance to domestic courts, 271, 276-285
defence attorneys, 276-283
fair trial, 220-252
gender diversity, 262-265
judicial nomination, 255-257
judicial selection, 271-276
substantive legal and procedural issues, 252-254
training, 257-262
trial observations, 254-256
victim compensation, 283-284
victim and witness support, 265-271
investigation,
national investigation, 3, 7, 26, 32-34, 44, 64-70, 77, 78, 82, 86, 93, 111, 124, 127, 133, 139, 150, 176, 179-182, 194, 200-216, 220, 222, 237, 240, 241, 242, 248, 266, 285, 295
ICC investigation, 4-6, 20, 22, 23, 37-50, 54-56, 62, 71-74, 80-83, 90, 134, 152, 154, 183, 185-188, 200, 201, 222, 225-228, 235, 236, 245, 254
See also proprio motu, referral
Iraq, 7-8, 38, 95, 115, 150, 238-240, 253, 261, 271-273, 308
Dujail trial, 102-104, 277
judges, 7, 95, 101-103, 238-239, 248, 253, 261, 271- 273
lawyers, 7, 150, 238, 248, 277-280
Saddam Hussein, 7, 8, 100-103, 238-239, 271-278
War Crimes Court, 8, 100-103, 238-240, 253, 261, 271-273, 280
Israel, 44-48, 88, 289, 307, 309

joint criminal enterprise, 253

judges, 7, 24, 53, 67, 93-111, 132, 144, 196, 202, 236, 238, 239, 250, 253, 257, 274-277
dismissal or removal, 102-103, 258-260
disqualification or recusal, 100-103, 260-261
gender diversity, 262-265
international judges, 104, 271-280, 295
judicial independence, 53, 94-98, 100-110, 114-115, 253, 257, 258, 295
judicial misconduct, 258-261
judicial nomination, 101, 104, 105, 250, 256-257, 275
judicial selection, 67, 94, 95, 101, 104, 105, 108, 256, 257, 262, 271-275
training, 54, 67, 115, 247-249, 254, 257, 258, 267
judicial independence, 53, 94-98, 100-110, 114-115, 253, 257, 258, 295
UN Basic Principles on the Independence of the Judiciary, 98-99, 259, 261
jurisdiction,
national jurisdiction, 2-9, 15, 16, 22-32, 35, 37, 39, 63-67, 72, 73, 80-83, 87, 90, 109, 113, 123, 194, 212, 220, 229, 241, 242, 289, 298
ICC jurisdiction, 2-6, 12, 19-23, 26, 31, 35, 36, 40, 42-48, 51, 54-58, 62, 69, 71-74, 77, 117, 124, 125, 129, 150-157, 162, 183-185, 188, 193, 194, 198, 200, 227, 228, 231, 247, 285, 289, 290, 297, 298
See also ad hoc jurisdiction, domestic jurisdiction, international jurisdiction, temporal jurisdiction, territorial jurisdiction, universal jurisdiction
jurisdictional nexus, 28-29
Jurisdiction, Cooperation and Complementarity Division (JCCD), 235-236
Justice Rapid Response Initiative (JRR), 243-245

Karadžić, Radovan, 168-172
Kenya, 5, 10, 50, 66-68, 71, 72, 80-83, 95, 109, 116, 134-140, 155, 160, 167, 181, 224, 225, 228, 231-233, 246, 273, 316
Waki Commission, 81
Truth, Justice and Reconciliation Commission (TJRC), 81-82, 246
Kenyatta, Uhuru, 137-139, 224, 231-232
Kirk McDonald, Gabrielle, 21-22
Kony, Joseph, 65, 173, 186-189, 194-196
Kosovo, 141, 148, 174-176, 269, 286, 296
See also International Criminal Tribunal for former Yugoslavia

language issues, 24, 31, 253
lawyers, 7, 24, 54, 103, 109, 145, 148, 150, 189, 216, 221, 236, 238, 239, 248, 249, 254, 256, 258, 263, 264, 276-280
See also attorneys, counsel, defence attorneys
League of Nations, 17-18
Lebanon, 6, 283, 307, 309
Liberia, 174-176, 297
Libya, 5, 6, 10, 25, 50, 69-71, 93-96, 109, 110, 115, 116, 127, 128, 130, 150, 180-182, 197-222, 229-231, 240, 249, 290
United Nations Support Mission in Libya (UNSMIL), 201-202, 249-250

Lubanga Dyilo, Thomas, 56-57, 60, 63-65, 97, 129, 197, 217

major war criminals, 15, 16, 171
Malawi, 126, 155, 157-160, 176
Mali, 191, 232, 307, 308
Meron, Theodor, 251, 252, 292
Milošević, Slobodan, 75, 88
mixed or hybrid courts, panels or tribunals, 104, 115, 133, 144, 245, 252, 255, 265, 271-276, 281-283, 295
Mladić, Ratko, 87, 168-172, 297
Moreno Ocampo, Luis, 3, 66, 196, 201
Moscow Declaration, 13, 15, 16

nationality and personal jurisdiction, 43, 265, 291
NATO, 167- 169, 204
ne bis in idem. *See also* double jeopardy, 62-63, 137, 184-185
NGOs (non-governmental organisations), 34, 38, 105, 126, 168, 170, 233, 236, 243, 245, 247, 256, 257, 295, 301-304
Nigeria, 38, 158, 160, 174, 308
non-cooperation, 88, 125, 140, 141, 153-158, 160-167, 226, 228, 297
non-compliance, 88, 138, 155, 157, 165, 176
Norway, 13, 14, 122-123
Nuremberg tribunal, 287

Office of Public Counsel for the Defence (OPCD), 69, 70, 93, 109, 110, 127, 181, 204, 209
Office of the Public Counsel for the Victims (OPCV), 9, 93, 116, 128, 181, 182, 213, 214
Office of the Prosecutor
ICC, of the, 9, 32, 33, 34, 38, 45-50, 54, 70, 80, 87, 137-139, 181, 182, 185, 189, 213, 233, 235, 245-246, 254, 255, 284
ICTY, of the, 164
Organisation for Security and Co-operation in Europe (OSCE), 8, 87, 133, 148, 255, 274, 277

Palestine, 44-47
preliminary examination, 32, 34, 38, 39, 41, 81, 200
preliminary investigation, 39, 41, 42, 45, 200
Preparatory Committee, 20, 113, 184, 229
personal jurisdiction, 291
Pillay, Navanethem, 85, 263
Pocar, Fausto, 3, 164, 298
political will, 7, 74, 76, 85, 87, 167, 169, 223, 241, 295-297
popular support, 295
post-conflict environment, 4, 7, 10, 24, 115, 128, 130, 134, 192, 217, 262, 294, 295
post-conflict states, 72, 95, 113, 115, 117, 238, 241, 254, 256, 255, 256, 258, 265, 266, 275, 277, 284, 295
principle of complementarity, 2-16, 19-26, 35-37, 47, 51, 55, 61-73, 92, 112, 116, 117, 120, 123-131, 143, 144, 149, 152, 162, 167, 176, 182, 183, 186, 187, 189, 192-197, 204, 211-213, 226, 229, 235, 240-243, 264, 285, 289-291, 294-298
propio motu investigation, 38, 47, 71, 72, 82, 228, 233, 235

rape, 30, 116, 176, 119, 200, 210, 263, 277, 287, 296
ratione materiae jurisdiction, 37
reconciliation, 8, 81, 85, 118, 128, 188, 189, 201, 202, 246, 284
referral,
  Assembly of States Parties, 125, 153-160, 228
  national jurisdiction, to, 117, 122, 231, 274

UN Security Council, *See* UN Security Council
withdrawal, *See* withdrawal
reparations, 51, 201, 202, 250, 283, 284
See also compensation
Republika Srpska, 163-164
restorative justice, 51, 129
retributive justice, 51, 129
Rome Conference, 21, 28, 29, 229
Rome Statute of the International Criminal Court, 29, 34, 39, 49, 53, 55, 58, 60, 61-67, 69-72, 77-90, 94, 96, 97, 113, 115, 123, 125, 129, 130, 136, 154, 155, 177, 181, 183-187, 193, 197, 204-209, 212, 217, 218, 221-228, 234, 235, 254, 276, 288
Article 1, 3, 12
Article 5, 44, 73
Article 11, 27
Article 12, 27-32, 39-48
Article 13, 198, 204
Article 14, 187
Article 15, 39, 42, 235
Article 16, 223-227
Article 17, 42, 53, 57-73, 77-105, 112-113, 120, 127-130, 181-187, 196-197, 204, 209, 212, 213, 218, 221, 234, 255, 271, 276
Article 18, 72, 73, 184, 254
Article 19, 66, 98, 177, 183, 185, 186, 195, 206, 208
Article 21, 129, 130, 217
Article 34, 27
Article 35, 184
Article 38, 262
Article 43, 235
Article 53, 42, 49, 54, 55, 183, 254
Article 54, 235
Article 66, 136
Article 86, 124
Article 87, 153, 154, 158, 162
Article 88, 123
Article 94, 206, 208
Article 95, 207, 208
Article 127, 227, 228
complementarity, 3, 12, 13, 21, 35, 56, 62, 125, 129, 195, 204, 241, 242, 294, 298
See also principle of complementarity
creation and establishment of ICC, *See* International Criminal Court
enforcement, 37, 116, 151, 152, 162, 163, 173, 228, 258, 285, 288
See also enforcement
gender, 262-263
implementation of, 5, 35, 113, 123-127, 225, 243, 249, 255
non-States Parties, to, 4-6, 27-34, 39-46, 156, 197-199, 222,
obligations, 23, 27-30, 44, 82, 123-125, 145, 152, 155, 157, 158, 161-163, 181, 196-199, 211, 227, 228, 242
Preamble, 3, 12, 19, 22, 90, 298
ratification of, 2, 6, 35, 42, 44-48, 123, 124, 165
States Parties, to, 2, 4, 6, 11, 16, 21, 26, 35, 37, 41, 44, 73, 80, 123-126, 152, 153, 157, 160-162, 173, 191, 198, 227, 242, 245, 262, 289
Russia, 30-35, 289, 306, 315
Ruto, William Sameoi, 140, 177-178, 180, 224, 230-234
Rwanda, 51-54, 76, 114, 116-123, 142, 166, 225, 229, 234, 258, 263, 274, 282, 288, 289
See also International Criminal Tribunal for Rwanda, *gacaca*

sanctions, 154, 155, 160-163, 169, 176, 261

Schabas, William, 9, 63, 64, 70, 128, 190, 191, 195, 291
SCSL. *See* Special Court for Sierra Leone
self-referral, 191-196
See also referral
Senegal, 91-92
Serbia, 8, 24, 25, 87, 88, 132-134, 163, 164, 168-173, 176, 251, 252, 266, 282, 287, 289, 296, 297
domestic war crimes court, 24, 88, 132
Šešelj, Vojislav, 140
sexual violence, 176, 247, 263, 303
sham trials, 7
shielding, 77-83, 87-90, 277
Sierra Leone, 89, 149, 174, 248, 256, 268, 282
See also Special Court for Sierra Leone
social alarm, 56, 57, 88
South Ossetia, 30-33
sovereignty, 3, 4, 20, 21, 22, 24, 26, 27, 29, 35, 48, 179, 224, 230, 288, 290, 293, 294, 298
Spain, 293
Special Court for Sierra Leone (SCSL), 89, 149, 174, 248, 256, 268, 297
Srebrenica massacre, 168, 296
Sri Lanka, 75, 83-86, 142-143
statute of limitations, 125, 290
Sudan, 6, 33, 36, 59, 126, 155-157, 160-162, 187, 198, 222-223, 226, 234, 245, 246, 249, 306, 317
See also Darfur
Syria, 116, 244, 306

Tadić, Duško, 146-148
Taylor, Charles G., 174, 297
Taylor, Melinda, 110, 230-231
temporal jurisdiction, 43, 204
territorial jurisdiction, 21, 28, 29, 31, 35, 47, 191, 204, 293
third-party States, 27, 28, 30, 38, 82, 118, 229-237
Tolbert, David, 131, 133, 134, 143, 267-269, 282
transitional justice mechanisms, 9, 51, 53, 128, 202
trial observations, 248, 254-256
Truth, Justice and Reconciliation Commission (TJRC), 81-82, 246
truth commissions, 51, 80, 202, 246
See also accountability mechanisms
truth seeking, 51, 147, 202

Uganda, 95, 173, 186-197, 246, 269, 273, 289, 307
United Kingdom, 83, 119, 120, 273, 316
unjustified delays, 69, 77, 90-94
unwillingness, 6, 8-10, 16, 18, 21, 26, 36, 37, 51, 62-65, 68-74, 77, 78, 82, 90, 94, 112, 168, 181, 216, 218, 229, 239, 285
See also willingness

United Nations (UN), 3, 29, 38, 46, 47, 57, 88-85, 103-105, 107, 121, 126, 127, 167, 176, 209, 239, 240, 245, 247, 257, 261, 283, 298, 304
Human Rights Committee, 3, 99, 298
Human Rights Council, 85, 86, 202
Members States, 32, 36, 46, 162, 163
UN Charter, 26, 35, 36, 154, 163, 197, 198, 223, 288
Chapter VII, 26, 35, 152, 154, 163, 165, 197, 223, 288
UN Security Council, 46, 76, 147, 163-167, 170, 197, 199, 200, 204, 222-227, 232, 236, 245, 288, 297

referral, 6, 26, 33, 35, 36, 39, 45, 87, 126, 152-162, 165, 166, 187, 197, 198, 200, 204, 222, 224, 226
United Nations War Crimes Commission (UNWCC), 13-20
United States, 18, 28, 45, 47, 133, 170, 172, 199, 238, 239, 250
Universal Declaration of Human Rights, 98, 131
universal jurisdiction, 35, 36, 121, 291-294

victims, 1-3, 49, 56, 59, 60, 74, 76, 95, 129, 131, 142, 143, 208, 236, 280, 286, 293-305
compensation, 202, 250, 283-284
protection, 133, 188, 295
victim and witness support, 143, 265
Victims and Witnesses Unit, 132, 265, 267
victors' justice, 24, 95, 145

War Report 2012, The, 299-318
Waki Commission, 81
war crimes, 5, 7, 14, 17, 30, 41, 44, 55, 57, 58, 75, 82, 83, 85, 87, 88, 114, 117, 118, 168, 172, 174-176, 187, 204, 243, 248, 249, 276, 286, 288
investigation and prosecution of, 2, 7, 36, 38, 84, 88, 109, 177, 235, 246, 294, 297
willingness, 7, 10, 18, 21, 25, 36, 27, 62, 66, 60, 74, 88, 111, 120, 122, 127, 138, 143, 150, 171, 176, 177, 182, 186, 192, 196, 197, 209, 216, 221, 230, 235, 238, 239, 289
See also unwillingness
withdrawal,
charges, of, 136, 137, 189
International Criminal Court, from, 5, 227, 228, 232, 288
referral, of, 190-195
witnesses, 4, 8, 23, 33, 68, 91, 93, 117, 118, 127, 130-132, 136-142, 138, 209, 215, 224, 255, 278
interference/intimidation, 119, 130, 135, 129-142
protection, 8, 9, 84, 125, 130-136, 140-143, 188, 218, 219, 220, 221, 244, 263, 265-269, 295
support, 236, 265-270
World War I, 74, 286
World War II, 13, 74, 286